Hart's Bridge

Hart's Bridge   *Sherman Paul*

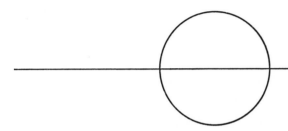

University of Illinois Press   *Urbana Chicago London*

For Austin Warren

Preface

Making a book is one way of remaking the mind. Or perhaps I should say that, whenever I undertake to enter another's world, I feel that obligation and in it find the challenge and reward of criticism. Why one chooses—is it chosen?—to enter a particular world at a particular time is another matter, one worthy of autobiography. Certainly I did not foresee this development, though I see now that its possibility was always there, awaiting developments, in myself and in our world. One of the things I regret is not having kept a journal, of a phenomenological kind, of this exploration.

There are enough traces of this, I suppose, for those who may be interested. Of more importance, since its mediation is apparent everywhere, is the method I have used. It is too eclectic to have a name, and the prominence of its elements change in keeping with the directive I find in Louis Sullivan's maxim—as good for making books as for making buildings—that every problem contains its own solution. (The problem with Crane, of course, is not only one of entering his world but of working through the criticism that surrounds it.) The constant, most essential elements are those for which Gaston Bachelard and I. A. Richards give me names. I have always worked *admiratively* and have always tried to read *vigilantly*; these activities, along with the equally demanding one of writing, constitute, for me, a discipline or way of criticism. Beyond this, I have always followed the phenomenologists' procedure of treating the entire work as a whole. I also share with them a predilection for spiritual adventure, but attend more to biography and milieu—to "life" and "times," the intersections of the individual and the common historical world—and to matters of symbolic action and form. Now, more than before, the work and play of imagination preoccupy me, and I would like to make "credible" —how difficult, as Rilke says—"the causes out of which a poem arises!"

The title of this study indicates this. I owe it to Kenneth Burke, who inadvertently gave it to me when we spoke together of his own long poem, "Eye-Crossing—From Brooklyn to Manhattan," a poem in which he considers the motives of Whitman's and Crane's poems of crossing. Burke knew Crane and belonged to the circle with whom Crane first discussed *The Bridge*; he had every right to speak of Crane familiarly. Had he said, "Hart Crane's bridge" or "Crane's bridge," I am certain I would have borrowed from Crane himself one of many suitable, if not perhaps so exact, titles. Of course my debt to Burke, having accumulated for more than thirty years, is greater than this. It is an outstanding debt of learning that I am happy to have this occasion to acknowledge.

Others to whom I am indebted have an expert's familiarity with Crane's work: Richard Hutson, for whom I first fully read Crane and whose book on Crane will be published soon; William Fine, Herbert Leibowitz, John Unterecker, Alan Trachtenberg, and Brom Weber, to whom my debt is also personal, greater than that indicated by the footnotes; and Edward Brunner and Ware Smith, both of whom are now writing studies of Crane and who, with the members of two seminars, engaged me, as only confreres can, in day-to-day, year-long discussion. To have such community of interest has been especially fortunate.

And there are others to whom I am always greatly indebted, companions, mentors, readers, who for a long time have been part of my work: James Ballowe, Warner Berthoff, James Guimond, William Rueckert, Austin Warren, Douglas Wilson, and my wife, Jim.

For various courtesies I wish to thank the libraries of Columbia University, Ohio State University, Southern Illinois University, the University of Texas, and the University of Iowa; and for time and money—necessities of scholarship—I am grateful to the Department of English, the Graduate College, and the Research Council of the University of Iowa.

Iowa City, May 1971

Contents

. . . the heart refuses to be imprisoned; in its first and narrowest pulses it already tends outward with a vast force and to immense and innumerable expansions.

Ralph Waldo Emerson

And one would not write were it not for this birth of words that gives us again the hope of a true life.

Yves Bonnefoy

. . . the poet Hart Crane was able to invent growth's likeness.

e e cummings

one

Mere Shadowings

The first memory that Hart Crane employs in his poetry is among the earliest and most important. It appears in the closing section of "Porphyro in Akron" (1921), where the poet, alone in his room, is moved to reverie by reading Keats's "The Eve of St. Agnes." The dawn with which the poet begins his poem has not fulfilled any miraculous promise. It has disclosed instead a smoky industrial world, a depressing urban landscape from which, in the course of the poem's diurnal action, the poet turns, first to an enclave of Sunday pleasure, then to the anonymity and isolation of a hotel room. The progression is retrogressive: it inverts the poet's development in the earlier poems. In them, though hesitantly, he turns outward from a self-enclosed world. But now, having faced the world he feels to be adversary—the world he would learn later to celebrate but that now, he believes, needs not "the oil of song"— he retreats to his room, to the interior world where, in one sense, he had started to grow, and poetry, not ironically, had been his "bedroom occupation."

The irony of the title and the poet's self-ridicule in the closing section of the poem express more resilience than one finds in the early poems, excepting perhaps the exuberant "tirade" on the imagination in "The Bridge of Estador" (1921). The early poems are necessarily imitative and exploratory; the poet seeks his role in experience by posturing. On this account one might dismiss them, as Yvor Winters did the early poems reprinted in *White Buildings*, as "relatively simple" imagistic poems of "the more fragile variety, calling to mind the brittle Parnassianism of H. D. or the slim symbolic flame of Ezra Pound's shorter poems. . . ." [1] But the posturing is not so important as the posture chosen, and Crane, in "Porphyro in Akron," finally names the posture that personal disposition had already seized on and the resistant conditions ("Akron, 'high place,'— / A bunch of smoke-ridden hills") that confirmed him in it. Although he acknowledges the beauty of the commonplace in "The Bridge of Estador" and knows the penalties of his romantic position, he elects to be "Beauty's fool." And so, driven back on himself, we find him reading "The Eve of St. Agnes," a poem about his successful namesake.

The fragment of Keats's poem—

> Full on this casement shone the wintry moon,
> And threw warm gules on Madeline's fair breast,
> As down she knelt for heaven's grace and boon

—this is more than identifying tag or ironic contrast with the present situation of a romantic *manqué*. As the reverie it awakens shows, it is an especially appropriate passage. For it leads, by way of another fragment of verse ("Connais tu le pays . . . ?") that defines and augments the longing associated with the first, to a memory of childhood:

> Your mother sang that [the French version
>   of Mignon's song] in a stuffy parlor
> One summer day in a little town
> Where you had started to grow.
> And you were outside as soon as you
> Could get away from the company
> To find the only rose on the bush
> In the front yard. . . . [2]

This memory, which comes up so strongly and whose force is increased rather than diminished by adult perspective ("a stuffy

1. "Hart Crane's Poems," *Poetry*, XXX (April, 1927), 47.
2. John Unterecker believes that the incident recalled in this passage occurred in Garrettsville, that is, during the first four years of Crane's life. (*Voyager: A Life of Hart Crane* [New York: Farrar, Straus and Giroux, 1969], p. 19.) Whether Crane remembered the incident or only remembered having heard of it does not alter its importance.

parlor": stuffy in a double sense) and bitterness ("Where you had started to grow"), belongs to the profound movement of imagination Gaston Bachelard calls reverie.[3] This memory is at the very heart of the poet's interior world. Here he discovers the source of his romantic attitude as well as the reason for its persistence. Declaring both the bondage of this memory and his willingness to be bound by it, the poet, in an earlier version, concludes: "You will never forget the song nor the rose." [4]

The depth and dangerous recognition of this memory, represented by ellipsis, is the immediate occasion of the self-protective irony that follows ("But look up, Porphyro,—your toes / Are ridiculously tapping . . ."). For the poet, though a lover—the memory is resonant because it tells *his* love—is not the Porphyro of Keats's poem, a romantic lover who wins Madeline and carries her off to be his bride. He is not romantic in that sense but in another: his longing is fixed at the stage of wondrous beholding and adoration of Beauty; he is still content, it seems, with the "soft adorings" promised in the sixth stanza of Keats's poem and fulfilled in the stanza from which the passage he reads is taken:

> Full on this casement shone the wintry moon,
> And threw warm gules on Madeline's fair breast,
> As down she knelt for heaven's grace and boon;
> Rose-bloom fell on her hands, together pressed,
> And on her silver cross soft amethyst,
> And on her hair a glory, like a saint:
> She seemed a splendid angel, newly dressed,
> Save wings, for heaven—Porphyro grew faint:
> She knelt, so pure a thing, so free from mortal taint.

The situation, we know, is erotic, yet at this point spirituality contests it. And this is what Crane, replacing Madeline with his mother, wishes. Summoned by name ("heaven's grace") and golden hair ("her hair a glory") as well as by "Rose-bloom," she is the "splendid angel," the forever virginal mother whose beauty moved the small

3. *The Poetics of Reverie*, trans. Daniel Russell (New York: Orion Press, 1969).
4. See Brom Weber, *Hart Crane: A Biographical and Critical Study* (New York: Bodley Press, 1948), p. 92. In the early version he returns with the rose. The revision emphasizes this memory.

boy to bestow a rose and moved the fledgling poet of "C 33" (1916) to justify his suffering and song:

> O Materna! to enrich thy gold head
> And wavering shoulders with a new light shed. . . .[5]

Devotion is the price of love her unattainableness exacts. Like the paradisal land to which Mignon wishes to go with her beloved father, she, too, is beyond—the paradise which, in fact, is already behind and stirs the deepest longing.

"Had started to grow" suggests a possible arrest in development and conveys the poet's recognition and reproach. The remembered incident antedates the fiercer quarrels of Crane's parents and may recall a lost harmony, though the boy's romantic gesture, so important to his mother, may also be the reflex of her possessiveness. The memory expresses not only a powerful emotion but a sensitive dutifulness little expected of a four-year-old unless the very world of his being rehearsed it for him.[6] It is not a memory of his mother's love for him; there are none in Crane's work. And his reproach, still alive in the present, comes from his awareness that his predicament as a poet—his being a poet as well as his inability to find himself as a poet in the contemporary world—is somehow connected with this memory. To him it may be *the* image of his arrest, of the emotional dependence he ascribed to his "fated" life of "parental absorptions."[7] In "Voyages," where Crane relates a history of love and reveals his lack of basic trust,[8] he warns the children frisking on the beach of a cruel maternal sea, one both too possessive and too little concerned ("too lichen-faithful . . . too

5. Even in a mood of hostility, Crane spoke of his mother, still in youthful middle age, as "a rather (for her) ductile and seductive woman with a certain aura of romance about her." *The Letters of Hart Crane, 1916–1932,* ed. Brom Weber (Berkeley: University of California Press, 1965), p. 33 (March 6, 1920). Hereafter cited as *Letters.*

6. John Unterecker says that as a boy Crane was desperately eager to please everyone and that "he needed the love and affection of his parents, who seemed always out of reach and whom nothing could quite please." *Voyager,* p. 10.

7. *Letters,* p. 40 (May 25, 1920).

8. The term is Erik Erikson's and the condition to which it refers may account for the imagery of breasts and nurture in Crane's work. Consider "Interludium," a poem "To 'La Montagna' by [Gaston] Lachaise." This statue of a recumbent

wide a breast"). And at the end of the voyage of love he himself hazards in these poems—that he finds the voyage fearful and seems compelled to make it because of what he has learned of the duplicity of mother love is to the point—he seems aware of the cheat the summoning ideal of Beauty has been. Though Crane's poetry may be viewed as a record of his long way home, his memory of home is sometimes apprehensive, as in "Repose of Rivers" ("the black gorge / And all the singular nestings in the hills / Where beavers learn stitch and tooth"). Even when he lived within its protection, as during most of the period when the early poems were written, he was aware that the Beauty he adored was double-faced.

How Beauty appeared to him in the awakening of adolescence is evoked by the dream woman of "In Shadow" (1917). This impressionistic poem, with its wonderfully suspended atmosphere and moment of radiance ("distill / The sunlight"), contains some of the central elements of Crane's work: the garden (both home and the American past, or pastoral), the night (darkness and modern industrial civilization), and Beauty (the feminine presence of the garden). Like "Harbor Dawn," it provides a visionary account of the advent of the woman or Beautiful Thing, to use William Carlos Williams' phrase, that the poet at this stage of his development believes it is his mission to serve and protect. The period quality of the poem is appropriate, for Crane found his ideas of woman and poetry—Beauty combines them—in just such a *fin de siècle* ambience. The woman of the poem is of the shadows, of the darkness that belongs to an interior world; she is a shadowy mysterious silent being who wills her radiance by standing forth. Her reality is spiritual, and in her accord with nature she is a presence,

---

woman has the self-subsistent quality of—is—Nature. The concluding quatrain is:

> Madonna, natal to thy yielding
> still subsist I, wondrous as
> from thine open dugs shall still the sun
> again round one more fairest day.

This poem suggests the more than literary maternalizing of Nature which enabled Crane to maintain his profoundest emotional values while advancing beyond the small domestic world of their origin. As we shall see, this development had the greatest consequences for him: it permitted him to become a cosmic poet (like Whitman), a poet of the heavens and the earth, of a world living and vast enough to complement the tremendous energy of his love; and it enabled him to fulfill one of the offices of literature—to create confidence in the world.

almost its divinity. We may think of her, as the poet does, as an ideal subject to time, to the loss of light in the darkening of civilization that Crane, always exact in his borrowings, expresses here in the idiom and cadence of Edwin Arlington Robinson. "The earth may glide diaphanous to death"—this line from "For the Marriage of Faustus and Helen" evokes her again. And we may think of the poet, who pledges himself in the poem, as a chivalric knight of the kind one finds in Lanier's "The Symphony" or in Yeats's early poems, as he still is in "Pastorale" (1921), where, dusty and travel-worn, he bears an "image" of pristine beauty and youth "beyond this / Already fallen harvest. . . ."

Poems such as these tell of the poet's persistence in behalf of an ideal or condition that he knows is already lost in time ("'Fool— / Have you remembered too long . . .'"). The persistence, though serving to preserve the ideal, argues arrest, a refusal, as in "Pastorale," to accept the inevitable sundering, the natural course of growth and experience. Spring, the season of childhood, innocence, and pure (unconscious) love, is over. The violets are gone, and the year, formerly an uninterrupted continuity of life connected with an infant's springtime "ritual of sap and leaves," is now, in a harsh phrase of recognition that expresses the meaning of time, "Broken into smoky panels." "Broken" and "smoky," which recur in Crane's work, here have the meaning of sundered and soiled. Beauty for the poet is the original condition of unity with Mother Nature; experience and maturity, agents seemingly external to him, bring the "fallen harvest," a terminal or dead condition of "Bronze and brass" and a loss all the more regrettable because, like Emerson in "Days," the poet was not surfeited in that happy time ("What woods remember now / Her calls, her enthusiasms"). But estrangement is necessary. The very "ritual of sap and leaves / The sun drew out" prompts it, the sun being a masculine power associated with time and the reality of the outside world (external force) and with the poet's growth and emerging manhood (interior, sexual force). The poet knows that he must enter the world, however "dusty," and that to some extent he wishes to. An exigency of his own being prompts him to do so; this is why he suggests that perhaps there was "too little said / For ease or resolution. . . ." And yet the feeling of loss, whose cadences here as elsewhere Crane has mastered, pre-empts the poem. The world he has entered does not compensate the loss of Beauty, and he travels *through* it, a chivalrous knight who is quixotic not only because he remembers Beauty and bears its image, as on a shield, as the sign of his destiny, but because he persists in finding it, in seeking it "beyond."

The chivalric knight, the romantic visionary, is Crane's first quester, and only when he reaches the limits of consciousness by discovering Beauty's naturalistic face will he turn back to the world to find her. Consider "North Labrador," probably written in 1917 or 1918, and placed by Crane in *White Buildings* in significant relation to "Pastorale" and "In Shadow." The landscape of this poem is polar—vast, forbidding, and, above all, unresponsive. It is a visionary, interior landscape, the landscape of consciousness itself, the complement of the darkening landscape of "In Shadow." For the poet who dramatizes his attempt to possess it, to transform it by giving it meaning, the unresponsive landscape is the unresponding mother, who, in the springtime of "Pastorale," had been benign (like Pocahontas, the vernal goddess, the transformed glacier woman of *The Bridge*). Much of the point of the poem is in the reversal of values usually associated by Crane with "cool" and "white." They may still signify purity and spirituality but now they are connected with a desolate, formidable, overwhelming anti-life. This landscape of hopelessness is so desperate it "Flings itself silently / Into eternity." Yet the poet has come here, and the very questions by which he tries to transform it protest the injustice done his constancy:

> "Has no one come here to win you,
> Or left you with the faintest blush
> Upon your glittering breasts?
> Have you no memories, O Darkly Bright?"

Having come so far in search of Beauty, the poet expects to be rewarded with an answer. But the Darkly Bright goddess (who anticipates the imperious divinity of "Voyages") is unresponding. Her silence—or rather *the* silence—is as awful as the presence of the solitary speaker in the terrible vastness, for vastness as much as silence is the measure of unresponsiveness, of meaninglessness and emptiness. And so the poet's own voice, by filling the emptiness, answers him. He cannot transform the "other," make it respond (correspond); the very vastness shows the separation of subject and object. "In answer"—the phrase is the subdued, suspended line closing the poem with finality—he sees only the shifting ice, the meaningless change of a changeless eternity, an icy landscape out of time and bereft of life ("no Spring—/ No birth, no death, no time nor sun"). That Crane may have borrowed this landscape from Poe or Coleridge matters little. It is his own, revealing a post-romantic awareness of the "nothingness of consciousness when consciousness becomes the foundation of everything" and of the necessity of turning elsewhere in order to find the sustaining forces of life.[9] It would not be inappropriate to say that he has discovered the death of God—discovered this in the death of the goddess, the death of love. For the whiteness which Melville said was the all-color of atheism is here the all-color of lovelessness. It is the face of romanticism inimical to growth.

Impasse and arrest of growth inform Crane's poetry from the beginning and are closely connected with his conception of the poet and his need to be one. As a way of being-in-the-world and as the calling of the self, poetry must satisfy the need for emotional security and the need for growth. Lacking the first, the other becomes difficult, for the self retreats rather than advances, turns inward on itself rather than outward to the world. These directions are irreconcilable until the poet turns the interior world inside out and finds in the work of poetry itself the values of security. Take, for example, "The Moth That God Made Blind" (1915), an Icarian fable that Crane wrote in his sixteenth year.[10]

This poem of adolescence, with its galloping anapests, might be cursorily dismissed were it not for what it tells us of the young poet's "world" and his attempt to understand and come to terms

---

9. J. Hillis Miller, *Poets of Reality: Six Twentieth-Century Writers* (Cambridge: Belknap Press of Harvard University Press, 1965), p. 3; see also pp. 1–12. The poem may also be considered in the light of Kenneth Burke's association of "ice" with punishment for an incest-wish. See *Attitudes toward History* (New York: New Republic, 1937), II, 170–71, where he also associates "incest-awe" with purification by fire and thus provides a bridge to "The Dance," *The Bridge*.

10. Unless the dating is wrong, the poem was not influenced by Joyce's *A Portrait of the Artist as a Young Man* (1916), a novel Crane later praised.

with it. What is impressive here is not the fable by which he fables himself but the fact that he uses it to accommodate an awareness of complexity. The poet's sense of himself is of one "scorned" though divinely favored. The moth that God made blind he also endowed with "signs mystical / And rings macrocosmic"; the poet is special, a divine fool, as the curious use of Pierrot in the verb "pierroting," instead of "pirouetting," suggests. His blindness permits him to go beyond the customary limits of his species; the "others" are "blinded by all waking things"—by the daylight world and to the waking powers by which he would claim it. But his blindness also covers the fact that his flight is instinctive, a divine impulsion, a necessity of his being. Of this impulsion the narrator of the poem speaks knowingly: it results from the pressures of growth, among them pressures both sexual and vocational ("But once though, he learned of that span of his wings,— / The florescence, the power he felt bud at the time"). Because of this the moth's world is one of parental dominions and powers and his flight is accompanied by a sense of guilt.

The moth's flight enacts the desire for freedom that for Crane is already a condition of poetry and the thing it achieves. It is already, like the bird flight of later poems, a symbol of his desire for all that is "consummate and free." [11] That he gives it an Icarian pattern tells of his awareness of youthful pride and overreaching— the powers are not yet fully his—and of the guilt he feels in leaving the maternal paradise and in defying the father (sun-storming is *son*-storming). His cosmos is explicitly ruled by mother (moon) and father (sun), and its nighttime and daytime associations are pretty much those of the late nineteenth- and early twentieth- century world noted by Freud.

The moth's messianic role is also connected with his blindness to the "small oasis" of his birth. (He will eventually see "what his whole race had shunned"—a vast and beautiful sunlit world, the glorious earth, a natural yet still maternal world.) He is blind to "that circle of paradise cool in the night," though we are not be- cause the narrator and the resonance of the phrase insist that we see it. He is blind to the nighttime exotic world of a "race" of

11. "The Dance," *The Bridge.*

moths limited in vision by the moon ("Their mother, the moon")
and by attractions they are unwilling to forego:

> Some say that for sweetness they cannot see far,—
> That their land is too gorgeous to free their eyes wide
> To horizons which knife-like would only mar
> Their joy with a barren and steely tide—

Conceived in the light of the moon and born in "mosaic date
vases," these moths live in an enclosure as confining yet as sufficient
as the "yellow cocoons" from which they emerge. They live in a
mother-dominated world whose soft sensuousness and concavity
Crane renders exactly, and, having the "lunar sensibility" he later
mocked by way of translations of Laforgue, they see only threat,
as Crane often did, in the "steely" reaches of the daylight world,
the industrial "desert," beyond. They lack the masculine desire of
intellect that Crane, like Melville, knew would force them to
leave the vernal isle. They do not wish "to free their eyes wide"—
"wide," a word of special import, having, as in the "wide from"
construction in "Voyages," the meaning of vastness painfully
recognized as incurring loss because experienced from a secure
place. They do not desire the umbilical severance hinted at by the
"knife-like" horizons, though the blinded moth, the "honey-thick
glaze" over his eyes suggesting a surfeit of sweetness, does.

The maternal power is represented as a condition from which
escape depends solely upon the moth. This condition is one of
suffocating dependence that growth cannot endure nor sexual
awakening permit. Knowledge is irreversible ("But once though,
he learned"); he must venture the desert, take flight (the poem
itself is a trial flight), deliver himself. What is interesting here is
the dichotomy of oasis and desert, the fearful sense of the outer
world as a world to be entered and its association with the vast
daytime world of the father; this, and—how terrible and premoni-
tory—the fact of flight, a self-sustaining act in which being free is
all in transit and never in rest, the space entered ("that wide mesh-
less blue") providing no purchase.

Yet to venture—to take the risk of imagination—is to be mirac-
ulously released. The quickened verse renders this. And the act is

sanctioned by two things that attend it: the dawn, which is usually promissory for Crane, and the dance ("pierroting," "Swinging in spirals," "gyrating"), the upward vortical motion of flight. It is an ecstasy, kinesthetic and visionary—a dizzying ascent to vision, an agony in which blindness is burned away by the heat of the sun and for "a little time only" he beholds a paradisal world: "Great horizons and systems and shores all along / Which blue tides of cool moons were slow shaken and sunned." What "sight burned as deep" is a vision of a felicitous, heavenly world—it is contrasted to his earlier "Hell"—a vision of Beauty, as the narrator interprets it, maternal in value (blue, cool, associated with "the fresh breasts of day") yet separate from the oasis he has escaped. Beauty, so often the ideal possession of the interior or enclosed world, is now connected with the external world, with a loving and sustaining earth. But it is still beyond reach. As the visionary glimpse indicates, it can only be attained by imaginative flight, by the act (art) of poetry.

Of this ascent, the sun, a "black god" to the blind moth, is witness ("The sun saw a ruby brightening ever, that flew"); of this consuming experience, the sun is the tropic power, drawing the unseeing (innocent) moth to him in "octopus arms." Though the sun is the agent of vision—the sovereign of all seeing—he seems to permit sight only on penalty of punishment. The upward vortex of flight is as fearful and death-dealing as the downward vortex more common in Crane's poetry, and the moth who attempts it is "atom-withered." When he falls, it is not to earth, the radiant world of his vision, but to the desert. This is probably to be explained by the reason that also explains why we are told "still lonely he fell." His ascent is to the enabling father, who, by only momentarily permitting him a glimpse of the lovely possibilities of poetry, condemns him, as had his mother by her possessiveness, to the "desert," the wasteland, business world of work.

It is to be noted that the mother's world is not favorable to poetry either. There the moth is "like a grain of sand, futile and dried." This subtle identification with the "desert" to which flight from home constrains him reveals the poet's awareness of his parents' insistence on worldly success. Neither permits him the world of poetry, the natural world, the fitting place to be. This accounts for the double resentment and sense of impasse expressed in the poem.

The last stanza as well as the probable biographical occasion of the poem supports such an interpretation. In the last stanza the narrator says:

> I have hunted long years for a spark in the sand;—
> My eyes have hugged beauty and winged life's brief spell.
> These things I have:—a withered hand;—
> Dim eyes;—a tongue that cannot tell.

The poet's identification with the moth, his own poetic "spark" or psyche, is not necessary to the fable, which does "tell," but to the symbolic action it completes for the poet. It expresses his own perseverance and reveals the nature of his strivings, which are inordinate and sexual ("My eyes have hugged beauty") and under the compelling enchantment of poetry ("winged life's brief spell"). It expresses his awareness of the heavy penalties entailed by this quest: "a withered hand" (hands, in Crane's work, are conspicuous in passages celebrating love; here, associated with the moth's "atom-withered" wings, the hand symbolizes castration and loss of creative power); "Dim eyes" (this penalty is not so much the result of gazing on beauty as of ascending toward the sun); "a tongue that cannot tell" (again, the denial of expressive, creative power).

Much of this is attitudinizing, for the poem itself is a flight, a vision, and a telling. Of more interest is the fact that it derives from present experience and portends the future. The poet's life—a winged, rare life—is connected with sudden release and abandonment, with loneliness, suffering, and diminishment (spent life). To undertake it incurs disapproval and chastening. Its possessions ("These things I have") are losses. No one, it seems, understands its necessity, and he himself is powerless to say.

The autobiographical ground of much of this belongs to the immediate past of the adolescent who, at fifteen, had told his friend William Wright that in poetry he had found his life's work, and who, in the winter of 1915, had lived on the Isle of Pines with his mother and grandmother. Not Arabia, but this tropical landscape, always associated with his mother, is the setting that informs the

poem. Crane's father had accompanied them there but soon re-
turned home because of a violent quarrel with his wife. There
Hart Crane had a traumatic experience; twice, we are told, he
attempted suicide.[12] This accords with the illnesses with which he
sometimes responded to his parents' quarrels. They were probably
extreme because the occasions were extreme, and those that occurred
on the Isle of Pines may be connected with his choice of vocation
and the impasse to it presented by his parents' marital crisis and
their middle-class expectations for him. With this in mind, the
last stanza of the poem becomes necessary for the poet because it
announces what is otherwise not expressed in the fable: that know-
ing the cost, he is still determined to be a poet. Although the
stanza is in the past tense, its declarative force and tone convey
the poet's resolution to continue the quest. And this, in turn, may
be immediately autobiographical in origin. After his parents' di-
vorce, in December 1916, Crane left home for the first time, pre-
sumably to prepare for college but actually to continue his life's
work, which, in his eyes, may have begun with the publication of
"C 33" in *Bruno's Weekly*, in September 1916. The holograph in-
scription to "The Moth That God Made Blind"—"(Harold) Hart
Crane / 25 E. 11 St. / N. Y. C. / 1915"—contains a significant
error: the misdating links his present liberation to the earlier un-
happy flight of the poem.[13]

In none of the other early poems is there such daring or is escape,
whatever the consequences, so fully achieved. For the most part,
the poet struggles with the need to emerge from a protective en-
closure and with his fear of doing so. He struggles with the desire
to be and the dread of being born. These powerful contending
emotions are related to his conception of the outside world as a
hostile place, as something to be feared, and to the way in which
his culture polarizes night and day, feminine and masculine. The

12. See Philip Horton, *Hart Crane: The Life of an American Poet* (New York:
Viking Press, 1957), pp. 24–25, 27–28; Unterecker, *Voyager*, pp. 30–31, 35–38.
13. *The Complete Poems and Selected Letters and Prose of Hart Crane*, ed. Brom
Weber (Garden City: Doubleday & Co., 1966), p. 279. Hereafter cited as P. The
date of composition is uncertain. Unterecker believes that it was written "just after
Christmas of 1915," but this seems unlikely. *Notes to First Edition of Voyager*, no.
42.

emergence of the poet—the always difficult birth into vocation—
is thereby complicated by the need to emerge as a "man," by the
need to reconcile in himself a world that presents itself to him as
irreconcilable. Perhaps for Crane the dawn is a special time of
dreaming-and-wakefulness and of love indeterminately hetero-
homosexual ("The Harbor Dawn" is a later instance of both) be-
cause it is, for its moment, a bridge that forecloses neither night nor
day.

"Fear" (1917), a curiously truncated ballad of two stanzas, de-
picts his dread. The speaker of the poem, who, like a child, should
be comforted by the food, warmth, and light of the inn and by the
parental solicitude of the host, who assures him at the start that
"all is well," still cries out for the protection of physical embrace
("Give me your hands," "But hold me . . ."). His fear, he says,
is not of the night that licks the windows;[14] it is a dreadful appre-
hension—the tense imperatives of the second stanza convey it—
of something less definite and more insistently present. The inn, we
suddenly realize, is only a transient shelter: the protection of night
will be followed by the exposure of day, by the necessity of entering
the "wild" romantic landscape established by the archaism of the
poem. For as the speaker explains—the vague reference and past
tense express the ambiguity and anxiety of his situation, a terrible
suspended moment of the immediate present—"somewhere I heard
demands. . . ."

These demands are both internal and external, of the self and of
the world. They are the impulsions of birth that in "Annuncia-
tions" (1917), a dream poem of vital quickening and severing,
trouble the poet's sleep with the stirrings of "day's predestiny." He
must be born as surely as day follows night. But here he does not
welcome the annunciations of dawn, even though the title of the
poem, with its reference to the Incarnation, seems to express a posi-
tive value. The earth of this poem *is* Mother Earth, her "anxious
milk-blood" striving "to sever" the tenacious child ("the girth / Of
greenery"). Earth does not sever the life it sustains, but mothers
do, and though the anxiety attributed to the mother, who "strives

14. Crane is already familiar with Eliot, in this instance "The Love Song of
J. Alfred Prufrock" (1915).

long and quiet" to deliver her child, may be hers, it is more likely a displacement of the poet's. In this waking dream, the poet-child imagines a mother-wife at his side ("The moans of travail of one dearest beside me"), an imagination whose purity is perhaps prepared for by the title of the poem and the dove of the previous line. In this regressive dream, he even imagines his own birth, the very birth some of the dream work—for example, the image of the descending moth—tries to avoid; and the cry that awakens him from his dream of the womb is the cry of his own birth trauma: "Then high cries from great chasms of chaos outdrawn. . . ." The image is of the vortex and connects the womb with death, while "outdrawn," by its awkwardness and position, calls attention to the act of being drawn out or delivered. Fortunately, the poet's fears of life and death are quieted by the comforting presence of the mother. "Hush!" she says, assuring him of the dawn—"Hush! these things were all heard before dawn." [15]

The theme of this poem is treated again in "Stark Major," a "strange psychoanalytic thing," Crane said when he sent it to Gorham Munson a month or so before his decisive departure from Cleveland.[16] A more accomplished poem than "Annunciations," Crane used it in *White Buildings* to represent the kind of experience he had been concerned with in the early poems. This "strange, compelling poem of childbirth," as Philip Horton characterizes it,[17] anticipates that "time of sundering" in a double way. Crane depicts it as a "lover's death" and links it with the lover's supplanting at the birth of a child. But he is both lover and child—a situation comparable to that revealed in his correspondence with his mother, who often reminded him that to leave her was to deny her a lover-son. And he must yield the pregnant woman, likened to nature and her "lifting spring" ("Beneath the green silk counterpane / Her mound of undelivered life"), in order that new life may be born. That birth, so inevitable—as "regular" as spring and "starker / Vestiges of the sun"—is final yet reluctantly accepted because it is

15. "Heard" explicitly ties this poem to "Fear," a companion piece published at the same time in *The Pagan* and printed on the same page.

16. *Letters*, pp. 117–18 (January 23, 1923).

17. *Hart Crane*, p. 141.

accompanied by loss. Now the lover must descend from the bedroom to the street; no longer is he permitted to remain in the cool dark room where joined hands "answer," in the Whitmanian sense of love and solace, the "heat and sober / Vivisection of more clamant air. . . ." Now he is debarred ("only to look / At doors"). And like the moth of his earliest poem, whose vast daylight world has now become the city street, the place of work ("the daily circuits of its glare"), he has "broken eyes," an affliction here owing more to severance than to its worldly consequences and recalling the "broken . . . panels" of "Pastorale." Though he adjures himself, a child confronted with the world of work, to "walk now," the irony is quickly dissolved in the concluding lines by the finality of loss expressed in the play of possessives ("her," "yours") and in the despairing belief that paradise is beyond the reach of both "cries" (the child's clamor) and "ecstasies" (the lover's art of poetry).

Crane did not welcome the dawn of manhood. The dawn he desired is, it seems, the one described in "The Bathers" (1917), a poem presumably about a painting that is less significant in this regard than for what it tells us of Crane's awareness of the arrest of life achieved by art. In this poem, the tropical landscape is again maternal, associated with a "milky sea" and with milky-white colors denoting purity. Two "ivory women" appear to be the guardians of a silent female world whose only threat, made visible by the restless dawn, is a "black mountain-spear." The observer who describes the landscape enters it as a dreamer ("A dreamer might see these, and wake to hear"), but unlike the dreamer of "Annunciations," he remains undisturbed, at least during the act of contemplation treated in the first stanza. There are no cries because nothing impends; this world is fixed, arrested by art, in a perpetual soothing, subtly erotic motion: "Only simple [innocent] ripples flaunt, and stroke, and float— / Flat lily petals to the sea's white throat." Yet the poet, who has sometime heard and knows that a dreamer might wake to hear, recognizes the eruptive force of the black mountain-spear and what it conveys of sexual agitation, masculinity, and the demands to be up and doing. He may enclose the silent sea-washed paradise in a couplet, but his own feelings, already at work in the poem, are not so easily contained and burst forth with unusual vehemence in the closing quatrain. Here he repudiates the notion of beauty commonly held by the world:

> They say that Venus shot through foam to light,
> But they are wrong . . . Ere man was given sight
> She came in such still water, and so nursed
> In silence, beauty blessed and beauty cursed.

Beauty, he insists, is not a birth, a violent emergence into (of) light. Beauty is uroboric. It belongs to the darkness, to the wholly enclosing embrace of the nurturing womb. To a resplendent Venus he prefers the dark mother, who cannot, however, satisfy the love of child and man, and whose beauty, bestowed only in the natal condition, is the blessing birth turns to curse.

The ambivalence of awakening is evident also in the way Crane treats sexuality. There is, for example, the convention of light and dark lady, a convention still vital in the puritan ethos of Crane's youth and useful to him in transforming what he considers lust into love—in purifying and spiritualizing erotic energy. Of the early poems, "Carmen de Boheme" (1918) explicitly employs this convention. Like other early poems, this finds its occasion in art. It describes the gypsy girl's entrance—a sexual advent to be compared with the chaster moment of "In Shadow"—and the sensual excitement accompanying it. The setting is decadent ("Bright peacocks drink from flame-pots by the wall"); the senses are stirred by "sweetened cigarettes," the sinuous smoke and shimmering light, by intoxication ("wine-hot lips"), and by the mounting, swirling music. With the altered tempo ("crescendo's start") there is a startling change from the sentimental "andante of smooth hopes and lost regrets," a change signaled by the women, whose "brown eyes blacken, and the blue drop hue." In keeping with these blackening eyes are the "smouldering eyes" of Carmen and the "fire's birth in each man's heart," a sudden erotic flaming-up that begins and ends with Carmen's entrance and exit—with the "tapestry [that] betrays a finger through / The slit, soft-pulling" and the "gloom / Of whispering tapestry, brown with old fringe. . . ." Images so explicitly sexual need no comment except to note that everything connected with them is characterized as the "Dis-

quieting of barbarous fantasy" and that the intensity they produce
is of the kind Crane sought as the stimulus to and end of poetry:
"The pulse is in the ears, the heart is higher, / And stretches up
through mortal eyes to see." These lines preceding Carmen's en-
trance express a visionary expectation at once sexual and spiritual.
The straining to see is inordinate and voyeuristic ("lipping eyes"),
a reaching readily associated with the visionary impulse of other
poems. (The "Bent wings" mentioned later are the consequence
of erotic flight and recall the moth whose budding impelled him
to try his wings.) Yet the intensity of this experience may trans-
figure or transcend the sensuality that prompts it. The heart may
see in Blakean fashion, not so much with the eye ("mortal" con-
notes the physical and sensual) as through it. And so, in the pure
"Morning," the poet, who has participated in the barbarous fantasy
of the night but obscured his sensuality by merging it in the general
response to Carmen, is one of the few who "dream still of Carmen's
mystic face,— / Yellow, pallid, like ancient lace." The "dream" of
which he speaks is not comparable to his agitated beholding; it is a
still after-image, a spiritualization of it, representing an activity for
which the young poet prized poetry. This is better understood
when we realize that the poem describes the beholding of an
exciting presence beyond reach, a gypsy, a dark lady, whom dream
transforms into holy mother.

Sexual importunity is not always so easily diverted. In "Modern
Craft" (1918), a poem depicting an encounter with a prostitute,
it figures as "My modern love. . . ." Here, and in the title, "mod-
ern" seems to refer to the vulgar or antipoetic subject of the poem,
to the prostitute and to the poet's lust. Unlike the prostitutes of
Wilde's poems, which Crane knew, she identifies the urban world
of masculine pursuits which the poet cannot move, which remains
unresponsive to his touch and even to the "craft" of the poem,
the imaginative concern with her that does not transform his lust.
(So, as the place of lust, the city becomes infernal, as in "Posses-
sions" and "Repose of Rivers.")

The poem seems to be an imaginary encounter because the
prostitute is less an object of the poet's concern than an object for
the play of his own feelings. The emotional development from
the romantic (innocent, naive, sentimental) to the realistic, though

literary ("Ophelia had such eyes"), represents a growth from self to world, a growth of compassion as much for himself as for her. The poet transforms the prostitute by himself becoming aware of the casualties of casual love, by investing her feelinglessness with his feeling, and by associating her with Ophelia, whose innocence, like hers (and his), has been betrayed by love. Even Ophelia, he says in an authentic phrase, "sank in love and choked with flowers." Yet this awareness, this sympathetic transformation of the dark lady, does not alter his desire. "This burns," he says, speaking also for Ophelia's betrayal—"This burns and is not burnt. . . ." We are reminded of the "fire's birth" in "Carmen de Boheme," of a desire so insistent, and guilty, that it calls up an image of terrible phallic punishment: "Charred at a stake. . . ." [18]

In "Echoes" (1917), the title itself indicates the stratagem, for echoes are tremulous reflections, spiritualizations. The stormy occasion of the poem is outside it, and the delicately wrought, numbered quatrains, each a more distant echo of the storm, provide, in terms of clearing weather, echoes of the lover's state of mind. Passion is not denied, but it is transformed. One wonders about the quarrel, distanced now in the lover's soulful gaze. Do the last indications of the storm, the "slivers of rain," suggest male aggression, and the "stain" and "strain," now vanished, impurity and physical intensity? Had the lover tried to force the moment to its crisis? Or was the crisis of another kind? No matter: for, again, all is "Fresh and fragile" and "your arms now / Are circles of cool roses. . . ." Purity is restored, and the lover once more is spiritually embraced. Recalling the "circle of paradise cool in the night" in "The Moth That God Made Blind" and noting the reverie of love that closes "Echoes," one suspects that the poet has again been reconciled—reconciled with his mother.[19]

The spiritualization that Crane achieves by such transformations

18. The concluding images suggest the possibility that "craft" refers to the poet's craftiness in talking about one kind of love in terms of another.

19. There may be another echo. Allen Tate says that the quarreling of Crane's parents and "the violent sexual reconciliations . . . had given him a horror of the normal sexual relation." (Cited by Unterecker, *Voyager*, p. 38.) Perhaps in the poem Crane is describing a reconciliation more to his liking, as well as possible for him. The emotional pattern of quarrel and reconciliation also has its counterpart in Crane's intensity and rhythm of creation.

is achieved also by stressing the spiritual terms of the polarities that constitute this poetic universe. Most often he prefers to set the self—all that is interior and enclosed, feminine and natural—against the world—all that is exterior and exposed, masculine and urban. He puts the old and the past against the "modern" and the present, the passive and suffering against the active and joyful, the constant (betrayed) against the inconstant. These polarities are familiar in the poetry to which Crane first turned for tutelage, and he did not soon overcome them because he believed that poetry itself, in its nature and in its work, was spiritual. At this time, poetry, for him, was not a mediating agency but an agency of the spiritual. It was just what the poet of "Porphyro in Akron" said it was—a bedroom occupation.

The chivalric aspect of Crane's early poems is conspicuous. As Herbert Leibowitz says in regard to "Carrier Letter" (1918), he is "love's acolyte." [20] He languishes and suffers, and he spiritualizes love in order to prove his purity of feeling and constancy. The threat to love—a private world that here recalls the sanctuary of "The Bathers"—is not only lust but separation and distance, or, as it is realized in "Carrier Letter" and "Legende" (1919), the world of space and time represented by the sea. And once betrayed, as in "Postscript" (1918), the poet withdraws to an "imagined garden," not the classic garden of urn and fountain—presumably the bright open erotic place that sexual trespass has destroyed (the marble urns *are* marble now, the "fountains droop," and all is darkening, cold, and painful)—but a wild romantic melancholy private place, the interior landscape of the self. The self itself becomes a refuge that the poet hugs protectively; and if he no longer wishes to admit the inconstant one to it, it may be not only because of its desolation but because it is homoerotic ("grey with sundered boughs / And broken branches"). Though the poem is both literary and sentimental, Crane seems truly to inhabit it. In it he provides a touchstone of much of his work: "Mine is a world foregone though not yet ended." Paradise has been lost in the betrayal of love.

Suffering is congenial to Crane because it expresses the spiritual merit of his constancy to the paradisal world. It is also the sign of

20. *Hart Crane: An Introduction to the Poetry* (New York: Columbia University Press, 1968), p. 29.

his vulnerability and passive endurance. Yet it is inwardly active and self-transforming, enabling him to create poetry, his precious gift to the world. "C 33" (1916), a poem about Oscar Wilde's "penitence" and "song," speaks also for the work of his own imprisoned self, for the transforming power he had discovered in poetry, and for the connection he recognized between poetry and pain. In speaking of this, especially of the unspecified wound that empowers his bow, it is important to notice that he dedicates poetry to the "Materna" in the hope that she will respond with guilt-absolving comfort. The logic of this sometimes confusing poem of supplication is fairly clear: the poetry that transforms "the desert white" (recall "The Moth That God Made Blind") and "form[s] / The transient bosoms" links associatively to the "Materna" of the second stanza, where the excalamatory mode furthers the work of religious exaltation, and this, in turn, links to the petition for maternal response in the last stanza ("But you who hear the lamp whisper thru night / Can trace paths tear-wet, and forget [forgive] all blight"). The mother, whose power is imputed but not realized in the poem, is asked to do what poetry itself must do for the poet: assuage the emptiness, or, in a phrase that begs for literal reading, fill the "empty heart of night." And this becomes permissible because the poem transforms—spiritualizes—a prohibited demand (one senses it the image of the "thorny tree" from which the "bosoms" must be taken) and is itself a token of requisite suffering, a "song of minor, broken strain."

More dramatic because of the shock of the metaphor is the depiction of suffering in "The Hive" (1917). Here the poet is a "bleeding heart" over whose "chasm-walls" all "Humanity pecks, claws, sobs and climbs. . . ." He is indeed the suffering Jesus, a sacrificial being, the very heart of the world ("the hive of the world that is my heart"). Thus, though he is withdrawn, the world comes to him, the watcher and sayer, and, in the heart-hive that passively accepts the world's suffering as it too suffers it, all the woe of the world is redeemed, transformed: "And of all the sowing, and all the tear-tendering, / And reaping, have mercy and love issued forth." What he gives and believes rewards his "anguish" is what he seeks for himself—"Mercy, white milk, and honey, gold love—." This line is as authentic as it is resonant, for these are the paradisal goods

—and colors—that Crane associated with his mother. If love and mercy are the fruits of suffering, then, according to the logic of the poem, his suffering deserves to be similarly rewarded.

In "The Hive" the poet makes the most of his vulnerability. He returns good for ill. But the poet who makes so much of suffering is also proud of it because it is somehow allied with the power with which he defends himself. In "Forgetfulness" (1918) that power may "bury the Gods"; in "Chaplinesque" (1921) it is the power of "meek adjustments" not unlike that depicted in "Interior" (1919), the most explicit treatment of what may be considered the second stage in the poet's early development.

In the initial stage the self is not independent; it is identified with an interior, maternal world, which it both clings to and tries to flee. In the second stage the self has acquired a secret independence; without taking flight like the moth, it has discovered itself and within itself the incalculable power of poetry. "Forgetfulness," for example, treats the freedom and glory of the imagination, a power connected with positive emptiness and unconsciousness and represented here in images of what the poet cherishes most. The poem, which defines forgetfulness, begins with song itself, with its liberating power, and this, in turn, is associated with a soaring bird whose wings are "reconciled." Following these images of release and self-possession, as if to mitigate them, are images of comforting, fairy-tale sanctuary, and innocence: rain at night, an old house in the forest, a child. These possibly regressive but certainly harmless images are followed by the blasting whiteness of the imagination's destructive-creative lightning. Partly because of the definitional mode and the cleverness of the concluding line, which closes the poem with its beginning word ("I can remember much forgetfulness"), the poem seems weak. But its progression of images declares an absolute strength, which may be what the poet wishes most to remember.

This strength is secret and putative: it "may stun . . . / Or bury. . . ." Nearer the poet's actual powers are the "evasive victories" Crane mentioned in an account of "Chaplinesque," one of the best early poems on the situation of the poet. It is only necessary to note here that, though Crane considered Chaplin the "prime interpreter of the soul imposed on by modern civilization," he saw in the clown, who is forced to play a "game," the situation of a child as well as a poet, a situation that is bearable because, as with the kitten, a symbol of innocent, defenseless childhood, there are still "Recesses . . . from the fury of the street. . . ."[21] The opening line of the poem enacts the defensive tactic it declares ("We make our meek adjustments"); the cadence falls—adjusts downward. Yet the tone of the poem is not, until the last stanza, as desperate as the situation allows, but somewhat jaunty and defiant. There is cumulative force in the declarative sentences ("we can still love the world," "We will sidestep," "We can evade you, and all else . . .") as well as the force of unimpeachable argument ("What blame to us if the heart live on").

This line, as a letter to Gorham Munson indicates, is a signature ("And yet, the heart [the poet] lives on . . .")[22] and speaks for the kind of vital persistence expressed in "Interior." The title of this poem names the familiar protective enclosure. It is not a garden, though "love blooms" in it, but such a room as Prufrock might have inhabited—one which justifies Leibowitz's characterization of "feminine narcissism" in referring to the world that Crane, following the models of Wilde, Dowson, and Yeats, created.[23] Here, perhaps guiltily, the poet escapes—steals an hour—from the world, his thrice-mentioned adversary; like a truant, he escapes or withdraws from the world—the "real," masculine world—he is expected to enter. For having found in poetry a means of evasion and a space of his own, he is no longer under the necessity to break out. Now it is the world that breaks in.

Though "poor"—small rather than bare, not poor like the cellar-limbo of "Black Tambourine"—his room provides a refuge from the "wide" world. It is not, it seems, an especially erotic place so much as a feminine place of rare spiritual experience, some precious good he feels every right to claim. The plural reference is probably the poet's way of speaking of his own self-unity—the reconciliation that makes the soaring of the bird in "Forgetfulness" so grand.

21. *Letters*, p. 69 (November 3, 1921), p. 85 (May 6, 1922). Crane says that the kitten is his image for the "infinitely gentle, infinitely suffering thing" of Eliot's "Preludes." *Letters*, p. 66 (October 6, 1921).
22. *Letters*, p. 66 (October 6, 1921).
23. *Hart Crane*, p. 26.

And the blooming of love is probably the tardy emergence, permitted by withdrawal into favoring gloom, of the genius of the self. (One remembers Thoreau, in "Wild Apples," protecting the "interior shoot," which, beyond the reach of foes, "darts upward with joy.") The inviolable privacy and special quality of this interior are suggested by the fact that "none [no one else] may know" the mysteries of growth that take place there and that the world must, as it will, "break in"—enter intrusively and aggressively, more thief than he with his stolen hour, and by means, familiar enough to Crane, of "jealous threat and guile." But when it does break in, the blooming of the stolen hour has prepared him to triumph in what otherwise would be defeat: a conclusive victory of spiritual superiority that he enjoys in the hovering turn of the second last line ("The world, at last, must bow and win / Our pity and a smile").[24]

The poem itself is an even greater victory because its artifice creates an aesthetic space, an appropriate interior of the poet's own making, and its accomplishment certifies the mysteries of love's blooming. It may be too smoothly rendered to convince us of actual worldly threat, but it does convince us of his antipathy to the world and his need to protect and nurture the emerging self by means of poetry, his interior work. He would live within a world that he has made and bloom there. That may be why the early poems have so much interior life. Crane's deepest concern in them is with the conditions of love's blooming, with the fostering of the heart to be found not in contact with the exterior world but in contact with the interior world of his own imagination.

The interior of this poem is the self's preferred place, a small world at one remove from the mother but still feminine and closed. It provides the poet's creative necessities; because of such "recesses," it is possible, as he says in "Chaplinesque," to "still love the world." And when he leaves it, as he may be said to in leaving home in March 1923, he tries forever afterward, as the first condition of work, to repossess it. Crane wrote to Charlotte Rychtarik a few months after his departure from Cleveland of his cherished tower room in the house on East 115th Street: "When I think of

24. The cadence of "and none may know," the handling of the last quatrain, and the theme of the poem remind one of Emily Dickinson.

that room, it is almost to give way to tears, because I shall never find my way back to it. It is not necessary, of course, that I should, but just the same it was the center and beginning of all that I am and ever will be, the center of such pain as would tear me to pieces to tell you about, and equally the center of great joys! *The Bridge* seems to me so beautiful,—and it was there that I first thought about it, and it was there that I wrote 'Faustus and Helen,' which Waldo Frank says is so good that I will be remembered by that, whether or not I write more or not. And all this is, of course, connected very intimately with my Mother, my beautiful mother.
. . ." [25]

Allen Tate is right when he says, in the Foreword to *White Buildings*, that "the poems of Hart Crane . . . refer to a central imagination . . . which is at once the motive of the poetry and the form of its realization." That central imagination is of the self and world; and Crane's problem, which Tate worried in several critical essays, is, though not so exclusively a matter of tradition as he maintains, one of the "dissociation of the modern consciousness. . . ." [26] Growth—poetic growth—beyond the confining and finally empty enclosures of the self; the risk of being: this is Crane's problem. Finding himself at home in the congenial world of *fin de siècle* romanticism, a world that embraced him while its melancholy atmosphere of loss anticipated his greatest fear, Crane faced a problem common to the poets of his time: that of giving up the security of a familiar world for a new and chaotic, yet vital modern world. He asks the question of his age in "The Bridge of Estador" (1921): "How can you tell where beauty's to be found?" [27]

Crane's early poems represent a chrysalis stage. Their small, tight, carefully made forms protect interior growth. They are often meditative and subdued. Their lack of intensity is noteworthy; they seem somnolent or dreamy because the poet is withdrawn, not

25. *Letters*, p. 140 (July 21, 1923).
26. Hart Crane, *White Buildings* (New York: Boni & Liveright, 1926), pp. xii–xiii.
27. Crane has not yet reached the point reached earlier by Williams, who asked, in "The Wanderer" (1914), "How shall I be a mirror to this modernity?" Perhaps his appreciation of Williams' *Kora in Hell* (1920), which he read in 1921, is one of the signs that he is beginning to. See Unterecker, *Voyager*, p. 190.

yet ready to burst out. In turning to *fin de siècle* models, Crane found a fitting environment for his nascent imagination. Yet the growth they fostered pressed beyond them, and the poet, who as his letters show is responsive to the outside world, is forced outward. Crane recognized, in "Forgetfulness," that the interior experience of art is itself expansive and shattering and requires a larger space ("freed from beat and measure"), but he avoided the challenge by enclosing the poem in a circle. In "Episode of Hands" (1920), a poem in freer form where he discovers that love exists in the outside world, love itself works the desired miracle ("And factory sounds and factory thoughts / Were banished . . ."). And in "The Bridge of Estador," where the incident of the previous poem is the strongest argument for the beauty to be found in the commonplace everyday world, he still prefers to go the private way of his visionary imagination ("High on the bridge of Estador / Where no one has ever been before") and to remain "Beauty's fool." Crane knows the deadliness of stasis ("Black Tambourine") and the pathos of childlike evasion ("Chaplinesque"), and he notes the limitations of the early poems when he writes that they are "mere shadowings, and too slight to satisfy me." [28] Yet in "Porphyro in Akron," the most ambitious of the early poems and the most "modern" in matter and form, he still tries to maintain a romantic posture.

His tenacity is remarkable. But so is his genius—his capability of growth. These, along with remarkable intelligence and critical awareness of what mattered to him—and mattered to the world and to literature in his time—account for the aspiring works in which the imagination of the early poems, without relinquishing what it values, turns outward to the world and includes the world in its widening circle.

28. *Letters,* p. 71 (November 26, 1921).

two   The Apples, Bill, the Apples!

I

"But the circumstances of one's birth, the conduct of one's parents, the current economic structure of society and a thousand other local factors have as much or more to say about successions to such occupations, the naive volitions of the poet to the contrary." So Crane told Yvor Winters in angry response to Edmund Wilson's admonition to poets to enter public life and follow larger careers than the writing of lyric poetry. He had not found it easy to become a poet nor to survive as one, and though he thought of advertising, for which he had modestly prepared and at which he sometimes worked, as his profession, it was not the kind of profession Wilson had in mind. But Crane had—and this may have prompted his anger as well as the intimation that his case was otherwise—been "born into easy means" and "suavely nourished." He might have gone to a "fashionable university" and succeeded in finding a "courtly occupation." This, rather than Wilson, who was not as uncharitable toward Crane and his work as Crane's response suggests, was probably the cause of his anger; this, and the fact that his career as a poet, in almost every aspect—from its choice and pursuit to its directions and goals—had had so often to be made against advice. Wilson, whose injunctions the poet was actually trying to meet, had merely reminded him at a time of frustration over his work of the frustrations that were his life.[1]

1. *Letters*, p. 298 (May 29, 1927). Wilson's article, "The Muses Out of Work," gave special notice to Crane's *White Buildings* and addressed his own desire to press beyond the influence of Eliot. Reprinted from *The New Republic* (May 11, 1927), the article is in Wilson, *The Shores of Light: A Literary Chronicle of the Twenties and Thirties* (New York: Farrar, Straus and Young, 1952), pp. 197–211.

There was nothing for Crane to complain of in the circumstances of his birth but much to complain of in the conduct of his parents. Like Wilson, he came of New Englanders of colonial lineage who had moved to the West. Both the Cranes and the Harts had settled early in the Western Reserve and established themselves as leading citizens. Garrettsville, Ohio, where Hart Crane was born on July 21, 1899, was dominated by his grandfather, Arthur Crane, who owned a maple-sugar cannery, served as director of the bank, and held the controlling interest in the largest store; and Warren, a larger nearby town to which the family moved in 1904, when Hart's father opened his own maple-syrup factory, had been the home of the Harts, a merchant family that had gone on to Chicago and prospered there. The circumstances of Crane's birth were good, and though his family was not professional, it belonged, like Wilson's, to the comfortable classes and enjoyed the large houses and spacious lawns of that now remote and confident world of solid affluence and respectable culture.[2]

His parents were the favored beings of that world, representatives of the types—or habits of thought—that Veblen brilliantly described in *The Theory of the Leisure Class*, the sociological landmark published in the year of Crane's birth. Clarence Crane had entered Allegheny College only to leave in his second year in order to get on with the business career in which he quickly and admirably succeeded. Grace Hart was the always fashionable girl whose beauty and sentimentality contributed to the genteel idealism that moved others besides her son to chivalric devotion. Both were more complex than the stereotypes which to some extent created their tragedies by limiting their awareness. But both were so much the realization of the stereotypes that they call to mind various characters from the critically realistic literature of the time. In his ardors and boosterism, for example, Clarence Crane is very much like the Lowell Schmaltz of Sinclair Lewis' *The Man Who Knew Coolidge,* and in her coldly selfish gentility, Grace Crane is like the Editha of Howells' story. Hart himself eventually understood them by seeing them in the terms presented to him by the literature and criticism of the cultural coming-of-age that coincided

2. The most detailed biography is Unterecker, *Voyager,* upon which I have relied.

with his own. In *Winesburg, Ohio*, he recognized the puritan world of his boyhood ("I could understand it perfectly myself, having lived for a while in a small town of similar location and colour").[3] And he learned from cultural studies, chiefly those by Van Wyck Brooks and Waldo Frank, how the marriage of his parents perpetuated the union of business and idealism that Brooks said was the foundation of the "acquisitive life"—that pervasive meager "life" against which Brooks summoned the artist to oppose the "creative life," the way of art.

It is easy to see Crane, as he himself sometimes did, as a classic instance of Brooks's theory of the ordeal of the artist. Within these terms his boyhood was "American"—he did not need to create an American background for himself as Williams did—and were one clever enough a case comparable to Twain's, rather than that of errant romanticism advanced by Allen Tate and Yvor Winters, might be made for his "failure." For Crane did not repudiate the goals of his parents: he shared them sufficiently to feel guilty of failing them. To them he owed the boosterism of his comments on the advertising work he hoped to do for *The Little Review* ("To a certain extent I would be my own boss with unrestricted initiative[,] freedom to develop my department systematically and along my own lines"), the chivalric protestations of constancy ("I am always faithful to your love") as well as his liberality with money, hedonistic self-indulgence, sometimes puritan attitudes toward sex, and need to be justified by success.[4] Though he became an artist, he never fully acquired another style of life, but lived, or tried to live, in the large way of his youth, when there was never a question of means and he was suavely nourished. Like Wilson, he saw the economic situation of his manhood from above rather than below —saw it from the vantage of the boy who, when the Cranes moved to Cleveland in 1911, had lived in a substantial house in an excellent neighborhood, had taken the collegiate course at East High School, and toward the proper finishing of his education had

3. This review of Sherwood Anderson's work (P, 208–13) was written in Cleveland in 1921.

4. The quotations are from letters to his mother (October 26, 1917; April 2, 1919) in Thomas S. W. Lewis, "Hart Crane and His Mother: A Correspondence," *Salmagundi*, no. 9 (Spring, 1969), 72, 76.

been given dancing lessons. This world, turning on the house on East 115th Street—on a warm and loving grandmother, a lovely but neurotic mother whose travels interrupted his education, and a father whose assertive masculinity and captaincy of industry probably stand behind the poet's recollection of "Captain Smith, all beard and certainty"—this world was an emotional center impossible to repudiate and was simply lost when the house, upon which Crane for so long fastened for anchorage, was sold in 1925.[5]

Crane criticized the conduct of his parents, all that precipitated their divorce in December 1916, and all that divorce did not, mostly because of the needless misunderstandings of Grace Crane's meddling, conclusively end. That his own profound emotional dependence contributed to "parental absorptions" does not alter their force. He told his mother in an aggressive early letter asserting his right to live that "my youth has been a rather bloody battleground for yours and father's sex life and troubles," and he explained a later episode of disruption and desolation with the following accurate account: "Family affairs and 'fusses' have been my destruction since I was eight years old when my father and mother began to quarrel. That phase only ended recently, and the slightest disturbance now tends to recall with consummate force all the past and its horrid memories on the pretext of the slightest derangement of equilibrium." [6] The divorce of Crane's parents provided the occasion of his first residence in New York City. It freed him for the trial of art but it did not, as his complaint to Winters indicates, set him free.

When Crane came to New York City in December 1916, he entered immediately on what Brooks called "the literary life." His determination to be a poet was already known to his parents; they had encouraged it to the extent of permitting him to visit Elbert

5. Crane sought similar centers in Mrs. Addie Turner's farmhouse in Patterson, New York, and at his grandmother's plantation on the Isle of Pines, where Mrs Sally Simpson cared for him. The house in Cleveland had been his grandmother's. With Mrs. Turner and Mrs. Simpson he found a similar world. Neither generous woman was like his mother. Bessie Meacham, his father's third wife, who made a home for him in the village of Chagrin Falls, belongs with them.

6. *Letters*, pp. 18, 108 (May 19, 1919; December 10, 1922). The first quotation, along with accounts of his reading, shows his familiarity with Freudian ideas.

Hubbard and by bringing him to the attention of Harriet Moody (Mrs. William Vaughn Moody), who confirmed him in his choice of vocation. Now he was sent to New York City in order to be free of family strife and to follow a course of collegiate and artistic preparation, the latter under the informal guidance of Carl Schmitt, a young painter whose study in Europe Crane's Aunt Zell had sponsored. Within a week or so, Crane reported that "things [were] progressing splendidly"—yes, literary things. He had got on with the Colums and had had some poems accepted by Alfred Kreymborg and William Carlos Williams (accepted by *Others* but never published) and he told his grandmother that "my intention is to go right on studying and working at my poetry, and next autumn to enter in for a special course at Columbia." [7] One may read this statement as a declaration of his double purpose and proper goal but also, in view of the actual accomplishment, as a single declaration of intent followed by a dutiful afterthought concerning the expectations of his parents. For both insisted that he be a success and that he find a way to succeed by other means than poetry—the acquisitive life was primary and underwrote the creative life. And his mother, to whom his success had now become necessary to her plans ("our plans," she said, tying to her by terrible bonds the distant boy she called "orphan"), reminded him almost immediately, as she went off to vacation in the South, that "you must not give up the college plan for a minute." [8] Crane's

7. Lewis, "Hart Crane and His Mother," p. 66 (January 7, 1917).
8. The letters of Crane's mother in Thomas S. W. Lewis' article and Unterecker's *Voyager* reveal the cruelty and sentimentality of her claims on a boy of seventeen. In the letter from which I quote, Grace Crane made Hart the consoling burden of her broken married life ("You in my trouble, have been able to pay me for all the care and anxiety I have had for you since you came to me nearly eighteen years ago"). She demanded that he send her his love every day ("I have acquired some specially sized paper for your letters," he told her); the ritual became a matter of "Sunday Specials," special delivery letters to be received promptly on Sunday on penalty of reproof. And she possessed him ("*my* boy") in words both romantic and possessive ("If we dance my partner will not be there—but I shall dance & be happy in thinking of how rich I am in having you—"). Not unwillingly, Hart understood his part in this play of courtly love. In reply to his mother's resentment at his new free life and her reminder that he had a duty to her, he wrote: "Well I haven't seen anybody as fine as you, Mother, and probably won't. . . . How I do long for your ultimate, complete happiness! You are a queen, and shall have it too" (January 2, 1917). He wrote often to his "blessed virtuous Mother" of her beauty

preparation for college was dilatory, and he later regretted it. He advised William Wright to complete his studies because he felt that he had forfeited the security he needed for his art and was frequently distraught by what continued to be his double responsibility.

Still Crane was wise in the way of genius. He seems to have known what Emerson said in "Spiritual Laws": "Each man has his own vocation. The talent is the call. There is one direction in which all space is open to him." And in following his own vocation he was wise to see that the kind of education it required was not to be had at a university—certainly not at Columbia, which Randolph Bourne, a few years earlier, had found so inadequate. Crane did not regret the education he might have had at college, only the certification he needed for a "courtly occupation"; college, not publication in the little magazines, was the sign of his class and the passport to employment. He was not damned by lack of education, as many of his critics maintain, but by lack of dollars, or, since he sometimes had enough of them, by the discipline of getting them and the loss of self-respect he felt on failing to get them. He knew how to educate himself, to find the nurture he needed— one of the reasons his example is attractive to poets. To read his letters—great letters whose lively intelligence repudiates his critics, valuable letters, too, because they record this education—is to see that in a few years the education in the arts he had acquired was as good as that to be had in any university, and far better in respect to contemporary developments. It might even be argued that the genteel literary education provided by the universities would have shored up the weakest element of his early poems and hindered his already difficult emergence as a modern poet.

Now that the university (the university-city) is so much the center of the arts we may forget that in Crane's time the center was elsewhere, outside the university and, actually, spread over the city. How, for example, shall we estimate the importance to Crane's education of Richard Laukhuff's bookstore in the Taylor

---

and, having suggested that she enter the movies, may have awakened the dream of glamorous youth in which she persisted. And at this time he conceded her wish, in fairness to the Harts ("your mother's side of the house"), that he sign his poetry "Hart Crane." That signature is his mother's lasting mark.

Arcade in Cleveland, where Crane discovered *Bruno's Weekly* and *The Pagan*, the little magazines in which he was first published, and the places (also bookstores) to which he turned when he arrived in New York? In those days—the phrase *is* nostalgic—bookstores were literary institutions comparable in importance to "291," the little gallery of Alfred Stieglitz, to which Crane turned later. The proprietor of such places was often an editor and exhibitor, and always a teacher, and "any time of day," as John Unterecker says of Laukhuff's, "one could drop in on what became a kind of continuing seminar." [9] Crane used the city, as European students still often do, as an artistic resource; he went to plays, concerts, exhibitions, dance recitals; he bought books, current novels as well as expensive art books, and records; he discussed art with artists, writers, and editors—a mere boy, he did not postpone the literary life but lived it now. Within a short time of his arrival in New York, he became an associate editor of *The Pagan* (from 1916 to 1919 he published ten poems and four prose pieces in this magazine, a "fetid corpse," he later called it), and he became well known to the editors of *The Little Review*, who carefully criticized his work and eventually published some of it.[10] Brom Weber is right, in a chapter of his study of Crane entitled "Emergence," to treat the literary milieu and, in particular, the little magazines of the time. These magazines were a cultural sign of the times, and by contributing to Crane's education contributed to his emergence.

Crane's first residence in New York City, like almost every period of his life, was disturbed by the demands of his mother. In the spring of 1917, when she came, with Grandmother Hart, to live with him in a small apartment in Gramercy Park, she diverted much of his literary life to her own social and personal needs. In the summer Hart returned to Cleveland to witness the terrible fiasco of her hoped-for reconciliation and remarriage, and in the following months, once again in New York, he helped her through a nervous breakdown. He didn't enter Columbia, and the instruction in French he began to take that fall seems to have been directed toward his literary career rather than college entrance

9. *Voyager*, p. 47.
10. *Letters*, p. 31 (January 28, 1920).

(Latin, German, and philosophy were the subjects he once intended to get up).[11] The following spring he returned home in answer to his mother's personal and patriotic pleading and worked for some time in a munitions plant and for the Cleveland *Plain Dealer*; but finding his mother difficult to live with because of her distress over Clarence Crane's remarriage, he returned to New York early in 1919. There he remained until November, when another summons—an invitation from his father to work his way up in the candy business—brought him home again. This ended Crane's first attempt to lead a literary life—"this trying time," as he once retorted to his mother's complaints about money, "when I am making every possible effort to get started in something." [12]

Crane got a footing in New York and saw the literary prospect. But the education and literary experimentation that did most to bring him forward followed his first residence there; it took place in Cleveland. There is little indication of growth in the poetry he had written or published in New York, and his literary recognition there was partly due to this. His first literary acquaintances were well-meaning but already old-fashioned teachers who confirmed him in the old rather than helped him to find the new. Padraic Colum, for example, gave him a ticket to a reading by Vachel Lindsay and presented him to the Poetry Society of America, and in one of their frequent talks told him to read Arthur Symons' *The Symbolist Movement in Literature*, the book published in the year of Crane's birth that had introduced the French symbolists to the English-speaking world and that now provided him with a persuasive guide to the kind of literature or the literary goals to which he had already given his allegiance. Guido Bruno, the sentimental genteel bohemian and Village apostle who edited *Bruno's Weekly*, revered Oscar Wilde and published his poems and work about him, along with the poetry of others less revered but also "decadent" (the word first used to describe the symbolists), like Ernest Dowson and Edgar Allan Poe. Of contemporary native poets Bruno promoted those, like Charles Keeler, who had the gift of "poesy." Keeler's poem, "I Sing," printed in the July 19, 1915,

11. *Letters*, p. 5 (January 5, 1917).
12. *Letters*, p. 18 (May 30, 1919).

issue, is an example of the kind and quality of verse being published during Crane's apprenticeship:

> My songs are incense
> Burning up my heart
> In this temple of love,
> All for thee, my dear one.
>
> If they give joy
> Unto thee in the burning,
> Let them be wafted afar
> When the ashes of my heart are cold.

This poem is a fair indication of the general state of American poetry and helps one understand why Crane's first poems, so much more advanced and accomplished, were readily printed. Joseph Kling's choices for *The Pagan*, gathered later in *Pagan Anthologies*, though better, were similar and represented little that was new.[13] Even *The Little Review*, which accepted Crane's "In Shadow" in September 1917, stood in need of the admonishment Ezra Pound gave Crane upon its publication: "Beauty is a good enough egg, but so far as I can see, you haven't the ghost of a setting hen or an incubator."[14]

What progress Crane was making toward the new was for the most part unexpressed or unapparent in his poems. One begins to notice it in his interest in Pound and Joyce, in his appreciation of Cézanne and the post-impressionists, and in his praise of Baudelaire and Joyce for having "a penetration into life common to only the greatest."[15] And this progress, though prompted by many things and in many ways in that heady time of cultural resurgence, owed most, undoubtedly, to Gorham Munson and Matthew Josephson, young men also at the beginning of literary careers, whom Crane met, one at the office of *The Pagan*, the other at *The Little Review*. They gave him, as only youth can, the immediate sustenance of enthusiasm, ideas, criticism, and recognition—of a high and wholly shared destiny. Of the two, Munson was the closest,

---

13. They included Crane's "October–November," "Fear," and "Forgetfulness."

14. Cited by Horton, *Hart Crane*, p. 57. Pound had recently become foreign editor of the magazine.

15. P, 199.

the most helpful, constant, and generous, as Crane, back in Cleveland, acknowledged in November 1921, when he told his distant friend that his "bright kindly letters" were "a lantern of hope" (the allusion is to Queequeg's situation in *Moby-Dick*) and that he wondered "if, without you, I should have kept writing so long." [16]

The desolation remarked in this letter refers more to Crane's confusion of direction than to any lack of stimulus or accomplishment. New theories had filled his head every day, as he told Munson on his return home, and in the following months he had reached "blind alleys and found no way out of them. . . ." [17] But the desolation, to which a long period of joblessness and family difficulties also contributed, was, as often with Crane in his early years, the ebb from a full tide that foretold another. When he quit working for his father in April 1921—a decisive break, at least from his father's business expectations for him, and a break in employment not unusual with Crane when pressed by creative necessity—he turned immediately to the cultural resources of Cleveland, from which the demanding routine of the factory had kept him for more than a year. That spring he met William Sommer, a painter who answered his needs for a surrogate father as well as articulate aesthetician (Sommer himself had been recently "liberated" by the cubist revolution and introduced Crane to Roger Fry's *Vision and Design*). And soon Crane was part of an art circle so stimulating to him that he did not feel deprived, at a time when Munson and other friends had gone to Paris, by being in "Cleveland, Cuyahoga County, God's country." [18] For Crane was learning not only that "genius . . . may walk in Cleveland," as he said of Ernest Bloch, but that it could be nurtured there. [19] The excitement of this quickening time is conveyed in his letters: "A new light and friend of my friend, the Swiss-French painter, Willy Lescaze," he wrote Munson, "has arrived in town,—Jean Binet, teacher of Eurythmics in our very alive Cleveland School of Music which Ernest Bloch heads. I am to meet him tonight and with some anticipations, as I am told he is a remarkable and in-

16. *Letters*, p. 69 (November 1, 1921); see also pp. 75–76.
17. *Letters*, pp. 25, 29 (November 22, 1919; June 12, 1921).
18. *Letters*, pp. 54–55, 57, 78–79 (April 10, May 16, 1921; January 23, 1922).
19 *Letters*, p. 82 (March 2, 1922).

spired pianist, playing Erik Satie, Ravel, etc., to perfection. Lescaze has proved an inspiration to me. Knowing intimately the work of Marcel Proust, Salmon, Gide, and a host of other French moderns, he is able to see so much better than anyone else around here, the aims I have in my own work. We have had great times discussing the merits of mutual favorites like Joyce, Donne, Eliot, Pound, de Gourmont, Gordon Craig, Nietzsche, etc., ad infinitum. After this it goes without saying that I never found a more stimulating individual in N. Y." [20] The months that followed, during which he wrote "For the Marriage of Faustus and Helen" and began to contemplate *The Bridge*, were the most rapid and concentrated in his development. They remind one of Melville's sudden growth and of his comment on it: "Three weeks have scarcely passed . . . that I have not unfolded within myself." [21]

Matthew Josephson remembers that when he first met Crane and they had exchanged poems, his response to Crane's had been unfavorable: "They were 'old-fashioned' or 'Swinburnian,' I declared, and what could be worse? In my youthful arrogance I even recommended that he throw them away and do something 'modern.' " [22] The spirit and point of this recollection are exact. Josephson, soon to become an advocate of dada, was a gadfly in behalf of current developments. He forced Crane, as the resistance of his letters shows, to confront them and carefully test their usefulness to him. He made the "modern," which he rightly sets off in quotation marks, the desideratum of the new poetry.

Crane was already aware of this.[23] It was part of the creative confusion he felt when he returned to Cleveland in November 1919. But for all the excitement of new theories, he was not yet ready to abandon the kind of poetry he had been writing; his poetic development followed inner necessities rather than programs. So he made his way home—his way back—over the bridge of a still

20. *Letters*, pp. 66–67 (October 6, 1921).

21. Letter to Hawthorne, 1851, in *Herman Melville: Representative Selections*, ed. Willard Thorp (New York: American Book Co., 1938), p. 393.

22. *Life among the Surrealists* (New York: Holt, Rinehart and Winston, 1962), p. 64.

23. In 1919 Crane published three poems in *The Modernist* and one in *The Modern School*.

somewhat old-fashioned poem. "My Grandmother's Love Letters," which he began on the eve of his departure and completed sometime after his arrival, expresses his uncertainty over this transition. In it one recognizes his familiar impasse: his love and his need for love, the eager reaching out of the one and the doubtfulness of response to the other. The desire that moves his memory of home and love unerringly finds the object that best represents the assurance of both. It turns to his grandmother and not to his mother, who is evoked but dismissed (or if not dismissed, instructed in motherliness) in the phrase, "my mother's mother," and by the act of calling his grandmother by her regal name and giving it the sovereignty of a single line. But this desire-moving-memory creates, in turn, the vast "space" (or time) that memory itself must span and fails to span because it is checked, in the attempt, by the poet's knowledge of fragile connection and difficult repossession. Like Whitman in "A Noiseless Patient Spider," Crane proceeds in the certainty of doubt. As the careful sensitivity of the poem and the acknowledged need for gentleness indicate, he is not confident that "the bridge you need will be form'd" or "the ductile anchor hold"; and having failed to reach backward to the certain ground of love, he feels uncertain of moving forward ("And so I stumble").

When he did move forward it was always because love moved him. We sometimes overlook this agency of Crane's development, but he did not. He was never reticent about his feelings of love or his love affairs because love, as he told Munson, was "the strongest incentive to the imagination, or, at least, the strongest in my particular case." [24] He reports his love affairs with the same candor and intensity that he reports the writing of poems, and they belong in the chronology of his creative life because they contributed so much to it.

His first affair followed his homecoming. He "embarked" on it in Akron, where he had been sent to tend his father's recently opened candy store, and he celebrated it in "Garden Abstract." [25] The first version of this explicitly phallic poem is spoken by the poet in unimpeded lines of simple purity; the final version is both more formally shaped and objectified (as a woman's experience)

24. *Letters*, pp. 46–47 (November 23, 1920).
25. *Letters*, p. 26 (December 13, 1919); see also p. 37.

and, if lacking the immediacy of the first, is superior in its expression of the kinetics of possession and of living in the fullness of the suspended moment of the eternal now ("She has no memory, nor fear, nor hope / Beyond the grass and shadows at her feet").[26] These lines closing the poem, bringing desire to its end, also bring an end to beyonding. The poem is an "abstract" in the Blakean sense; it relates a universal fable of desire and consummation, the fable of innocent emotion, of Edenic timelessness and bliss, that underlies Crane's poetry.

Another poem of this time—of the months immediately following the brief period in Akron, when Crane worked in his father's factory—tells of his discovery of love in the adversary world he had now entered. The world of "Episode of Hands" is new to Crane. It is not the world of "Interior," but the "real" world, the man's world of the factory, the machine, the worker, and the relationship here is not one of Love's tardy blooming but of a warm, comradely affection that is satisfying to him because of its open responsiveness. The incident of the poem, or "episode," Crane told Munson, was autobiographical but not, as Munson believed, of sociological significance; Crane was not concerned with class war but with other suspicions.[27] He may have used the poem as an oblique way of telling of his homosexual love. It dramatizes homoerotic discovery, and makes it an occasion of the external world. He knew and admired Sherwood Anderson's story "Hands" and sent the poem to him (as much for that, perhaps, as for the honesty of the narrative approach he had employed); and he was probably familiar with Whitman, with the "Bunch" poem alluded to here, Whitman's fondness for "roughs," and his role as a wound dresser. For the poem involves both: the initial reluctance or suspicion of male contact ("The unexpected interest made him flush"—the reference is rightly ambiguous) and the wound-dressing by which the "knot [of love] was tightened / [And] the two men smiled into each other's eyes").

"Episode" speaks for the brevity and singleness of the occasion but not for its importance to Crane. The lines just cited provide the poem with one of Crane's happiest and most consummate

26. For the first version, see Weber, *Hart Crane*, p. 76.
27. *Letters*, p. 37 (April 14, 1920).

closures—with an end beyond which he needn't go because there is nothing beyond it; with an experience, in its reciprocity, richer even than that of "Garden Abstract." "The two men smiled into each other's eyes": more than anything for Crane, the smile—it will become obsessive—is the seal of love, the touchstone of response with which he tries it, as later, in "Van Winkle," where the poet recalls the "unconscious smile / My mother almost brought me once. . . ." It figures now in another relation, an episode of hands in which the homoerotic associations, like the suspicion, give way to filial-parental feelings—to a purity of feeling like that of "Garden Abstract." The poet evokes this relationship by naming it ("the factory owner's son"), by noting the signs of experience in the "wide / Deep hand," "that larger, quieter hand / That lay in his," and, most of all, by investing it with pastoral significance, indeed making it a pastoral assuring world powerful enough (as love is powerful) to "banish" the actual world of "factory sounds and factory thoughts. . . ." [28] But even with its power to banish the industrial world, this imagery of the pastoral world is not necessarily a way of escape from it; we are in fact recalled to it by the very lines that "banish" it, and it is subtly connected with it by the imagery of sunlight. Instead, the pastoral imagery is the sign of the poet's recognition of the wonder of the new emotion and its values, the wonder of a new world of love, which reminds him of the earliest universe of love. The pastoral restores a preferred world, the free landscape of peace and play, of childhood, when the father was loving, when one was not under the necessity of withdrawing into an interior world or of having "factory thoughts"; and for the poet who has entered the industrial world it represents the condition (actually lacking in Crane's account of working for his father) that would make it acceptable to him. The significance of this episode for Crane's development, as we see in his attempt to write more directly of the exterior world and in the prominence he gives this episode in "The Bridge of Estador," is in his willingness, because of this emotional discovery, to make the exterior world a part of his experience.

A poem's importance is not, of course, the measure of its achievement. "Episode of Hands" is a new departure for Crane, a break

28. See "Fear": "Give me your hands, / Friends! . . ."

into a new world of experience, and he is not yet expert in dealing with it. He relies most for narrative example on Anderson, but also on Frost (the matter-of-fact directness of the opening stanzas recalls "Out, Out—" published in 1916) and Edwin Arlington Robinson (for the cadence of the lines beginning "And as the fingers . . .").[29] The poem belongs with other "entering" poems of the time, with "Porphyro in Akron," which follows the example of Eliot in *Prufrock and Other Observations* (1917), and "The Bridge of Estador," which follows that of Williams in "The Wanderer," published in *Al Que Quiere!* (1917). And we must remember that at the same time he was working in other ways and considering other elements of his experience. Sometimes, though more skillfully, he worked in familiar ways, as in "A Persuasion" and "Pastorale." More often he worked in ways new to him both in materials—again in more direct response to the exterior world—and in manner of treatment—more classically objective and formally rigorous—as in "Black Tambourine" and "Chaplinesque," poems in which the difficulties of form encountered in "Porphyro in Akron" and "The Bridge of Estador" seem to be resolved in ways more agreeable to him.

Neither "Porphyro in Akron" nor "The Bridge of Estador" provided models sufficiently suitable to Crane to be developed further by him. But both experiments contributed to the making of "For the Marriage of Faustus and Helen," the poem that concluded Crane's residence in Cleveland with a climactic creation whose importance actually lay ahead of him in *The Bridge*, the poem to which it gave birth. These poems constitute a development—contain each other, as *The Bridge* may be said to contain "Faustus and Helen." They represent a major thread of concern, for all of them treat the problem presented to the poet by the "modern."

It is easier to tell how the "modern" stood to Crane than how he stood to it, the latter requiring nothing less than a full account of his work. When Whitman said that "the direct trial of him who

---

29. Milne Holton also notes the debt to Frost as well as other debts in the early poems to Stevens and perhaps to Sandburg. See " 'A Baudelairesque Thing': The Directions of Hart Crane's 'Black Tambourine,' " *Criticism*, IX (Summer, 1967), 219.

would be the greatest poet is today," he stated a condition that the greatest poets of Crane's time, he among them, acknowledged, if not always in Whitman's fashion of open acceptance.[30] The "modern" was "today," the immediate external world. But it was also those aspects of today that were most contemporary—newest, most vital (and "vulgar") and overwhelming. The "modern" was the democratic or popular culture of industrialism, all that the critics designated by "the Machine." This is what Josephson meant by "modern" and what Crane meant when, in the case of Cuthbert Wright, he expressed exasperation with "the *young* [who] turn their heads and wag them despairingly at every modern manifestation." [31] This was the "modern" to which Josephson pressed Crane in their correspondence and to which Crane responded in poems like "Chaplinesque," a "sympathetic attempt," he said, "to put in words some of the Chaplin pantomime, so beautful, and so full of eloquence, and so modern." [32] To the extent that he accepted such materials of contemporary society Crane becomes a "modern." Robert Lowell seems to regard him as an urban poet, and others, taking Crane seriously at his word, think of him as a *"Pindar . . . of the machine age."* [33]

But the "modern" for Crane, as his letters to Josephson show, was a troubling situation rather than a simple issue of materials to be solved in Josephson's fashion. His reservations were profound and anticipate those of Edmund Wilson's imaginary dialogue between Josephson and Paul Rosenfeld, where Crane would have found himself on the defensive, in the more traditional position of Rosenfeld, upholding as modern *Ulysses* and *The Waste Land*, which Wilson has Josephson, the dadaist *provocateur*, cavalierly

30. Preface (1855), *Leaves of Grass*.
31. *Letters*, p. 100 (Summer, 1922).
32. *Letters*, p. 65 (October 1, 1921).
33. "Robert Lowell," a *Paris Review* interview reprinted in *Robert Lowell: A Collection of Critical Essays*, ed. Thomas Parkinson (Englewood Cliffs: Prentice-Hall, 1968), p. 32; *Letters*, p. 129 (March 2, 1923). Crane is an urban poet as much or as little as Boris Pasternak, whose hero in *Doctor Zhivago* writes of this time that "cities are the only source of inspiration for a new, truly modern art" and that "the living language of our time, born spontaneously and naturally in accord with its spirit, is the language of urbanism," but whose own imagery is taken mostly from country life. *Doctor Zhivago*, trans. Max Hayward, Manya Harari, and Bernard Guerney (New York: New American Library, 1958), p. 406.

deny. Though imaginary and intentionally discordant, this dialogue speaks for a major cultural crisis and for the difficulties of reconciliation presented by polarities, especially, as in this instance, where "old" and "new" accord more with differences between humanist and "modern" views of culture than with the critics' actual partisanship in the cause of new art. The point of Wilson's dialogue respects the continuity of culture: that the smart-alecky young, represented by Josephson ("I tell you that culture as you understand it is no longer of any value"), consider Rosenfeld, an ardent proponent of the new who refused to countenance a break in culture, an old fogey to be dispensed with. This point, with all it meant in cultural violence and chaos, was not lost on Crane, whose own emotional needs gave him a stake as large as Rosenfeld's in much that Josephson thought obsolete.[34]

Crane did not easily accommodate the "modern" because his own experience of the machine and of advertising neither matched Josephson's claims ("It is the writer of advertising who forges its [America's] literature") nor altered the adversary aspect of the industrial world, and because Munson, the critic closest to him, had shown him both its challenging centrality and complexity. At the time of Crane's initial experiments with the "modern," Munson was developing the critical point of view of his first book, *Waldo Frank: A Study* (1923); and during the time of Crane's efflorescence—the period of composing "Faustus and Helen"—he read the book twice, once in manuscript when Munson came to Cleveland in July 1922, and again, early in 1923, when he went over the proofs in preparation for reviewing it. The importance to Crane of this small essay in criticism was enormous—of a focal, seminal, and catalytic nature. It not only turned him to Waldo Frank (Crane first wrote to Frank in November 1922, and was heartened by the older writer's sympathetic response); it established for him the literary connection that he had not been ready to make during his first residence in New York, and at the opportune moment charted the direction and dimensions of his most ambitious work.

Munson begins his study by noting the appearance, in November 1916, of *The Seven Arts* and by rehearsing the elements of its program for an American art. What Crane either missed or neglected

34. "The Poet's Return," *The Shores of Light*, pp. 125–40.

earlier he was now reminded of: the isolation of the American
artist and his need for an audience, the necessity of the artist's
work in bringing America to consciousness, the primary example of
Whitman—and reminded of them as continuing, still-crucial issues.
Munson brilliantly summarized Frank's *Our America* (1919),
which Crane had read on its appearance when he was keeping
shop in Akron. Then he had found Frank's analysis true but terribly
pessimistic and had been disturbed by his "extreme national con-
sciousness"; and he had fended off its influence or program—he
called it propaganda—by noting how creatively restrictive the book
would have been to "men like Dreiser, Anderson, Frost . . . in
their early days." [35] Now he read this "unanswerable" book in
fuller awareness of the fact that its cultural diagnosis was not orig-
inal with nor limited to Frank but represented a school of critical
thought—"synthesize[d]," as Munson said, "the researches of Ran-
dolph Bourne and Van Wyck Brooks"—and that the issues it
raised were general and were becoming his own.[36] This response to
Our America is one of the signs of Crane's emergence.

Munson's study of Frank, which he wrote on returning from
Europe, declared his allegiance to *The Seven Arts* group.[37] It was a
sign that some of the youngest generation had espoused its ideas,
and more than any of the critical studies by the older writers
(themselves the original younger generation of the pre-war period)
it helped Crane place himself and see his development in terms
of the cultural situation and focused for him, within those
terms, the profound significance of the Machine. These critics,
according to Munson, had shown in their psychological histories
of puritan-pioneer-industrial America how "service to Machinery
ha[d] adopted the pioneer-puritan life-denying attitudes and ha[d]
stratified them into a permanent extraversion." Frank, especially,
had shown, in Munson's resumé of *Our America*, how the dom-
inant "rhythm" of such an industrial society had "perverted talents
like that of Jack London and genius like that of Mark Twain,
devitalized church and university, theater and press, buried Amerin-
dian culture, distilled the air-brew of transcendentalism, spawned

35. *Letters*, pp. 26–27 (December 13, 1919).
36. *Waldo Frank: A Study* (New York: Boni & Liveright, 1923), p. 19.
37. Van Wyck Brooks accepted Munson's articles for *The Freeman*.

the limited philosophy of utility called pragmatism, produced Los Angeles, the city without a voice, discarded the inner life of man." [38]

The Machine, in this view, is identified with the "extravert," the sometimes brutal but always inescapable force of the external world, and set against Life, the vital, spiritual force of the inner world. And as Munson maintains, it is conspicuously modern and disruptive, the new alien factor in the balanced equation of man and nature ("It is Machinery that has broken up our former equations"). But granting this, Munson refuses to reject the Machine or accept it, as Frank does, as a "necessary evil" to be offset by "native counter-forms." He resists the melodrama of capitalized forces, the "pernicious antagonism between the values of [L]ife and Machinery" because, like many of the youngest generation, he has felt the attraction of the Machine ("such phenomena as our skyscrapers, bridges, motion pictures, jazz music, electric light displays, advertising"—phenomena that may be "the peculiar genius of the American people thrusting up into a new age"), and he prefers, with the dadaists, to recast the cultural equation and "bring the Machine into the scope of the human spirit." He shares the dadaist's positive rather than negative aim ("to destroy the existent counter-forms to Machinery") but only because America, unlike Europe, is already too far advanced in mechanization (the dadaists, Rosenfeld says in Wilson's imaginary dialogue, "have made a sort of cult of America") and too little possessed of counter-forms to resist it. And so, while encouraging an attitude of acceptance toward the Machine, Munson proposes as "our immediate task" the "creation and strengthening of our counter-forms, the building up of our reserves." [39]

Our America was one of these counter-forms, and a most instructive one to Crane. Munson's treatment of it stressed its spiritual significance: its connection with Whitman's belief that "the real and permanent grandeur of These States must be their Religion" and its advocacy of Frank's own concern with "mystical realism"— with "the hierarchy of Consciousness," the "dimensions" of experience entered by great mystics like Whitman, and the religious

38. *Waldo Frank*, pp. 20–21.
39. *Waldo Frank*, pp. 21–25.

man's awareness of himself "as a parabolic force. . . ." Munson said that it reasserted the values of Life and gathered into a tradition those writers who "inspire us with faith, help us find new gods to replace the old we cannot worship." The book, he noted, was a synthesis and a history—characteristics that Crane found applicable to *The Bridge*. And its purpose, which Munson described in Frank's words ("to lift America into self-knowledge that shall be luminous so that she may shine, vibrant so that she may be articulate"), was one that Crane grandly fulfilled in "Atlantis." In this section of *The Bridge*, the first he set down, he tried to overcome the dualism of subject and object represented by Life versus the Machine, and to avoid the extremes of solitary vision and "American Fact," against which Frank had warned, by transforming the Machine itself into a counter-form.[40]

At first the Machine was resistant, and Crane's counter-form was romance.[41] In both "Porphyro in Akron" and "The Bridge of Estador," the world of the Machine is introduced and recognized but, finally, not accepted. "Porphyro in Akron," the longest of the early poems, is clearly a new departure, an attempt to make something of the Akron experience by using the "modern" poetic means with which the Machine had been treated in poetry. For these means Crane owed most to Eliot and Laforgue—and perhaps to Apollinaire.[42] Formally the poem has a "modern" appearance, the "broken effect" Crane identified with literary cubism;[43] and like many modern poems it employs a persona (the poet), a subjective center and associational mode, and takes up "vulgar" or antipoetic materials. But of most importance, perhaps, is its indebtedness of

40. *Waldo Frank*, pp. 21, 28–29, 20, 11–12. Crane's suspicion of sentimentality in Frank's mysticism did not countervail its influence. See *Letters*, pp. 98–99 (Summer, 1922).

41. Romance, Munson noted, was a counter-form neglected by Frank. *Waldo Frank*, p. 28.

42. Eliot's "The Love Song of J. Alfred Prufrock," "Preludes," and "Morning at the Window" seem to have been the most important examples. For Crane's comment on the first two poems, see *Letters*, p. 90 (June 12, 1922); for his debt to the last, see the early version of "Porphyro in Akron," in Weber, *Hart Crane*, pp. 89–92.

43. *Letters*, pp. 121, 51 (February 9, 1923; January 14, 1921). This "crudeness of form," he says in the last letter cited, was "deliberate."

theme: the "traditionalist" modern theme of the sterility of the modern world.

The title itself establishes the ironic attitude of the poem, the elements of romance and reality that only irony can bring together, and only briefly, in the poem. Composed of three sections (like "Faustus and Helen"), the poem moves in a temporal sequence that will become characteristic—here that of morning, noon, and night, a sequence which is also one of consciousness-turned-outward drawing back to itself. In the first section, the poet, who it seems would be at least an observer of the industrial scene, or in some way make significant contact with it, is from the opening line its ironic commentator. He strives in the first stanza for a descriptive neutrality, but this is compromised immediately by his awareness of the anomalous: the night shift of factory workers who, dead-alive like the crowd that flows over London Bridge in the winter dawn of *The Waste Land*, greet the dawn with weariness and spiritual heaviness. And this is compromised too because he has chosen a phenomenon of industrial life—not the Machine itself but one of its consequences—that can be exploited for cultural shock and the exasperation with it that he expresses in the next stanza:

> Akron, "high place,"—
> A bunch of smoke-ridden hills
> Among rolling Ohio hills.

By restoring the Greek meaning of Akron and suggesting its religious import in "greeting the dawn," Crane sets up the fundamental opposition of the poem between the old and the new civilization, the past and the present—an opposition that includes on the side of the old both the pastoral ("rolling Ohio hills": the Indian name is meaningful) and the romantic or poetic.[44] The third stanza ex-

---

44. The image of "muddy water" anticipates "The River." Time, in its flowing over the "cross-lines," evokes a vague sentiment of religious loss—loss of the eternal, represented by the hills. The suggestion of an imposed grid system prefigures the opening stanza of "Faustus and Helen." The imagery also recalls another poem by Keats—"Sleep and Poetry":

> The visions all are fled . . .
> .   .   .   .
> A sense of real things comes doubly strong,
> And, like a muddy stream, would bear along
> My soul to nothingness. . . .

plicitly names the Greek in reference to the present strife of immigrants—exists mostly for this and the poet's ironic comment on present and past: "And the Fjords and the Aegean are remembered." And this irony turns the poem to the more desperate irony of the last stanza, where, in syntactically similar lines whose dying fall emphasizes his defeat or spiritlessness, he confesses his uselessness and alienation—a forced exclusion, it seems—from the modern.

> The plough, the sword,
> The trowel,—and the monkey wrench! [45]
> O City, your axles need not the oil of song.
> I will whisper words to myself
> And put them in my pockets.
> I will go and pitch quoits with old men
> In the dust of a road.

Each stanza of this sequence develops the same fundamental contrast, while the pauses between them add to their cumulative weight. At its close the poet, who presumably stands in South Main Street, will seek out some anonymous road (or, actually, by way of a compensatory Sunday, an anonymous room). But his defeat is too easy: he grants too soon the inutility of poetry, which is thereby placed with the old in opposition to the new, and he too readily adopts the attitudes of others, as the echoes of Eliot, Williams, and Anderson show. He is too willing to address only himself, to follow the unhappy example of Dr. Reefy, who put paper pills in his pocket (the allusion to *Winesburg, Ohio* summons that book with all of its tremulous adolescent feeling about the city); too willing to join the old men in their old-fashioned, Old World sport or, like Williams in "Ballet," to see in the loneliness of the poetic vocation defiance of those who do not need him. His pessimism is facile, and fashionable. He knows the modern theme too well and is not, like Williams in "An After Song" or Eliot in "Prufrock," sufficiently disquieted by it.[46] And his irony is a matter

45. The image is perhaps less shocking to those who remember Chaplin's *Modern Times*.

46. "Ballet" was published in *Others*, III (December, 1916); "An After Song" was first published in *The Tempers* (London: Elkin Mathews, 1913).

more of tone and posture than of awareness. It is defensive and self-protective, exclusive rather than admissive, not used to reconcile the old and the new, the romantic and the modern, but to maintain the former in the face of the demands of the latter.

The second section of the poem treats the poet's experience of the immigrants introduced in section one and, by contrasting the goals of their Americanization with their Old World culture (the theme of Bourne's famous essay on trans-national America), confirms the cultural detritus, the emptiness the poet has already found in the modern world. Crane himself had enjoyed just such relief from prohibition America and his mother's prohibition as the episode recorded here presents—relief from the Machine that critics claimed was allied in America with life-denying, puritan attitudes.[47] The good feeling of this occasion is evident in the easy narrative sweep that ends with the certifying line: "And we overpayed because we felt like it."

This section depicts the poet in contact with a world, an Old World community, where he can abandon irony. His host will not be an American ("Using the latest ice-box and buying Fords") but, when rich enough, will return to his native countryside, while his wife, the mountain of a woman who perhaps portends Crane's "Interludium," will undoubtedly continue her fertile career. Against this background, so earthy in its warm humanity, both the first section but especially the last are set. This, the last section, connects profoundly with the previous sections: to the poet's resignation in the first and, by way of the pastoral configuration in the second, to all that "Among rolling Ohio hills" means to him. Sections one and three probably belong to the same present time—all of the poem, in fact, is in the present of meditation and may have had its origin in the poet's situation at the end and be the journey of thought in which he goes back to discover how he got there. But section two is reminiscent of another time and, as reminiscence and for what it remembers, is associated with the memory of childhood that the poet finally recalls. This memory is at work throughout the poem and represents a reverie more vital to the poet than that on modern civilization, though it is connected with it because it holds

47. See *Letters*, pp. 28, 29–30 (December 27, 1919; January 9, 1920). Harry is Harry Candee, whom Crane met in Akron.

for him those reasons of the heart that explain his persistence in romance and his inability to give himself to his own time. The poet who remembers the fjords and the Aegean may be said to remember too much, and if his poem seems inconclusive, it is most likely because of his refusal to explore this deep and dangerous memory. And irony, again, is his recourse, although now it is not directed at the modern world but, in terms of the realities of that world, at himself, alone in the enclosure that he knows can no longer protect him and that represents his defeat.

"The Bridge of Estador," finished in April 1921, about the time Crane left his father's employ, treats the "modern" with bravado, perhaps because of this. ("The best thing is that the cloud of my father is beginning to move from the horizon now," he told Munson, ". . . and in time we *both* may discover some new things in me. *Bridges burn't behind!*") [48] The bravado takes the form of "An Impromptu Aesthetic TIRADE," as Crane subtitled the poem, probably in the manner of Williams' "The Wanderer: A Rococo Study," and it is to be seen most in his repudiation of Williams' proposal to ground poetry in the everyday world of one's immediate contacts and in the decision instead to follow the high road of vision.[49] Crane admired Williams' early poems and was pleased with his comments in *Contact*.[50] But the question that "The Wanderer" inspired him to ask was not quite Williams' "How shall I be a mirror to this modernity?" but "How can you tell where beauty's to be found?" How crucial the difference in emphasis was for Crane, Williams himself noted in an obituary article on Crane's career in which he pays him the genuine respect of unsparing criticism: "Crane didn't write as low as he knew, or should have known, his life to be. Instead he continually reached 'up,' out of what he *knew*, to that which he didn't know. . . . He grew vague instead of setting himself to describe in detail. . . . His eyes seem to me often to have been blurred by 'vision' when they should have been

48. *Letters*, p. 55 (April 20, 1921).

49. For an association of aesthetics with "tirade," see *Letters*, pp. 71–72 (November 26, 1921).

50. Their relation, which began with Crane's submission of poems to *Others*, in 1916, is treated by Joseph Evans Slate, "William Carlos Williams, Hart Crane, and 'The Virtue of History,'" *University of Texas Studies in Language and Literature*, IV (Winter, 1965), 486–511.

held hard, as hard as he could hold them, on the object. . . ." [51]
Williams, of course, is advocating his own remarkable attentiveness
and his willingness to answer the question of "The Wanderer" by
giving himself, as he does in the marriage of that poem, to his
environment in all of its sordidness and vulgarity. Beauty for him
is as much the goal of quest as it is for Crane—"Rigor of beauty is
the quest," he says in the Preface to *Paterson*—but for him it is to
be sought in things, in the rigorous imaginative engagement with
them by which they are revealed, and not, as he thought was always
so with Crane, in a misdirected, careless imaginative leap beyond
them.

Crane's tactic in this poem, which follows the free form of "The
Wanderer," is to grant Williams' point but, dialectically, move
beyond it. The poem, comprising six stanzas, breaks in the middle,
where its opening lines ("Walk high on the bridge of Estador, /
No one has ever walked there before") in slightly altered form act
as the refrain that resumes its argument. These lines summon us to
the bridge, which, as an explicit image, now enters Crane's work.
This bridge is an imaginary bridge serving the imagination. "Esta-
dor," according to Weber, is a neologism, in Spanish, meaning one
who views or measures; [52] the bridge of Estador is a visionary span
of vision, as Crane, lifted by love, actually found later in the case of
the Brooklyn Bridge: "we shall take a walk," he told Waldo Frank,
from whom he had learned of the relation of love and mysticism,
"—we shall take a walk across the bridge to Brooklyn (as well as to
Estador, for all that!)." [53] Being imaginary, it is the poet's private
bridge untrod by others, an arch pulling him into the sky, into a
space vaster than the world's, into the unknown. And not without
reason; when we think of this and the fact that it spans the abyss,
we recall such dedicated visionaries as Rimbaud, who was willing to
disorder his senses and to suffer in order to arrive at the unknown,
and Baudelaire, who ends "Le Voyage" with "Plonger au fond du
gouffre, Enfer ou Ciel, qu'importe? / Au fond de l'Inconnu pour
trouver du nouveau!" [54]

51. "Hart Crane (1899–1932)," *Contempo*, II (July 5, 1932), 4.
52. *Hart Crane*, p. 103.
53. *Letters*, p. 182 (April 21, 1924).
54. "But plunge into the void!—hell? heaven?—what's the odds? We're bound
for the Unknown, in search of something new!" Translation by Edna St. Vincent

Crane's aestheticism may be said to reach its apogee in this visionary quest, in the reliance on the visionary powers of the imagination. The poem begins with the poet's attempt to come to terms with lesser, available beauties, things of this world which he recognizes and appreciates but, like Ahab refusing the attainable felicities, turns from in search of a beauty (Beauty) both spiritual and absolute. For his notion of beauty, derived from such sources as Yeats and Symons—and even Roger Fry[55]—is of something transcendent; and though it may be revealed in things or events, sprung from them like love, it can be secured only in an absolute beyond them. That the bridge arches skyward is important: the unknown it leads to is spiritual (a divine Love, Unity, Reconciliation, Repose), and symbolism—imaginative transcendence of the real and the earthly—is the bridge to this end.

In an essay on transcendence, Kenneth Burke observes that consolation is one of the seven offices or functions in the spectrum of human needs and that this priestly office may be designated by "pontificate; that is, to 'make a bridge.' " To bridge, he finds, is the symbolic function of transcendence; it is the "building of a *terministic bridge* whereby one realm is *transcended* by being viewed *in terms of* a realm 'beyond' it." As an example of the pattern of such beyonding, he cites Virgil's lines about the dead whom Charon refused to ferry across Cocytus and the Stygian swamps to the final abode: "And they stretched forth their hands, through love of a farther shore." [56] We find lines of an equivalent kind in Crane's pontificating poem, brilliant lines that declare the visionary fufill-

---

Millay, in Charles Baudelaire, *Flowers of Evil*, trans. George Dillon and Edna St. Vincent Millay (New York: Washington Square Press, 1962), p. 199.

55. In *Vision and Design*, which Crane read in the spring of 1921, Fry argues that art develops more in response to its own inner logic than to the life of the times; that the impressionists, to whom he traces the modern spirit, while concerned with actual life, upheld "the complete detachment of the artistic vision from the values imposed on vision by everyday life"; and that art belongs to "the imaginative life," not an "actual life." A transitional figure, Fry preached an aesthetic moralism as well as the "modern" notion that art need not be representative. In stressing the idea of "significant form," he stopped short of yet suggested "the depths of mysticism."

56. "I, Eye, Ay—Emerson's Early Essay 'Nature': Thoughts on the Machinery of Transcendence," *Transcendentalism and Its Legacy*, ed. Myron Simon and Thornton

ment he has known and above all hopes to regain: "Nor the Gods that danced before you / When your fingers spread among the stars." This, we might say, is his transcendental or visionary gesture, the reaching-up Williams mentioned. He depicts it in "Carmen de Boheme," and in "Faustus and Helen" he lifts his arms to Helen, but in "The Broken Tower," where he leaves the "visionary company," he "lift[s] down the eye." The loss of such visionary scope, of the possibility of love originally associated with it, is what we feel at the end of "Porphyro in Akron" in the poet's compaint that "The stars are drowned in a slow rain. . . ."

From the bridge, which provides a vantage between earth and sky (it is ladder-like, or like the segment of a rainbow), the poet invites us to look down to the sublunary, to either nature or civilization: perhaps to a lake, which may be ("perhaps" works doubly) radiant with the sun lapped under it, or to a dismal industrial landscape such as Paul Rosenfeld depicted later in *Port of New York*. The contrast of pastoral and urban, of bright and free and dark and enslaving, is of consequence only because the poet wishes to negate it. Both scenes are beautiful: each is complete, a concord of things and their relations, because seeing from a height, the everyday analogue of visionary seeing, composes and thus transfigures them.

Like Emerson, the poet, who in the poem has demonstrated this aesthetics of relation, knows the value of distant seeing—and perhaps the value of the intense white light that Emerson said made all things beautiful. He advises us not to "think too deeply," that is, not to follow the Understanding in pursuit of particulars, but to follow the Reason (Imagination): "Do not think too deeply, and you'll find / A soul, an element in it all." The spiritual element matters, the *all* of it—something not unlike the "radiant gist" that Williams, in his different way, tries to recover from the pitchblende of ordinary things.

That beauty may be found in such ordinary things is granted by the question "How can you tell where beauty's to be found?" and

---

H. Parsons (Ann Arbor: University of Michigan Press, 1966), pp. 3–23. Transcendence, one of Burke's pivotal terms, is not necessarily transcendental or visionary; it covers other modes of "surmounting," among them that of widening inclusiveness.

proved in the example, not hypothetical now, that the poet takes from his own experience—the factory incident of "Episode of Hands."

> Yet a gash with sunlight jerking through
> A mesh of belts down into it, made me think
> I had never seen a hand before.
> And the hand was thick and heavily warted.

Beauty, he agrees, is not a matter of subject, of what or where or kind of material, but of how one sees it: "I had never seen a hand before." The bridge of Estador is a vantage from which one sees, but a vantage, we now learn, best secured by love.

At this point the tirade begins again on a higher level, and the opening lines that serve as the refrain acquire an incantatory quality. The poetry is agitated by expectation. The poet says that he doesn't know what we'll see, but clearly it will be something wondrous, for it will be disclosed by the kind of seeing he now calls "vision." The stanza, in fact, describes the kind of visioning one associates with the symbolists, or with the profound imagining, not dreaming, that Bachelard calls poetic reverie:

> —your vision
> May slumber yet in the moon, awaiting
> Far consummations of the tides to throw
> Clean on the shore some wreck of dreams. . . .

In every way, and especially rhythmically, these lines are inimitably Crane's—and inevitably, because they touch the deepest source of his poetic being. The seascape, to be sure, is that of many romantic and visionary poems, and he will fully exploit it in "Voyages." But he could do so only because it was already his.

These lines, and what follows them, recapitulate the history of Crane's vision and are poetically a kind of reminiscence or reverie (movement of images) which renews his faith in it. The vision slumbering in the moon is of a different—and earlier—kind than that which, in the sunlight, saw the beauty of hands. The image suggests a child in utero, in repose, awaiting birth into experience, those fearful tides that the poet knows grant only the wreck of dreams. The imagination is the romantic visionary kind ("dreams") that belongs to the moonlit, the feminine world. It is the imagination we find enclosed in the earlier poems, especially in "The Moth That God Made Blind," an imagination whose destiny, once given birth, will be to search the wider universe, the eternity of the sea, for tokens, the sea drift of its dreams. These tokens, the wreck of dreams, are the result of time, the tides (the time of life, of growth, dependent on the mother, the moon) which, in their rhythm, may be said to consummate (reach a momentary eternity, as in love) as well as wreck. The consummation of time and eternity is at the heart of this vision; so is the wreckage that accompanies inordinate desire. And as the previous stanza on hands suggests—and our knowledge of "Voyages," too—the consummation and the wreckage apply to a dream of love.

Knowing this, the poet still chooses to follow his vision. The fifth stanza, offered in explanation, begins with "But," as if to say, I know all this, but nevertheless. . . . For he is one of those who "are twisted with the love / Of things irreconcilable"—the love of the things of time and the things of eternity, of the real and the ideal, the sun and the moon, the flesh and the spirit ("Clean" on the shore), the heavily warted hand and the "dream" of love.[57] And he knows the discrepancy, and the *falling*: "The slant moon [the descending, fading dream] with the slanting hill"—"slant" being an appropriation from Emily Dickinson, for whom it means discordance or want of correspondence, and the situation Robinsonian. Still he chooses to be "Beauty's fool," a Pierrot whose "everlasting eyes" have seen the everlasting, as well as the fool of Beauty, because, as we learn also in "Forgetfulness," he has seen "them"— things reconciled—has known a *"world dimensional"*;[58] and this experience, so glorious, so ecstatic, he "won't [can't] forget."

The poem might perhaps have ended here, for the closing stanza is didactic, flat, and heavy-humored. The "others," the "you others" the poet now disdainfully addresses, are told to follow their "arches," to go their pedestrian way. He has chosen the way of Pierrot, and they, perhaps like Williams in "Ballet," may go Gargantua's way of laughter. These lines, however, are a necessary re-

---

57. "Twisted" probably comes from Eliot, in this instance "Rhapsody on a Windy Night."
58. "For the Marriage of Faustus and Helen."

statement of the polarities the poem has helped the poet resolve. And for him, at least, the introduction of Pierrot as the exemplar of his choice is necessary. It refers to love: to be Beauty's fool is to be the fool of love, to be the poet who has seen the beauty of a wounded hand and whose fingers, like the fevered hands of "Garden Abstract," have been granted the ecstatic fulfillment of the dream of love (and who, later, during his affair with Emil Opffer, will remember "Estador" as a *place*, the achievement of vision to which love brings him). This is what "Pierrot" tells us—and that the poet admits the painful consequences of his choice, a choice, however, that he must make because only that choice, it seems, will fulfill his poetic destiny.[59]

In both "Porphyro in Akron" and "The Bridge of Estador," Crane makes us feel that to be Beauty's fool is a predicament particularly modern, the predicament, as he said of Chaplin, "of the soul imposed on by modern civilization." [60] In the poems of this time, this predicament begins to acquire the definition it will have for "Faustus and Helen" and *The Bridge*, and we see how profoundly it is connected for him with emergence and poetic identity.

Between the writing of "Porphyro in Akron" and "The Bridge of Estador," he wrote "Black Tambourine," a poem in three quatrains, whose tight form enclosed—was—the death from which the tirade of "Estador" released him. In point of experience, as polarities, these poems are complementary; they represent a scale of being, from vastation to exaltation (or its visionary promise). And they should be brought together if only to remind us of Crane's awareness of *experience*—of the "darkness" that he said later was a part of the poet's business.[61]

59. The poem may have been prompted by the concluding lines on Pierrot and Gargantua. Crane set them down in a letter of January 28, 1921, with this comment: "Maybe it is my epitaph, it is contradictory and wide enough to be." Actually, as they stand here, they are used in "Praise for an Urn," his "epitaph" to Ernest Nelson. In keeping with the necessity of choice, "Or" replaces "And" in "The Bridge of Estador." And there Pierrot, as the theme of love in the poem suggests, is probably to be connected with a love affair of early 1921. Crane speaks of the "very soul of Pierrot," of the "beauty and happy-pain," the suffering and ecstasy of his experience. *Letters*, p. 53.

60. *Letters*, p. 85 (May 6, 1922).

61. *Letters*, p. 260 (June 20, 1926).

"Black Tambourine" (1921) is a very dark poem—none quite so dark before it except "North Labrador," whose whiteness is comparable. This depressed and almost wholly hopeless poem about the black man in the cellar concerns his minstrelsy as well as situation in the dark "mid-kingdom." And the poet, who in the objectivity of the poem may be trying to avoid the sentimentality at risk in this theme, by this means secures his identification with the black man of the poem, enters his darkness, lives in his situation, and attempts to overcome the death presented there. The poet looks at the black man as closely and to the same despairing end as the black man looks at the roach on the floor—at the abyss: "a crevice in the floor." He looks downward, a direction in which Crane's acuity (see "O Carib Isle!") is notable; and since so little lifts the spirit, the poem seems static, the "carcass quick with flies" at the end being an image not of life arising from death but of quickened deathfulness that turns the poem back to—encloses it in—the minimal parasitical insect life of its beginning.[62]

The black man in the cellar reminds one of Pip in *Moby-Dick*.[63] Like Pip, he may become a visionary by losing his mind, and, like Aesop, he will get mostly kicks for his vision of truth. As critics have noted, the poem concerns the poet, his neglect and suffering, and not the rewards of love and immortality that Crane recognized. It also concerns the powerlessness of the poet to raise himself out of the cellar, the cell and the pit, the prison of despair (in which he shut himself in "Porphyro in Akron"). The poem is a "black song."

Crane considered the word "mid-kingdom" the key to the poem. He told Munson that it referred to the brutal placement of the Negro in the modern world and to notions of his position between man and beast.[64] But "mid-kingdom" also describes a space of betweenness and, in consequence, a state of arrested being. The structure of the poem supports this too: the second, the middle stanza on Aesop, a historical example of the condition of the black man, arrests the poem, whose static quality is increased rather than over-

---

62. The vertical arrangement of the poem and its relation to its meaning is noted by Holton, " 'A Baudelairesque Thing,' " p. 223.

63. Weber, *Hart Crane*, p. 95. The black man is also an invisible man.

64. *Letters*, p. 58 (Spring, 1921).

come by the references to time and by the similarity of the initial lines of the first and third stanzas.[65] And these, ending with "cellar," suggest an enclosure as fearful as any the poet has found himself in: an underground place, a cell of dark consciousness, the womb that stanza two suggests may also be a grave.

It is not pressing the poem too hard to read it in this way. "Porphyro in Akron" concludes with a bitter memory of arrested growth, and it recalls the poet to childhood, which is also present in "Black Tambourine": in Aesop, who, Monroe Spears says, reminds us of Uncle Remus [66]—that is, of the world of fables we heard as children as well as the fabulous world of childhood, whose loss might drive one to ponder fables of his own. "Black man"—not "Negro," Crane's usual word in his letters—also evokes childhood, its threats and its fears.

The dark world of this poem is limbo. We are in a space like that of "The Tunnel," but there is no outlet; the door is "closed." This world is small and squalid, the habitat of insects whose diminutive movements both define the general lack of movement and signify diminished states of being. The gnats "toss," the roach hangs over the abyss, the flies pullulate in the carcass of death (with no suggestion of the beauty Baudelaire taught us to see in that). The black man does not find in these insects the heaven Aesop found in small animals—in writing fables about them. He has not found, like Aesop, a way to transform his suffering. Where Aesop, "driven to pondering," found a way, he "wanders" in a mid-kingdom of forlornness. Because it is "stuck on the wall," his tambourine is black.

The hopelessness of the poem follows not only from the world's lack of concern but from the poet's desire for another world, the "Heaven" Aesop knew, the "Africa" of the black man's imagination, where, as "carcass" suggests, the great animals, the truly fabulous animals, once were found. Africa is a place of romance—a place of the past, of the black man's origin, the happier place of

65. Because of its verse form and syntax, the poem, according to Leibowitz, is always halting. See *Hart Crane*, p. 196.

66. *Hart Crane*, University of Minnesota Pamphlets on American Writers, 47 (Minneapolis: University of Minnesota Press, 1965), p. 17.

childhood. But now the imagination cannot possess it; the romantic object is "quick with flies," a carcass of death that he cannot alter by song. His tambourine is "stuck" in what we feel is the terrible immobility of poetic death—the death, we said, from which his "tirade" released him. Commenting on the germinal lines of "The Bridge of Estador," the lines he called his epitaph, Crane said that he hoped "to make [them] into a poem and thereby, like Lazarus, return." [67] That poem helped him return by exalting upward—it has the "upward slant" of his imperative to Tate: "Launch into praise" [68]—and it located him in another mid-kingdom somewhere between heaven and earth, an open place of the imagination, a place of vision and freedom.

"Chaplinesque" also treats "Beauty's fool," a Pierrot, and a clown, perhaps like the Negro minstrel of "Black Tambourine." It belongs with this poem—and with "Pastorale" and "Voyages I" ("The Bottom of the Sea Is Cruel"), other poems of this time— because its treatment of the poet's predicament is overwhelmed by concern with childhood, by the double concern with its losses and need to go beyond them and with its splendors—with the "reverie toward childhood" that often moves at the heart of poetry.[69] Pierrot, with his everlasting eyes, eyes on the beauties of the ever-lasting, inalienable childhood within us, is indeed Beauty's fool, a great fool, like "blind Pierrot" in "To Portapovitch." whom the poet commands to "Despair until the moon by tears be won. . . ." So is Chaplin, the fool-as-child.

What is noteworthy in this poem besides the virtuosity of putting Chaplin's pantomime into words is the way in which Crane treats the ordeal of the artist under the aspect of childhood and yet avoids sentimentality. In writing an ostensibly modern poem, a poem about one of the popular arts, he creates a counter-form, a poem about the *maladie moderne*, the condition of the romantic artist. Like the critics whom he had read, he uses the opposed catchwords —sets poet-poetry-heart-spirit against the "fury of the streets," the

---

67. *Letters*, p. 53 (January 28, 1921).
68. *Letters*, p. 94 (July 19, 1922).
69. See Bachelard, *The Poetics of Reverie*; Edith Cobb, "The Ecology of Imagination in Childhood," *Daedalus*, LXXXVIII (Summer, 1959), 537–48.

"mechanical scramble," as he explained to William Wright, that crowds out poetry.[70] He accepts the romantic notion of the poet as outcast, sufferer, and redeemer. Yet like the black man of an earlier version of "Black Tambourine," he "Sees two ways, too, —with less gay eyes." [71] He knows that Chaplin may be childish, that he "may be a sentimentalist, after all . . ."; and he knows that he, too, may be a sentimentalist unless, like Chaplin, he can make sentimentality "transcend itself into a new kind of tragedy. . . ." [72]

This is what he tries to do in the concluding stanza, where the desperation of the situation is admitted and the limitations of romanticism are measured in the very act of persisting in them. The situation in the moolit alley—the "modern" romantically, picturesquely seen—especially the echo of the cadence of the run-on lines, is deflationary, a "collapse" that supports the poet's earlier assertion that we can evade everything but the heart. For these lines recall Edwin Arlington Robinson's "Mr. Flood's Party," where the moonlight does less transfiguring than the drink, and the laughter, gaiety, and quest do not silence the *cri de coeur*. Now, instead, the imagery of emptiness and space in the previous stanzas acquires terror: wilderness. The poet-as-clown is now abject, a lonely poet-as-child, a poet who knows that childhood is this side of the line of experience and that we play the "game" not merely because we are privileged to know the transfiguring power of art but because we know that it does not always save the kitten in the wilderness. The transfiguring light of this stanza reveals a genuine, not sentimental situation and feeling. Like Robinson's, Crane's romanticism becomes tragic.[73]

II

A tragic spirit also informs "For the Marriage of Faustus and Helen" (1923), the most ambitious poem Crane had yet undertaken. Writing it—the work of perhaps the most intense and ex-

---

70. *Letters*, p. 68 (October 17, 1921).
71. Weber, *Hart Crane*, p. 95.
72. *Letters*, p. 69 (November 3, 1921).
73. At this time Paul Rosenfeld was writing critically of the moonlit worlds of Arthur B. Davies and Albert P. Ryder. See "American Painting," *The Dial*, LXXI (December, 1921), 649–70.

citing year of his life—confirmed him in his high ideal of poetic vocation at the same time as it marked his emergence. This, rather than any special excellence, is the achievement of the poem. For Crane, it dramatized his majority, he being-in-the-world and his response to the vision of its beauty. No longer is he Porphyro, for whom romance is a matter of books and poetry a bedroom occupation; no longer a child-clown. Though still a devotee of Beauty, he does not stand off from or try to evade the adversary world. Finding himself in it, he tries to make contact with it. He has begun to heed the admonition that Williams addressed to the poet in *Contact* (1921): to "know his own world, in whatever confused form it may be" or risk failing to perceive the "disclosures" that will "then come to him as reality, as joy, as release." [74] Almost every element of the Machine that Munson felt expressed the American genius—skyscrapers, jazz music, electric light displays—now captures his attention and is used to the end of bringing the Machine within the human spirit. His method of doing this is not dadaist but one that Waldo Frank had learned from Alfred Stieglitz, its great exemplar: that of finding the spirit in (of) the materials of the immediate world.[75] That Crane found himself to some extent capable of doing this largely accounts for his exultation, for the celebratory note of the title of the poem, which is to be read also as meaning a movement *toward* reconciliation or marriage with the world.

In this poem, the showpiece of an education in Eliot, Joyce, and the Elizabethans, Crane allies the vocation of poetry with Faustus, a representative in many respects of the inimical masculine daylight pursuits of the modern world. The very scope of the poem and the daring of putting it in competition with recognized masters exhibits a Faustian pride. Crane told Munson that he had taken Eliot, the teacher whose attitudes he had been working through and testing in earlier poems, "as a point of departure toward an almost complete reverse of direction." [76] For him the poem is a turning point, estab-

74. Reprinted in *Selected Essays of William Carlos Williams* (New York: Random House, 1954), p. 28.

75. See Bram Dijkstra, *The Hieroglyphics of a New Speech: Cubism, Stieglitz, and the Early Poetry of William Carlos Williams* (Princeton: Princeton University Press, 1969).

76. *Letters*, pp. 114–15 (January 5, 1923).

lishing a new direction, poetic posture, and role. He would contact his world, become a public poet, follow the upward slant to affirmation and praise. The extent to which he does this and thereby joins the writers of *The Seven Arts*—the exponents of a modern art devoted to the discovery and expression of the American spirit—is seen in *The Bridge*, the still more ambitious poem to which "Faustus and Helen" immediately led.

We may overlook this because Crane's formal debts to Eliot are so conspicuous in this poem and because its ground is pessimistic and he goes about the new enterprise in his old romantic clothes. Were it not for its appropriateness we might take the epigraph from Jonson's *The Alchemist* for a parody of Eliot's practice. And though accurate enough, the title seems pretentious. It advises us, of course, of the "mythical method" Eliot had employed in *The Waste Land* and explained in a review of Joyce's *Ulysses*, the method of continuous parallel between past and present that Crane himself commented on later in speaking of "Faustus and Helen" in "General Aims and Theories." [77] Though Crane expressed a double allegiance in this essay—to the "future of America" (*The Seven Arts*) and to the utility of "traditional literary elements," among them "the vocabulary and blank verse of the Elizabethans" (Eliot) —his stake in tradition, as one sees in his rejection of dada, has a different rationale than Eliot's. He did not set the present so radically against the past as Eliot did, nor use the past so much as Eliot did as a "way of controlling, of ordering, of giving a shape and significance to the immense panorama of futility and anarchy which is contemporary history," though his own poem treats contemporary history, "a period," he also found, "loose at all ends, without apparent direction of any sort." He did not adopt the mythical method in order to make "the modern world possible for art" [78]— there were other ways to do that. His use of "Faustus" and "Helen" neither controls nor condemns the present, but, in keeping with profound needs of his own, serves, as he said, as a "bridge" to connect him with past experience. "Helen" may remind us of the past but in the poem she is recognized as a "presence," as the vital ex-

77. "Ulysses, Order, and Myth," *The Dial*, LXXV (November, 1923), 480–83; P, 217–23.

78. *Letters*, p. 110 (December 24, 1922); Eliot, "Ulysses, Order, and Myth."

pression of something permanent and continuing within the
ground of the human spirit. What Williams said of the Greek gods
in *Kora in Hell* may be said of her: she dances now, only "few have
an eye for it, through the dirt and fumes." As important to Crane
as his thought of Helen in the past is the discovery of her presence.
"So I found 'Helen,'" he says in "General Aims and Theories,"
"sitting in a street car. . . ." [79]

The poem begins with the state of the general mind. The mind
as well as the urban scene that depicts it is the modern predicament,
and the poet, who shares and suffers its qualities, would quicken
and raise its consciousness. This mind is doughy, half-baked, and
also hard and stereotyped ("baked and labeled"). Crane provides a
gloss when he remarks in a letter to Stieglitz that his "mind is like
dough [he is on a business trip] and *The Bridge* is far away." [80]
This, then, is a lumpish mind, fixed, in Emerson's words, on com-
modity rather than spirit—lacking spiritus, as Thoreau says of a
similar mind in *Walden*—and as far from that salutary condition
as the imperfect stampings are from Plato's Forms. The reason for
this want of spirit—an imprisonment of dullness—is not intrinsic
but historical; it results from the conditions of modern life, among
them that tendency in mass society suggested by "Numbers" (ab-
stractions) and "accepted multitudes" (which calls up "plati-
tudes"). This mind is also both cause and effect of the world of
business, the office world associated here with our financial empire;
it has permitted and undergone the fragmentation and alienation
("partitions of the day": the schedule of nine-to-five). These
"stacked" partitions evoke the cell-by-cell rise of a skyscraper as well
as the meaning of "wrenched gold" in the similar context of "Reci-
tative." These partitions cheat us by dividing us from "day," the
radiant fullness of life.

This modern theme is notably commonplace. This is the heavy
world of "Porphyro in Akron." But now the poetry, even with its
direct quality of speech, condenses more detail and meaning. The

79. P, 217; *Kora in Helen: Improvisations* (San Francisco: City Lights Books,
1957 [1920]), p. 51.

80. *Letters*, p. 142 (August 11, 1923). Roger Fry observes that "in the practical
vision we have no more concern after we have read the label on the object. . . ."
Vision and Design (Cleveland: World Publishing Co., 1956 [1920]), p. 48.

skyscraper, the temple of business, a frequent symbol of both the degradation and aspiration of modern civilization (as in the work of Marin and Stieglitz), is evoked by the multiple association of words and the catalog of what goes on there: the paperwork, talk of baseball, mechanical flirtations and response ("stenographic smiles"), the ticker tape (and "stock quotations"), the smutty jokes. But "smutty" also means begrimed in respect to "wings," the soaring spirit that would fly athwart and above ("across") all this, that "flash out" (and flush out) deception. The mind here seems to have within it, as things have within them (the flashing reminds one of the garter snakes in "Van Winkle"), the power of "surprise," the power Emerson relies on in "Experience" to overcome or redeem ("a cross") its own spiritlessness.

The mind with which the poem opens is a limited faculty imprisoned by its own work—by its sterile rationalism and system. It awakens to its fullness only when it is released, when the imagination is liberated. This release—and with it the transition from the abstract world of day to the incarnate world of night—is what the initial stanzas enact. At the end of the day, in a twilight time somewhat like that of "Prufrock," it is released and, in its self-possession, discovers new "dawns," new spiritual possibilities. With this, the journey of the poem, a kind of Prufrockian "visit" of the world, begins.

Stanzas one and two are joined by "wings" as well as the sequence of time. The harbinger of imagination is the sparrow, a bird of the city sidewalk, where the mind, still disembodied and abstract, now finds itself. "Numbers" (picked up again in Part III) is tied to "crowd" (a verb): both bespeak anonymity. The evening crowd pours out, more than the walks can hold. The crowd is "rebuffed," jostled but also brightened by the street; it crowds "the margins of the day"—what's left of it as well as the wide freedom Thoreau desired. (The pun in "margins" on stocks and bonds—not just the work of the exchange but the gamble of it—is an example of the backward reaching meaning that is also involved in Crane's "dynamics of inferential mention. . . .") [81] And the crowds "accent the curbs": both sharpen the streets with motion and diverse speech and sharpen the sense of being and having been

81. P, 222.

curbed. But as the crowd moves on and breaks up, singularity emerges. The numbers "convoy" (carry and protect: enclose) the precious cargo of "divers dawns" (yes, the dawn returns in Part III), that is, the many individual states of higher consciousness whose goals, for the moment, are "druggist, barber and tobacconist," or, if we press the nautical meaning of the image, the ideal of Helen, whom Poe likened to a ship bearing the weary wanderer home to his native shore. This submerged meaning (to which "divers" may allude) is important because it suggests that the search for Beauty is a return, a homecoming to an ideal that once, in some earlier time and at a deep level of experience, was ours.

Gradually—all this is expressed in one sentence, a sinuous movement of leaving—we lose sight of "them" ("divers dawns"): "the graduate[d] opacities of evening / Take them away. . . ." The liquid line that follows describes a mysterious translation into another realm. From our vantage, the street is suddenly empty; the crowd has been spirited away, into the night, "to somewhere / Virginal perhaps, less fragmentary, cool." The ideal place, as often with Crane, is vague but the values are precise and define what has been lacking in the world of these stanzas. These lines speak for the restoration of wholeness, innocence, purity, spirituality—for a prior, perhaps childhood, condition. By working back into the stanzas they conclude, they remind us of the doubleness of experience, of two related states of being as necessary to each other as day and night, and of the change from one to the other (as in "Recitative," where "darkness, like an ape's face, falls away, / And gradually white buildings answer day").

This change opens the poem to night and to the poet's quest for Beauty. The italicized, set-in lines upon which the poem turns rise out of the text as an "ideal" rises out of life. Refreshing in sound and sense, they are a cool virginal thought of the timeless present— a verbal "image" of it—and affirm both the certainty of "somewhere" and its location in the gathering darkness.[82] And they declare the ideal being sought: *the world dimensional,* the unity of being realized in the reconciliation or marriage of the opposites the poem describes. These lines incorporate Crane's statement of

82. "Somewhere" is positive, as in Paul Rosenfeld's work, where it answers the negative, elusive "otherwhere."

visionary goal in "The Bridge of Estador" and recall "Forgetful-
ness," where, in the image of the bird used in the introductory
stanzas of "Faustus and Helen," this ecstatic state is compared to
that of "a bird whose wings are reconciled." "Twisted," also used
earlier, is best glossed in "Recitative," though the doubleness is as
much the result of the modern situation as of human nature (as in
Crane's remark about the penalty of advertising work: "I feel like a
thread singed and twisted . . .").[83] "*World dimensional*," a new
phrase, derives from Crane's recent reading in Munson's *Waldo
Frank* or perhaps in P. D. Ouspensky's *Tertium Organum* ("the
dimensionality of the world depends on the development of con-
sciousness") [84] and, with these glosses in mind, suggests the higher
consciousness that for him had become the end of poetry.

The poem turns on these lines because they summon the poet
in the visionary direction he is trying to avoid. He chooses not to
flee ("Walk high on the bridge of Estador") but to explore the
world; he enters night neither to escape in dreams nor to find a
haven but to search the present for Beauty. He seeks the vital prin-
ciple, the eternal feminine, upon which the city of man is built.
He wishes to know the fertile darkness from which day springs, to
find the ground of the belief, affirmed in Part III, that life rises
from death. And reconciliation, as he has been recently taught, is
marriage, the sensuous contact or intercourse of self and world. He
hopes to find a (the) way to "touch."

And yet the discovery of Helen's presence, the goal of this sec-
tion of the poem, remains hypothetical ("suppose some evening").
The poet doesn't touch her; he only imagines her presence in the
world and, in his old chivalrous way, declares his wish to serve her
and so deserve her touch. Crane accurately described Part I when
he told Munson it involved "Meditation, Evocation, Love, Beauty,"
and in the description he later provided Waldo Frank, he accu-
rately explained the movement of the poem at this point: "The
street car device is the most concrete symbol I could find for the
transition of the imagination from quotidian details to the universal

83. *Letters*, p. 145 (August 25, 1923).

84. Trans. Nicholas Bessaraboff and Claude Bragdon (New York: Alfred A.
Knopf, 1922), p. 5.

consideration of beauty,—the body still 'centered in traffic,' the imagination eluding its daily nets and self consciousness." [85] The shock of disorganized daily routine prepares "surprise" as does the losing oneself by which one finds oneself; the poet, "lost yet poised in traffic," is ready for an explosion like that of "Sunday Morning Apples." "Then," he says—discovery is conditional and depends on disorientation and readiness to attend—

> Then I might find your eyes across an aisle,
> Still flickering with those prefigurations—
> Prodigal, yet uncontested now,
> Half-riant before the jerky window frame.

The flickering eyes, the line ending in "prefigurations," call up the earlier lines: "Across . . . / Smutty wings flash out equivocations." The not yet extinguished flame of Helen "flash[es] out" prefigurations of love and beauty, signs of something "prodigal" (like the "lavish heart" of Part III), something, however, no longer contested in the old chivalric way. And the laughing, mocking eyes, framed in the window of the moving car—the eyes perhaps of a Mona Lisa—know this and prompt the poet's romantic declaration in what follows.

Whether the poet leaves the streetcar or views the city from it is inconsequential. What matters is the metamorphosis of the girl in the streetcar, the realization of her presence—or the presence she shares—in the nighttime city, and the fact that the imagination is asked to possess the world she animates. And to a considerable extent the imagination does this in the *poetry* of the poet who himself is still looking for a way to touch and who, in imagery not yet demonstrably erotic (stanza five), ardently proposes that she "meet" him because of his high spiritual credentials. For him it *is* her hands that "count the nights": hands that mean so much to Crane, and "count" in some sense other than that of the previous stanzas—count beads(?) or blink in the night like electric signs, those "flickering . . . prefigurations." And the streets, in a nice pun, are her "arteries." She is presence because she is incarnation, like the Christ of "Lachrymae Christi," the Pocahontas of *The*

85. *Letters*, pp. 116, 120–21 (January 14, February 7, 1923).

Bridge; she is the first example of Crane's deepening awareness that the world is feminine and that the restoration of vital culture in our time depends on our awareness of this.

And now before all shuts down for the night ("turn dark"), now before modern civilization signals its own demise, he would have her accept ("have you meet") his "bartered blood." The imagery of arteries and blood, as well as the submerged meaning of "have you," suggests vital meeting or merger. But his blood, his very vitality, is bartered, sold to "trade," as Lanier would say; hence his unworthiness. Yet it is bartered for something more precious than money ("better knows"): for his dream of her, a dream not *of* so much as immanent *with* sacramental-redemptive love.

> . . . none better knows
> The white wafer cheek of love, or offers words
> Lightly as moonlight on the eaves meets snow.

The imagery here, so virginal and cool, brings to a pure end the other meanings of communion already suggested; and it describes a spiritual development the poet might find "imminent" (threatening) because it moves away from his wish for sensuous contact. It returns him to the pristine world of mother (of Priscilla in *The Bridge*) and grandmother, too (see "My Grandmother's Love Letters"), and to his role of sufferer. "None better knows"—yes, the poet, willing to pay the old price to prove his worthiness, will, like the adolescent of "C 33," offer "words" to enrich the gold head of the "Materna." Contact will now be visionary.

As much as Crane disavows this attitude, he carries it forward into another attitude at once sensuous and spiritual. The Materna he worshiped in his youth becomes the Virgin of Henry Adams, the divine mother or goddess whose spirit is sexual, generative, the force that moves all things; she becomes Helen, whose beauty, compelling erotic love, creates history. This is what he recognizes in the "reflective conversion" that transforms the city of daylight masculine striving into the nighttime feminine city of pleasure—of dream, play, art, love—a conversion of religious significance signaled in the lights of electric signs and their rainbows as well as in the "deep blush" of sunset and light display. With this conversion the poet begins to see the world sensuously. Restored to life at

night, city and nature become one. The lights of the city are the
finery of the "body of the world"; its streets are her "arteries"
through which "ecstasies thread / The limbs and belly. . . ." The
stanza attends the body—its blush, its throat, breasts, sides, limbs,
belly—and awakens the Dionysian spirit of the rest of the poem.

To residents of Cleveland, which is presumably the city of the
poem, the rainbows (which otherwise would not be visible at night,
nor plural, nor "spread") are the winkings of the Sherwin-Williams
electric sign that stands high on the banks of the Cuyahoga River
and spells out over a waste of ore boats and mills the message
"COVER THE EARTH WITH PAINT." In the context of this stanza and
of this part of the poem, which Crane said signified "the rape of
Helen," [86] the message represents the ominousness of industrial
civilization. No wonder the body of the world, the pastoral world
of the bluet flower, "Weeps in [the] inventive dust," and the sign
"winks" at the spoliation! Crane uses the electric sign, a desidera-
tum of dada, with as much skill and point as Fitzgerald does the
sign of the oculist in *The Great Gatsby*, and with more than the
satiric intent of Edmund Wilson in *I Thought of Daisy*.

"Bluet in your breasts," the phrase with which this stanza ends,
restores the attitude of veneration associated with the pastoral
world. With it and the false promise of the rainbow in mind, one
reads back into the stanza some misgivings over the "ecstasies,"
which now seem to portend the frantic pleasure of Part II. The
phrase also provides the transition to the concluding, exalted dec-
laration of devotion and establishes the absolute point from which
the poet measures history. In the course of history (of time) the
earth, he says, "may glide diaphanous to death": the ideal, the pas-
toral, the feminine earth, which he associates with Helen, may sim-
ply vanish in the inventive dust; it may "glide . . . to death," a
downward motion at once suggesting the airplanes and warfare of
Part III and the movement of a Pre-Raphaelite woman. He knows
the industrial city, the masculine despoiler, and lifts his arms in
petition and prayer because he himself ignobly serves it. When he
had approached Helen before (was it in "Porphyro in Akron"?)
she had denied him because he was twisted by things irreconcilable;
in an image used again in "Recitative," he was too "alternate"

86. *Letters*, p. 120 (February 7, 1923).

with "steel" (the industrial city) and "soil" (not nature, but impurity): accordingly, he could not hold her "endlessly" (eternally).

The poet who lifts his arms—and heightens his speech—is, like Gatsby, a romantic in search of the ideal. The "eventual flame" is a green light beckoning from beyond, a consummatory liberating flame, like the fire in "The Dance," and, in a secular equivalent, the orgiastic future that follows in Part II. "Meet" is again a focal word, as in stanza four. The poet both postpones the meeting and redefines it: he will not seek or possess Helen in the present (at best a mixed condition) but in a visionary future. He will meet her when he is worthy; when, like the historical Helen, he is no longer "captive" to time, and vision, itself a flame, has freed him from the world presented in the poem; when he is "beyond"—"Beyond their million brittle, bloodshot eyes," the eyes of those who have lusted after her and failed to comprehend him. In this sharp and bitter phrase, the poet turns on the multitudes with whom he was once merged and turns to his own private goal. What he finally envisions is "White" and gathers up the previous values of the virginal and cool and of the "white wafer cheek of love. . . ." "White" is Helen transfigured, not the historical Helen but the spiritual Helen or the spirit of Helen transmitted through history by poets, like Poe ("Helen, thy beauty is to me"), transmitted through the "white cities," the eternal forms, of their poems. Helen is no longer the girl across the aisle; she is not even a person celebrated in poems, but, as Crane's own poem exemplifies, the spirit of poetry itself, moving the poets, the visionary company of love, to create and so possess, singly and in solitude, their own visionary worlds. For Crane, as for Poe, Helen's beauty brings him "home," brings him back to the world of the early poems and to their inalienable source. But—and this perhaps is a penalty of such achievement—it brings him back to an unendurable loneliness and incompleteness.

"Alone" in the penultimate stanza is insisted on in "a lone" of the concluding quatrain. Although the strained and grandiloquent imagery ("bent axle of devotion"; "orb of praise") mars it and another avowal of devotion is unnecessary, the stanza, with its forced mechanical imagery and its triple rhyme, shows the desperation of the poet, who by verbal force, if nothing else, would unify the hitherto irreconcilables of his experience. The imagery of machinery ("axle," "riveted") and of dimensions ("plane") picks up earlier themes and reminds us of the oscillation of impulses that characterizes the movement of the poem and also seeks reconciliation. But the reconciliation, like the movement of the poem, is deceptive: just as under the impetus to go forward and out the poet goes backward and in, so, in the end, he takes a visionary posture. The single eye he asks Helen to accept is, according to Philip Horton, the right eye that Jacob Boehme said looks to eternity—the everlasting eye of Pierrot.[87] The left eye—perhaps that of Gargantua—belongs to the world of time, and must bend, like the axle. What the poet desires is clear enough but not expressed well enough nor with as much justice to the alternations of experience as in "Recitative." The days, unlike the day of the poem, will be "hourless," an eternal now, not because "In alternating bells . . . / All hours [have been] clapped dense into a single stride" (an image of horizontal unity, one of equivalence) but because, in vision, he has risen above things (a vertical unity). It may be that "axle" is also "axis" and some idea of unity such as Emerson's of the coincidence of the axis of things and the axis of vision is being expressed. Perhaps the "glowing orb," which is disconcertingly Poe-esque, is Emerson's transcendental eyeball!

In resorting to the prospect of visionary reconciliation the poet denies his own best vision: he loses touch with his sense of present life. Rather than accept that intuition and transform his consciousness by accepting the world, he declares his desire to transform the world with "poetic" consciousness: that is, he declares his longing, like Poe, for supernal Beauty. And "vision," which is not achieved but only declared, leaves him dissociated, as much unreconciled as he was in the polar state of mind at the beginning of the poem. In keeping with the falling rhythm of the stanza, his being is not exalted but diminished.

Part II, which Crane completed first and entitled "The Springs of Guilty Song," seemed to him "a work of youth and magic." He was immensely pleased with it because he had fulfilled the injunction of his introductory letter to Allen Tate: "Let us invent an

87. *Hart Crane*, pp. 115–16.

idiom for the proper transposition of jazz into words! Something clean, sparkling, elusive!" He told Munson that he had done "something entirely new in English poetry, so far as I know"—certainly no one will deny the brilliance of his achievement. When he indicated its place in the total poem, he said (to Munson) it represented "Dance, Humor, Satisfaction" and (to Frank) "the DANCE and sensual culmination." And when he first alluded to it by way of jazz idiom in the letter to Tate, he seems to have thought of it as a successful example of breaking away from the "poetry of negation." [88]

This section of "Faustus and Helen" presents another stage in the journey through the poet's day. It may be considered as Crane's equivalent of the nighttime episodes of Joyce's *Ulysses*, the book that may have suggested to him the structure of the poem. From his own accounts of the structure, the movement of the poem seems to be less a matter of juxtaposition and dialectic than of mounting intensity: Part II, he says, accelerates the ecstasy of Part III.[89] But Part II is also juxtaposed to Part I, especially to its devotional conclusion, and its relation to Part III, granting the Dionysian connection, is the result of its concern with death and of the dialectic of purity by which it is transformed. Though it suggests "The Dance" in *The Bridge* because in it, too, the dance eroticizes space, it seems to have deeper affinities with "Three Songs." For the dance in "Faustus and Helen" is not celebratory. Having taken visionary flight, the poet attempts, in this part of the poem, to make vital contact; like "The Tunnel," it represents for him a descent into darkness. So the contact he makes is not without revulsion, and the possession of Helen, the recognition of her presence, which is what enables the poet to affirm life over death in Part III, requires considerable transformation.

The poem does more than transpose jazz into words: it comments as well as depicts. The "brazen hypnotics" are not only bold and brassy but probably Negro, copper-colored; in any case, their metallic character identifies them with the Machine. And they are "hypnotics" because they have abdicated to the trance of the music —nighttime counterparts of the baked and labeled minds of Part I.

88. *Letters*, pp. 89, 116, 121 (June 4, 1922; January 14, February 7, 1923).
89. *Letters*, p. 121 (February 7, 1923).

The dance is only a "blessed excursion," and the dancers, who taunt the gods, are not immortal but "breathless," in a condition of excitement that lasts only so long (in a wonderfully playful and witty image) as "nigger cupids scour the stars!" The dancers, moreover, are ghostly ("white shadows"), lucky (note the image of cards) to be released from the grave, and doomed, when dawn comes and the rooster crows, to return to it. They perform a *danse macabre.* Their spirituality is unreal, a shadow, or corrupted, as the interpenetrated white-black suggests. They may be Negroes behaving like whites—Crane's view of the Negro is not sentimental. Nor is he enchanted by mechanical paganism, for the release it provides is a cheat. "New soothings, new amazements" is not equivalent to "New thresholds, new anatomies!" in "The Wine Menagerie." The metallic idiom of jazz is the idiom of death, as in Edmund Wilson's *The Crime in the Whistler Room* (1924); and it is death's instrument because, as Paul Rosenfeld said, it weakens the lure of the actual by creating ready-made Elysiums ("metallic paradises").[90] It may soothe and amaze; it may license surrealistic behavior (falling down stairs, an inversion of popular Freudian symbolism; the humorous dreamlike floating before one's powerless relatives) but only momentarily, at fearful penalty.

For the poet, who participates in the dance, sees what the rest refuse to see. Like Prufrock he is familiar with the rituals of his world—"O, I have known metallic paradises"—and like Tiresias in *The Waste Land* what he sees is its central meaning. This paradise is a hedonist hell; the dancers are devils, grotesques out of the earlier world of Grünewald and Bosch ("incunabula"). The music has only a "reassuring way"—they are skating on thin ice. And the "cuckoos" are literally that, but also, like the "finches" (sirens), connected with death, as in the case of Odysseus, who was lured on by them. The dancers think themselves "above . . . catastrophes," but the poet has seen the vortex ("Beneath gyrating awnings"). The sensuality that evades death portends it.

These meanings are carried over in the "siren" of the last stanza.

90. *An Hour with American Music* (Philadelphia: J. B. Lippincott Co., 1929), pp. 14–15. Though Rosenfeld's views on jazz antedate this book, he seems in writing it to have remembered "Faustus and Helen." His own prose evocation is an excellent gloss.

The poet, perhaps because of these thoughts, hasn't found Helen in this metallic heaven, but a *femme fatale,* or maybe only a flapper.[91] She lures him, and he willingly "takes" her, not directly in a sexual sense, though that is implied by the dance. This is sufficient reason for "guilty song" because it represents the relinquishing of his ideal goal—in sexual terms, a fall from love to lust. As in "National Winter Garden," the poet recognizes the compulsions of flesh ("nervosities / That we are heir to" recalls Hamlet's meditation) and he speaks of guilt because for him Beauty must not be defiled by sexuality. Yet somehow, like Endymion, in yielding, he doesn't betray the ideal. Youth, it seems, is a sign of purity—of the need for care and devotion. And how can he refuse or "frown" when "she smiles," for him the most important token of love? And so, in dancing with her, he discovers that she is Helen (like the hero of *I Thought of Daisy,* who finds that the chorus girl is the Daisy, the *jeune fille* of his youth). In dancing with her, he experiences something of the "eventual flame."

With this transformation, the verse is transformed. It softens; its tone is pleasantly ironic, self-mocking. And its closing images of storm, garden, and sky now contrast favorably with "metallic." The siren promises nothing orgiastic; jazz modulates to waltz. She is sedate and demure ("dipping," "slim skaters"), managing the "cultivated" storm and suggesting to him the values of "gardened skies" —not those of the roof garden but those of a pastoral heaven. The vortex is now a cultivated storm. The Websterian-Eliot view of "Whispers of Immortality" ("Webster was much possessed by death / And saw the skull beneath the skin") is momentarily displaced by one that promises both a restoration of the ideal and a renewal of life. His dark experience is not disputed but relieved by the presence of Helen, who, like Mary in "Three Songs," recalls him to the innocent devotion of his youth and effects the spiritualization by which he overcomes "the fever of the bone."

Part III is apostrophe. The action is an act of speech, another virtuoso performance, richly Elizabethan, that reaches up to the pitch of praise. The poet who speaks it has left the roof garden and is alone in the street—in a De Chirico cityscape—as dawn ap-

91. Leibowitz, *Hart Crane,* p. 68.

proaches. Here he meets Death, whom he invites to accompany him in tragic song ("fear and pity") and its purgative-redemptive work of catharsis. As the "capped arbiter," Death is the hanging judge who arbitrarily decides the fate of "beauty." In keeping with the space in which the poet finds him, he initially represents negation and limitation, the conditioned circumstances of existence— what "flesh remembers," all that the poet in quest of Beauty would transcend. As the poem proceeds, however, the terms of address alter ("delicate ambassador," "brother-thief of time") and with them the powers of Death, who is recognized as an agent of the miraculous transformation by which he himself is overcome. In the concluding stanzas, the poet, a representative of the imagination and thus of life, addresses Death more boldly than ever before.

The scene already suggests this outcome. The opening lines present a "street / That narrows darkly into motor dawn. . . ." They situate us within a confining perspective, in the corridor of a tomb or in a tunnel. The prospect is dark and threatening, yet opens on the dawn—the dawn, Crane said in an early version, "That brings dismay and beauty to the world." [92] The darkness is fearful and promissory, perhaps of the fertile quiet kind that Crane later associated with this part of the poem: "it's like the moment of the communion with the 'religious gunman' in my 'F and H' where the edge of the bridge leaps over the edge of the street." [93] The "motor dawn" may be not only the futurists' world of destructive machinery into which the poem moves but the bridge of the imagination with which, in closing, it may be said to open.

In speaking of communion with the gunman, Crane describes an achievement of the poet's act of speech: he entertains Death, the spirit of death he recognized in Parts I and II. His companion, as Herbert Leibowitz says, is a doppelgänger.[94] But the "capped arbiter" also recalls, perhaps intentionally, the hooded figure of *The Waste Land*. Crane's "delicate ambassador" is not an unrecognized risen god, except to those who have not yet recognized him. The poet recognizes him and treats him according to this entry in Crane's notebook: "The agency of death is exercised in obscure

92. Leibowitz, *Hart Crane*, p. 72.
93. *Letters*, p. 181 (April 21, 1924).
94. Leibowitz, *Hart Crane*, p. 73.

ways as the agency of life." [95] For the movement of the poem is grounded in the idea of generative or process nature—an idea not yet fully unfolded in this poem. The poet is aware of the bipolar unity of death-and-life, destruction-creation; and the poem, as Crane explained to Frank, "is Dionysian in its attitude, the creator and the eternal destroyer dance arm in arm. . . ." [96] In private and public terms, the poem affirms the renewal of life. Crane answers Eliot's response to the destruction and death of World War I with his own faith in death's vital agency. By way of death, the imagination of the poem reaches toward the glorious beauty of Helen and a civilization of white buildings.

Death, whose credentials are spiritual, is the ambassador of another world. He delicately frees "numbers," the multitudes of Part I, from modern civilization ("steel") and releases them to heaven ("arise / In whispers"). As a "religious gunman!"—a gangster of the twenties, inspired perhaps by Apollinaire—he is an unrecognized "hero" of the secular, thrifty civilization. Simply because men without faith—unaware of the dimensions of experience the poem itself creates—have forgotten him, he will "fall." Having an unrecognized position, a faith in spiritual agency, and a power of embassy, he shares much with the poet. It is fitting, then, that they should join in tragic song, itself a form of expression little respected in the modern world, and that, as the brilliant phrase "unbind our throats" suggests, their act of song should be, in Whitman's words, "Death's outlet song of life. . . ." [97]

The tragic event that prompts their song is World War I, the first public occasion in Crane's poetry. It is represented by what was to become the most terrible aspect of war—aerial bombardment of civilians. Here the poem is unusually fine. Identifying with the pilots, the poet, Crane explained, describes from a moving position in the air the strafing and bombing, an apocalypse comparable to the "bursts in the violet air / Falling towers" of *The Waste Land*.[98] The airmen are flying horsemen, Cossacks enjoying

95. Cited by Leibowitz, *Hart Crane*, p. 70.
96. *Letters*, p. 121 (February 7, 1923).
97. "When Lilacs Last in the Dooryard Bloom'd," § 4.
98. P, 221–22.

a pogrom, rapists of cities. And identifying with his generation, the poet expresses the moral shock, the outrageousness of a civilization whose guilt he accepts and whose redemption he seeks. Having "survived," come through this death, he will "persist to speak"; he will affirm the spiritual necessity of Beauty and remind us of its destruction by Machinery—thrifty bridges, airplanes, dictatorship. The last belongs in this series because of the alliance of futurism and fascism; dictatorship, for Crane, is the political aspect of the Machine, the agent ("the ominous lifted arm"—ominous because the gesture of transcendence nullifies itself) that "lowers down the arc of Helen's brow / To saturate with blessing and dismay."

The image of saturation recalls another that may help us measure the poet's acceptance of public role. At the end of "Porphyro in Akron," the stars are drowned in a slow rain. Then the poet, who believed the Machine did not need his song, expressed dispiritedness; now he resists it with all the resources at his command—"the lavish heart," "the bells and voices," the upward-reaching hands. He accepts a threefold task: to leaven the mind depicted earlier, to spread the tidings, and to atone for the needless limitations men have imposed on mortal being. His office is religious, both Christ-like and Dionysian: to suffer (to spend the self beyond repair, to spend lavishly of the heart) and, by gathering the "blown blood" and "scattered wine," to prepare a new communion as the foundation of a new civilization. The Dionysian, marked in an early version by invitation to drink,[99] is prominent in the imperatives of the concluding stanzas ("Delve upward," "Laugh out," "Distinctly praise"). And it is also present in the poet's commitment to renewal: in his desire to be, like Anchises and Erasmus, a culture hero who, by transmitting a conception of Beauty, maintains the continuity of civilization. This is what Crane meant when he explained that the evocation of Helen consisted in "a reconstruction in these modern terms of the basic emotional attitude toward beauty that the Greeks had" and that, in doing this, he had built "a bridge between so-called classic experience and many divergent realities of our seething, confused cosmos of today. . . ."[100] And

99. Leibowitz, *Hart Crane*, pp. 71–72.
100. P, 217.

this is what he meant by myth—an imaginative construct by which the negations of history are (temporarily) overcome, the accomplishment by which the poet becomes a "thief of time."

This public motive is impelled by the familiar personal one evoked by "For golden, or the shadow of gold hair." The prodigality and suffering of the poet are of early origin, having been expressed in "C 33" and "The Hive." Behind Helen stands the "Materna." This is explicit in an early version of the poem, where the poet invokes Astarte, "mother of beauty— / mother of Saints!" and declares that "The lavish heart shall win [overcome] the rape [of Helen, civilization], in sight, / of ever-virgin Beauty, untouched, unatouchable." [101] This purification of Helen by maternal pre-emption is never directly disclosed, only hinted at in the way the obviously erotic is avoided in the previous parts of the poem. Perhaps this is necessary to Crane's conception of the poet-redeemer of ravished civilization. But the familiar imagery and the resonance of the line seem to owe their power to something else— to an occurrence which may even have prepared for the composition of this part of the poem.

Crane began Part III after a slack autumn during which he quarreled with his mother over having wine at home and, to win his point, moved to a hotel. But self-imposed banishment from his tower room left him "desolate," and he complained that "Life is meagre with me. I am unsatisfied and always left begging for beauty. I am tied to the stake, a little more wastefully burnt every day. . . ." [102] This episode, as the letter relating it shows, revived the world of the early poems, the image of unresponsive mother, and his own guilt. And it provided the emotional context of his excited response to Isadora Duncan, whom he felt called on to defend from a philistine audience and who, he said, was "now on her way back to Moscow . . . where someone will give her some roses for her pains." [103]

Locating this emotional source does not reduce the poem to it. Instead it reveals the double energy at work in the poem, an emotion so powerful that it draws the poet to it even as it moves him

101. Leibowitz, *Hart Crane*, p. 71.
102. *Letters*, pp. 107–9 (December 10, 1922).
103. *Letters*, p. 109 (December 12, 1922).

to turn from it. Such emotion, at once constraining and liberating, is the psychological equivalent of the death-and-life theme of the poem, and the poet is under the necessity of singing his tragic song because, as Whitman wrote of the thrush's "outlet song," "If thou wast not granted to sing thou would'st surely die." [104] The poem is not regressive. The poet returns to his source but also goes forward, and this exhilarating experience, known to the poet in his poetic activity, secures the concluding stanza in something more than the will to "launch into praise."

In commanding Death to "praise the years," the poet commands him to praise history—all of the crucifixions, suffering, temporal yet spiritual ("volatile") trials of mankind. He imagines all of history present now, as suffering "blamed" mankind, its bleeding hands extended toward and threshing heaven, delving upward to gather the new and scattered wine. This conception of history as the everpresence of all human experience is grand (it is present again in "The River" and "Atlantis"). All the anguish and undaunted search that Crane associated with the liberation of imagination are united in it and given more than personal significance. What was treated earlier in personal terms—the lifted arms and "troubled hands" of the poet who would "touch / Those hands of yours [Helen]"—now becomes what before was only implied: the motive of man's immemorial search, the motive of history and the reason for its continuity. The bleeding hands of mankind petition the heavens and by their reaching "extend" them, put them farther off (perhaps, as in "At Melville's Tomb," even create them). They petition with "bargain, vocable and prayer," each a more compelling form bespeaking greater need. For these forms of petition—all forms of petition—bring despair by opening rather than closing the distance. Like the anguished hands, they "extend . . . the height," they are unanswered. But this despair is a condition of imagination, the shore from which it throws its bridge, the shore beyond which it "spans." Despair defines man's spiritual consciousness; it follows from the demands he makes on the universe and the depth his petitions open. Imagination does not arch this space; it is not, like bargain, vocable, and prayer, a completed action. It "outpaces" such petitions, strides ahead of them, but to

104. "When Lilacs Last in the Dooryard Bloom'd," § 4.

no fixed end. It is characterized by lively motion, and the feeling that accompanies it is defined by the despair it overcomes, by ecstatic release. "Faustus and Helen" celebrates the imagination, the power that enables man to bear the burdens of his private and public history.

We must not forget how much death dominates "Faustus and Helen," how death-ridden Crane's generation was. *The Waste Land,* which Crane read before completing Part III and said was "so damned dead," [105] expressed and thereby confirmed this sense of sterility. It provided the test poem for those, like Crane, who still shared the hope of the generation of *The Seven Arts.* Crane's advice to Tate to "launch into praise," to follow the "upward slant into something broadly human," describes his own achievement.[106] So does the letter to Munson in which he says that "after this perfection of death [*The Waste Land*]—nothing is possible in motion but a resurrection of some kind," that he would "still affirm certain things," the kind of "spiritual events" he attributes to Blake, and would work "toward a more positive . . . ecstatic goal." [107] That he was able to some extent to express these intentions accounts for his own enthusiasm for the poem and for its acclamation by the members of Paul Rosenfeld's (*The Seven Arts–*Stieglitz) circle; and the latter, the first public recognition in his career, may account for his placing the poem with more accomplished work in *White Buildings.*

Crane did not will the faith expressed in the poem, though the straining of the poem is sometimes felt; he simply did not realize it fully there. That was to become the work of *The Bridge,* much of which is anticipated in or proposed by "Faustus and Helen." This faith is vital and resurrectional. It reminds one of Crane's older contemporary, Pasternak, whose sense of miraculous life has its source in a profound appreciation of the feminine mystery of nature, the humanity of history, and the revelatory power of imagination. Crane believes that history itself—human suffering—has within it the redemptive force of imagination. He believes in the natural

105. *Letters,* p. 105 (November 20, 1922).
106. *Letters,* p. 94 (July 19, 1922).
107. *Letters,* p. 115 (January 5, 1923).

miracles of diurnal and seasonal change and in "spiritual events," the miracles of experience. The men he celebrates reach "beyond despair" and are willing to spend themselves "beyond repair. . . ." They build bridges out of their very substance, from the "substance drilled and spent. . . ." The self, in an experience comparable only to the life-yielding sexual act of dying, makes its own bridges, and these, like Whitman's fancies ("I fling out my fancies toward them"), outpace bargain, vocable, and prayer because they are energized by love, sped on by the "lavish heart. . . ." [108]

During the period of composing "Faustus and Helen," Crane wrote "Sunday Morning Apples," one of his consummate poems, a poem, surely, that fulfilled his desire "to present a vital, living and tangible,—a positive emotion to [his] satisfaction." [109] He does not say it did; he hardly notices it, merely remarking to Munson that, balked in writing the long poem, he had written "a homely and gay thing . . . out of sheer joy." [110] Still, he chose to read it on the occasion of his coming-out at Rosenfeld's, and not perhaps only for the reason, as he explained to his mother, that it had everywhere been talked about since its publication.[111]

The poem is dedicated to William Sommer, whose art it presents in the supreme tribute of verbal equivalent. Crane seems to have written it easily and quickly according to "the 'Ding an Sich' method" that Sommer himself advised. "One must be drenched in words," Crane explained, "literally soaked with them to have the right ones form themselves into the proper pattern at the right moment. When they come . . . they come as things in themselves; it is a matter of felicitous juggling." [112] Crane speaks of words in the sense of materials, and in speaking of "things in themselves" (*Ding an Sich*) is speaking for the cubist theory of art he had read about in Roger Fry and Clive Bell and had been instructed in by Sommer and Lescaze. The words that come as things in themselves

108. "Song of Myself," § 33.
109. *Letters*, p. 71 (November 26, 1921).
110. *Letters*, p. 96 (August 7, 1922).
111. *Letters*, p. 195 (November 30, 1924).
112. *Letters*, p. 71 (November 26, 1921). Crane's notion of juggling words is similar to Williams' notion of "jostling" them in *Spring and All* (Dijon: Contact Publishing Co., 1923), p. 86.

are to be used in a nonsymbolic way, as things with which the artist constructs an object, which is also a thing in itself whose significance resides not in any "meaning" extrinsic to it but in its intrinsic formal relationships. Words, of course, are not devoid of meanings, but within the frame of the poem they may be juggled (dynamically placed or balanced) to help them "form themselves into the proper pattern"—a pattern intrinsic to them, constituting their own interior order or significant form.

Crane did not often exploit this theory to the visual ends that Williams did, though the title of this poem describes both Sommer's and his own still-life. He did not try, with Williams, to divest words of metaphorical meaning but, as the need to be drenched in words suggests, to use their meanings to cubist ends. One hesitates, for instance, to call the verbal art of the opening stanza of "Faustus and Helen" symbolical because the multiple associations are used to reveal the object, to present it instantly— simultaneously—in all its aspects. Not their ambiguity creates the obscurity one sometimes feels in Crane's poems but the crowding of the meanings of words, what Crane referred to when he said the poem is "packed with cross-currents and multiple suggestions. . . ." [113] And one understands better the reason for Crane's impatience with the sociological readings of "Black Tambourine." What disturbed him was not the imputation of sociological import but what it indicated about the total misunderstanding of the new art. He told Munson that he valued the poem for "what a painter would call its 'tactile' quality,—an entirely aesthetic feature," and he told Sherwood Anderson that it was an example of "interior" form.[114] The poem is cubist, and Milne Holton, who appreciates its "visualization" but treats it in imagistic terms, describes its cubist aspect when he says that Crane "sets before his reader a single image and requires that the reader contemplate that image with an imagination which exposes all of its implications." [115] The poem is arranged to reveal the black man in the cellar. Its movement is visual, opening out the central image, even using history to create a simultaneous order, and in its circularity

113. *Letters*, p. 121 (February 7, 1923).
114. *Letters*, pp. 58, 77 (Spring, 1921; January 10, 1922).
115. " 'A Baudelairesque Thing,' " p. 224.

enclosing or confining it. The restricted visual experience accords with its dark "meaning."

"Sunday Morning Apples" is more complex because it does what it talks about. It is one of the notable poems on art by an American poet, comparable to Williams' "To a Solitary Disciple" (1917). The title describes the painting Sommer is constructing as well as a central motif of his art. The catalog of the memorial exhibition of his work, which reprints Crane's poem, has for its cover and frontispiece pictures of apples; it even lists a water-color painting, "Hart Crane and Apple," probably done during the summer of the poem's composition—a painting that seems to have vanished.[116] The title of the poem, which awakens echoes of Stevens' "Sunday Morning," refers to the double freshness of morning and Sunday, to a paradisal time, a time renewed by art. In a more literal sense, since Sommer was only free to paint on weekends, it refers to the time during which he painted. And it may refer to his master, to Cézanne, from whom Sommer learned to value common objects and to make paintings of them. He had also learned to take up the materials of his place, and he did for the rural area surrounding his schoolhouse studio on the Brandywine River what Cézanne did for Aix-en-Provence.[117] Certainly Crane was right in pressing Sommer's claim to the attention of the partisans of the "American Moment"—the Stieglitzians who had fashioned a native art credo from cubist theory and a concern for the world of their immediate experience. An ardent champion of Sommer, he may even have read his tribute at Rosenfeld's in order to remind them of their neglect.

The poem not only characterizes Sommer's art, it captures its "dynamism," the quality of both man and work that had overwhelmed Crane on his first visit to Sommer's studio,[118] and treats the modernist issue of the relation of art to nature and to imagination. The dependence of the artist on nature is not one of

116. *The William Sommer Memorial Exhibition: Catalogue of an Exhibition of Works by William Sommer Held November First through December Tenth in the Cleveland Museum of Art 1950.*
117. William M. Milliken, in *The William Sommer Memorial Exhibition*, p. 13. See also Hunter Ingalls, "Genius of the Everyday—the Art of William Sommer," unpublished master's essay, Columbia University, 1963.
118. *Letters*, p. 60 (June or July, 1921).

imitation, though Sommer uses natural objects, but of inspiration: of contact with nature and the steady influence that moves through nature in her seasons.[119] The first stanza provides this condition of art, and evokes the equanimity, confidence, and quiet hope that come of relying on this ultimate resource. The organic rhythm of nature—the poet recognizes inevitable seasonal change ("the leaves will fall")—this rhythm also renews life and fulfills the artist's "purposes." For his purpose, the *work* of art, is to bring life out of death, movement out of stasis: to create, to transform one condition into another.

This may explain why the poet's meditation on a melancholy theme is untroubled. He is already in the presence of art, already responsive to the motion of the painter's remarkable draughtsmanship. Though he acknowledges the season of creative ebb and death, thereby establishing the necessary ground of art, he feels that the future is open, that what will happen will happen "sometime" in contrast to the "now," the absorbing vital present of aesthetic contemplation and creation. Taking its strength from time, from the decay of self and world, art overcomes time; and so, in the cycle of experience nature both symbolizes and enables the artist to work through, despair yields to joy. The poem exemplifies this and may be said to bear the "beloved apples of seasonable madness. . . ."

The verse, the single sentence in which the poet declares this assurance, has the easy, uninterrupted movement of the line of the good draughtsman. The rhythm is internal: there is a stress-pause at "sometime"; and "fill" runs over into line two, which, also with a shorter stress-pause on "purposes," runs into line three. The lines lack heavy stress and, aided by liquid consonants and long open vowels, run fully and smoothly to the end. The imagery, of fallen leaves and snow ("fleece"), is warm and gentle, not cold and hostile; and the natural action is of "filling," of providing a bounty. The "fill" of this stanza will be fulfilled in the "full" of the last.

The two stanzas that follow may depict both actual landscapes and paintings. Sommer painted just such landscapes, and the poet may be viewing them in the artist's studio, where the artist himself is perhaps painting a still-life. Along with this picture, treated in

119. Williams' idea of "dynamization" bears on this. See *Spring and All*, pp. 90–93. Williams is aware of the revolution in art since Cézanne.

the last stanza, they exist simultaneously. They are the elements of the poet's own composition, the composite canvas of Sommer's work that he is poising for the explosion, the instantaneous, radiant, immediate impact of art.

The first landscape presents a leafless yet budding tree ("ripe nude"). But this phrase in turn evokes a richly endowed woman: Nature herself, in motion, rearing her head into the opposing elements. "Nude" suggests the entire body of a late winter landscape and the naked and exposed new life beginning to emerge; "ripe" suggests a fullness at the point of bursting. One thinks of the landscape of Williams' "By the Road to the Contagious Hospital" (1923) with its "challenges to spring." "Challenges" may seem to be inappropriate unless followed by "of"—"challenges of spring"—but it is right if the verbal character of "to spring" and the motions of a spring landscape and the challenge of the art of painting are kept in mind. The tree-female rears its head into a realm of swords, a forceful motion of straining and opposing that the colors, purple against white, complement in purely visual terms, actually bursting and thus defying death, the mere whiteness of snow. And this motion is also conveyed by the poet in his art: by the strenuous, continuously pressing sentence, which, after the pause following "now," moves decisively, with stresses on "reared," "bursting," and "defiance," to its victorious culmination. This victory, an advent of beauty, is not represented immediately by the emergence of new infant life but by the overcoming of one aspect of nature by another, Mother Nature herself (defying what swords?) triumphing over her North Labradorian coldness. A regal powerful woman, the eternal feminine, dominates this landscape, and she can defy even the "winter of the world" because her stunning whiteness is everything that white meant for Crane—purity, spirit, the absolute. For him the supreme deity, the deity of life, is truly maternal.

What spring brings forth is the child—and childhood world—of the next stanza. The boy and dog compose another landscape that functions in the cubist design by presenting activities outside of yet intimately related to Sommer's studio. In this landscape we effortlessly, by immediate sympathy, enter a timeless universe of sun and flowers ("perennials") and spontaneous joyful play: "A boy runs with a dog before the sun. . . ." This landscape is radiant, spacious, open, free; it offers release into almost astronomical space, a world without limitation, without threat (unlike the childhood landscape of "Voyages I"), a world still within the protection of the mother ("valley") and comfortingly known (Brandywine).

The descriptive language of this landscape moves easily. Though it may seem difficult ("straddling / Spontaneities . . . orbits"), it also seems colloquial, perhaps because the poet addresses the painter and names his valley. Brom Weber glosses the stanza in terms of Ouspensky's idea of the different orders of consciousness in man and animal: a dog, for example, cannot grasp the kind of objective knowledge necessary to our understanding of astronomy nor the idea of recurrence; its world is always new.[120] But perhaps the point of the verse is that the boy does not grasp them either, that he is not yet twisted by things irreconcilable and lives fully in the sunlit present of his own spontaneous life. And there is no difficulty if we remember that the poet is describing a painting, that his brilliant plosive images present the compositional organization and its effect, especially the bursts of light, the flowers of light ("perennials of light") through which the boy runs in a landscape characterized by radiance, by Sommer's notable depiction of the motion of light.

In the concluding stanzas the poet turns to the painter he has just addressed and to the still-life he is either in the process of painting or being invited to paint as he has before ("again"). These stanzas take their departure from "Brandywine," the name of a variety of apple that also conveys the intoxicating (ecstatic) use to which it is put—a use Sommer appreciated and associated with art. "I have seen the apples there [in the Brandywine valley] that toss you secrets," the poet says to the painter, bringing their friendship, another condition of art, within the frame of the poem as well as reminding us of the seasons that ripen the artist's purposes. The logic of the poem is seasonal, moving from an imagined winter to late summer, the actual time of the poem; nature supports the artist's purposes—the very landscapes he has painted tell us that he knows and values her miracles of emergent life and spontaneous joy. But, in the poet's view, the logic expresses a related ripening that is intimately his own. Moving through landscapes maternal,

120. *Hart Crane*, p. 151.

youthful, and mature, it supports the poet's feeling that emergence is only truly possible when conditions are favoring and happy. To become an artist like Sommer, capable of contacting the world and following the method of nature, to enter the state of maturity the poem finally depicts—that of the absolute freedom of artistic creation in which one rivals nature—one must be able, like him, to acknowledge radiantly the sovereign female and the spontaneous child upon which one still depends. And one must acknowledge the good father, too, who, for the poet, is Sommer himself.

The apples of the title and of the last stanzas symbolize this by gathering to fullness the earlier seasons. They have Edenic associations—with blissful garden, with innocence, with woman and the secrets of life, with fulfilled desire (as in "Garden Abstract": "The apple on its bough is her desire"). Their connection with happy love is also conveyed in "toss you," which evokes the race of Atalanta and her lover. Their negative associations with sin and loss are dismissed by the poet's description: "Beloved apples of seasonable madness / That feed your inquiries with aerial wine." The apples of the beloved are breasts; they nurture the artist. They are seasonal and seasonable, and the madness they produce (since they themselves are the fruit of "seasonable madness") is the divine madness of poets, a spiritual intoxication or ecstasy caused by "aerial wine," the aroma of orchards, of sensuously filled space, that might make one, in Emily Dickinson's phrase, "inebriate of air." They afford a state of grace—of possession—in which the sexual and the spiritual are reconciled.

Having to this point treated the resources of the artist, the poet now instructs him to begin the work of felicitous juggling—to place the apples with the other objects of the still-life in such a way that the painting will be charged with life. "Full and ready for explosion" modifies apple; but the act of composing them, of "poising" them in relation to the knife and pitcher, also creates the unstable equilibrium of explosive situations. The artist, too, understands the dynamism, the vital power of nature; and he, like the poet who here emulates him, contributes to the explosion, the wonderful revelation of the thing itself rendered in the last line by the poet's ecstatic outburst: "The apples, Bill, the apples!"

In "Sunday Morning Apples," the poet tells his new confidence in the sources of inspiration and the miracles of art. He tells the faith without which he could not have written "Faustus and Helen" and *The Bridge*: that art brings life out of death—transforms *nature morte*—and provides the stay of "absolute experience" ("a formally convincing statement of a conception or apprehension of life that gains our unquestioning assent").[121] The poem enacts an aesthetic moment comparable to the sexual moment of "Garden Abstract." It is an *elan* of the imagination that convinces us that "vision is the release into pure being." [122]

121. P, 219.
122. Bachelard, *The Poetics of Reverie*, p. 6; William H. Rueckert, "Kenneth Burke and Structuralism," *Shenandoah*, XXI (Autumn, 1969), 28.

three

"And Gradually White Buildings Answer Day"

I

"Really," Crane wrote his mother during the early months of his return to New York—"really, I'm having the finest time in my life." [1] And this was so. He left Cleveland for good in March 1923, took the night train, and the next day found himself, as Scott Fitzgerald remembered he once had, in a great metropolis that "had all the iridescence of the beginning of the world." [2] Crane reported immediately to the Rychtariks the "salt air and clean sunlight . . . [the people] carrying canes and wearing bright clothes," [3] and in subsequent letters to Cleveland he told of his own equally splendid entrance to the literary life.

That Crane's arrival was a literary arrival had much to do with his exhilaration. He was not an unknown poet, and he brought with him a remarkable long poem, which he soon read publicly, and the idea of a still longer and more remarkable poem, which he soon began to discuss with his new-found friends. Having a base at Munson's, he established within a few weeks the relationships he needed. He met Waldo Frank ("it was great to shake hands and talk with you"), the older writer whose sympathetic response to "Faustus and Helen" had heartened him, the "brother" who more than anyone helped him get *White Buildings* published and, by going with him to the Isle of Pines, undoubtedly helped him get

1. *Letters*, p. 135 (June 10, 1923).
2. "My Lost City," *The Crack-Up*, ed. Edmund Wilson (New York: New Directions, 1945), p. 25.
3. *Letters*, p. 130 (March, 1923).

The Bridge under way.[4] And he met Alfred Stieglitz, another "brother," or father, whose work had overwhelmed him, had been a shock of recognition. He told Stieglitz that "that moment was a tremendous one in my life because I was able to share all the truth toward which I am working in my own medium, poetry, with another man who had manifestly taken many steps in that same direction in *his* work." [5] Trying to remain independent, Crane gladly bound himself to Stieglitz by identifying with his aims; and Stieglitz, whose photograph "Apples and Gable" (1922) fascinated Crane and perhaps reminded him of Sommer, stood in for Sommer, becoming at once another mentor whom Crane would serve, this time by writing about his art. Crane never completed the essay that, in eagerness to champion the artist he believed he had understood better than anyone, he promised he would write, and this may be the reason he never turned to Stieglitz for support and that Stieglitz disappears from his correspondence. But Stieglitz did not disappear from Crane's thought: the ideas that at this time he began to explore in his letters to Stieglitz were tried out in his work and set down in "General Aims and Theories" and "Modern Poetry."

By June he had also joined a circle of writers and artists that included William Slater Brown, Susan Jenkins, Kenneth Burke, Edward Nagle, Gaston Lachaise, Malcolm Cowley, and his old friends Gorham Munson and Matthew Josephson. He had found a job in an advertising agency, had taken over Bill Brown's room and fixed it up, had even acquired a Victrola. And so, with preparations made, he was, as he announced in his letters, "all ready to begin on *The Bridge* again." [6]

He did begin to work on the poem, on the last section, sending new drafts of it to Charlotte Rychtarik and Stieglitz. But summer in New York City—the loneliness as well as the press of work, the

4. *Letters*, p. 130 (Easter, 1923). Susan Jenkins Brown says that Frank, because of his "dozen or so years of seniority and his constant high seriousness," was able to restrain Crane's sometimes drunken behavior, and that his "labors on behalf of the publication of *White Buildings* . . . exceeded those of anyone else." *Robber Rocks: Letters and Memories of Hart Crane, 1923–1932* (Middletown: Wesleyan University Press, 1969), pp. 60, 63. Crane dedicated *White Buildings* to Frank.

5. *Letters*, p. 131 (April 15, 1923).

6. *Letters*, pp. 135, 136 (June 5, 10, 1923).

heat and the noise—enervated him. Toward the end of July, he complained, in a letter prompted by nostalgia for home and guilt feelings over his mother's suffering, that "I am forced to be ambitious in two directions . . . and in many ways it is like being put on a cross and divided." [7] He stopped working on the poem ("I know," he told Stieglitz, "what it is to be exiled for months at a time").[8] By September he no longer remembered the bright atmosphere of March; he noted the "insidious impurity in the air that seems to seep from sweaty walls and subways." [9] And by the end of October, claiming exhaustion, he resigned his job and went to live with Brown and Nagle in a farmhouse at Woodstock.

As a result of the conflicting demands of cash and creativity, Crane's life followed this pattern of advance on and escape from the city; and as the pattern was repeated the city lost the attraction it had had for him in that moment of liberation from home, that single happy expectant moment he perhaps describes in "Legend," the introductory poem of *White Buildings*, when he speaks of "all those who step / The legend of their youth into the noon." [10] Like Fitzgerald—like an entire generation of writers who associated the city with the fulfillment of dreams—Crane learned otherwise. With Fitzgerald, who discovered his mistake when viewing the city from the top of the Empire State Building ("the last and most magnificent of towers"), Crane might have cried out, as perhaps he does in the title of his first book of poems, "Come back, come back, O glittering and white!" [11]

In going to Woodstock, Crane was one of the early pioneers in the exodus of writers and artists from the city that Malcolm Cowley called "the Connecticut migration." [12] In time, the hilly countryside near Patterson, New York, which reminded him of the

---

7. *Letters*, pp. 141–42 (July 21, 1923).

8. *Letters*, p. 145 (August 25, 1923).

9. *Letters*, p. 147 (September 8, 1923).

10. The pattern enacts a major rhythm of Crane's life—that of new birth. When he explained to his mother the reasons for again quitting his job, he said: "I was ready for ANYTHING after the prolonged tension and confinement here. . . ." *Letters*, p. 207 (May 28, 1925).

11. *The Crack-Up*, pp. 32, 33.

12. *Exile's Return: A Literary Odyssey of the Nineteen-Twenties* (New York: Viking Press, 1951), p. 211.

Ohio landscape of his boyhood and of Sommer's place, and Addie
Turner's farmhouse, which he first shared with the Tates in 1926,
became the center of his otherwise homeless life. Crane went there
initially because his mother did not concur in his wish—clearly a
profound one—to go to the Isle of Pines, where later, in the sum-
mer of 1926, he was able after long delay to write a large part of
The Bridge. During his first retreat to the countryside he intended
to finish *The Bridge* and thus complete the materials for his first
book of poems. But *The Bridge* was not finished because its con-
ception was larger than Crane realized then; it required growing
into, and waited on other things besides time for composition. For-
tunately, as he told Charlotte Rychtarik during a period of little
progress on it, "some smaller poems . . . crop[ped] out from time
to time very naturally"; [13] and fortunately he was inspired by a love
affair to write "Voyages," a group of poems long enough and good
enough to replace *The Bridge.* By March 1925, about two years
after coming to New York, the manuscript of *White Buildings* was
ready, and search for a publisher began.[14]

Allen Tate and Yvor Winters, friends of Crane's who wrote the
most intelligent contemporary criticism of *White Buildings,* con-
sidered him "the poet of the complex urban civilization of his age,"
a poet who "accepts his age in its entirety. . . ." [15] Perhaps they
interpreted the title of the book to mean this, or read into it their
understanding of Crane's development and of his intentions for
The Bridge. Except for "Faustus and Helen" and a few of the
shorter poems ("Chaplinesque," "Possessions," and "Recitative"),
White Buildings is not notably urban. Nor is it openly accepting,
as the epigraph from Rimbaud's *Illuminations* clearly shows: "Ce
ne peut être que la fin du monde, en avançant." This line—"It can
only be the end of the world ahead"—concludes the section "En-
fance" ("Childhood"), gathering up in dismay a sense of loneliness

13. *Letters,* p. 148 (September 23, 1923).
14. The manuscript was altered during the year or more before it was delivered to
Boni & Liveright. See Kenneth A. Lohf, *The Literary Manuscript of Hart Crane*
(Columbus: Ohio State University Press, 1967), pp. 3–5.
15. Tate, Foreword, *White Buildings,* p. xi; Winters, "Hart Crane's Poems,"
p. 49.

and loss, of being abandoned and forced to leave the dark library
armchair, the enclosed world of childhood, for the high road of life.
"How far away are the birds and the springs!"—this is what Crane
is telling us, and how little he expects to find (or has found) in the
city, the modern world, ahead.[16]

This epigraph fittingly introduces a first book of poems whose
pervasive spirit, in consequence of the poet's advance from youth
to manhood and from innocence to experience, is valedictory.[17]
Crane used it for its resonance—not so much to identify with Rim-
baud, though it enables him to, as to suggest the spiritual adventure
in terms of which he organized the book. And it helps to define the
White Buildings of the title, the inalienable ideal of the poet's past
that he places in the future and hopes, by going ahead, to repos-
sess.[18]

Jean Guiguet, in *L'Univers poétique de Hart Crane*, treats build-
ings as an aspect of the city and of civilization. In this context they
seem to carry all the weight of Crane's antipathy to modern life;
for the city, Guiguet says, is a place for Crane of agitation, hostility,
and exile—"a trench of stone." [19] Yet to Crane and his generation,
the city, with its soaring skyscrapers, meant something more, some-
thing that Rimbaud again defines: "Et, à l'aurore, armé d'une
ardente patience, nous entrerons aux splendides villes." [20] Crane's
earliest response to New York captures this splendor ("It is very
cold but clear, and the marble facades of the marvelous mansions

16. *Illuminations*, trans. Louise Varèse (New York: New Directions, 1957), pp.
6–13.

17. The phrase "innocence to experience" alludes to the letter in which Crane
tells of his enthusiasm for Donne and his desire to sing the "beauty of experience
[rather] than innocence." This letter also contains a statement of intent applicable
to the poems in *White Buildings*: "Unless one has some new, intensely personal
viewpoint to record, say on the eternal feelings of love, and the suitable personal
idiom to employ in the act, I say, why write about it?" *Letters*, pp. 67–68 (October
17, 1921).

18. For the sources of Crane's interest in Rimbaud, see Weber, *Hart Crane*, pp.
144–50.

19. (Paris: M. J. Minard, 1965), pp. 58–59; my translation.

20. "And, at dawn, armed with an ardent patience we shall enter the splendid
cities." *Une Saison en Enfer*, trans. Delmore Schwartz (Norfolk, Conn.: New
Directions, 1939), pp. 96–97.

shone like crystal in the sun").[21] So do the lines of "Recitative"
from which he took the title:

> Then watch
> While darkness, like an ape's face, falls away,
> And gradually, white buildings answer day.

Written several years later, out of the anguish of experience, these
lines still express the poet's expectancy, his sense of wonder and
assurance in the radiant transformation that restores the purity of
aspiration. The white buildings answering day, emerging from
darkness and taking the morning light, belong to the world of Stieg-
litz' later photographs, to an art that sometimes celebrates the
beauty of the modern city.[22] If the city is a play of horizontals and
verticals, as in Guiguet's account, then buildings, which whiteness
will not permit to be squat, are vertical, of the aspiring dimension,
the dimension that Ouspensky, in speaking of towers, said was "per-
pendicular to time." [23] In answering day, white buildings overcome
the darkly bestial, the less than human; they are not so much
phallic images as the cool and clean images of purified desire,
images of a paradisal world, of the fully responsive maternal, re-
deemed world of innocence. They are Crane's Jerusalem.[24]

The white buildings of "Recitative" become in the course of
the day (in time) the skyscrapers of a "fallen" business world, the
tower the poet enjoins us to leave for the bridge ("yet leave the
tower. / The bridge swings over salvage"). But in its morning
splendor the tower is equivalent to the bridge. Crane associates
them in "General Aims and Theories," when he says that "language
has built towers and bridges." [25] And this statement reminds us that
for Crane the poems by means of which he took account of and
lived into his experience were constructs, white buildings and
bridges, triumphs of the imagination that granted him the redemp-
tion Blake called "Eternity." [26] White buildings belong in the

21. *Letters*, p. 4 (December 31, 1916).
22. They belong to the world exhilarated by the Eiffel Tower. See the paintings
of Robert Delaunay and John Marin, and the poems of Blaise Cendrars.
23. *Tertium Organum*, p. 47.
24. See Norman O. Brown, *Love's Body* (New York: Vintage Books, 1966), p.
36. Brown cities both Freud and Blake ("Jerusalem, 'a City, yet a Woman'").
25. P, 223.
26. See also Crane's poem to Emily Dickinson, with whom he associates Blake.

"white cities" of "Faustus and Helen"; they are the "pure pos-
session" of "Possessions," the "bright stones"—raised (an essen-
tial pun on "rase": achieved in suffering) by the "white wind"—
"wherein our smiling plays." For Crane, poems, characteristically,
enact the loss and stress and the intense attainment and reconcilia-
tion which are also the larger rhythm of his work and the reason for
his perseverance; they are the forms in which he tries to unite him-
self and have his being. And so it is right that the city represents
both the good he seeks and the loss he suffers, and that, in calling
his book *White Buildings*, even in the face of the suffering acknowl-
edged in "Legend" and of the love lost in "Voyages," he is assert-
ing that he will not be subdued. As he told Charlotte Rychtarik,
"I want to keep saying 'YES' to everything and never be beaten a
moment, and I shall, of course, never be really beaten." [27] Poetry,
"the imaged Word," as he says in "Voyages VI," is a landmark of
imagination, the sign of the unconquered spirit.

"Language has built towers and bridges." The imagery of con-
struct is not adventitious with Crane, who thought of poetry as an
architectural art and took as much care in building a book as in
making each poem a "single, new *word*. . . ." [28] He arranged
White Buildings with the same concern for structure, for a mean-
ingful sequence and not a miscellany of poems, that he showed in
preparing for publication another first book of poems, Malcolm
Cowley's *Blue Juniata*. Cowley later rearranged in an autobiograph-
ical sequence the poems Crane had placed in an emotional se-
quence; [29] but these sequences are not mutually exclusive, and
Crane employed both in *White Buildings*. Except for "Legend,"
the initial poem whose function is given in its title, and "Emblems
of Conduct," whose theme of "spiritual gates" accords with its posi-
tion, the first thirteen poems, roughly half of the book, are early
poems, work of the apprentice years before Crane finally left Cleve-
land for New York. In point of time but not in point of develop-
ment and significance, "Faustus and Helen" belongs with the early

27. *Letters*, p. 148 (September 23, 1923). Crane's affirmative posture here bor-
rows from Joyce, but it is also one of the things that relates him to Emerson, who
wrote that "I am *Defeated* all the time; yet to Victory I am born."
28. P, 221, 223.
29. *Robber Rocks*, pp. 103–5.

poems, but Crane placed it at the end of the book, with "Voyages," to indicate its importance. Though written earlier, the first of the "Voyages" necessarily belongs with that group of poems. Of the eight remaining poems, all written after Crane's arrival in New York, seven ("Repose of Rivers" to "Recitative") comprise the middle section of the book, and the eighth, "At Melville's Tomb," appropriately prefaces "Voyages," the group of poems, most recently completed, that resumes many of the themes of the book and concludes it.

It is possible to consider the structure in a wholly thematic way and within these sections to find significant groupings of poems, like "My Grandmother's Love Letters," "Sunday Morning Apples," and "Praise for an Urn," which may have been placed together not only in the interest of spiritual chronology and emotional and formal contrast but to call attention to the poet's awareness of other people.[30] Still, the contrast of the early poems, which Winters characterized as relatively simple, and the later poems, which are more complex and intensely confessional and often more ambitious in scope, is decisive.

Having already examined the early (not so simple) poems and discovered their common concern with the poet's difficulties of emergence, we may now turn to the later poems. "Legend" tells us that they will be concerned with his advance and that they will be complicated by the necessity he feels to bring his past with him and to re-enact it. For the legend named in "Legend" is of two kinds. The title of the poem may be construed as designating nothing more than the key to a chart or map; here, the poet says, is an inscription (as in Whitman's *Leaves of Grass*), the key to the kind of reality the book contains. But the key itself is a legend ("The legend of their youth"), a legend in the sense of fable, of a story of the past—old and romantic, unverifiable, *legendary*—that we must nevertheless carefully attend to because it is, in Emily Dickinson's meaning, the poet's letter to the world.

What is the poet's legend? Can we believe it?

30. For example, see William F. Fine, "The Pure Possession: Theme and Technique in Hart Crane's *White Buildings*," unpublished master's thesis, University of Wyoming, 1967, pp. 63–66.

Crane begins the poem not with the legend but with the matter
of belief connected with it, with a kind of reality and the experience
of it that supports the subsequent declaration, "I am not ready for
repentance; / Nor to match regrets." The opening lines

> As silent as a mirror is believed
> Realities plunge in silence by . . .

assert, as unquestionable, an absolute experience in an absolute
present. The poet, as if in the act of beholding, is certain of "Reali-
ties": the placing of the word, the stress it requires and its capitali-
zation, insist on this. These "Realities" are plural but that in no
way lessens them; they are not pieces of Reality or, like the images
in a mirror, reflections of it, but its refulgent presence, rapid, end-
less, comet-like explosions (as the plosives indicate) within the vast
and otherwise empty cosmos of the mind. They are explosions of
inner light, the bursts of imagination—we derive from "mirror" that
they occur within the mind, are events of the mind. The inverted
phrasing and the noise of "plunge" tell us that they are not silent.
They come out of the silence that surrounds the poem—listen to
the sizzling fuse of the first line—and they plunge into silence as
into an extinguishing sea. When they come they fill all space; but
their coming is brief, and they are lost: their motion is downward
("plunge") and out of the line of sight ("by"); and their passing,
indicated also by "by" as well as the ellipsis, determines, as much as
the certainty of their wonderful presence, the poet's resolution
to continue his quest until, again, as he says later, "the bright logic
is won."

"The bright logic" is the fully achieved poem whose "evocation,"
Crane says in "General Aims and Theories," is "toward a state of
consciousness, an 'innocence' (Blake) or absolute beauty," and
whose truth, like that of the "Realities," is immediate experience.
Such a poem is itself a Reality. Crane explains, in what may serve
as a gloss of the opening lines, that "It is as though a poem gave the
reader as he left it a single, new *word*, never before spoken and im-
possible to actually enunciate, but self-evident as an active principle
in the reader's consciousness henceforward." [31] Reference to the

---

31. P, 220–21. This essay was written during the same period as "Legend." It
depends heavily on Blake, who also figures prominently in Crane's letters to

"mirror" merely emphasizes the self-evidence of seeing, of the imaginative act or vision; belief is the issue ("Unwhispering as a mirror / Is believed"). All notions of reflection, of an image indicating a hidden Reality, are secondary, to be entertained, as in "Recitative," but dismissed in preference to a Reality revealed directly to the imagination. The poems of *White Buildings*, accordingly, are Realities that plunge silently, that is, self-evidently, through the reader's mind; they are not to be taken as symbols of anything but as things in themselves, explosive events, like "Sunday Morning Apples," bursts of the "active principle" of imagination that affects henceforward our relation to the world.[32] And when poems are strung like pearls—an image of gathered lusters that picks up the plunging Realities of the opening lines—they may be said to be the perfection of the imagination, the White Buildings of the Jerusalem to which Crane, in praising the "clairvoyance" of Stieglitz' art, said great imaginative work would lead us. Crane, too, would give us ("those who step / The legend of their youth into the noon") "the end of a golden string" that we might be led to "Heaven's gate" and in the joy of poetry ("Relentless caper") find "innocence." [33]

Because the poet's experience of "Realities" is one of freedom and consummation he is unwilling to accept the limitation and diminishment implied by "repentance" and "regrets"; his very statement of this, which may seem portentously romantic, is a declaration of liberty befitting an outsetting poet, who puts behind him both the world of his early poems and their aesthetic. He seeks the "only worth," the worth that all grant and that grants all: the ecstatic possession, passionate and pure—the consummation of

---

Stieglitz. In the Foreword to *White Buildings*, Tate associates Crane with Blake when he refers to Crane's desire to release "the imagination as an integer of perception" and to realize "the maximum of poetic energy," and by naming Blake as an example of Crane's most serious failure. Blake's influence is central. Because of it one understands better Crane's dislike of obscurity and his pleasure in the clarity and outline of Sommer's and Stieglitz' work. Crane came to Blake indirectly in his relationship with Waldo Frank and directly by reading S. Foster Damon's *William Blake: His Philosophy and Symbols* (1924), an important and curious work important to Crane also for its references to Whitman. According to Weber, Crane read Blake as early as 1917 (*Hart Crane*, p. 25); and Crane himself reports reading "the Damon book on Blake" in 1922 (*Letters*, p. 100).

32. "A poem," Stevens says, "is a meteor." "Adagia," *Opus Posthumous* (London: Faber and Faber, 1957), p. 158.

33. *Letters*, p. 132 (April 15, 1923).

moth-and-flame, which he now knows is the answering of mutual desire, and the cooler but no less intense consummation of lovers whose pure love (in the setting of snow) is like melting, tremulous flakes ("In the white falling flakes / Kisses are"). Both instances speak for the self-annihilation of ecstasy, the consuming consummation, and the latter, which evokes the epiphany of Joyce's "The Dead," suggests a tender redemptive love.

In the developing argument of the poem, the poet refers to this experience as "burning" and "cleaving," thereby introducing the idea of suffering which is so important in his view of consummatory experience—the experience of love and art.[34] The participial nouns indicate both actions that come to an end and the intense pain involved. And when he says "It is to be learned," he means that it must be and is still to be learned—that he must accept the brevity and the pain and learn also that to seek such consummation requires repeated suffering, the complete expenditure of self. The poet insists on the total price and clarifies the special sense "spend" has for him by adding "out" to the phrase: "Spends out himself again." To spend the self is to suffer, to give up one's very substance—a sexual loss, the burning in which we are burned, a transformation of being.

And this is the challenge the poet, not without pride, accepts in his own call to win the fight for "the bright logic":

> Twice and twice
> (Again the smoking souvenir,
> Bleeding eidolon!) and yet again.

Now, however, the suffering is not only the "burning" in the "imploring flame" but its absence, its loss, the "smoking souvenir"— the unsubstantial image (as in a mirror), the "eidolon," whose bleeding, the flesh spending itself, evokes both fire and crucifixion. To these images of extremity the desired prize is juxtaposed, joined by the preposition "until," as if to show that by enduring such suffering "the bright logic" will be won.

A similar assurance is conveyed by "Then" in the concluding stanza: *then*, in consequence of enduring, he shall attain the victory

---

34. See *Letters*, p. 140 (July 21, 1923), where Crane says that he is only happy when "writing or receiving a return of love."

—his tears ("caustic drop") shall become pearls and his ecstatic cry ("a perfect cry") shall sound a "constant harmony." Compression of meaning unites these consummations. The "perfect cry" also strings the beads, the transformed pain, into a poem (song: "constant harmony"), or into a bridge.[35] For the apposite phrase, "Relentless caper," suggests, even more than some Chaplinesque antic, the heroic leap of the imagination that spans beyond despair, the ascending arc that compensates for the descending "Realities" with which the poem began.

In form, theme, image, and symbolic action, this is Crane's legend, the legend he addresses to both those who merely "step" into the noon and those, like the poet, who daringly leap. The form is a rising one, an argument in behalf of faith in imaginative "Realities" and endurance in their quest. The poem advances from a state of loss, it mounts abruptly in resolution, and it concludes with a fairly regular quatrain, the formal sign of the harmony or reconciliation the poet seeks. The essential action of the poem is the mastery, the transformation, the "possession," of difficult experience. By means of such poems, by the repeated poetic act, the poet survives his experience and achieves his highest being-in-the-world. But much of his legend concerns the suffering he willingly and confidently endures for such moments, the suffering that for Crane is the poet's signature, the evidence of his worthiness and the ground of his work. This romantic posture belongs especially to the legend of his youth, but it persists into his maturity.

The smaller poems that Crane said cropped out in the meantime make clearer the kind of experience to which "Legend" refers. These poems—"Repose of Rivers," "Paraphrase," "Possessions," "Lachrymae Christi," "Passage," "The Wine Menagerie," "Recitative"—are well characterized by Crane's declaration of preference for poems "at once sensual and spiritual, and singing rather the beauty of experience than innocence." [36] They are at once sensual and spiritual because they treat the need to reconcile these con-

---

35. R. W. B. Lewis notes the Whitmanian allusions of the poem, and, in this instance, "glories strung like beads" from "Crossing Brooklyn Ferry." *The Poetry of Hart Crane: A Critical Study* (Princeton: Princeton University Press, 1967), p. 138n.

36. *Letters*, pp. 67–68 (October 17, 1921).

traries, and they may be said to sing the beauty of experience if we think of experience as necessarily involving the attempt to achieve this reconciliation. In this respect these poems are new (their placement in the book emphasizes this). But they are also new in their honesty, the directness with which they treat experience, make *experience* their concern. The distance one sometimes feels in the early poems is closed, and the experiences in which we now participate are extreme, desperate, anguished, the "privatest," as Thoreau demands, of the poet's very soul.[37] The poems, in a phrase from "Possessions," are "piteous admissions"; more than hitherto with Crane, they are openly confessional and autobiographical; they comprise the "too well-known biography" he knew his friends would look for in them.[38] Their personal as well as poetic density is heavy. They record a "new, intensely personal viewpoint" in a "suitable personal idiom" and so arrest our attention (and easy progress through the book) and strike us not as small but as large, even major, poems. For they are formidable and bring us to a center. Knowing them, we see the previous poems with new understanding and move on better prepared to understand the more extensive treatment of these themes.

The contrast of "North Labrador" and "Repose of Rivers," both of which concern the poet's quest in symbolical landscapes, marks these differences. The poet of "Repose of Rivers" speaks directly in his own voice, with more authority, with the maturity of one looking back over his life's experience, seeking there the ground of being. This may be one of the reasons that Crane used it to introduce this group of poems. He meditatively narrates a spiritual fable, and though he tells of agitation, he is not, in the present of the poem ("this summer"), agitated. Yet the telling has the authority of experience: the pressure of what he relates is still felt because it is the emotional burden that the very work of the poem helps him carry and because the telling is more than an act of memory. It is an act at a deeper level than memory, at the level where memory, according to Bachelard, joins with imagination and rivals "in giving us back the images that pertain to our lives." [39] It is poetic reverie,

37. "Life without Principle," initial paragraph.
38. P, 21.
39. *The Poetics of Reverie*, p. 105,

as the title, changed by Crane from "Tampa Schooner," indicates; for this change, unusual with Crane, locates the meaning of the poem in a state of feeling rather than an object or place, and the title, itself a brilliant addition to the poem, awakens a powerful resonance by naming a deeply desired condition and, in the ground tone of its sound, picked up immediately in the poem, inviting us to it, or rather to the reverie toward childhood that restores it. Bachelard speaks of the waters of childhood, making explicit the repose we remember as having been at the source and that we hope to find again at the end of the river of life. Our reveries turn to childhood because "childhood remains within us a principle of deep life, of life always in harmony with the possibility of new beginnings." [40]

The poem moves through four symbolical landscapes in order to tell (recollect) an achieved repose like that of the present. These landscapes are not presented in the natural order of the river of life, the course depicted in "Key West," an inferior poem, whose first stanza is especially relevant to "Repose of Rivers":

> Here has my salient faith annealed me.
> *Out of the valley, past the ample crib*
> *To skies impartial,* that do not disown me
> Nor claim me, either, by Adam's spine—nor rib.[41]

They figure instead in the order of reverie that is awakened by the poet's present awareness of the sound of the sea—reverie and water are wedded together—a reverie that turns on the sound of the willows with which he associates it, the sound of repose (innocence and well-being) that encloses the poem. The willows, prominent thematically and structurally (they appear in stanzas one, three, and five), are a "poetic image," a "wonder-filled image" that "bears witness to a soul which is discovering its world, the world where it would like to live and where it deserves to live." This image belongs to the poet's past—"the reverie toward childhood returns us to the beauty of the first images"—and it is a sign of the recovered innocence of the pressent.[42] Invariably it is linked with sound (the

---

40. *The Poetics of Reverie*, pp. 112, 124.
41. My italics.
42. Bachelard, *The Poetics of Reverie*, pp. 3, 15, 103.

solemn sound of the opening lines, the "singing" of the "willow rim," the steady flaking sound of the sea), linked, that is, even though sadness is also conveyed, with the inspiriting wind and the full motions of inspired life. The willows are such an image and belong, it seems, not to infancy but to youth, to the time—in memory, the season of summer—of innocent sexual awakening; and only when "age," in its inevitable course, brings the poet to the sea, its landscape counterpart, and to another summer season, does he remember it.

In the lines with which the poem begins, the image of the willows is detached from any place, floats freely before us, and we entertain it fully, satisfied by its low music and slow stately dance, the completeness of its being. The past tense places it for us in the world of memory, and the archaic "mead" and the courtly "sarabande" contribute the dignity of pastness, as does the evocation of a pastoral landscape. Only with the poet's admission that he had not remembered this landscape until time (of life) had passed—only with the vivid memory now present, intensified by the further description ("That seething, steady leveling of the marshes"), do we realize that for the poet this landscape is mediated by awareness of spiritual loss. The mowing and the leveling portend the death of innocence.[43] For the poet who meditates on this landscape its resonance resides in the fact that age has brought him to the sea, that he now recalls the willows from a long perspective of experience, that they arise in imagination in answer to the needs of the soul.

The sea is not yet granted the restorative repose associated with innocence and eternity. It is the place of death to which age brings us. The terminus of all rivers, it concludes the stanza. The marshes are not necessarily sea marshes but perhaps only the meadow in its watery aspect—there is a logic in the end words "mead," "marshes," "sea." We do not know whether the meadow and marsh belong to different landscapes or whether the willows belong to both. And for the moment we remain unaware of the sexual import of willows, the gentle, virginal value they acquire by contrast with the poet's experience.

43. Lewis finds the source of the imagery of mowing in ch. 58 of *Moby-Dick*, but overlooks a fact that may have impressed Crane: the mowers are "morning mowers." *The Poetry of Hart Crane*, p. 213.

That experience, associated with either the sea or the agitated waters that bring him there, is violently sexual. The sharp, vivid initial images of the second stanza ("Flags, weeds") are abruptly sexual, breaking into the poet's consciousness, and ours, with all the force of memory finding an immediate focus. These are the phallic images given prominence by Whitman in the *Calamus* poems, associated there with the pond that Crane introduces in stanza three; and, as with Whitman, they announce one of the burdens of the poet's confession:

> I proceed for all who are or have been young men,
> To tell the secret of my nights and days,
> To celebrate the need of comrades.[44]

They direct the poet's memory to a more immediate, tropical landscape (we surmise from the turtles that figure also in "O Carib Isle!" that he has in mind the Isle of Pines), a landscape that heat and hellishness link with the city of stanza four. And now he remembers an erotic experience of such intensity that it presents itself expressionistically. This landscape of love (of "happy-pain" and wonder) [45] needs no gloss except to note the similarity of its "steep alcoves" and the "steep floor" of "Voyages III," where the ecstasy of love again demands of the poet an utmost resourcefulness of language. His experience is passive, under the "tyranny" of noon; it is a signal chapter of his legend, a part of the destiny that, he says, "drew me into hades almost." Its hellishness, or the beastliness that relates it to the "ape's face" of "Recitative," is depicted in the "mammoth turtles," primordial animals whose world of love is the hot sand and warm sea. But so is its glory: the marvelous struggle of love in the bright light, the grandeur of these great beasts who here, as in "O Carib Isle!," are moved by a fierce, inextinguishable desire to live. The consummation of their love in the sunlit sea conveys the poet's sense of sexual wonder, the wonder of an imperishable innocence; and this climactic moment of yielding retains its supreme value for him even though it is followed —he represents it as simultaneous and apparently inevitable—by

44. "In Paths Untrodden," *Leaves of Grass*. Isadora Duncan may have brought *Calamus* to Crane's attention. See *Letters*, p. 109 (December 12, 1922).

45. *Letters*, p. 53 (February 11, 1921).

sundering, the loss (and betrayal) indicated perhaps by the ellipsis.[46]

The ellipsis also sustains a significant pause that brings us back to the present of the poet's exclamation in stanza three: "How much I would have bartered!" Yes, he knows that once, not now, he would have bartered everything ("How much!") for that glorious experience. And the implication is that he did barter, and (in contrast to the barter of "Faustus and Helen") gladly. For what he bartered, though necessary goods of the spirit, did not serve him; the landscape of home is bitterly recalled:

> the black gorge
> And all the singular nestings in the hills
> Where beavers learn stitch and tooth.

From this frightfully female world, the valley source, the nest, he escaped, it seems, by means of sexual adventure, an innocent initiation (it prompts a feeling of coolness and purity) that he himself undertook: "The pond I entered once and quickly fled— / I remember now its singing willow rim." Juxtaposition suggests a causal relation, and the serial character suggests that he even bartered his innocence, the spiritual glory of it that he remembers now because he is once again liberated—and at repose.

This innocent love, associated with the willows of the opening and closing lines, is most likely the "memory all things nurse," the memory which sustains him, like a mother—and more than his mother—because it is, presumably, a memory of both liberation and complete response. "Finally," however, suggests that this memory is part of the more immediate memory of another moment of release, that of the monsoon at the end of his journey to the sea. This memory, the reiteration of "finally" tells us, is of a great difficulty overcome, passed through: "After the city that I finally passed / With scalding unguents spread and smoking darts. . . ." It is a memory of release once again nursed by the memory of furious sexuality, only now, in the recollection of the infernal city, there is nothing to mitigate it. The city, evoked here with terrible

---

46. Crane may have known Lawrence's tortoise poems, especially "Tortoise Shout." Lawrence's *Tortoises* was published in New York by Thomas Seltzer in 1921.

surrealist immediacy, is, like that of "Possessions" and "Recitative,"
a place of lust. It is the final trial of the poet's pilgrimage, bringing
him to "gulf gates," where a natural force commensurate with the
enormity of his need destroys, cleans, and cuts him free, delivers
him from the abyss into new life.[47]

That memory of rebirth is rendered brilliantly as a spiritual
liberation:

> The monsoon cut across the delta
> At gulf gates . . . There, beyond the dykes
>
> I heard wind flaking sapphire, like this summer,
> And willows could not hold more steady sound.

After the sharp wind arrives at the place of birth, there is an ex-
pectant pause, followed by release, by wonder-filled expression. The
eye is pointed seaward "beyond the dykes" of all restraint to the
vast openness suggested by hearing sound out of the silence of great
distance—the eternal vastness or creative void indicated on the
page by the visual space dividing expectation and answer. And the
way the words are placed (the initial "I heard" of the concluding
lines) and their accuracy to experience ("flaking sapphire") authen-
ticate a memory of almost present vividness. Sound supports the
sense and image of waves in "flaking sapphire," an image of cool
gemlike beauty, of precious brightness, that is visual as well as
aural. The eye and ear entertain a reposeful steady sea, and the
cosmicity of childhood, a union of self and world, is restored. As
Bachelard says, "Water, water always comes to calm us." [48]

It brings repose, but also, as a result, renewed creativity, that
"flaking sapphire," which may be the making of poems, the very
poem before us which verifies the "improved infancy" the poet has
achieved.[49] This experience, known again now ("like this summer"),
is related by the reverie of the poem to the willows of an earlier
experience of being; but, as the last line tells us, it is a possession
of maturity, the joy of the man who has surmounted a trial of
experience. "Steady sound" nicely closes the poem by inviting com-

47. For the importance of this larger wind, see the following *Key West* poems:
"O Carib Isle!," "The Hurricane," "The Air Plant," "Eternity."
48. *The Poetics of Reverie*, pp. 108, 128.
49. P, 21.

parison to the "steady leveling" of the first stanza and by evoking the Arnoldian phrase, "steady and whole." [50] And yet, in what might be called the after-sound of the poem, there is a hovering sense of loneliness and immense otherness. The landscapes through which the poet has passed, unlike those at the beginning and end of the poem, are landscapes, whether terrible or not, of love. Repose, like innocence, seems to involve deprivation—"could not hold" is perhaps too insistent. Though the poet achieves "that still-ness ultimately best, / Being, of all, least sought for"—though he achieves "being of all," one feels, as in the poem "To Emily Dickinson" cited here, that for him something is still wanting.

What is wanting is indicated perhaps in the other face of eternity presented in "Paraphrase." This tidy poem, both Dickinsonian and Poe-esque, seems at first merely curious and virtuosic, a brilliant exercise in conveying the dread of approaching death and of being dead—a terror whose magnitude is measured by the fear of naming it. The experience is familiar to us from anxiety attacks, and Crane's exactitude in rendering it is the immediate reason for our interest. The sound of the heartbeat with which the poem begins, though "steady" like the sound of the previous poem, occasions anxiety, and the repose of this poem is the "purposeless repose" of death, just as its eternity, first suggested by "winking" (recalling "wink of eternity" in "Voyages II") and later evoked by "antarctic blaze," is the terrible white glory of nothingness, the illumination that an-nihilates.

During the "dark hours" (the phrase is Fitzgerald's),[51] the poet becomes aware of time; the clock-beat of the heart and the turning wheel awaken his sense of mortality, the death that is already lodged within him and he cannot flee, "the record wedged in his soul." "Wedged in" conveys the undislodgeable pain of anxiety and the terrible entering, the onset that nothing can guard against ("What skims in"). And "uncurls," a characteristic Crane usage ("unrocking" is another instance), conveys the active power of death's negation of life. To die, the poet realizes, is not to tell time (like a bell: the rigid tongue is the clapper) nor to be aware of the regularly recurring cycles of life—that the "systematic morn

---

50. The image of the river is also appropriately Arnoldian.
51. See Fitzgerald, "Sleeping and Waking," *The Crack-Up*, pp. 63–68.

shall sometime flood. . . ." It is to be stunned by a stunning light, to see suddenly the cold whiteness of endless space. It is not to be deliciously whispered to, rocked in a cradle, answered. It is to be unrocked and, spirited instantly into a "white paraphrase" of the polar landscape, to find oneself inhabiting the enclosed spaces of life as a ghostly presence ("Among bruised roses on the papered wall").

"White paraphrase" may be read in conjunction with "bruised roses" as the ultimate evidence of irreparable, gratuitous injury. But because of the quiet power of the images and cadence of the concluding line, it seems to stand in opposition, and the poem may be said to end by summoning our attachment to life, whatever its limitations and injuries. The resonance here qualifies an otherwise clever poem and directs us to the source of anxiety that moved Crane to write it. He placed the poem within easy remembrance of "North Labrador" and probably expected "antarctic blaze" to recall the unanswering landscape and lovelessness of that poem. The images of bedroom (enclosure), roses, and cradle ("unrocking") also reverberate with maternal memories and help us realize the extent to which Crane's imagination of life without maternal response precipitated the poem and prompted him to cling to painful images of dependence and restriction. Better this than nothing: for, as he had shown in the earlier poem—paraphrased now—life without love is death.

The love for whose lack only death is an adequate measure is the "pure possession" of "Possessions," the poem that follows "Paraphrase." This is the spiritualization of love his trust in which he now asks us to witness in a poem relating the possession (madness) of wayward homoerotic desire, or lust. "Trust" may also refer to the expectation of response with which the driven sexual adventurer sets forth, and in view of this and the pitiful outcome, the imperative ("Witness now this trust!") has an accent of mocking bravado. Yet trust is tested by failure, and the poet does trust—believe in—the spiritual efficacy of desire. It may, he knows, prohibit "pure possession," but the suffering it causes may also work that miracle. This belief is one of his "possessions."

When erotically possessed the poet is lost, directionless. He seems enveloped by the soft rain, which also depicts the way erotic feeling "steals" upon and overwhelms him. We see him sexually ready—key in hand—but without an object, uncertain to cruise for one, maddened almost by the peremptory "flesh" and the torment of failure: "Through a thousand nights [the allusion to the Arabian Nights suggests sensuality] the flesh / Assaults outright for bolts that linger / Hidden. . . ." The imagery is explicitly phallic, and "linger" describes the posture of those he petitions but who refuse, as Paul Goodman would say, to come across. What he seeks —the shattering experience of the sacrificial moment, the phallic lightning evoked by "bolts"—is denied him both by those he "assaults outright" and by the stormy heavens ("black foam"), the latter representing also his own turbulent emotion as well as his sense of guilt (the "sky . . . has no eyes / For": doesn't countenance). Such anguish of frustration and dismay finally forces him to cry out for relief from his oppressive burden ("O undirected. . . . this fixed stone of lust").

Though the stanza following modulates this anguish into a contemplative "metaphysical" key, it turns on his knowledge of the complete trajectory of this experience ("I know"; "account the total"). By anticipating the furtiveness and the outcome in sexual ordeal ("stabbing," "mercy"), it expresses the quiet yet insistent desperation of one whom knowledge cannot deter, who, weary as he is, must take up again, as he subsequently does, the heavy stone. The metaphysical wit is in the verbal play of his initial imperative to our imaginations. If the first stanza represents a "moment," how excruciating an hour of "such moments" would be! "Accumulate," here, comments sardonically on his "possessions" and, with "Account," asks us to count up and in consequence take account of the sum, the accumulated intensity of his anguish. And though the lines that follow are not readily glossed they are clear enough because their Prufrockian overtone summons our sense of abortive experience.

This knowledge is part of the burden he takes up on entering the inferno of Bleecker Street (in Greenwich Village). Here, he tells us, he goes quietly—"As quiet as you can make a man [be quiet]" —and perhaps in the stress on "make" he explicitly tells us his goal. Still penetrant in the emptiness around him ("still trenchant in a void": the phrase recalls the directionless man with the key but

evokes also an unbearable cosmic sense of unresponsiveness);
"Wounded" by his own fears and speechlessness as well as by the
speech of others, he experiences the torment of the damned:

> I hold it up against a disk of light—
> I, turning, turning on smoked forking spires,
> The city's stubborn lives, desires.

In the upward-reaching imploring gesture of raising the stone of
lust to the light, the poet both declares his need and beseeches the
heavens, reduced to a disk of light (like the sun seen through an
overcast sky), to take up his burden, to transform desire into a
pure possession. But this moment of greatest sexual anguish—of
dying in the vortex of the stabbing fires of his own lust—goes un-
heeded in the city with which he associates it and which seems to
provoke it.

The end of this experience is the leaden aftermath expressed by
the first sentence and the apocalyptic hope expressed in the last
sentence of the concluding stanza. These are the horns of his
dilemma, the duality, like that of "Recitative," upon which he is
tossed. Though trite, the imagery of the bullfight is sexually
graphic. It evokes the unsuccessful (feminine?) matador, the
animal fury of his dangerous opponent, and the goring, the dying
which does not gratify desire in the sense of the Elizabethan pun
but only, if that, the poet's predilection for suffering, for spending
himself. (The last two stanzas gloss the "smoking souvenir, / Bleed-
ing eidolon!" of "Legend.") Yet his suffering and the "Record of
rage and partial appetites" are genuine, attested to by the "piteous
admissions" of the poem.[52] And because its images are authentic
and its movement full and serene, so is the apocalyptic close, the
redemption of desire in which he trusts.

The poet awaits the purifying fire of the "inclusive cloud," the
whirlwind, the "white wind" that shall burn away and transform
his "appetites" ("rase" and *raise*), that shall destroy the stone of
lust and leave only the "bright stones wherein our smiling plays."
The pervasive biblical imagery of this vision gives "bright stones"

---

52. By reading "piteous admissions to be split / Upon the page" in the Joycean
fashion of Kenneth Burke, one may discover a compensatory gratification of poetry.

the redemptive significance of white stone in Revelations 2:17; and "stone," which still retains its earlier sexual meaning, in the plural and modified by "bright" becomes the radiant mutuality of love, its habitation. Sexuality remains; the vision of redemption here is solely sexual. But it is spiritualized by the complete responsiveness of "our smiling," by the innocence and happy play of childhood.

This vision of love is one of Crane's "possessions": love is an absolute, a supreme good. The "pure possession" he seeks is the "return of love." [53] He would be "answered" ("changed and transubstantiated as anyone is who has asked a question and been answered"), and he had been during the period when "Possessions" and "Lachrymae Christi," companion pieces placed together in *White Buildings*, were written. In the letter to Waldo Frank in which he tells of being answered, he describes the happiness he found with Emil Opffer, a possession that he felt was pure, "where flesh became transformed through intensity of response to counterresponse, where sex was beaten out, where a purity of joy was reached that included tears." This letter, one of the most wonderfilled in his remarkably open correspondence, should be read in full as a touchstone of Crane's spirit. It shows not only how much he depended on religious imagery to describe his exaltation, but how much the happy pain of love is at the heart of his vision.[54]

The answering and the transformation of love are celebrated (consecrated) in "Lachrymae Christi" in inextricably spiritual-physical terms of resurrection and natural renewal. Because love is doubly redemptive of soul and body, both Christ and Dionysus are evoked—actually united, as in the title and symbolic action of the poem. The tears of Christ (*Lachrymae Christi*) may have

53. *Letters*, p. 140 (July 21, 1923).
54. *Letters*, pp. 181–83 (April 21, 1924). Both John Unterecker and Susan Jenkins Brown confirm the identification. Elizabeth Jennings provides the best comment on Crane's religious imagery: "Crane employed many Christian words, signs and symbols. But, as with Rilke, he removed these things from the realm of strict orthodoxy and gave them a free life of their own. His imagination unyoked them from the bondage of dogma. . . ." *Every Changing Shape* (London: Andre Deutsch, 1961), p. 232.

recalled for Crane his own tears of joy as well as the persistent theme of sacrificial suffering first introduced in "C 33." But the title of the poem, by way of "'Lachryma Christi," a Neapolitan wine, contains a Dionysian significance and announces, in shorthand, that the tears of the suffering Christ are wine, have a Dionysian efficacy and occasion a Dionysian joy. The Passion is passion. Part of the poet's legend, we remember, is the repudiation of repentance; he no longer wishes to believe, as he did in "C 33" and so many of the early poems, that penitence is singularly good and must be endured for "song of minor, broken strain." Such song, dedicated to the "Materna," bargains for love, springs from denial rather than joy. Instead, in "Lachrymae Christi," where the moment of transformation is the experience presented and suffering is joy and joy is suffering, everything, enabled by male divinities, declares for joy, for release whose gladness (overflow of powerful feeling) translates immediately into song, *is* song: "Not penitence / But song, as these / Perpetual fountains, vines. . . ." [55]

This is the theme developed simply and directly in the early versions of the poem, love poems to the redemptive Christ—or lover. The first version begins as follows:

> Recall to music
> and set down at last
> what stain could hold mine eyes
> so long in perjury . . .
>
> What have I asked
> but silence that containd'st
> Thee, newly bright to bear
> no penitence—but song,
> as these, thine everlasting fountains here!

And it tells how this presence, evoked here, has delivered him from the rending experience of "Possessions":

> Yea—every margin wide
> with fear, with scorn or terror
> clasps no more now, nor rends
> my substance. . . .

Christ is a stream (the fountain of joy) he implores to flow on and,

55. See "Postscript" for "fountains droop in waning light and pain. . . ."

in what is perhaps most interesting in these early versions, to answer the rose:

> Stream, Thou,—
> most flowing, and best knowing
> what call the rose
> obtains in thee,—flower
> most bright—Rose, waiting,
> of most clear attendance, white.[56]

In the early versions the springtime landscape and the Dionysian aspect of the final version of the poem are absent. And so is the industrial setting of the opening stanza, which helps to explain the "stain" alluded to in the early version, and the conspicuous use of "smile" in the opening and closing stanzas. Noteworthy, too, is the fact that the action of the poem, controlled by "while" in the first and third stanzas, involves the almost instantaneously brief duration of transition or transformation, and that the initial transformation, under the auspices of moonlight (a transfiguring, purifying power of imagination like that in "Chaplinesque"), introduces the natural landscape, that is, the setting of vital renewal. The poem, accordingly, may be said to begin with wonder, with a motion toward renewal and purity ("Whitely"; "Rinsings") and toward the prior and innocent (the pastoral condition of childhood). The season celebrated in the poem is spring, with its miracle of rebirth; and the action of the poem is toward the unity of Christ and Dionysus in the concluding stanzas: toward the unity of being of childhood, toward innocence and wholeness, the "improved infancy" of "Passage."

In the first stanza Crane may have had in mind Vaughan's lines (cited in Edgell Rickword's *Rimbaud*):

> I saw Eternity the other night
> Like a great ring of pure and endless light,
> All calm as it was bright.[57]

But Crane's eternity, though bright and even visibly calm, is in

56. Weber, *Hart Crane*, pp. 225–27.
57. *Rimbaud: The Boy and the Poet* (New York: Alfred A. Knopf, 1924), p. 146.

process, is renewing. It is a memorable crisis of the kind Thoreau speaks of in *Walden* in reference to the pond, which "was dead and [suddenly] is alive again." The poem itself enacts renewing by "dissolving" the parenthetical passage on the mills in its own forward motion and description of nature's concomitant vital activities. It turns from death to life—away from the mills which represent industrial society, the city as a place of lust, and (given the inside concern with machinery, which recalls Melville's "The Tartarus of Maids," and the images of "curdled" and "unyielding smile") the mother.[58]

Crane does not describe nature in maternal terms, but in terms of Christ's suffering (stanza two) and his own restoration (stanzas three and four), and his description of renewal and rebirth is splendid, quite as good as Thoreau's, in "Spring," which also ends in "recovered innocence." Christ is not explicitly mentioned until the fifth stanza, in the single isolated line that brings this part of the poem to its peak and turning: "Thy Nazarene and tinder eyes." For "Nazarene" carries with it the "benzine / Rinsings," the cleansing and transfiguring of stanza one, and "tinder," compressing tender and fiery (fire-making), covers the double aspect of renewal (as in the "pure possession" of "Possessions") and points ahead to what the remainder of the poem treats.

The following stanza in parentheses repeats explicitly in personal terms, as the poet's inner experience, much of what has already occurred. The poet, also identified with the natural landscape, has been (as suggested earlier in "the nights opening / Chant pyramids") released from the grave, has been restored to life by the cordial of death. ("Borage," a weed with medicinal, purging properties, is also a cordial. Crane may have taken the word from a sentence in Rimbaud's *A Season in Hell* that also seems to have suggested the image of the urinal in *The Bridge:* "Oh the little fly drunk from the inn urinal, in love with the borage. . . ." But he employs the word in a context whose meaning is perhaps best glossed by Ouspensky, who, with Waldo Frank, seems to have done most to alter Crane's puritanical attitude toward sex. In chapter 15

58. These associations are not random but related. For a helpful comment, see Brown, *Love's Body*, pp. 70–71.

of *Tertium Organum*, Ouspensky cites Nietzsche on "Voluptuousness": "to free hearts, a thing innocent and free, the garden-happiness of earth. . . . the great cordial, and the reverently saved wine of wines." [59]) As a consequence of his resurrection the poet regains his poetic power (the tongue of "Paraphrase" is no longer rigid); he is no longer bound by "vermin and rod" (the first image recalls the vastation of "Black Tambourine" and the second a punitive situation perhaps of childhood). Like the spring freshets of stanza two, tears, the gentle rain of heaven, reanimate his body, truly the blood of the lamb that "flocks" through him; and because of this, "Betrayed stones slowly speak"; he is no longer overcome by lust, as in "Possessions," but, in the words of stanzas three and four, is "Anoint[ed] with innocence" and, his "perjuries" retrieved, again able to sing.

By establishing the new condition (as well as what had been the old), this stanza prepares for the invocation with which the poem ends. In these stanzas the poet both describes the consummate glory of the new condition and petitions the gods who grant it to sustain him in it, to make it last, to "spell out . . . Compulsion of the year. . . ." "Spell out," of course, supports the suggestion of Word in "Names" and the bell-like annunciation that rings it out. It helps us hear the glory of a moment that is bright ("undimming," "luminous") and full (streaming, "Unstanched") and celestially harmonious and radiant ("as the nights / Strike from Thee perfect spheres"). The moment is one of the most brilliantly rendered in Crane's work; it has for him the direct impact on consciousness he considers the end of poetry. And the concluding stanzas are one of his supreme endings. This is so because the poet implores the lover (Christ-Dionysus) from the fullness of answered love. The sacrificial aspects—the "sable slender boughs," even the "charred and riven stakes"—do not seem terrible because their sexual significance is salutary: they belong to the "passion," to the joyous condition he already wishes to renew. "Lift up," he entreats —"Lift up in lilac-emerald breath the grail / Of earth again—."

59. Rickword, *Rimbaud*, p. 229; *Tertium Organum*, p. 173. Ouspensky also cites Schopenhauer on the connection of Death and Eros, and Edward Carpenter's Whitmanesque rhapsody, "The Ocean of Sex," both of importance to "Voyages."

Yes, and as the syntax compels us to read the concluding stanza, lift up "Thy face":

> —Thy face
> From charred and riven stakes, O
> Dionysus, Thy
> Unmangled target smile.

The poet ends by asking for the responsive sign of love (it is comparable to the "undimming" eyes of the crucified Christ), and by asking us, in the final phrase, to recognize, in contradistinction to "unyielding smile," the resurrectional power of love.

None of the subsequent poems attain such fulfillment. "Passage," which follows "Lachrymae Christi," tells of a troubled, difficult passage from one condition of self to another. This "Rimbaudian autobiography," as L. S. Dembo calls it,[60] belongs to the period of Crane's residence at Patterson, New York; it was begun in the summer of 1925, but was "improved," according to Crane, during the time he spent in Cleveland helping his mother and grandmother quit his boyhood home. Although the rancor of the poem may be attributed to Crane's failure to get his first book published, it is probably better accounted for by the trip to Cleveland that stirred up memories that he preferred to forget. ("I may decide to evade the moving," he had written Waldo Frank earlier. "I can't at present see my way to make any definite plans without risking some kind of unpleasant entanglement. . . . There is always some other immediate duty or requirement for me to perform than creation. I've had only above [about?] five hours at the writing table since I came out here. . . ."[61])

Memory is the burden of his story, and, as in "Repose of Rivers," which it immediately suggests, the poet tells it in the past tense, the tense of memory. The hilly landscape, presumably that of Patterson, recalls the sea because the poet has come to it from the city in order to begin anew and it offers him the freshness and repose of the sea in "Repose of Rivers":

> Where the cedar leaf divides the sky
> I heard the sea.

60. *Hart Crane's Sanskrit Charge: A Study of* THE BRIDGE (Ithaca: Cornell University Press, 1960), p. 78.
61. *Letters*, pp. 212–13, 215 (July, 1925; August 19, 1925).

> In sapphire arenas of the hills
> I was promised an improved infancy.

The poem wonderfully begins where "Repose of Rivers" ends. The poet has come to a bright, redolent, steady-sounding open landscape, and momentarily it grants the repose he seeks, the redemption from past experience that the desire for innocence, an "improved infancy," suggests. And yet, as the last line tells us, it is already foreclosed: "was promised" sneers at a promise not kept, and "improved infancy" carries the angry awareness of an infancy that in some way was not what he wanted it to be.

The natural landscape, so glorious and restorative, should work a miracle comparable to that of "Lachrymae Christi," where nature, more than ever before, is assimilated to Crane's vision of redemption. For it reminds us of the Emersonian belief that "in the woods . . . a man casts off his years, as a snake his slough, and at what period so ever of life is always a child." [62] But memory, the poet finds, is not so easily sloughed and jeopardizes this promise. Memory is left in a ravine, "Sulking, sanctioning the sun": dark memory, not only left in the unconscious but of it, memory of the ravine ("the black gorge" of "Repose of Rivers"?), and memory of the dark, the repulsive, the sexual, the furtive. And because he tried to repress these deep and disturbing memories, the summer, the passing time, "Dangerously . . . burned," and the elemental life of sun and wind and rain merely hardened him physically. Time itself, as if mocking his attempt to deny it, worked against restoration: the rain did not refresh him, his cheeks became "bronze gongs," and the wind moved him about at its will, leaving him in the desolate condition best glossed by "Pastorale":

> The ritual of sap and leaves
> The sun drew out,
> Ends in this latter muffled
> Bronze and brass. The wind
> Takes rein.

What the wind spoke to him is not clear. "It" ("It is not long") may refer to summer, the brief period of attempted for-

62. *Nature* in *The Complete Works of Ralph Waldo Emerson*, Concord Edition, vol. I (Boston: Houghton Mifflin Co., 1903), p. 9.

getfulness, for the ripening grapes in the valleys tell of the fruition of time and are signs that with summer's passing the sexuality of maturity cannot be denied. Wind is spirit, the inner creative voice of the poet, who confesses that the wind stopped because he, with his "chimney-sooted heart," still secretly cherished his past and the memories of impurity that inevitably belong to the loss of innocence. The image of the chimney recalls Melville and Hawthorne, but the cadence is Eliot's out of Ezekiel ("Son of man . . ."), and the smoke, obsessive as it is with Crane, is Thoreau's, advertising the dangerous burning of these summer months, the smoldering hidden fire that, though it burns in the heart of everyman, characterizes the "well-known biography" of the poet. With the passage of time, before which he is helpless, the poet is "turned about and back," forced finally to meet the memory—confront the self—he had tried to leave behind.

This passage as well as reversal is indicated also by the evening of the fifth stanza. Now the poet recognizes the darkness, the persistence and force of erotic memory ("a spear in the ravine / That throve through very oak") and wonders if, in fact, he had ever left the ravine. Here, after all, is the laurel crown and the book by which he hoped to win it—the book stolen by that part of himself that refused to acknowledge the creative depths of memory; and the laurel is "opening" and the book that he had lost during the summer is "found."

We learn from this confrontation with memory that he has come "back here" to "argue with the laurel," to find the sources of poetic achievement. These, though released by repose, as in "Repose of Rivers," are not necessarily natural or conditional on innocence. As all the poems of this group show, the sources are within the troubled depths of the self. Not innocence but experience—or the desire for innocence it awakens—is the source of poetry. And poetry itself defeats time and restores the innocence of maturity when the poet, as he does here and in "Repose of Rivers," works through rather than denies memory, the time-bound and burdened human condition. By committing memory to the page of the poem, the poet breaks its hold; by means of his own creative effort he breaks the fever of the dangerously burning summer. And with that breaking, comparable in function to the monsoon in "Repose of

Rivers," he experiences a vertiginous ascent which, unlike any other ascent in Crane's poetry, does not overcome the troubled condition of memory but presents, in wonder, its deepest stresses to him. The poem does not relieve the poet of his responsibility: it is an enabling act, a *rite de passage*, of continued growth and maturity.[63]

Such willingness to confront oneself is a notable aspect of these poems, and of none more than "The Wine Menagerie," a companion piece to "Possessions" in which Crane again, with even greater thoroughness, gives an account of as well as accounts for his aberrant behavior. The title of this poem is not necessarily ironic; it may be descriptive of the intoxicated condition, comparable to lust, with which the poem begins. For the poem begins, as Herbert Leibowitz says, in "the middle of an already started process" [64] ("Invariably when wine redeems the sight"), and describes a complete curve of rising and falling exaltation, the latter corresponding equally well to the omitted beginning. The opening line clearly states the theme and tells us that the poet, who uses the present tense of recollected experience, is depicting something familiar to him. The poem, of course, is about intoxication but is not necessarily the result of intoxication, and the poet is not saying that intoxication always redeems the sight but that when it does what he experiences "invariably" happens.

The redemption of sight is vision. Crane's theme is Blake's but the mastery with which he treats it is his own. Vision begins with the release and intensification of perception—with wakefulness, attentiveness, a fully summoned being:

> Invariably when wine redeems the sight,
> Narrowing the mustard scansions of the eyes,
> A leopard ranging always in the brow
> Asserts a vision in the slumbering gaze.

The narrowing of the eyes describes the sharpened focus of attentive seeing—the sharpness being conveyed also by "mustard" and the deliberate motion of seeing by "scansions." "Mustard scansions" is heavily compressed; it may refer to the sharp, alert, yellow eyes of the "leopard . . . in the brow," for eyes that move

63. Lewis, *The Poetry of Hart Crane*, p. 188.
64. *Hart Crane*, p. 183.

like a leopard are leopard eyes.[65] The eyes "always" caged in the brow belong to the active imagination and restlessly await release, are always ready, like the powerful, beautiful, and dangerous beast, not only to pounce on an object of sight but, in keeping with "ranging" (as going beyond rather than pacing), to assert a "vision." "Asserts" conveys the explosive energy of perception; "vision," here, is substantive, that is, a positive, active seeing different from the mere seeing of "the sight," which is blindness and stands in the same relation to vision as "slumbering gaze," sight as withdrawn, absent, unseeing. Perception, then, is not passive but active; as Crane noted in Blake, it is seeing through, not with the physical eye ("the eyes"; "asserts a vision *in* the slumbering gaze"). Vision is of the imagination, the power by which we really see. And, since it belongs to what is most vital in us and requires the full participation of being, it presses, like a caged animal ("ranging" here takes up "narrowing"), for release. Vision belongs to liberated being. And liberated being is part of Crane's "vision": "I nearly go mad," he told Stieglitz, "with the intense but always misty realization of what *can* be done if potentialities are fully freed, released." [66]

Perception-redemption is aided by drunkenness, which builds up out of the experience of the several stanzas preceding it to the vision of stanzas six, seven, and eight. In the first stages of drunkenness, the poet is closely occupied with objects, perhaps, as Samuel Hazo says, with the rhythm of mustard pots lined up on a bar.[67] Then ("Then" in stanza two indicates process), the showy, glossy, flattering bottles that literally and figuratively "reflect the street" reflect him, "gloss" him. His relation to them is intimate, passive, voluptuously sensual ("Wear me in crescents on their bellies"),[68] a condition that seems to be connected also with being cradled in

65. See Rilke's "Der Panther" and Blake's "The Tyger."
66. *Letters*, pp. 138–39 (July 4, 1923).
67. *Hart Crane: An Introduction and Interpretation* (New York: Barnes & Noble, 1963), p. 44.
68. "Visions from the belly of a bottle"—this line from Malcolm Cowley's "The Flower in the Sea," dedicated to Crane, seems to allude to this poem. Crane acknowledged the receipt of the poem on January 3, 1926. (See *Robber Rocks*, pp. 47–50.) Perhaps Cowley's poem, so richly Crane's in its imagery, suggested "Cutty Sark."

the moon, in the protected maternal world of his "romantic" imagination. In "Slow / Applause flows into liquid cynosures" we hear and see the glasses being filled, and sense the flowing, passive experience of the poet, who is now slowed down, happily approving ("Applause"), and transfixed ("conscripted") by the glowing reflection of the glasses on the bar.

Then—the way the stanzas end establishes the discrete moments of attention—then, perhaps turning from the bar and his own self-involvement, the poet begin to notice his surroundings, again with remarkable attentiveness ("the imitation onyx wainscoting / [Painted emulsion of snow, eggs, yarn, coal, manure]"), and observes ("Regard" gives the exact sense of aloof looking on) the significant detail of a human encounter that is terrible to him. The man and woman, whose combat he witnesses, are modern replicas of Judith-Holofernes, Salome–John the Baptist, and the poet himself as victimized Pierrot-Petrushka, and probably even more to the point of the poet's concern, they are father and mother seen from the "distance" of childhood. Fascinated, he watches "the forceps of the smile that takes her"—the smile here is a forceps used instrumentally and sexually with extreme care and awareness of danger; watches the "percussive sweat" that beads the brow beaten on by the "mallets" of her angry eyes; watches the insistent drumming (we hear it in the last line) not only destroy his composure, but "unmake" his world.[69] Here, in what the poem insists is a paradigm of experience, man is undone by woman—by the "feminine will," according to Blake, or the murderousness that Michel Leiris attributes to Judith and Salome.[70] This condition, too, needs redemption. It is the sight that wine later redeems for the poet when his "blood dreams a receptive smile / Wherein new purities are snared. . . ."

Meanwhile this sight turns him inward and prompts his meditation on the redemptive power within man himself. He ponders (in question form) mankind in its fallen, temporal condition—mankind subject to the ravages of time, of experience and mortality (the serpent-worm)—yet somehow, like the serpent that sheds

69. The mechanical and jazz imagery fit this "modern" situation.

70. *Manhood: A Journey from Childhood into the Fierce Order of Virility*, trans. Richard Howard (New York: Grossman Publishers, 1963).

its skin, capable of renewal, of the redemptive transcendence of time. In images, by now obsessive with Crane, he suggests the religiously freighted moment of eternity as a wondrous seeing ("sapphire transepts round the eyes") and hearing ("whispered carillon");[71] suggests not only the goal but the intimations of it that "assures / Speed to the arrow into feathered skies." For man himself—to answer the question ("What is it?")—is moved by the desire for eternity. The "feathered skies" represent the unity of time and space, serpent and eagle, as in *The Bridge*, and also, naively, a cloud nest, eternal bliss, an at-one-ment such as that accorded by "receptive smile." And the arrow not only intends this target and, with the speed of sight, rushes to it in its upward flight, it is a Blakean arrow of desire sped on from within. Creature of desires, fallen man has this desire too; he does not want a world "broken and in heaps" but yearns for an "instant of the world. . . ."[72]

When he resumes observation (the "Sharp" motion of the man has caught his eye), the poet sees him evade the woman by turning from her eyes toward the window where, presumably, he has noticed the "urchin" about to enter the saloon. Though he is moved by guile ("guile drags a face" renders his fallen state), the man turns toward the light, away from the "alcove of her jealousy," the possessive emotion that confines him as much as the booth in which he sits. With this release the appearance of the boy coincides wonderfully, as if he were the asserted vision of the man's longing for innocence. Perhaps the Dickensian-Wordsworthian description of the boy is maudlin[73]—this "urchin" whose summery pastoral "somewhere" (distant for us) contrasts with the bleak "here" of winter and who still trails the clouds of glory of the "feathered skies." But, in any case, his appearance, embracing the contraries of innocence and experience, is doubly poignant for the poet who grieves for his own lost childhood, the redemptive power represented by infancy, which Emerson said pleads with fallen man to return to paradise,[74] and for the terrible deprivation of experience,

71. The former picks up "Names peeling from Thine eyes" from "Lachrymae Christi," while the latter picks up the bell imagery of "Lachrymae Christi" and "Recitative."

72. The first phrase is Emerson's, in *Nature*, p. 74.

73. Are we to recall Tennyson in "across the bar"?

74. *Nature*, p. 71.

which makes wine not a mild pleasure but a necessity of the spirit.

Loss is the primary emotion the poem reaches into and probably accounts for the poet's sympathy with the drunken derelicts to whom he now gives his attention. In stanza six, where he presents hell, he stresses their isolation and (in the act of finding the right change) the value of their resolve to rise, to wreathe "up and out," almost to flee by becoming spirits. For him their difficulty in rising has religious significance ("stigma," for example) and, as his compassion grows ("Poor streaked bodies" recalls King Lear's "unaccommodated man"), he begins to understand better the questions he had meditated earlier. These "bodies" seek release in drunkenness; it is the "stigma" of spiritual desire. Recognizing this in the case of others, he more readily accepts for himself the spirituality and beauty he sees in degradation: "Between black tusks the roses shine!" This exclamation of wonder climaxes the stanza with a vision of spiritual ordeal—with a Websterian sentiment that Crane, as Herbert Leibowitz says, learned on his pulses.[75]

And it leads to the joyous exclamation of the next stanza ("New thresholds, new anatomies!"), where the "whispered carillon" of stanza four begins to ring out the fulfillment promised there. In noting the incantatory charm "new" has for Crane, Herbert Leibowitz says that "it peals out [as in this instance] whenever an exceptional feeling has passed into him. . . ."[76] The Elizabethan quality of the diction accords with the previous line and evokes the excitement of the prospect of a new world, a vast free territory of being. This, the poet explains, is the result of "wine talons," for wine, like an eagle, grips him and bears him aloft, in spiritual flight, to "feathered skies"; and this ecstatic experience "Builds[s] freedom up about me and distill[s] / This competence. . . ." The positive quality of a liberated yet protected existence, of freedom itself as an enclosing, strengthening, and comforting thing, a fortification, perhaps, or tower, is exactly rendered in the first phrase, while the second, nicely punning, tells of the spiritual process that

75. *Hart Crane*, p. 48. The symbols have sexual significance.
76. *Hart Crane*, p. 115. One hears Rimbaud's "O saisons, ô châteaux!" in Crane's line. R. P. Blackmur uses this stanza as an example of Crane's way of using words. See "New Thresholds, New Anatomies: Notes on a Text of Hart Crane," *Language as Gesture: Essays in Poetry* (New York: Harcourt, Brace and Co., 1952).

produces both the sparkling tear and the "competence" (confidence) to travel in it. For the sparkling tear is the distillation of the poet's vision in the previous stanza, the vehicle as well as sign of his projective sympathy. Its sparkle picks up the "shine" of roses, and "alone" speaks for the loneliness, which the poet, in his vision, recognizes and overcomes. Unlike the derelicts "minting their separate wills" (divisiveness and money are associated here, as in "Recitative"), he has distilled (by spiritual transformation) the elixir of projective sympathy which permits him to close the vast distances of separation and to enter into "another's will." [77]

It is important to recognize that the poet, identified at the end by exile, is not saying that drunkenness is a necessary condition of writing poetry; poetry, rather, may be for him an intoxication like drunkenness. He is saying that, by freeing him, drunkenness makes projective sympathy possible. It gives him an enveloping security and permits him to escape from himself and to enter the world of other people—to identify himself, as Crane told Charlotte Rychtarik he wished to do, "with *all of life*." [78] "To travel in a tear" is indebted to Blake, as R. P. Blackmur first pointed out, but it also owes something to the tear Ahab dropped into the sea and much to one of the great examples of projective sympathy in American literature—Whitman's, in section eleven of "Song of Myself." The sadness conveyed by the image is fitting: one reaches this state and acquires this power by knowing loss, isolation, dereliction. The movement of exaltation is upward but the vision depicted here is lateral. The vision the poet asserts is of mankind (comparable to Wordsworth's "still, sad music of humanity") and, with that of "The Idiot" and "A Name for All," is one of the supports of Crane's reputation.

What the vision kindles is a dream of love that purifies and redeems. Sympathy quickens and warms the entire being of the poet and awakens the desire for total response, for the "receptive smile," the answering, the supreme testimony for Crane of love. This image derives its force not only from contrast with "forceps of a smile" but from its visionary nature, its source in profound longing, and the fact, suggested by "snared," that it is a violent

77. One may also interpret these lines to mean that he enters another's tear.
78. *Letters*, p. 140 (July 21, 1923). See also *Letters*, pp. 138–39, 191.

physical power of the kind evoked by the leopard and the eagle ("talons"). For the poet wishes to be redeemed by physical means (by "intensity of response," we remember, "flesh became transformed").[79] In love as complete as this, "new purities" would replace the "old lusts" that contrast compels us to read into the phrase. But the duality upon which this visionary desire depends defines its perilousness, and the very vision of sinners in hell momentarily redeemed by love contains the hellish anguish into which it fades. From the height of exaltation the poem turns precipitously, and the poet, no longer in the grasp of "Wine talons," falls to despair—finds himself, like the anguished humanity that had once known innocence, guiltily burning.

"Wit" speaks the poet's anguish, and it speaks sardonically. In the phrase "the wit that cries out of me," the awkwardness of "wit that" seems necessary to represent wit as a separate aspect of the self, the spokesman of its deprivation. Wit, here, is mind, an agency self-concerned and lacking the fullness of being needed to assert a vision. It is best characterized by what it says and by the sudden transformation of the imagery to the cold, mechanical, and naturalistic. In "these frozen billows of your skill!" wit mocks the poet's competence to travel in a tear (may even mock his verses); in "Invent new dominoes of love and bile" it makes a fanciful worthless game of the poet's vision and derides the newness he had entertained; in "Ruddy, the tooth implicit of the world / Has followed you" it reminds him that his awareness of redemptive power ("Between black tusks the roses shine") does not belong to the permanent, naturalistic way of things and that the leopard in the brow is not for long equal to the actual survival of the fittest. Wit spares him a complete nihilism by acknowledging his faith in some future reward but only to emphasize the cruel reality that intervenes:

> Though in the end you know
> And count some dim inheritance of sand,
> How much yet meets the treason of the snow.

The "inheritance" the poet both counts (as money) and counts on

79. *Letters*, p. 181 (April 21, 1924).

is a matter of time and money as well as the warm paradisal place
(the Isle of Pines, for Crane) that "snow" helps to evoke. He may
yet survive, as Crane hoped to, by going there, but that possibility
of redemption is "dim," far off, and not as clearly seen or evident
as the betrayals of life, "the treason of the snow," which calls up
the present winter situation of the poem (and the fact that Crane's
mother did not permit him to go there). Much of "North Labra-
dor" and "Paraphrase" is carried over by these lines and supports an
autobiographical reading. Crane, whose evocation of the island is
associated with the urchin's pastoral world and belongs to the
cluster of supreme goods that includes "feathered skies" and "re-
ceptive smile," knew the treasons of life and, by alluding to per-
sonal instances of them, establishes the human condition and
actual occasion in which the poem may have had its start.

An autobiographical reading is indicated also in the concluding
stanzas. Here, wit advises him to "Rise from the dates and
crumbs": to summon resolution, as the derelicts had, and to leave
the rich yet stingy provision of his parents—to "walk away," as he
had tried to do. But nothing secures such a reading so much as
the sense of betrayal, the "treason," the capital crime he associates
with other men who have been victimized by women. (The mi-
sogyny of this passage is matched only by that of "Southern
Cross.") The humor of the context does not relieve the grimness
evoked by Holofernes and John the Baptist, who remind us now of
the earlier situations of the poem. They recall the episodes of the
man and woman and of the derelicts (which we now see truly
follows), and by recalling the former, with its vaguely Eliotic
quality, Holofernes and John the Baptist supply the link to "Their
whispering begins." For this forcefully calls up Prufrock, a victim
of the women who talk of Michelangelo and who, Prufrock fears,
will—in that frightening image of man diminished and crucified—
pin him to the wall.

Entering the poem in this way, Prufrock identifies and checks
the poet's lapse into self-pity. He establishes another register of
anguish, which, after all, is genuine, and permits the poet to move
from Holofernes and John the Baptist to the Pierrot figure of
Petrushka, the representation of whose hopeless love—his suffering
heart—contains the essential aspect of Prufrock's situation: "Pe-

trushka's valentine pivots on a pin." [80] The very references to Holofernes and John the Baptist suggest the Prufrockian character of the poet who, for the moment, in his fear of whispering, seems about to regress to genteel sufferer. But rather than succumb to ignoble fear, the poet, it seems, will follow the admonition to "fold your exile on your back again. . . ." Once an eagle carried aloft on outspread wings, he is now earthbound, reduced to carrying them folded on his back as the sign, the burden of his exile. This burden is stigmatic and visually identifies the poet with Petrushka, a hunchback, who, in turn, by way of Pierrot, presents him with the more acceptable if still outcast posture of "Chaplinesque." But even more acceptable, perhaps even ennobling, is the posture suggested by the Daedalean-Joycean connotations of winged flight and exile. These better fit the determination we hear in the cadence of the concluding lines and the resolution to endure suffering that "again," reminiscent of "Legend," declares.

"The Wine Menagerie," like "Paraphrase," is unusual because it does not end, as the rest of these poems do, in affirmation. The poem passes through this moment and, at the close, reaches again only a low plateau of resolve. Although it is one of Crane's finest poems, it is not—or perhaps Crane did not think it was—the poem with which to conclude a sequence depicting the poet's legend. In choosing to end the sequence with "Recitative," he seems to have waived considerations of quality for those of architecture: he placed at the end a somewhat brittle poem that reached the characteristic affirmation and, in its "reflexes and symbolisms," [81] inventoried the previous poems. "Recitative" is a summary poem, comparable in function to "Legend," except that it implicates us in the poet's experience. It closes the sequence by treating the common theme of duality, of man's doubleness and desire for unity, and, at the same time, by evoking modern civilization, provides a transition to "Faustus and Helen."

As Crane explained to Allen Tate, in this poem he addresses not only himself but us—"Humanity, Man (in the sense of Blake)." [82]

---

80. Crane heard Stravinsky's *Petrouchka* during the 1924–25 season. See *Letters*, p. 200 (February 28, 1925).

81. *Letters*, p. 176 (March 1, 1924).

82. *Letters*, p. 176.

"Here," in the mirror of the poem, he asks us to face the fact of his and our doubleness (and duplicity), the anguish it causes ("twist," added in revision, evokes the important italicized passage of "Faustus and Helen"),[83] its unbearableness, and our desire to avoid it by refusing to recognize it. Everything in the first two stanzas insists on our double nature and experience: on duality, division, and separation, on appearance and reality, on polarities and contraries. And the second stanza, while making us especially aware of our fragmentation or brokenness, also describes the wholeness, however brief ("the breaking second holds"), of identification—the very possibility that the poet, in the sympathetic spirit of "The Wine Menagerie," offers us in his broken poem.

For identification is necessary if we are to do what the poet asks of us: accept the "fragment smile" that demands a total response of love, and ignore the lust that attends it. The "fragment smile" recalls especially Dionysus' "target smile" in "Lachrymae Christi" —recalls the entire conclusion of that poem and so helps us see in the "fragment smile" the "one crucial sign" of redemptive suffering that deserves our sympathy. The poet asks that we "travel in a tear," as he had done in a similar instance in "The Wine Menagerie." For tears too are crucial signs, and he would have us generously shed them in acknowledgment of the spirituality of his love rather than withhold them ("revocation" suggests a denying legalism) because of his lust.

And he asks us to defer that revocation because sometimes we transcend our fragmentary nature. "Look steadily"—look *again*, he implores, until you see the whole. The wind is not always an infernal Dantean one blowing the "darkest . . . leaves"; it may "feast and spin," make whole, in its upward vortex, the "disk shivered against lust."[84] The white wind of "Possessions" may come—indeed the logic of spiritual events is as certain as the yielding of darkness to light:

> Then watch
> While darkness, like an ape's face, falls away,
> And gradually white buildings answer day.

83. Another version was printed in *The Little Review*. See Horton, *Hart Crane*, p. 171.
84. See the manuscripts of "Atlantis" in Weber, *Hart Crane*, pp. 425ff.

The assurance of this radiant prospect carries through the remainder of the poem. Because of it the poet is no longer dismayed by the modern world, which is represented here as the chief cause of the loss of wholeness. Having beheld the white buildings, he can endure the terrible separation and loneliness ("same" establishes this as the condition of the previous stanzas), and the unsuccored anguish. He can endure a heartless acquisitive civilization ("atrocious sum," "Wrenched gold") and the competitive stress within it ("The highest tower") that he seems here to consider feminine ("her"); he can endure, though the catch in the movement of the line suggests that this way madness lies. So rather than endure passively he would follow another course, one that the declarative sentences tell us is there and his to take: "The bridge swings over salvage, beyond wharves; / A wind abides the ensign of your will. . . ." This is the course of imaginative beyonding first set down in "The Bridge of Estador" and modified in "Faustus and Helen." And it is the course that promises connection and wholeness: for the bridge reaches out over the "nameless gulf," over the wreckage (the brokenness), and it "swings," a motion not only of soaring outward flight but of the "alternating bells" of the last stanza. It is a way and points a way, if only the soul's ship will run up its flag (and sails) and accept the favoring inspiring wind (the abiding spirit).[85]

And there is no reason to question this summons to imaginative voyaging because, as the poet's question implies, the unitary experience it intends is not unfamiliar to us. All of us have heard the sound of bells merge into one sound, have known the cessation of time in a moment of the eternal now, and have experienced the kinetic harmony of a single motion: "In alternating bells have you not heard / All hours clapped dense into a single stride?" That is why the poet asks us to forgive him this poem, this "echo" of the real experience, and, in the fraternal gesture of the closing line (a rather weak line), invites us to walk with him "through time with equal pride." In the certainty of such experience he would have us

85. See ch. 135 of *Moby-Dick*, and, especially, Whitman's "Passage to India." "Ensign" puns on "one . . . sign" in stanza three; the most significant gloss is "A Postscript," where Crane speaks of the "ensign of my faith / toward something far. . . ."

walk with the proud stride of the bells, with the swing of the bridge (its stride is noted in *The Bridge*), and not only walk throughout time and proudly endure it, but walk "through" it in the sense that "through" acquires from Blake's notion of vision—with a splendid readiness of imagination.

Why should we hesitate to call such masterful poems mature? [86] They demonstrate a remarkable attainment of craft—"Repose of Rivers," "Lachrymae Christi," and "The Wine Menagerie" belong with the finest poems of the age, and all of the poems exhibit the complexity of awareness and composition involved in the "logic of metaphor" at the same time as they fulfill Crane's motto from Donne: "Make my dark poem light, and light." Nothing in these poems, as Crane said of "Recitative," is "wilfully obscure or esoteric," and when we come to know them we realize how much the "more perfect lucidity" Crane sought in his art served the "spiritual honesty" he claimed for himself.[87] By grouping these poems together—poems written during the same period of development— he shows us how far he has come on the pilgrimage toward his inner self,[88] how willing he has been, and how necessary it has become for him, to use poetry to explore, to order, and to consolidate his experience. In these poems, which support Elizabeth Jennings' belief that Crane's poetry is "inward, spiritual at an extremely deep level," [89] he searches out the primary concerns of the soul and, in treating them, provides an anatomy of love. Their intense autobiographical quality and their daring are due to the fact, as Robert Lowell said of the poems of his own *Life Studies*, that these poems are about "direct experience, and not symbols," and that the poet who wrote them, to cite Elizabeth Jennings once more, "put on no masks, had no public face. . . ." [90]

86. Milne Holton indicates the legacy of Crane criticism when he remarks that "after R. P. Blackmur's 'New Thresholds, New Anatomies' . . . one hesitates to use the word 'mature' in connection with Crane." " 'A Baudelairesque Thing,' " p. 216n.
87. *Letters*, pp. 176, 150 (March 1, 1924; October 5, 1923).
88. Ben Shahn, *The Shape of Content* (New York: Vintage Books, 1957), p. 42.
89. *Every Changing Shape*, p. 227.
90. "Interview with V. S. Naipaul," *Listener*, LXXXII (September 4, 1969), 304; *Every Changing Shape*, p. 223.

II

Crane's legend is not a saint's but a lover's legend whose motto might be "Make thy love sure. . . ." [91] In "Voyages," the brilliant sequence of poems with which he concluded *White Buildings,* he "plunder[ed] himself" [92] to tell it—turned to the causes of his need for response and surety in love and to the romantic expectations that he persisted in even as they failed him.

"Voyages." The title itself establishes a new landscape and reverberates with all we remember of voyages or the sea in Melville, Whitman, Poe, Coleridge, Tennyson, Baudelaire, Mallarmé, and Rimbaud, to cite only those writers of whom Crane was evidently aware. It awakens our sense of the primal universe—of all that is vast, chaotic, and perilous. It is, of course, one of the grand metaphors of experience and destiny, which makes all the more daring —and wonderful—Crane's use of it to create a universe of love (the sea as an erotic realm) and to treat all experience under its aspect. Nothing shows more the centrality of love for Crane.

We do not think of the voyage as high adventure because Crane defines it in Melvillean terms. In "At Melville's Tomb," a poem written after "Voyages" was completed and used to preface it, Crane identifies himself with Melville and thereby appropriates for these poems a specific controlling vision of life—of the sea, of the seer (as in "Voyages VI"), and of the voyage itself. This superb monody is one of the best examples of Crane's profound understanding of the writers he made part of his own work. Poe, for instance, is explicitly acknowledged in "The Tunnel" and Whitman in "Cape Hatteras"; and there are poems to Shakespeare and to Emily Dickinson, the latter worthy of comparison with the poem to Melville. But, with the exception of Whitman (and Blake, whom Crane acknowledged in epigraphs), no other writer seems so pervasive an influence, to count for something, as Joseph Warren Beach says, "in the direction taken by Crane's imagination." [93] This powerful influence may be explained by kinship: Melville—"orphan" and voyager—is Crane's older brother, someone

91. Lewis, *The Poetry of Hart Crane,* p. 239n; P, 114.
92. Jennings, *Every Changing Shape,* p. 224.
93. "Hart Crane and Moby Dick," *Western Review,* XX (Spring, 1956), 186.

whose work, like his, exhibits a terrible lack of basic trust. This persistent quester verifies Crane's darkest view of experience, tells him what reality is, while Whitman, another writer of the sea and, for Crane, Melville's complement, sustains his innocence, the hope that "the long way home" [94] will end in homecoming. In Melville, Crane appropriated a naturalistic vision that countervails Whitman's "Sea eyes and tidal, undenying, bright with myth!" [95] Whitman assured him that the "deepest soundings" would be answered; Melville spoke for the damp, drizzly November of his soul.

Crane identifies with Melville by standing at his tomb, the sea, and by taking Melville's view of it, thus making the vision his own. This vision, which R. W. B. Lewis believes involves "one of the greatest religious statements of modern poetry," and which Crane himself, in a letter to Harriet Monroe, may have confirmed as religious in glossing "frosted eyes," is not religious so much as naturalistic.[96] The religious figures in it, but desperately, as part of man's unwillingness to accept the naturalistic view of his condition; it figures because God is absent. In this respect it reminds us of Stephen Crane, who seems also to have contributed to the poem.

Because the sea is unchanging, the poet, standing where Melville stood, sees what he saw. Vision, here, spans history. We are given the dimension of space but not of time. The present tense, used only in the last stanza, brings together past and present in the recognition of naturalistic "eternity." What Melville saw and Crane now sees is universal, timeless: the cosmic seascape of the direful voyage that Melville said was the longest ever known to man. As he stands above the sea, looking out ("wide from this ledge") and into the depths ("beneath the wave," where, as in "The Mast-Head" chapter of *Moby-Dick*, visionary dreaming yields to the terror of truth), he contemplates man's naturalistic destiny.[97] The opening line establishes cosmic dimensions, and

94. "Voyages V."

95. "Cape Hatteras."

96. *The Poetry of Hart Crane*, p. 208; P, 239.

97. Denis Donoghue cites this as "one of the recurrent 'moments' of American literature [where] the imagination confronts reality in the guise of a poet gazing at the sea." *Connoisseurs of Chaos: Ideas of Order in Modern American Poetry* (New York: Macmillan, 1965), p. 26.

"Often," the opening word, tells of obsessive preoccupation with an invariably repeated, changeless spectacle.

What did Melville see? That chance and death rule life and that nature is cruel ("beat"). He saw the bones of drowned men washed up by the sea.[98] A key word in stanza one is "dice," not only evoking an image of white rolling bones ("bones" is slang for "dice") but suggesting the gamble of voyaging, the chance involved—even calling up a poem of dice and sea and stars: Mallarmé's *Un Coup de dés*. Melville pondered the meaninglessness of chance and the fact that there is death in this business of whaling, of going beyond the "dusty shore." This is the "embassy" the bones "bequeath," the end of voyaging. It is all that the dead have to give us (tell us); their bones are their ambassadors, not from another world but from the death-dealing world. "Bequeath" and "embassy" also contribute to the ceremonial and funereal quality of the poem and sustain the somber tone, which, with the admirable control, reminds one of "Praise for an Urn." The syntax suggests that only Melville saw this, recognized the bones as ambassadors and received their testimony, and that this was so because he had come to the sea in search of an answer. Now the bones are both numerous (this fate is common) and numbered, like dice; and these numbers, marks of identity, are worn away. Life, in this stark view of it, is attrition and disintegration, as much for the cosmic reasons associated with the sea as for those associated with the "dusty shore." (Crane keeps Melville's root metaphor of sea-and-land.) We may attribute the obscurity of the numbers to the neglect and indifference of the shore, as in Stephen Crane's "The Open Boat," as well as to the actions of the waves.

Melville also saw the "wrecks" (the wreckage that life is) pass untolled by bells ("without sound of bells"), pass, that is, in silent procession and without presage of a spiritual world—and pass untold, though he himself told it in the concluding chapter and epilogue of *Moby-Dick* that count for so much in the second and third stanzas of this poem. These stanzas take us outward to a scene of shipwreck on the heartless immensity of the sea. Here the

---

98. Melville merges here with the Whitman of "As I Ebb'd with the Ocean of Life."

vortex created by the sinking ship figures ironically as the calyx of a flower, a dreadful association of the greatest significance for Crane, who connects the downward vortex with ultimate destruction and cosmic evil and the flower with ultimate fulfillment and cosmic good.[99] Though the thought of death is seldom absent from Crane's desire for fulfillment, and sometimes becomes the metaphor of fulfillment, as in "Voyages II" and "The Return," the association of calyx-vortex works here to deny the universe any good, any "bounty." Taking life, the vortex takes everything and gives back precious little, certainly not the answers, the spiritual assurance, Melville sought. It gives back only portents of doom: the "scattered chapter," where "scattered" recalls the image of dice and, with "chapter," suggests the destruction of order and unity, a chaos without clues, especially those to faith that "chapter," in its biblical sense, seems to indicate; the "livid hieroglyph," where "livid," punning on "lived" and conveying also the blue-black color of the sea, symbolizes ("hieroglyph," a Melvillean word charged with his anger at inscrutability, and also associated with tombs—an association picked up at the end in "sea keeps") the bruising "demeanors" of life at sea, the injury called up in the off-meaning of "wound" in the next line; and the "portent wound in corridors of shells," where the vortex is again evoked in the winding of the shell, itself a calyx-vortex form, and portends the doom we hear when we hold the shell to our ears. This is not the assuring portent Holmes heard in "The Chambered Nautilus" ("Thanks for the heavenly message brought by thee / Child of the wandering sea / Cast from her lap, forlorn"), a poem Crane seems intent on having us remember for its generous faith and especially for the maternal imagery which, even at this remove, binds his poem to "Voyages I." [100]

In the third stanza the sea becomes calm, in mood like the peaceful Pacific of *Moby-Dick*. But the "circuit calm" is not only the calm of the vast seascape, the circle of the horizon, but the limited space in which the sea's "lashings" and "malice" are

99. See Guiguet, *L'Univers poétique de Hart Crane*, pp. 74–75.
100. As in Holmes, the shell, washed on the shore like bones, is a "crypt," a "tomb." Crane's "corridor" covers Holmes's idea of mansion or chamber, and his use of "coil" may have been prompted by Holmes.

"charmed" and "reconciled." We are still aware of the dangerous vortex in "one vast coil," an image which defines the limited space of shipwreck while extending its character to the entire sea: the sea is a vortex, a sea serpent, leviathan, whose calms are limited in space and momentary in time. The emphatic words "lashings" and "malice" admirably convey the sound of an angry (personified) sea, and the internal rhyme of "charmed" and "reconciled" enacts the quieting they denote at the same time as they remind us that it will not last. (The very language does the charming and reconciling: "Its lashings charmed and malice reconciled. . . .")

Now when the calm comes and the sea relents, some sailors—how few, how derelict the phrasing makes them out to be!—lift their eyes in supplication, an act not to be found in *Moby-Dick* but in "The Open Boat," where the reporter learns that personification and entreaty are unavailing in a godless world. Their "Frosted eyes," like the "spindrift gaze" of the seals in "Voyages II," may be covered with brine and so unseeing; or having seen and felt the full impact of experience they may be chilled by the North Labradorian nature of things ("silent answers"); or they may be the eyes of dead men ("Where icy and bright dungeons lift / Of swimmers their lost morning eyes"), and, if not, they may be, as much in the early stanzas of "Voyages VI" suggests, eyes not unlike those of the poet, the "derelict and blinded guest," whose voyage has also ended in shipwreck. That the sailors "lifted altars" does not mean that they have religious faith—if they still do, after their experience, the phrase is ironic—but that they would like to. This phrase indicates the depth of their despair, the extent of their knowledge; the phrase depicts only a posture or gesture. The sailors themselves create the spiritual dimension of "heaven," the religious idea that would make their experience "meaningful," much as our instruments "contrive" what we measure; and if this wholly subjective determination is in fact the case, then the altars they have raised are those upon which they have been sacrificed. For their prayers are not answered; and if there is a God, there is no consolation in knowing that silence is his attribute. The sailors do not find "silent answers" in the stars—in the heavenly order, Emerson's last outpost of God. The line—"And silent answers crept across the stars"—is perfectly in the spirit of Stephen Crane, an impressionistic statement of what they felt, with finality: answers not even directed to them and of a space more vast and indifferent than the sea; furtive answers that "crept across the stars," the answer of silence itself, negating whatever spiritual significance the stars have had.[101]

This explains why the instruments of navigation mentioned in the last stanza "contrive / No farther tides. . . ." The sailors have learned in this extreme and final experience that there is no spiritual port. They have come as far into the nature of things, farther, in fact, than man's instruments—those instruments that orient us by means of the stars yet only "contrive" or, as Crane explained, extend the space they were designed to measure.[102] Dependent on the "heavens," these instruments still cannot "contrive [that] farther tide." They declare man's radical helplessness. Eternity is the ultimate "vision" of man. There is no heaven, only the sea, the natural condition that Crane ironically depicts in terms of heaven ("High," "azure," and the implied idea that we have our sleep in heaven). And there is no "waking" into another world. The poet, looking to sea, knows now and says, declaratively, that nothing, not even the dirge of the sea—the sea that rocks the mariner in (to) his final rest! (perhaps whispering death)—"shall" (in the sense of "ever" and "can") wake the mariner (here Melville) lost at sea, lost in this kind of voyaging. This kind of voyaging, the quest for ultimate assurance, is heroic and grand—"fabulous": yes, the stuff of fables. But, again with finality, which rhyme insures, only the sea "keeps" his "shadow," his "fabulous" soul, his ghost. "Keeps" ends the poem conclusively: the sea is a tomb. Giving up his bones, it may "keep" his shadow in the sense of cherishing it ("monody"), but in another sense, that of the dungeon, it keeps it from going heavenward, toward all that it desires. "Keeps" closes out the quest with an image of an eternally present guardian sea that, at the same time, is possessive, confining, and dark—an image whose vaguely maternal character is strengthened by the personification of the sea

---

101. "Crept" recalls the rat of *The Waste Land*, in the passage where the protagonist muses on his "brother's wreck." The borrowings from Eliot are heavy: "contrive," "corridor," "circuit" are probably from "Gerontion."

"A high cold star . . . is the *word* he feels that she [Nature] says to him. Thereafter he knows the pathos of his situation." Stephen Crane, "The Open Boat"; my italics.

102. P, 239.

in "Voyages" and made frightful by our realization that for Crane love, alluded to also by "monody," which recalls Melville's "Monody," was the voyage that enabled him to share Melville's vision.

The maternal character of the sea is established in "Voyages I," the earliest poem of the sequence. Crane wrote it before coming to New York and entering on the love affair treated, specifically, in "Voyages II-V." When he wrote about it to Munson, in 1922, he thought it merely a "kind of poster," a " 'stop, look and listen' sign," [103] but by the time he put the sequence together he seemed to know that its right to be included was due to more than mere reference to the sea—that it belonged because it "explained" the subsequent voyage and the course of experience depicted in it. Edwin Honig says of "Voyages" that "the private place where the poetic vision rediscovers its source and from which it goes forth to do its work is associated with the sea"—an especially accurate observation in terms of his theme ("the search in American poetry for an island of promise, a spiritual garden, a personal refuge enclosed in reality") and in terms of what Crane would not have us forget: that his vision has its source in the difficulties of love and is a vision of love and that the "private place" is also the primal place, the mother, identified in these poems with the sea.[104]

"Voyages" is a psychological progression. The sequence presents, and moves through, phases of love, and the despair of the concluding poem reaches back to the first, where the most notable thing is the poet's feeling of urgency and bitterness. Even in "Voyages II" the hope of consummated love is not without distress; and in the sequence as a whole what impresses one most is the fearfulness of love, the poet's expectation of betrayal and shipwreck. The extremity of Crane's response to the joy and pain of love is perhaps unusual, but he prepares us for it by considering its etiology in "Voyages I," the report of his first voyage in love.

Although "Voyages I" concerns the deception and hidden malice of a maternally guarded world, it begins directly and descriptively, seemingly without any hidden meaning, and lets us discover it.

103. *Letters*, p. 99 (Summer, 1922).

104. "American Poetry and the Rationalist Critic," *Virginia Quarterly Review*, XXXVI (Summer, 1960), 429, 427. Honig is treating what Bachelard calls "reveries toward childhood."

The scene of childhood play on the beach is bright and gay. The children are not playing in the water but "above" it—"Above the fresh ruffles of the surf": an image at once domestic but, on second reading, jeopardized by "surf" and by the fact that the "ruffles" easily translates into the "folds" of stanza two ("The waves fold thunder on the sand") and that their curtain-like character, while connoting an enclosed world, defines a boundary and hides things from view. The children, described as "urchins" (summoning all that "urchin" conveyed in "The Wine Menagerie," but also, as Leibowitz notes, because of syntactical ambiguity, suggesting sea urchins),[105] are in brightly striped bathing suits, though again it is the urchins, too, who are "bright" (and shining—"brilliant") and whose "stripes" may be due to the sun or to their play, "flay[ing] each other with sand." Children's play is often cruel—that the poet is not sentimental about them strengthens his later claim on truth.[106] Moreover, reminded of it by "At Melville's Tomb," we realize that unknowingly they have already set out on the adult quest; their children's games imitate ours, prepare for ours: "They have contrived a conquest for shell shucks"—have created their own world of play, one of sand forts and battle, of aggression, conquest, limits, and going beyond limits. They are incipient Ahabs playing at (with) the destiny awaiting them—the "shell shucks" that, with "scattering," evokes Melville's world of shipwreck.

Already they ask questions of the universe, or of the mother; at least the poet considers their "treble interjections" in that way. And they are "answer[ed]": by the sun that "beats lightning on the waves," an exact yet ominous description of the sunlit sea, where "beats" recalls the final return to shore in "At Melville's Tomb"; and by the sea, whose "waves fold thunder on the sand," where again the accuracy of image, sound, and cadence includes the intimation of imperious force in the nature of things, the storm that thunder and lightning portend.

Now the fact that all along the poet has been speaking is emphasized by his wish, at the end of stanza two, to speak to the

---

105. *Hart Crane*, p. 84.

106. And children's play is sometimes innocently homosexual. See Beach, "Hart Crane and Moby Dick," p. 187.

children, to tell them what *he* knows, to guard their innocence with his experience, a thing he urgently wishes to do—the urgency powerfully transforms the poem—because he knows that, being innocently trusting, they cannot hear (understand) him, or for that matter the sun and the waves. They belong to the scene he describes, his very distance from it marking his own experience; and the scene, which for us at first may have been only one of childhood play, mediated by our own sentiment of childhood, now provides the evidence for the poet's warning. In his injunction to them he initially describes the scene in just such terms ("O brilliant kids, frisk with your dog, / Fondle your shells and sticks"), and even as we become aware of the irony in "brilliant" we remember the happy boyhood world of "Sunday Morning Apples"— and now begin to see how much Crane needed someone like Sommer to reassure him about nature's "purposes." But the shells and sticks, as the subsequent phrase insists, are "bleached / By time and the elements"; like the "fragments of baked weed" in stanza one, they are tokens of death. And so he verifies his truth: that the universe, even that of childhood, being in time and of the elements (and being elemental), is not to be trusted. Childhood doesn't last. Yet—cruel paradox—do not cross the line to experience ("but there is a line / You must not cross nor ever trust beyond it"); do not go to sea, as Melville said, do not push off from the vernal isle; and do not "ever trust beyond it"—trust to beyond it. For the sea is a cruel mother, at once too possessive and indifferent. ("Too lichen-faithful from too wide a breast"). The love she offers is superficial and deceptive. A bottom, in its depths, in its very nature, the sea is cruel. This is the certain truth of the final line, a single declarative sentence: "The bottom of the sea is cruel."

This is not an exceptional truth about experience. Were it not for the maternal imagery and the poet's bitter conviction, we would consider it shortly as a truism. The children will learn it because they will grow up; "Spry cordage of your bodies" suggests that they are already at sea or intended for it. Being in time, they cannot protect their innocence. No, what the poet really wants to say is the burden of his own growing up and of his greatest love, which is why it is fitting to begin "Voyages" with it: Do not trust love, not even a mother's love. It is a counsel he hasn't followed and isn't about to follow. He speaks here as a disillusioned voyager, one who, trusting, had gone beyond the securities of childhood; and now he knows that love is not to be counted on, is dangerous and death-dealing. Still, the voyage beyond limits is one he will continue to make because the very love he has been denied urges him to it.

For Crane the voyage is explicitly connected with love and, whether because his love is homosexual or oedipal or inordinately demanding, figures as a transgression, a going beyond limits in the metaphysical sense of attacking or searching out the nature of things. Crane refused to follow the wisdom of the poem—that "there are," as Leibowitz says, "boundaries to the exploration of self and experience. . . ." [107] Perhaps he did not know when he spoke of the poem as a poster, a "skull & cross-bones insignia," that he was flying his flag of piracy. Joseph Warren Beach reads the poem as a warning against homosexual love, [108] but it may also be read as a declaration of it. The subsequent voyage, enacted within the maternal sovereignty and presence, and apparently with approval, may repay the betraying mother with betrayal.

Although the poem treats childhood, it does so not objectively but in the context of adult experience. In this respect, as in others (the relation of shore and sea, of happiness and loss, love and death), it reminds one of Whitman's "Out of the Cradle Endlessly Rocking." And though it brings Whitman and Melville together over the central issue of trust, and Melville is clearly ascendant, it is most like Whitman in telling us what prompted the "outsetting bard." By the time Crane placed it in this sequence he was aware of the oedipal significance of his relationship with his mother and its relation to homosexuality. And he had found a sanction for it in Munson's study of Waldo Frank—in those passages cited from Frank's *Dark Mother* where we learn that Tom's revolt "against the source of his father's hold, [was] his own deep identity with his mother," that in his relation to other women he "fought her betrayal of him," and that "Directly through her [his sister], indirectly against his father, Tom grew in love with imagery, with color, with

107. *Hart Crane*, p. 82.
108. *Letters*, p. 99; Beach, "Hart Crane and Moby Dick," p. 187.

the Symbol—the artist in Tom grew." [109] In going to sea, Crane does not—cannot—forget his mother. He defies her on the very ground of love ("I'm engaged in writing a series of six sea poems called 'Voyages' [they are also love poems]"),[110] breaks her lichen-faithful caress, and enters the vast world of experience.

"Voyages II," beginning with a dash and the qualifying "And yet," continues the argument of "Voyages I." The sea is cruel; "this great wink of eternity," the incomprehensible vastness of "rimless" and "unfettered," may be offered in proof. Still, it is enticingly beautiful. From the shore of the bright childhood world of "Voyages I" we are moved by love to turn seaward. Under the spell of its rapture and of the moonlit seascape we enter a romantic universe, and the vastness upon which the poem opens is transformed into an erotic realm justifying the Melvillean recognition that sometimes the visible world seems formed in love. And formed for love: the "demeanors" of the sea are womanly and, like the "floating flower," invite consummation.

Nowhere in Crane's mature work is the erotic attraction of woman so fully and genuinely evoked, though the seductive female presence, the imperious goddess who permits the voyage of love, has been little appreciated in this much-noticed poem. The sea in "Voyages II" is the cruel mother in another aspect: the mother feared yet lovingly regarded as a woman, as one who knows every motion of love and may therefore be expected to sanction it. Not the lover with whom the poet is embarked but she, variously celebrated, is the source of the poem's eroticism. In the extended primary metaphor of the poem, that of marriage and consummation, we are asked to "Take this Sea," to consider *this* sea, arrayed for marriage and full of longing, to take her in marriage—and in the vulgar sense, too. But this is a forbidden act for the poet who has established the maternal character of the sea, and even voyaging, the metaphor here of his love of another, is fear-ridden and death-burdened because it involves her. In an early version of the poem the poet says that "She / is our bed" and "enlist[s] us / to her body

---

109. *Waldo Frank*, pp. 32–34. Crane also found sanction in Remy de Gourmont, *The Physiology of Love*, where all forms of love are accepted and love is related to growth of intellect and sensibility.
110. *Letters*, p. 192 (November 16, 1924).

endlessly." [111] Her presence not only suggests to us that the poet's lover is a woman (a confusion similar to that of "Harbor Dawn") and provides an analogue for their affair, it is so necessary and intimate a part of it that we feel its pre-emption. [112]

It is fitting also that the setting is tropical—specifically the paradisal Caribbean island world of Crane's boyhood—and that "undinal," used in the root sense of "wave" and admirably conveying the sensuous motion of the "vast belly [bending] moonward," has maternal associations. One remembers the water sprite who becomes mortal and acquires a soul by accepting human love and bearing a child. The sylph becomes a woman, a mother, is domesticated—as the soulless sea world of the poem may be said to be because of the maternal presence. And perhaps one remembers Fouqué's *Undine*, where the water sprite is betrayed by her husband (as Grace Crane felt she was) and repays him with a fatal kiss before returning to the sea. Undine, whose experience of love is here its paradigm, may well laugh at "the wrapt inflections of our love." But the poet himself, rehearsing family history, has not forgotten the duplicity of love nor the "sceptred terror" of the cruel sea to whom his being is committed. His romantic expectation is poised on this naturalistic awareness.

From the very outset suspicion marks the voyage. Though "this great wink of eternity" may be considered the summons of a flirtatious woman, the goddess as whore, [113] it suggests also the awareness that transience is a cosmic joke made at the expense of the poet's attempt to transform the sea and love to the eternal demands of his desire. In its changelessness and vastness, its "rimless floods, unfettered leewardings," the sea is an eternity of space, a flux impossible to contain or hold; the phrases are adopted from Melville, and their cadence and sound support the sense of endless motion. In the context of sexual consummation, which offers a "wink" of eternity, these phrases may have the psychological equivalence of spontaneity and freedom, may be images of the abandon welcomed in love: "leewardings," a fitting participial noun of longing, con-

111. Leibowitz, *Hart Crane*, p. 87.

112. The poet's return to the goddess in "Voyages VI" seems to support this.

113. Judith S. Friedman and Ruth Perlmutter, "Explication of 'Voyages II,' " *Explicator*, XIX (October, 1960).

tains "lewd," and the impression of the sea's motion as under the compulsion of tidal desire is almost immediately strengthened by the graphic force of "Her undinal vast belly moonward bends." The sea of this introductory stanza is wonderfully sensuous, exotic, oriental perhaps—"samite" echoes "semite," a people who wore raiment of gold and silver cloth. But even as this splendid word begins the work of romantic transformation, it reminds us of the death that Poe said was mingled with romantic love. Most likely Crane took this word from Tennyson's *Morte d'Arthur*, where the Lady of the Lake is "clothed in white samite, mystic, wonderful." [114] Like "sheeted," samite renders not only the whiteness of the smooth moonlit sea but the ambiguity of white in its Melvillean resonance; it is the forbidding white of "North Labrador." And "Samite sheeted and processioned," which in the erotic context we read primarily in a nuptial sense, has an equally strong funereal meaning.

The concluding line ("Laughing the wrapt inflections of our love") is also equivocal. Its descriptive accuracy is not in question: "Laughing" gives a jewellike, tinkling sound as well as a sense of the visual play of moonlight on water. The sea, according to the syntax, is not laughing at the lovers but *laughing them*, or *laving* them (see "Voyages III"), supporting and washing and cradling them in the waves whose very movement depicts their ardor. "Wrapt inflections" evokes the image of waves breaking and flowing back on themselves—waves as innocent-seeming as those in "Voyages I"—and "wrapt" contains the several meanings of *wrapped* (as in embrace), *rapt* (the complete involvement of being "wrapped," the rapture in which time and death are forgotten), and the protection love grants (a notion advanced in the next stanza by "All but the pieties of lovers' hands"). The "inflections" are the movement, of both the waves and "our love," that causes the laughing. Laughter is the language, the "inflection," of love.

But laughter is not the register of this poem—nor of the "Voyages"—and the poet is never wrapt in love's blessed forgetfulness.

---

114. See Paul Goodman, *The Structure of Literature* (Chicago: University of Chicago Press, 1954), p. 221; Beach, "Hart Crane and Moby Dick," p. 188. In *Morte d'Arthur*, the Lady of the Lake, who emerges with Excalibar in hand, is the source and keeper of manhood.

No sooner has he depicted the loving-laughing aspect of the sea, its open sensuous favoring nature, than he recalls its imperiousness and remembers that its protection, a matter of whim, may yield as quickly as, in the equation of the poem, love becomes death (laving and wrapping having ominous meanings too). This sea answers Ouspensky's description of the deity of love: "sometimes terrible, sometimes benevolent, but never subservient to us"; [115] and, as Crane, who served this goddess, knew, she rules according to the code of courtly love. So he presents her, the grander music of this stanza and its reverential close paying her appropriate homage.

Now the waves, whose majestic motion and sound are depicted ("whose diapason knells / On scrolls of silver snowy sentences"), tell of death. "Knell" here is funereal and prompts us to read "Samite sheeted and processioned," which as seascape the subsequent phrase recalls, in its darker meaning. The "scrolls" bear "sentences" of death, as do the "snowy," crested waves. And in keeping with the either-or of the waves, the "well or ill" of her "demeanors," we are asked in this stanza to recognize a sea "The sceptred terror of whose sessions rends"; a fierce sea—we hear it especially in "whose sessions"—that renders sentence (of death), rends (tortures), and is perhaps most truly death-dealing to the poet (the injunction to "Bind us" picks up this meaning later) because it tears apart or separates. To take *this* sea, which the pivotal injunction of the two-stanza sentence also asks us to do, is to love in fear of death, indeed to love death, to accept the romantic merger of love-and-death and seek the fulfillment of the one in the other.

In the voyage that follows, the demeanors of the sea motion well, though the poet, almost immediately, anticipates—and dreads —its turning, thereby creating the mounting excitement-anxiety of the desire for consummation that fills the remainder of the poem. The lovers, on their voyage of discovery, move "onward" through the pastoral ("crocus," "poinsettia meadows") paradise of the Caribbean ("San Salvador" secures both meanings). Their passage is triumphal, celebrated, it seems, by festive bells and fireworks, or cannonade, the bells that "Salute the crocus lustres of the stars"—a visually rich line including a sense of pristine erotic

115. *Tertium Organum,* p. 168.

awakening ("crocus") and heavenly sanction ("stars"). But the bells, which perhaps signify unitary fulfillment of the kind desired in "Recitative," or the risen Atlantis of love's fulfillment in "Belle Isle," also remind us of "knells"; and they may summon, as Philip Horton says, the legend of "the sunken city off the island of San Salvador" [116]—the lost Atlantis, death-possessed in Poe's "The City in the Sea." Even in the "poinsettia meadows" and in the slow movement of passage through the islands of these tropical waters (the "Adagios of islands" Crane glossed in "General Aims and Theories"); [117] even as the springtime love ("crocus") becomes the fully sensuous love evoked by red tropical flowers, music, dance—all associated with the sea, whose sensuous body, indicated by "veins," [118] is that of a dark lady and moves the poet to demand both the prolongation of enchantment ("spell," spell out, and spelling, the last recalling "inflections" and "sentences") and its swift consummation ("Complete," and make complete); even then there is foreboding, in "tides" and "dark confessions," of death, of the "far consummations" first associated with the sea in "The Bridge of Estador."

This perturbation is not shared by the poet's lover—his "Prodigal"—who seems to enjoy the enchantment of the voyage and must be reminded by the poet, ever more desperately, to bring it to a timely close. For the anxious poet is aware of the turning tide ("Mark how her turning shoulders wind the hours"), is aware of time, the destructive agent of his felicity. The tides are "her demeanors" and they "motion well or ill" by telling time. "Mark," "wind," "hours" all refer to time; and "wind," in relation to "sheeted," suggests a winding sheet, while "Mark" reminds us that the ever-changing sea not only marks but keeps time, keeps life, as in "At Melville's Tomb." "Hasten," which the poet twice implores his lover to do, evokes the sound of the incoming waves that threaten to cast them on the shore, the "earthly shore" upon which the poet would not be wrecked ("to throw / Clean on the shore some wreck of dreams," as in "The Bridge of Estador") before he experiences, at sea, a heavenly consummation. The shore is

116. *Hart Crane*, p. 175.
117. P, 221.
118. Recall "arteries" in "Faustus and Helen."

already evoked by "palms," whose primary meaning seems to be benedictory ("Pass superscription") and to refer to the safe passage accorded devout lovers ("All but the pieties of lovers' hands"). And this passage the poet would conclude in time: "*while* they ["her penniless rich palms"] are *true*," [119] and also, since he fears betrayal, "sleep, death, desire" are "true"—truly efficacious of the fulfillment that, in impatience, he denotes in a series of apparent equivalents.

The verse moves too quickly to the poet's own wonderful vision of consummation for us to remember that death is a sleep from which there is no waking (on that account perhaps a blessed sleep) and that desire is a condition of longing rather than appeasement. Initially, we take "sleep, death, desire" as completed conditions, though "desire" makes us suspect this. But "desire," a vital force, is rightly placed, and modifies the series, because the poet finds its common property in the act of completing which is the completion: sleep and death become their own agents and here perform a loving action. The poet emphasizes "one instant," the wink of eternity, that contains the glory of that action—that which happens so instantly, so miraculously, that "desire" might now be accepted in the series without misgiving. He also emphasizes—how deliberately we must read "Close round one instant in one floating flower"—the intimate act of enclosing and completing ("Close round one"—recalling "wrapt") and the unity or oneness (in "one instant," "in one floating flower") that are of ultimate importance to him. And the "one instant" he seeks is the "one floating flower" because, like it, it affords these satisfactions.

In its urgent appeals and deliberate quiet closure, the concluding stanza parallels the preceding one. The poet implores the "Seasons clear," the propitious occasion of this voyage (comparable to the goddess in her "demeanors" and therefore hypostatized), to "Bind us in time . . . and awe": to unite in time, while there is time, in the time of life, and in the wink of eternity Emily Dickinson called "awe." Now is the time, he says, while they are passing among the islands and are in the sway of "minstrel galleons of Carib fire"—their love boat, so much like the "floating flower," as well as the vessel of the poet's song. Let love be consummated now,

119. My italics.

let longing have an end, even in "the vortex of our grave," which, with "Bequeath us to no earthly shore," recalls "At Melville's Tomb" and the "calyx of death's bounty." The rhyme of "our grave" and "our love" insists on the equation of love and death. The poet welcomes a consummatory death because only such total experience will "answer" his paradisal longing, the demands he makes on love. For, like the seal with his "wide spindrift gaze toward paradise," the poet has been moved by cosmic loneliness and unbearable longing and willingly would bring love to the fearful yet desired end in which both the immediate voyage and its profound necessity are satisfied. Where the sea has been so closely identified with the mother as in this poem, shipwreck is a fitting conclusion.[120]

The consummation so fervently sought in "Voyages II" is never achieved, though "Voyages III" and "Voyages IV" give more extended, particular, and arresting evocations of it. Both poems, occasioned by the lover's absence, involve the visionary enactment of consummation and thereby declare—pledge and prove—the poet's love. In these poems, the poem itself is the agency of love.

Of importance in "Voyages III" is the poet's determination on relationship and connection: the way he employs the idea of consanguinity to nullify distance and separation and to direct the poem successfully to the visionary goal of unity ("this single change"). Both the sea and "This tendered theme," the poem, have this quality; for the poem, like the sea, whose primal salty substance (bloodlike: "veins" in "Voyages II") reaches everywhere, is a bearer of tidings, an element of connection, especially here, where

---

120. Beach reminds us of the "young seals," in ch. 126 of *Moby-Dick*, whose cries were due to their having "lost their dams." "Hart Crane and Moby Dick," p. 195.

By calling up "At Melville's Tomb," the closing lines remind us of the fateful end of Ahab's voyage and of the "lovely leewardings," the "soft showers" Ahab once saw to leeward and said "must lead somewhere—to something else than common land, more palmy than the palms." These leewardings portend the "paradise" of Crane's poem, the paradisal isles so much like the Isle of Pines, the "one insular Tahiti" from which he should never have cast off and to which he would now return. And it should be noted, in anticipation of "Belle Isle" in the last poem of the sequence, that Ahab said of these leewardings that they were "An old, old sight, and yet somehow so young; aye, and not changed a wink since first I saw it, a boy, from the sand hills of Nantucket!"

the sea, in another of its "infinite" aspects, separates the lovers. Like a ship at sea, the vessel of the poet's love, it tenders the tender theme of "Infinite consanguinity," a theme that the poet, looking seaward in longing for his sailor-lover, finds imaged in the universal embrace of sea and sky ("the sky / Resigns a breast that every wave enthrones").

Though at first the poet seems to be standing at the sea's edge, as in "At Melville's Tomb," he is already in the intimate element of the poem, at sea, the sea which simultaneously "laves" him and "lifts" his distant lover. This connection, of a physical kind, makes the idea of consanguinity real to him, but there is a closer one of memory, which enables the poem to do its work. By being at sea, the poet is able in the poem to remind his lover of their voyage together in "Voyages II": "While ribboned water lanes I wind" recalls the "samite" sea and "Adagio of islands" of that poem; "lave" recalls "Laughing," and "wind," followed two lines later by "hour," recalls "wind the hours"—an urgent time, not, as now, an idle, empty one. "Lifts . . . reliquary hands" plays on "enthrones," and both recall the court of love and the exemption granted "the pieties of lovers' hands"—hands acquiring now, however, a more explicit erotic meaning, in readiness for the admirable closing line of the poem. And finally, the present impossibility of mutual ship-wreck ("scattered with no stroke / Wide from your side") recalls the terrible vortex of "At Melville's Tomb" and the ecstatic vortex of "our grave" in "Voyages II."

By voyaging in memory the poet's imagination of love reaches visionary intensity. By giving himself totally to the sea, in death-by-drowning, he is "admitted through black swollen gates," the vortex of death (and separation) from which he is delivered to new life (and ecstatic union). He undergoes a sea change. In imagined consummation—an experience so cosmic in its glory that it fills all space—he ovecomes all distance. The moment of release that brings him to his lover in the "rush of feeling" noted by Leibowitz is itself consummative.[121] This voyage enacts the erotic experience ("whirling," "wrestling," "kissing," "rocking") and is notable for the clarity with which we are made to see the frenzy that carries the

121. *Hart Crane*, p. 179.

poet beyond the pillars of the world, beyond the Apollonian to the Dionysian.

In this experience death is not dying but transformation. For death is not "shed" in the sense of bloodshed but in the sense of cast off. Sex here, as Crane once said of it, is "beaten out" and the poet is "transubstantiated." [122] The change that "destroys" the body is the spiritual change that unites and glorifies the lovers ("this single change"). It is the miracle for which the poet coins the word "transmemberment," a word, Leibowitz says, that expresses "the tension in the poem between creative and destructive process, between love and death," and, like love, "is made up of transubstantiation and dismemberment, the one impossible without the other." [123] In its immediate visual sense, however, "transmemberment" evokes the intertwined limbs (members) of lovers (as in the case of Queequeg and Ishmael in *Moby-Dick*), the union that the poem, this "song," accomplishes. And the concluding lines call up "At Melville's Tomb" only, in the light of this experience, to countervail the dark vision that underlies it. For with love, the lovers in the "azure steeps" bridge the peaks of the waves ("from dawn to dawn") and avoid the abyss.

In respect to the poem itself, "transmemberment" also countervails another vision that underlies it: Whitman's of unappeased love. The poet's "song," which love creates out of its despair in the way a spider creates a filament out of itself (a kind of "spending"), is the "silken" thread the poet, in Whitman's words, "flings" "to connect them." In this poem, unlike Whitman's ("A Noiseless Patient Spider"), the thread catches, bridges from ecstasy to ecstasy. "Silken," recalling "samite" in "Voyages II," confirms the erotic aspect of the sea, while "skilled" refers to the art by which the poet achieves the miracle of the poem and thus creates the earnest of his love. Having risked so much and demonstrated so splendidly in his vision what he would like their love to be, the poet is justified perhaps in asking his lover to "permit" the voyage he has imagined. But that voyage, we now realize, depends on the lover, whose presence is especially evoked in the direct address of

122. *Letters,* pp. 181–82 (April 21, 1924).
123. *Hart Crane,* p. 101.

the last line—an imploring line, standing in isolation and ending with ellipsis, that opens the poem again to the vast sea and the fearful "black swollen gates" that need not admit ("permit" echoes "admitted") the poet to desired life.

The occasion and argument of "Voyages IV" is similar: the poet addresses an absent lover whose favor he asks, in a poem of such ardor and skill that the logic of his request seems undeniable. Passionate petition now takes the more conventional form of love letter, in keeping perhaps with "signature," a conceit of the poem, and as a token of love, of the "secret oar and petals," at once the sexual symbols and code words of the voyage and its destination.

Again the poet is looking to sea, waiting, counting the "hours and days" of his lover's return (another reference to "wind the hours" in "Voyages II") and counting on his lover's "smile," which he hopes will bring him a fuller time (the "hour" of stanza two) and which he knows, in all its colors, as a rainbow of promise, as well as he knows the sea, whose changes he has been carefully attending. Light, which "retrieved" the "theme of you" in the previous poem, is refracted here, giving a spectrum of time and states of feeling. In a literal sense, the poet may be said to count on his lover with an assurance equal to his knowledge of wave lengths and frequencies. (Distance and consanguinity are involved here, too.) But "spectrum" contains "spectre"; the remembered "smile" is only the phantom of the lover, only a pledge, like the rainbow. The poet, who declares his trust, is uncertain of his lover, and toward his "smile" and all it represents certifies his love in the pledge of this poem.

"Smile" also depicts the wave motion of the sea, which parts or intercepts the circles of frequency made by the dipping wings of gulls ("gulf" echoes "gull")—gulls in whose descent the poet, looking intently for the signatures of things, sees another spiritual pledge, the descent of doves. But "parting" again introduces an element of distrust (like "suppose" earlier) and occasions the second, asserted, "I know." Yes, the poet knows that the circle, radiating endlessly, "bridges"; but the bridge, in the qualifying parentheses, is *from* the "palms," the bliss of the tropics in "Voyages II" and the "Blue latitudes and levels" spoken of later, to "the severe / Chilled albatross's white immutability," the polar state of

"Voyages V." With its recollection of Coleridge's *The Rime of the Ancient Mariner* and of Crane's own North Labradorian landscape, this measured, weighty, irrevocable line acknowledges an assured development. Fearing this, the poet contains it in the pressing movement ("stream") of the poem and in the love he pledges now because writing this poem quickens love in him and reassures him and negates the icy "immutability" (as in the play of "mortality" and "immortally"):

> No stream of greater love advancing now
> Than, singing, this mortality alone
> Through clay aflow immortally to you.

"Now / . . . singing" cancels the earlier "now parting," for poetry is unific and life-giving, an act of being that transforms the mortal (the physical and perishable) into the immortal (the spiritual and permanent). The poet sings his "mortality," too— his physical desire, his loneliness ("alone"), his heaviness of spirit ("clay")—and transforms rather than transcends it, sings it into life, makes it flow. This flowing ("Through clay aflow") is comparable to being admitted "through black swollen gates," and recalls the passage on the thawing railroad cut in *Walden*. For the flowing, like the streaming, is a sign of life, of the immortality of nature. It is also an example of creative art, the process by which poems such as this poem bring love "immortally to you." And it is Neoplatonic, an effulgent stream of love. "Singing" is that streaming and so is the love flowing in his body: his body sings, love transforms his clay, and thus his song, unlike the questionable pledge of his lover, is an immortal pledge.

Nothing attests this transformation so much as the stanza that immediately follows, where, as in "Voyages III," the poet proves his love by a vision of its fulfillment. The stanza lacks predication but needs none, according to Leibowitz, because "the poet is experiencing an unduplicable voluptuous magic sensation. . . ." [124] Though not in itself especially confusing, the stanza conveys a sense of sensual riot, presents a confusion of senses as an image of ecstasy. "Fragrance" (its undeniable power maintained in "ir-

124. *Hart Crane*, p. 243; see also p. 181.

re*fragibly*") [125] is the essence of flowers (connected with the tropical meadows and "floating flower" of "Voyages II" and the "June" of this poem); and such fragrances, spiritual yet sensual, fill all space and therefore meet, and meet "Madly," in the sense of intoxicating perfumes and, as in "Possessions," of being possessed. And just as such essences "wreathe," so will the spirit and flesh ("eyes and lips") of the lovers in what the poet previously called "transmemberment."

Yet even in this depiction of reunion ("again") and consummation the poet expresses desire for assurance and permanence. In the significant pun of this stanza, insisted on in "port" and "portion," this poem, unlike the others, except for "Voyages V" which hideously fulfills it, is "Portending": port-tending and port-ending. Making port is, of course, explicitly sexual, and the imagery of the marriage ceremony in a church (with "bans" and all the rest) may work to spiritualize it and insure its keeping with "fragrance." But, unlike the marriage evoked in "Voyages II," this marriage forsakes the voyage or brings it to an end—seeks the security of the shore and, in Melville's words, "all that's kind to our mortalities. . . ." [126] The poet not only wishes to reach the port "of our June," the blissful time of marriages and presumably of "Voyages II," but to have a "portion" of it. And in connection with the paradisal aspect of June, "portion" may be read as "part" and, by extension, "island": the desire to make port represents a desire to return to the verdant land.

In the subsequent stanza that completes the sentence begun by the preceding one, the poet imagines the wedding that "eyes and lips" portend—the music and flowers (more exactly, a music and light of flowers, a fragrance plucked from them), the march to the altar, the kiss that seals, and the "aye" of "eyes"—imagines all this as a vortex ("stem and close"), as wonderfully self-enclosing sexual ecstasy. But this vision of happy vortex depends on, is guaranteed or pledged by, the experience of another: the "fatal tides" not only of fated attraction (thus he declares his abiding love) but of the doom, the "black swollen gates," to which it

125. My italics.
126. *Moby-Dick*, ch. 23.

brings him, and admittance through which, as in "Voyages III," enables him to "tell" the "making told" of his desire.

In signature of this arrival, which the poet imagines again in stanza five, the poet composes this letter, this poem, his marriage pledge. And in the meaning of "signature" associated with Boehme, it is indeed a "signature of the incarnate word," a symbolic correspondence of the word made flesh—the word become deed. Both meanings of "signature" are expressed in the visible action of the sea ("The harbor shoulders to resign in mingling / Mutual blood"): the tides have turned ("shoulders" in "Voyages II") and come to port, and have accepted there the burden of love ("shoulders" as used here); in coming to port, the sea yields ("resign," and as in "Resigns a breast" in "Voyages III") but also, in keeping with the earlier meanings created by "port," it "re-signs," signs again, pledges itself in blood, enacts a sacrament of consanguinity that (to take up "mingling") is the "incarnate" equivalent of mingling fragrances. The blood pact of the sea (associated also with their piracy) is exemplary, the hopeful end of "fatal tides."

For the tides need not be fatal if, as in this instance of the sea's return, the lover responds by accepting the burden of the poem, by "widening noon within [his] breast" to receive the harvest ("gathering") of the poem: "All bright insinuations that my years have caught / For islands. . . .") [127] Here his lover will find, he says, his intimations of islands—the vision of successful voyaging, the voyage that leads, he claims, "inviolably" to the heavenly tropics of his lover's eyes (the blue eyes are a sea) and to their consent ("ayes"). And if he calls these intimations "insinuations" it is because a goal so supreme belongs to the courtly love the poem enacts and, specifically, to the convention of deifying the lover, by skillful art, in order to win love, a convention Crane learned from and associated with his mother ("my years have caught," where the pun on "my ears" is also significant). But "insinuations" also insinuates the homoerotic meaning that the marriage imagery may disguise. That is the "secret" whose signs the poet reveals to the

---

127. The rushing-then-quieting parallel periodic structure of stanzas two and three and of stanzas four and five conveys the sea motion of the poet's desire, and the gift of the closing lines may be said to answer the question of stanza three.

initiate and bestows on his lover in the concluding and final signature of the poem.

The doom that threatens throughout the earlier poems, even in "Voyages II," "Voyages III," and "Voyages IV," which reach and maintain a peak of expectant visionary exaltation, comes suddenly with the transition to "Voyages V." Now everything is transformed—remarkably so in terms of the previous imagery. Instead of vision, which in the usage of "The Wine Menagerie" is related to dream ("I dreamed"), there is, as the poet himself puns in "clear rime," the cold clarity of sight. The pitch of voice changes too, and the verse moves with the deliberate quiet of intense pain. Here, where we hear, as in none of the other poems, the speech of the lovers, the poem tells of anguish and resignation.

Now the landscape of love is not the imagined "widening noon" of the receptive heart, as in "Voyages IV," nor the paradisal tropical island seascape of "Voyages II" and "Voyages IV." Prefigured perhaps in "Frosted eyes" in "At Melville's Tomb" and certainly in the "Chilled . . . white immutability" of "Voyages IV," the landscape is one of vastation, "past midnight" and North Labradorian—a bitter, bleak, cold, unanswering darkness of soul. In this poem the lovers have reached port, but now the harbor "shoulders" ("Voyages II" and "Voyages IV") a destructive tidal change—"this tidal wedge," the "Meticulous" and "smooth" ice of a "merciless white blade" that executes the "sentence" of "Voyages II." Images of cutting, the death not of consummation but of parting (one recalls the marriage vow, "Till death do us part"), are conspicuous: "blade," "sword," "filed," "shred," "cleft." And there is imagery of metal ("cast") and stone ("fleck")—of hardness, of a rigid death of feeling where nothing flows or streams, of merciless unresponsiveness and infrangibility. The colorless ice contrasts with the "mingling / Mutual blood" of the harbor waters in "Voyages IV"; and the sky has become close and "hard," the horizon appearing now as a limit ("limits" makes it discrete), a boundary beyond which sight cannot go. Now unity is terrible, a shut-in, unalterable, irrevocable condition. The lovers are bound by the icy sword of their suffering, a relationship "too brittle" and "too clear" and, as with an icicle, beyond the reach of touch, which would shatter before it could melt it.

The poet himself desires to touch—to caress and warmly unite with his lover—but their relationship no longer permits this talismanic gesture ("I cannot touch your hand"). For the "cables" that once united them in "sleep, death, desire" in "Voyages II" are now cut ("filed"): "sleep," the cover word, declares the absence of the others—dismemberment, not transmemberment. And the "cables," the poems with which he communicated and bound himself to his lover in "Voyages III" and "Voyages IV," are filed away. Now the cables "hang, shred ends from remembered stars": hang in a phallic sense as well as that of "despatches me" in "The Broken Tower," and hang from the stars to which the poet's vision, recalled in this line, fixed them, the heavenly anchorage of their love. These stars are the "crocus lustres" of "Voyages II" and the "star kissing star" of "Voyages III"—remembered stars that measure the lapse of being and well-being conveyed by "shred ends" with its Prufrockian echo ("butt-ends of my days and ways").

Another evidence of change is the "one frozen trackless smile," which contrasts with the "counted smile" of "Voyages IV" and the laughing sea of "Voyages II" and, rhyming in cadence with "one merciless white blade," evokes the vast wastes of love. This smile, made by the play of moonlight on the ice, is especially cruel because it mocks the poet's faith in its romantic and visionary agency. The sudden vehemence of "What words / Can strangle this deaf moonlight?" expresses his anger at its unresponsiveness, while the subsequent lines express the outrage of his feelings of victimage (powerlessness) and betrayal. The lovers, he feels, "are overtaken." A terrible power wills their separation, a "tidal wedge" as overwhelming and irresistible as a glacier. "Tidal" identifies this power with the sea and the moon, with the tyrannical goddess of "Voyages II," who had once motioned well but now, as he says of the moonlight he had loved—and shows us in the run-over line and its stress —has "changed."

Another run-over line at the stanza separation emphasizes the excruciating nothingness of situation and feeling. So do the thrice-reiterated "nothing" and cluster of negatives ("no," "not," "never"). Speaking for his lover, the poet defines their condition in an apparently compassionate but cruel commonplace: " 'There's / Nothing [no thing] like this in the world.' " For he is denied the assuagement of touch and experiences nothingness—looks "into that godless cleft of sky," not into a visionary heaven nor into the blue of his lover's once-responding eyes but into the vortex "where nothing turns but dead sands flashing." The imagery recalls that of "Passage" but expresses more explicitly the relation of lovelessness and godlessness, nothing and nothingness. Here the vortex is not "the vortex of our grave" ("Voyages II"); it is sterile, empty, lonely, meaningless death.

At this point in the poem, the dialogue renders the disparity of words and feeling and reminds us of the similar situation in Eliot's "Portrait of a Lady"—a situation whose enormity the poet refuses to accept. To his lover's inconsequential words (" '—And never to quite understand!' ") he replies vigorously, expressing his sense of betrayal in terms of the high expectations and fulfillments he had had:

> No,
> In all the argosy of your bright hair I dreamed
> Nothing so flagless as this piracy.

By recalling the "minstrel galleons" of "Voyages II" and all the poet, in "Faustus and Helen," declared he would gladly spend for "golden, or the shadow of gold hair," he fully evokes the dream of love he had identified with his lover.[128] In the line brilliantly suspending it, he even suggests that the dream had been occasioned by his lover. And so the abrogation of the dream expressed in the turn to "Nothing," more than the withholding of erotic joy specified by "flagless," is the treachery for which he blames him.

But this turning is accompanied by another. The tyranny of love, first attributed to a deity and then to the lover, passes to the poet, who acquires the power of the true and the injured. Moving through the stages of the poet's anguish, anger, and resignation, the poem represents the transfer of power that accounts for the bitter generosity of his relinquishment at the end. Now he gives his lover to the sea, enjoins his departure, somewhat in the elemental way of "Song of Myself," [129] though to the end of identifying the lover with the alien seascape, and also, faintly suggested, with the solici-

128. Crane called Emil Opffer "Goldylocks." See Brown, *Robber Rocks*, p. 87.
129. § 52.

tude of a mother putting her child to bed. In yielding his lover to sleep and death, to the sea that already possesses his eyes and spirit, the poet twice asks him to withdraw his head, the last token of the dream of love. The lullaby suggested by the rhythm and the rhyme and, especially, by the refrain, is elegiac: it expresses the poet's loss. "Slant" not only recalls Emily Dickinson, from whom Crane borrowed it, but "Praise for an Urn," an elegy in which he used it; and "sealed," describing the entombment of ice, and "ghosts" recall the unavailing monody of "At Melville's Tomb." But even here, the recognition of the lover's eagerness to be gone and of his unresponsive eyes and determined silence is accusing. "Sleep the long way home," the poet's final words, may be read as generous permission to sleep through this winter season, the poet in his steadfastness counting on time to bring in again the summer of love ("our June") and bring the lover back to him ("home"). Yet it may be read at the same time as a vindictive taunt to sleep the long joyless sleep, which, unlike the short or timeless way of ecstasy in "Voyages II," is the lonely way of unrewarding death.[130]

Meanwhile, with the death of love, the poet continues to voyage —not in search of the immediate rewards of love but in search of Love, the idea that sustains him in his hope of love.[131] In "Voyages VI" the poet is a "seer." Again he is outward bound, but on icy waters that belong to the winter seascape of the previous poem and also, as a place of shipwreck and lost innocence ("lost morning eyes"), to the naturalistic seas of "At Melville's Tomb." Like Melville—and Whitman in his despair—he seeks a token in guarantee of faith, "Some splintered garland" (the image depends on "The secret oar and petals of all love" in "Voyages IV" and unites oar and petal in a sign of separation and death), or, as in "The Bridge of Estador," some wreckage from the "wreck of dreams."

The verse itself conveys his particular anguish. No longer free but in rhymed quatrains, like those of "At Melville's Tomb," it tells an emotional truth expressed by Emily Dickinson's "After great pain a formal feeling comes. . . ." Yet within this deadness desire is still acute ("afire" recalls "Carib fire" in "Voyages II") and asks

---

130. The concluding phrase echoes *The Long Voyage Home*, the title of an early, starkly naturalistic play by Eugene O'Neill, a friend of Crane's.

131. See Beach, "Hart Crane and Moby Dick," p. 194.

to be relieved, as in "Voyages II," by apocalyptic experience. "Let thy waves rear / More savage than the death of kings," he cries, perhaps in self-pity, willing to endure more than Richard II and all that Lear did.

The structure of the poem confirms the totalism of the poet's demands, the all-or-nothing attitude with which he confronts experience. The first four stanzas of the poem, those depicting the "Where"—the here—of the actual wintry present, are answered in the next three stanzas, not by an actual token but by the poet's own vision of the "Beyond," the "morning" vision of paradise that, we learn now, initially prompted the search. We may consider heroic the poet's endurance if we take the search, as he would have us, in the romantic context of quest. But he himself is too self-aware to believe wholly that it is, and the structure of the poem rehearses the hard truth of his experience: that the vision he now raises up by means of poetry to solace himself has in fact already betrayed and will continue to betray him. He knows that poetry—these poems are the wreckage, the "splintered garlands" he has salvaged from the voyage—is not as rewarding as the experience it contains and completes; poetry, as Joseph Warren Beach says, is his "consolation prize." [132] But he also knows that poetry is as necessary to him as life, is the ultimate resource with which he meets it. For him it is a vital action, a self-preserving impulse in strength like that of the death-resisting terrapin of "O Carib Isle!" Poetry keeps alive the heart's vision, the profound reasons of the heart, by which he lives.[133] And so, though his recognition of the truth is noteworthy, the truth he recognizes is unavailing, and he will continue to voyage. Perhaps he calls the poems "Voyages" because the voyage they chart follows the course of all the others he has known or will know.

Shipwrecked in love, blinded by looking into nothingness, the poet is bereaved of all that might inspire faith. Like the sailors in "At Melville's Tomb" and the "swimmers" with whom he here identifies himself, he is now "derelict," at the mercy of a sea whose

132. "Hart Crane and Moby Dick," p. 193.

133. In distinguishing this vital imagination from "mind," Rilke speaks of the "heart's range of vision. . . ." *Letters of Rainer Maria Rilke, 1910–1926,* trans. Jane Bannard Greene and M. D. Herter Norton (New York: W. W. Norton & Co., 1948), p. 199.

tyranny is indifference. Though the sea holds promise of the lovely leewardings of other seasons and places ("Green borders under stranger skies"), the poet no longer entertains the distant hope of them. He is a "stranger" to them, though his own vision has been one of eternal spring and verdant isle. Such renewal and beneficence are now attributed to the illusory aspect of things; to the loveless and disillusioned the sea is mechanical ("churning," "shift"), she merely shifts scenery. In this seascape, characterized by monotony of color, sound, and motion, nothing portends a sea change; and the signatures he recognizes—the reddened sea, the mingling waters—merely mock him because now they signify betrayal. Troughed in "many waters," the sun tells not of consanguinity but of piracy: it is a red ship denying Whitman's belief that "a kelson of the creation is love," the setting sun of death, of a Götterdämmerung.[134] And the ocean rivers with which he moves do not admit to love; they are not, as in "Voyages IV," bound for the harbor of his lover's "breast," but move outward "toward the sky / And harbor of the phoenix' breast"—toward an unattainable haven, the ideal harbor where love, according to legend, is forever renewed. He himself, in the desperation expressed by the negative turn of these images and by his self-characterization ("My eyes pressed black against the prow"), is driven not so much by the hope of a phoenix-like recovery as by the hope of an assuring sign, a visible proof of the goddess he serves. For he knows—and accordingly beseeches and defies the sea to do her worst and so test his merit and reward him, if only with a minimal sign of favor—that he has no right ("cannot claim") to demand so much of her, to claim all that his vision tells us belongs to the "name, unspoke."

The sudden shift in scenery, the vision the poet himself raises up in answer to the unanswering goddess, represents the poet's way of escape from impasse and despair—not just the "after-word" of "Belle Isle," the earlier poem from which much of this part of "Voyages VI" derives,[135] but the after-image produced by intensity of search, the "eyes pressed black against the prow. . . ." In a double sense, it may be considered a miracle of vision. And it is miraculous, having for the reader the same wonderful radiance of

134. "Song of Myself," § 5.
135. See Weber, *Hart Crane*, p. 391.

something distant yet fully and serenely beheld that it has for the poet. These stanzas of vision tell as much as the poet, confessional as he is, ever permits us to know of the secret places of his heart. To enter the landscape of these verses—and they enact the entering—is to come to the penetralia of the self. Their vision attests the poet's reverence, is an act of devotion to his dearest and earliest image, that of the goddess-mother whose sovereignty within his heart nothing, not even North Labradorian silence, can alienate. But these verses of praise are not celebratory in tone because they serve also to admonish the goddess—not the lover, whose absence from the poem reminds us that the poet's sense of betrayal has other grounds, but the goddess, who has not been true to his own true image of her.

The poet's vision is of the birth of Beauty, of an Ideal doubly pure—"white echo of the oar!"—and it belongs to the placid waters of the interior world of "The Bathers." Though connected with the cruel mother of "Voyages I" and the capricious sovereign of "Voyages II," this vision is anterior. Like the "Belle Isle" with which the goddess is identified, the "Belle Isle" of the poem of that name, it is identified with the redemption of the fallen Atlantis ("a place / The water lifts to gather and unfold").[136] This vision is the poet's "wink of eternity" and fills the "godless cleft of sky"; it is beyond time and experience, the passionate winds and storms of experience, and, as "crept away" reminds us by recalling the un-answering stars of "At Melville's Tomb," it answers him. Its advent is miraculous, an opening and entering, as if the veil of Nature parted and one found himself suddenly within her reality, at the very heart of spring and paradise. The image of the "cliff swinging" has the surreal quality of Poe's *The Narrative of Arthur Gordon Pym*, from which it may have been taken, and, with the image of the ship at sea suddenly finding itself ("flung") in vernal meadows, belongs to a vision of return to the verdant isle, the Edenic glory and security of the beginning.

In his vision of the birth of Venus,[137] the poet beholds the

136. Weber, *Hart Crane*, p. 391.

137. We think especially of Botticelli's painting, much esteemed by the Pre-Raphaelites and others during the latter half of the nineteenth century; and "blithe," we remember, is a Pateresque word.

"imaged Word," a revelation that sustains his faith in Beauty, and Love. For Beauty, though represented here as the recipient of "Creation's blithe and petalled word," is the Creation, what it forever renews at its heart and speaks in the language of love, in flowers—in the "Unfolded floating dais" of the goddess, which is "Belle Isle." And love is what the goddess concedes in the "smile" of her eyes, though the smile, reminiscent of Helen's in "Faustus and Helen," is enigmatic, promising "unsearchable repose," the most profound and complete but perhaps still-unattainable "sleep." The ambiguity here—and elsewhere in "fervid," in the imagery of flowers (especially that of the "floating dais" veiled by the hair of "rainbows," which recalls what it would deny, the experience of piracy in "the argosy of your bright hair"), and in "white echo of the oar," where "echo" is read as "answer to"—the ambiguity is sexual and belongs to the poet, whose emotions, even now, are not simple but intermixed. "Belle Isle" is depicted as a holy place, but its "unfolded, floating dais" is the "one floating flower" of "Voyages II," and its "covenant," pledged again by "rainbows," is a promise of marriage, of ecstatic fulfillment such as the poem of that name ("Belle Isle") describes.[138] There the poet covertly speaks the "name, unspoke" when he says that "Belle Isle [is] the grace / Shed from the wave's refluent gold"; and he tells us why "Belle Isle," probably taken from Baudelaire's "Un Voyage à Cythère," is not inappropriate.[139]

Though the "imaged Word" is "Belle Isle," it is also the poem, the "after-word" (and "afterward"). And it "holds / Hushed willows anchored in its glow" because poetry, which permits him to compose his experience, can only compose it when it is completed —when, all passion spent, the willows are hushed and willing to repose. Poetry is absolute ("Word"), beyond the betrayals of time; it is a refuge from the passionate encounters of experience, like the sea in "Repose of Rivers."[140] But in saying this the poet is also

138. This important image appears again in "—And Bees of Paradise," a later poem celebrating love: "Sea gardens lifted rainbow-wise through eyes / I found."

139. There are other likely sources: Eliot's "Gerontion" and Emerson's "Works and Days," the latter noted by Maurice Kramer, "Six Voyages of a Derelict Seer," *Sewanee Review*, LXXIII (Summer, 1965), 420–23.

140. The image of the willows was taken from "Belle Isle," which seems to have provided Crane the scenario of "Voyages" and "Repose of Rivers."

saying that he prefers the fire of experience. For the "unbetrayable reply" knows "no farewell" in two senses: no farewell to Love—that love quiescent, secure, enfolded—and no farewell or risk—no faring forth on voyages of love.

Shipwreck, dereliction, uncertainty. The "Voyages" end by reminding us of "At Melville's Tomb"—of the calyx-vortex, the portent of the shells, the sailors who "lifted altars" to the silent stars. The poet's vision of "Belle Isle"—his lovely leewardings—is the petition of his heart, not its answer. That he purifies the flower of "Voyages II" and imagines love under the spiritual aspect of Beauty does not alter the fact (to adapt Melville's words to the poet's condition) that there is death in this business of loving. "At Melville's Tomb" reminds us of the foolhardiness of the poet's dangerous quest. But "Voyages VI," by withholding the "vision"— the secret of persistent search—until the end, forces us to measure its strength and acknowledge its necessity and even to appreciate its "fabulous" character. "At Melville's Tomb" might have served as an epilogue, for the poet has earned a Melvillean vision. But "Voyages VI" makes a better close, to the sequence and to *White Buildings*, because it apprehends in their extremes Crane's romantic idealism (his "innocence," the visionary) and his naturalism (his "experience," the "clear rime") and because its theme is love, the touchstone of all his experience and the determinant of his world. It remains true to the extremity and tension of his complex confessional poems and to the challenge of his "Legend."

In "Voyages" Crane most fully enters and explores his experience and faces its truth. He does not break the downward curve of the poems with a "perfect cry." Recognizing the vast power of negation and the limited power of art, he is subdued, without the usual spirit to affirm, somewhat in Ishmael's situation, holding the balance of his world with an "equal eye." [141] And this is mastery, as when we say that poetry enables the poet to master his experience, to "face it by naming it." Crane seems to have learned that "stratagem of poetry" early: "The old betrayals of life," he remarked of *The Duchess of Malfi*, "and yet they are worth some-

141. *Moby-Dick*, ch. 85.

thing—from a distance, afterward." [142] From that distance, as poetic accomplishment, the "Voyages" affirm the honesty and resolution of the human spirit. And this, even more than the skillful use of the "logic of metaphor," which he demonstrated in single poems but now extended as the unifying thematic element of a narrative sequence of poems, gave Crane the creative assurance he needed to complete his task.

142. Austin Warren, "Emily Dickinson," *Connections* (Ann Arbor: University of Michigan Press, 1970), pp. 73, 85; *Letters*, p. 90 (June, 1922).

Crane's "task" is what Rilke would have called *The Bridge*, the large work that had become his destiny, that took up all his growth and, by expressing all that he had been given to express, completed his development. And Crane recognized this when, in the act of desperation that brought him a benefactor, he wrote Otto Kahn that "besides the poems collected into my forthcoming volume I have partially written a long poem, the conception of which has been in my mind for some years." In saying this he allowed himself a poet's license—or merely that of applying for grants—for only "Atlantis" was "partially written," and the conception, which had been in his mind since the spring of 1923, had simply been there, advanced not at all, to judge from the way he put it—"a new cultural synthesis of values in terms of our America. . . ."[1] This vague description derives from Waldo Frank, or from what Munson had written about him, and it is important, less for what it tells us about the completed poem than for the way it locates its beginning in Frank's thought and invokes the tutelary friend upon whom Crane relied most in the long travail of getting it written. He wrote Kahn, too, for the same reason he talked so much about *The Bridge:* to bind himself to it. He asked Kahn's help not only because his condition was unusually desperate—he was "foot-loose in the world," the Cleveland home having been sold, he was without a job and living off friends, and he was distressed by his mother's silence—but because he needed in a decisive way, at this critical creative moment, to precipitate his fate. By accepting

1. *Letters*, pp. 222–23 (December 3, 1925).

Kahn's stake, he staked his life on this poem. (And Kahn's stake was insured by his life!) That he had, as he wrote his mother in a pompously defensive letter telling of his good fortune, "the first real opportunity to use my talents unhampered by fear and worry for the morrow" was itself, he soon learned, a severe condition.

Crane began and ended the year 1926, during which the conception of *The Bridge* was finally worked out and much of the poem was written, at Patterson, New York—at Addie Turner's farmhouse, his new home, which he shared, not necessarily unfortunately, with the Tates. Conditions of work were especially important to him. (How often he expended time and money in making a room his own and placed himself within the shelter of a beneficent maternal presence! The Isle of Pines, he told his mother, was "the most ideal place and 'situation' I've ever had for work," chiefly, he went on to say, because of Mrs. Simpson's interest in his work and generous attention to his needs.) [2] But just as important for creativity as this security, this enclosing of the self, was an attendant risk—the challenge of the task, those "tests" of materials and imagination he speaks of, which were set him by the age but which, it seems, he sometimes put in his own way by reading (Spengler's *The Decline of the West* is the immediate example), by correspondence (at this time he resumed with Munson their discussion of the nature of poetry and of his limitations as a poet), and by the presence of friends (in this instance Allen Tate, whose conviction of the wrongness of *The Bridge*, based as it was on Tate's allegiance to Eliot's views, was undoubtedly made known to Crane before the Foreword to *White Buildings*). [3]

2. *Letters*, p. 269 (July 30, 1926). A year later he recalled that room in a letter to Mrs. Simpson: "I liked my little study room there so much, with the mango tree to look at through the back window. . . . I achieved some triumphs in that little room." (*Letters*, p. 304.) During his chaotic stay in Europe he wrote to Isidor Schneider that "I can't help thinking of my room out there in Patterson"; and during the last flurry of work on *The Bridge*, he left the city, he told Caresse Crosby, "for a week's work up here in my old farmhouse room. It's lovely too." *Letters*, pp. 341, 346.

3. *Letters*, p. 236 (March 5, 1926). In the correspondence with Munson he included "General Aims and Theories," which he had written to provide Eugene O'Neill help in writing a preface to *White Buildings*. The uncertainty and delays of its publication, as well as the necessity of using his friends, was unsettling. He wrote this essay, he said, in order to ward against "biases and critical deficiencies

Though Crane began to work enthusiastically on *The Bridge*, he worked in fear of failure—in fear of failing to countervail Eliot's "poetic determinism of our age," that the world ends "Not with a bang but a whimper." [4] Mostly he read, in a fruitful eclectic way, in order to prepare a rich poetic soil—"to incorporate [the materials] in the subconscious," as he said of his reading of Marco Polo.[5] And mostly he worked on the Columbus section (later called "Ave Maria"), which was not the adventitious beginning it seems but the necessary beginning of the return to the self upon which the composition of *The Bridge*—"this structure of my dreams" he called it—depended.[6] In the letter to Otto Kahn in which he outlined his early progress on the poem and thereby put an end to the first period of concentrated work, he said that "mid-ocean is where the poem begins." [7] And that, in fact, is where his own creative activity began, and where creative necessity, not hindered but served by the quarrel with the Tates, brought him. An early letter to his grandmother foretells this outcome: "I have been reading the *Journal of Christopher Columbus* lately—of his first voyage to America, which is concerned mostly with his cruisings around the West Indies. It has reminded me many times of the few weeks I spent on the Island [the Isle of Pines]." [8]

By April Crane had reached an impasse. Intense pressure of commitment had prompted the premature account of the poem to Otto Kahn, and this, in turn, had blocked him. "I'm afraid," he told Munson, "that I've so systematically objectivized my theme and its details that the necessary 'subjective lymph and sinew' is frozen." [9] Though he never acknowledged it in words, he needed,

---

which I felt [might] lead to unwarranted assumptions, misplaced praises, etc." (*Letters*, p. 240.) As for Eliot, see Crane's unsent letter to Tate in Unterecker, *Voyager*, p. 434, and also *Letters*, p. 236, where he comments on the "easy acceptance of death" by "most of my friends. . . ." The strength of Tate's allegiance and the temper of his mind may be gauged by a statement in his letter to Crane on Crane's allegiance to Whitman: "I am unsympathetic to this tradition, and it seems to me that you should be too." Unterecker, *Voyager*, p. 621.

4. *Letters*, pp. 235–36 (March 5, 1926).
5. *Letters*, p. 242 (March 28, 1926).
6. *Letters*, p. 232 (January 7, 1926).
7. *Letters*, p. 240 (March 18, 1926).
8. *Letters*, p. 234 (January 27, 1926). He had spent a few months.
9. *Letters*, p. 244 (April 5, 1926).

after the initial creative sally, to descend more deeply into himself; the creative source of the poem was there and he had not yet reached it. And so, all unconsciously, he may be said to have brought on the crisis—an unduly severe but not uncommon one of bitter feeling, urgent creative necessity, and financial extremity —from which, in this instance, only his mother could satisfactorily deliver him. The letter in which he told her of the "hideous" situation in the Turner farmhouse implicated her in the fate of his poem; it put her affection to the test and made all but impossible the refusal of the island property ("this refuge," he now called it) she had always refused him before: "If you feel at all sympathetic to this situation of mine I wish you *this time* be generous enough to let me go to the Island and finish my poem there." [10] This time she did (reason enough for naming the Columbus section "Ave Maria"). Her generous act—even her wedding to Charles Curtis, which she arranged to take place in New York City prior to Hart's departure—contributed to his self-possession and to the repossession of his past. For the island was both family ground (he speaks variously of "the house my grandfather built," "my grandmother's place," and the "sure . . . ground" of "my parents' property") and "Eden." In reaching it he had journeyed back, had actually discovered the verdant isle: "To me," he told the Browns, "the mountains, strange greens, native thatched huts, perfume, etc. brought me straight to Melville." A profound compulsion of his being moved him to this journey, but he saw with new eyes—was "surprised," he said, "that I didn't carry away more definite impressions from my first visit 11 years ago." [11]

Was it necessary for Crane to discover the Caribbean world in order to write about Columbus? Probably not: no more than it was necessary for him to carry out archaeological studies in preparation for "The Dance." It is true that he spent much of his time assimilating that world ("Mine own true self has been chewing its cud, mostly, i.e., trying to imagine itself on the waters with

10. *Letters*, pp. 245–49 (April 18, 1926).

11. *Letters*, pp. 249–50, 251–52 (April 25, May 7, 1926). He liked to think that the mango tree, about which he wrote a poem, was "the original Eden apple" and that islands such as the Isle of Pines were the visible peaks of the lost Atlantis. *Letters*, pp. 255–56.

Cristobal Colon"), and that he was pleased that the voyage by schooner he made to Grand Cayman had enabled him to give the verses of "Ave Maria" a veritable sea rhythm. But his essential activity was at a deeper level, figuratively expressed by the remainder of the earlier sentence—"and trying to mend the sails so beautifully slit by the Patterson typhoon." [12]

He wasted little time in reaching the Isle of Pines and toward the restoration of his spirit wisely chose Waldo Frank to accompany him there. In his recently published *Virgin Spain* (the title "Ave Maria" may also allude to this), Frank had used Columbus, the "mystic mariner," as his spokesman and had placed him, at the end of the book, in debate with Cervantes over the spiritual future of America.[13] Frank, moreover, was the foremost exponent of the "mystic tradition" that for him began with Whitman, and positive faith for him was exemplified in art by what he called the "apocalyptic method"—the acceptance of the chaos of contemporary life and its transfiguration in new forms. It is to this faith that Crane referred when he told Munson, in the letter on Eliot's "stern conviction of death," that *Virgin Spain* was a "document of the spirit . . ." and when, later, at the height of creative excitement, he addressed Frank as "Dear repository of my faith. . . ." [14] On completing the book, he wrote Frank that " 'The Port of Columbus' [the concluding chapter] is truly something of a prelude to my intentions for *The Bridge*"; and the book, described by Frank as "Symphonic History," was very much in his mind when he wrote Otto Kahn that his poem would be an "eloquent document" with an "unusually symphonic form." [15] More than anyone, Frank, it seems, was necessary to Crane's task—and its resumption.

12. *Letters*, p. 256 (June 1, 1926).

13. Crane was reading *Don Quixote* a few weeks before the onset of creative work. *Letters*, p. 263 (July 3, 1926).

14. *Letters*, pp. 236, 268 (March 5, July 26, 1926). Frank developed these ideas in *The Re-Discovery of America* (an apt subtitle for *The Bridge*). Published in 1929, this book was made up of installments that Crane read when they appeared in *The New Republic* in 1928. Frank placed Crane in this tradition and later, in his introduction to Crane's poetry, fully discussed him in terms of it. For Frank's place in the Whitman tradition, see John R. Willingham, "The Whitman Tradition in Recent American Literature," unpublished doctor's dissertation, University of Oklahoma, 1953.

15. *Letters*, pp. 242, 241 (March 20, 18, 1926).

That Frank, usually preoccupied with his own writing, consented to come with him was an act incalculably generous, capping his always sympathetic attention to Crane's work. Without his encouragement, Crane probably would not have completed *The Bridge*.[16]

Crane later named the immediate work he had to do—"get into myself again"—and this was accomplished in several ways.[17] By mid-June he had written two of his finest poems, "O Carib Isle!" and "Repose of Rivers." The former commemorates the experience of elemental exposure at Grand Cayman, which provided him a landscape of vastation.[18] Like the best of the island poems—"Island Quarry" and "The Idiot," which were written later—it is death-haunted, haunted specifically by spiritlessness, powerlessness. It shows the depth of negation he had to reach and how writing itself—the creative force he wished to liberate—helped him to reach and overcome it. "O Carib Isle!" is not so much a poem of despair as of gathering strength. "Repose of Rivers" is similarly therapeutic, for in it Crane was able to work through and free himself (for the time) from the restrictive hold of the past. "Here," as he says in "Key West," an inferior poem devoted to the same end—"Here has my salient faith annealed me." The illness following the voyage to Grand Cayman was also salutary, and so was the skepticism concerning *The Bridge* to which the reading of Spengler had given full play. Referring to Spengler's book, he later told Frank that it was "a very good experience for ripening some of *The Bridge*," and so, he realized, had been the "many 'things' and circumstances that seem to have uniformly conspired in a strangely symbolical way toward the present speed of my work." The "ripening" he speaks of here was a consequence of the "rotted seed of personal will" (the phrase is from *Virgin Spain*).[19] Crane's spiritual dying had released

16. I say this hesitantly because even without Frank the exigencies of creation were great enough. We know very little of the friendship between Frank and Crane, but the psychological character of Frank's writing and the mixture of distance and confidence in Crane's letters to him suggest that Frank served a paternal role not unlike that of a psychoanalyst, where firmness is softened by accepting, unjudging understanding.

17. *Letters*, p. 336 (February 7, 1929).

18. See also a lesser poem, "The Air Plant."

19. *Letters*, p. 274 (August 19, 1926).

the creative self, the "positive center of action, control, and beauty" to which, he found, everything suddenly, wonderfully rushed.[20]

"A hurricane in the spirit"—Rilke's description of creative possession admirably conveys the overwhelming fury of the month during which Crane brought to some stage of expression all but three of the fifteen poems comprising *The Bridge*. Rilke was describing the "nameless storm" that overtook him and granted him in a few days the power to complete the *Duino Elegies:* "All that was fiber, fabric in me, framework," he says, "cracked and bent." [21] Except for the fact that Rilke finished his task, Crane's situation is comparable, marked by the joy and gratitude of the artist who has been given so much. "I feel an absolute music in the air again," he wrote Frank on July 24, less than a week after he had begun, as he said later, to "spill" over. Here he announced the writing of "To Brooklyn Bridge," and the receipt of the contract for *White Buildings*, which must have been as heartening as the "news of Allen Tate's generosity [in promising to do the Foreword]," a "truly beautiful" act, he said, that "refreshed me a great deal." [22] On July 26 he wrote Frank that "my plans are soaring again, the conception swells" and enclosed "Ave Maria"; on July 29 he sent the Cowleys "Cutty Sark"; on August 3 he sent Frank a new version of "Atlantis" and the gloss notes that "a reaction to Eliot's *Waste Land* notes put . . . in [his] head," commented favorably on Tate's Foreword to *White Buildings*, which Munson had sent him ("clever, valiant, concise and beautiful"), and told of how he was trying to steady himself in readiness for the several poems of "Powhatan's Daughter." Toward that pivotal section of the poem, on August 12 he reported his reading of Sandburg's *The Prairie Years* and noted that two of the "Three Songs" had "just popped out" and the third, "Virginia," was about to follow; that "The Tunnel" was nearly done, along with "Calgary Express" (a section omitted from *The Bridge* but partly used in "The River"); and that the poem he was constructing—he likened himself to a

20. *Letters*, p. 274. Crane had written William Wright that he seemed to be wasting his energy in a "kind of inward combustion" and would "continue to kill myself in my own way." *Letters*, p. 267 (July 16, 1926).

21. *Letters of Rainer Maria Rilke*, pp. 290–91. Crane wrote several poems involving the hurricane in fact and in spirit.

22. *Letters*, pp. 267, 277 (July 24, November 21, 1926).

"sky-gack or girder-jack"—though only half finished, was "already longer than *The Waste Land*. . . ." In this letter he wrote Frank that he was "happy, quite well, and living as never before"; and in a letter of August 19 he informed him that he was living completely in his poem and "having the time of my life. . . ." That phrase ended with "just now, anyway," and signaled cessation. "Work continues. 'The Tunnel', now," he told Frank on August 23; but by the time he wrote again, from Havana, on September 3, the storm was over.[23]

He had gone to Havana to recover himself after "doing more writing than all the last three years together (a glorious triumph!),"[24] but his mother, to whom he had written this, was undergoing the dissolution of her second marriage, and her emotional distress destroyed the benefit of his holiday and interrupted the course of his work. The hurricane that shattered the Hart plantation in October also forced him home to Patterson, but it was the lesser power, unmentioned in the list of things headed by his mother's "unrestrained letters," that, he confessed to Charlotte Rychtarik, "nearly killed me." He may have "managed to come through, at least with my skin," as he told her, and he may have been secure enough in his accomplishment to wait out, without worry, the subsequent doldrum, as he told Frank toward the end of November, but bitterness filled him and old guilts burdened him. "Nothing but illness and mental disorder in my family," he wrote Wilbur Underwood in December, "—and I am expected by all the middle-class ethics and dogmas to rush myself to Cleveland and devote myself interminably to nursing, sympathizing with woes which I have no sympathy for because they are all unnecessary, and bolstering up the faith in others toward concepts which I long ago discarded as crass and cheap."[25] Even the appearance of *White Buildings* at the end of the year did not lift his depression. In the letter telling his mother of its publication, he described the insomnia he was suffering in terms vaguely reminiscent of "Southern Cross" and "The Tunnel": "when I do 'sleep' my mind is plagued by an endless reel of pictures, startling

23. *Letters*, pp. 268–76 (July 26–September 3, 1926).
24. Cited in Unterecker, *Voyager*, p. 452.
25. *Letters*, pp. 276–77, 279–80 (November 1, December 16, 1926).

and unhappy—like some endless cinematograph." And then, re-calling what he had staked on his poem, he charged her with the fact that "I'm trying my best—both to feel the proper sentiments to your situation and keep on with my task." *"The Bridge,"* he reminded her, "is an important task—and nobody else can ever do it." [26]

Crane never again attained the creative situation—the explosive poise—he had known on the Isle of Pines. He remained at Pat-terson during much of 1927, working intermittently at both old and new portions of the poem, but he did not complete it. Family and financial worries distracted him. By August he was, as so often in the past, looking for a job, only now in dismay of delaying further the completion of his nearly finished poem. In September he sent Kahn the manuscript of all he had done, along with an account of his intentions (this prompted perhaps by the criticism of Tate and Winters), in the hope, it seems, of duplicating all that his earlier good fortune had brought him. And in October, when Kahn supplemented with travel money an allowance from his father, he looked forward to a winter in Martinique ("a much pleasanter island than the Isles of Pines"), where he expected to finish the poem.[27] But his mother, always reluctant to have him beyond easy reach, urged him to remain in New York City—which he did. And later, when Eleanor Fitzgerald found employment for him as the companion of Herbert A. Wise, a wealthy young man who was going to California for his health, he was able to join his mother, who, having secured her divorce, had, in her impetuous way, gone there to live.

The terrible quarrel with his mother in which Hart disclosed his homosexuality and following which fled California like a "thief in the night" is the most dramatic episode with which to mark the disequilibrium that had already become evident in the months following his return from the Isle of Pines.[28] Crane seemed unable to rally the creative force needed to complete his poem and, con-sequently, seemed unable, where decision was required, to decide in its favor. Perhaps Martinique would have helped him. But he

26. *Letters*, p. 280 (December 22, 1926).
27. *Letters*, p. 310 (October 11, 1927).
28. *Letters*, pp. 336–38 (February 26, 1929).

chose instead to honor his "responsibilities" and go to California, where he yielded to an environment whose decadence mirrored his own disgust and abetted his self-destructiveness. The letters from California, though sometimes heady with drink, are among his best: observant, serious, full of energy. They witness a great and greatly troubled spirit, whose reading in the prophets of the time (Wyndham Lewis, Ramon Fernandez, and Waldo Frank) and the essential critics (I. A. Richards and Jessie Weston) and the classic modern literature (Proust and Gide) indicates the disorientation he was trying to stem, and whose most demoralized and unguarded letters, like that to Slater Brown on February 22, 1928, expose the pristine sensibility only death would overcome.[29]

In the letters of this time Crane attributed to the "spiritual disintegration of our period"—a theme addressed by his friends Frank and Munson—his own inability to complete *The Bridge*. "When I get some of the points [of contemporary speculation] a little more definitely arranged," he told Isidor Schneider, "then maybe I'll have more nerve to continue my efforts on *The Bridge*." [30] Like the earlier skepticism over Spengler, this uncertainty over ideas was genuine but only symptomatic of deeper sources of difficulty. Where poetry was concerned—his discovery of Hopkins, for example—he showed no hesitancy, and even at his most defenseless ("As for Hart Crane," he wrote in reply to Munson, whose *Destinations* he had just read, "I know him too well to disagree on as many points as I once did") he held fast to his essential view ("I still stake some claims on the pertinence of the intuitions").[31] Put simply, his disorientation followed from the frustration of the profoundest claims of his being and was immediately due to the demands and disorientation of his mother, as the violence of their break-up indicates.

But break-up did not relieve it nor enable him, as he wrote Waldo Frank from Patterson in June, to complete *The Bridge* "this summer." [32] The shame of precipitate departure, the guilt of irresponsibility (he left his mother to care for his dying grand-

---

29. *Letters*, pp. 317–18 (February 22, March 4, 1928); *Robber Rocks*, pp. 83–85.
30. *Letters*, pp. 322, 323 (March 28, April 17, 1928).
31. *Letters*, p. 324 (April 17, 1928).
32. *Letters*, p. 325 (June 12, 1928).

mother), the fear that his father, with whom he was on good terms, would now learn of his homosexuality, the terrible emotional wound whose consequences he saw in the projected indifference of his friends—all this compounded it. So did the final contest with his mother over the legacy left him by Grandmother Hart, who died in September, and his further flight to Europe, where he was now free to go.

Writing to Frank from Paris, in February 1929, Crane said that the previous year, lost as far as *The Bridge* was concerned, was "the most decisive of my life," but that he now needed "more strength than ever." [33] A long letter to the Rychtariks, relating in detail all that had contributed to the break-up, accounts for this—and for the willingness with which he gave himself to the "carnival" life of Paris. The noteworthy news of this letter tells of Harry and Caresse Crosby's promise to publish *The Bridge* in a fine edition. But perhaps of greater significance for Crane and the subsequent course of his life is the plan he said he had had but in hatred of his mother had given up of "buying a little country place in Connecticut, for her ultimate home as much as mine." [34]

Crane accomplished nothing in Europe but his humiliation. He was jailed for disorderly conduct in La Santé and beaten, the necessary conclusion, perhaps, of the logic of return that moved him almost from the time of his arrival. At the end of July he embarked for home. And there—at Patterson and Columbia Heights —under pressure of deadline and at heavy expense of will and drink (and with the good offices of friends), he completed *The Bridge* during the months of the declining year that brought the Wall Street crash and the suicide of Harry Crosby.

From August through December Crane revised, in what he described as "fevers of work," the proofsheets of the poem and added to it "Cape Hatteras," "Indiana," and "Quaker Hill." In May he had written Isidor Schneider that the poem would be published in the fall "regardless"—that is, as it was then, without those sections which he said might be incorporated, should he ever write them, in a later edition.[35] But with publication impending he was more

33. *Letters*, p. 336 (February 7, 1929).
34. *Letters*, p. 338 (February 26, 1929).
35. *Letters*, p. 340 (May 1, 1929).

respectful of his poem and its conception. "Don't rush along too fast, though—please!" is the reiterated plea of his correspondence with Caresse Crosby: "Please be patient. The book must have these sections. . . ." [36] For they were not negligible, mere "accent marks" as he said of "Quaker Hill," [37] and their significance, not insignificance, explains his not having written them earlier. In them he had, finally, to resolve problems of faith and feeling whose centrality is suggested by the briefest labels: Whitman, mother, friends-community-home. By December 26 this difficult work was done and he was relieved at last of what he had come to consider "the 5-year load of The Bridge. . . ." [38]

In the spring of 1930 *The Bridge* appeared in two excellent editions, one published by the Crosbys' Black Sun Press and the other by Liveright. Except for his replies to its critics—among them friends who had shared in the work—Crane's task was done.

II

At almost every stage, *The Bridge* was a controversial poem. Criticism—opposition—seems to have mounted in ratio to the degree of its completion, and on publication it was for the most part greeted with openly hostile reviews, the most damaging, Crane felt, by his friends Yvor Winters and Allen Tate. Tate had already expressed his basic strictures in the Foreword to *White Buildings*, which he wrote during the year in which he had lived and quarreled with Crane; and Winters, who had reviewed *White Buildings*, had accepted Tate's "evaluation and definition of Hart Crane's genius" and made it his point of departure.[39] Their criticism—and that of Munson in *Destinations* (his essay on Crane is subtitled "Young Titan in the Sacred Wood")—is similar, having for its grounds an appreciation of Eliot's account of the modern sensibility and the ethical-religious demands made on poetry by the New Humanists, who, in the years Crane devoted to *The Bridge*, had again become prominent and powerful. With the later criticism of Crane by R. P. Blackmur, these vigorously held and

36. *Letters*, pp. 344, 345 (August 8, September 6, 1929).
37. *Letters*, p. 347 (December 26, 1929).
38. Unterecker, *Voyager*, p. 605 (October 30, 1929).
39. "Hart Crane's Poems," p. 47.

expressed views—position papers in the contemporary debate on the modern spirit—created the perspective in which *The Bridge* and the imagination that fashioned it have almost always been treated. With this encumbrance of criticism it has been difficult to see the poem freshly, or, as Bachelard would say, in an open, "admirative" [40] way, but this is what we must now try to do.

How splendidly the dedicatory poem opens and fills its imaginative space with the reverberations of its images—images whose invitation to poetic reverie can hardly be surpassed.

> How many dawns, chill from his rippling rest
> The seagull's wing shall dip and pivot him,
> Shedding white rings of tumult, building high
> Over the chained bay waters Liberty—

The poem begins with the renewal of creation and with its own birth. And in its beginning is its end. The point of departure is the place of return. *The Bridge*, constituted by all that occurs between "Proem" and "Atlantis," describes a circle, the most pervasive figure of the poet's world.

The opening lines evoke a familiar prospect—New York harbor as it might be seen at dawn when looking seaward from Brooklyn Bridge—and express the sense of liberation, the dilation of spirit, afforded by it. In pitch and rising rhythm suspending on "Liberty," they strike up for a new world, for the freedom and creation—the freedom of creation—depicted in the movement (flight, soaring, and dance) of the seagull, Crane's tutelary bird. ("Constantly your seagull ["the white bird"] has floated in my mind," he told Gaston Lachaise, "and it will mean much to me to have it.") [41] This is not the scavenging gull of *Paterson IV*, but the gull of

---

40. *The Poetics of Space*, trans. Maria Jolas (Boston: Beacon Press, 1969), p. xxii; and *The Poetics of Reverie*, p. 190: ". . . the maxim of our admirative critique of poets: admire first, then you will understand."

41. The harbor had been variously celebrated by Stieglitz, Marin, Williams, and, most recently, Paul Rosenfeld, whose *Port of New York* (1924), an account of artists sharing the Stieglitzian spirit, ends in a coming to port that represents the rediscovery of America by its artists and the hope of creative fulfillment. For Crane's response to this book, see *Letters*, p. 202 (April 9, 1925). For the seagull by Lachaise, which Crane took with him on his travels, see *Letters*, p. 234 (February 10, 1926); *Robber Rocks*, pp. 55, 58.

"The Wanderer," a poem opening also in New York harbor and treating a poet's dedication to America and to the renewal of creation, a poem whose importance to Crane may have been hinted at in the epigraph from Job with which he introduced *The Bridge*. Its kin are many, among them the bird with whose free spirit Wordsworth identifies in *The Prelude* and the hawk in Thoreau's *Walden:* symbols of "all that's consummate and free," of the self, fulfilled in and liberated by the powers of imagination and spirit.[42]

The scene, like that of "Crossing Brooklyn Ferry," is eternally recurring and warrants faith in the future. ("How many" suggests this, and "shall" invokes the future, bends the poem toward it.) The coming of dawn—the radiant hope of beginnings insisted on by the writers of *The Seven Arts* group—is the expectation of the poem. But the dawn does not come of itself so much as through the agency of the seagull, as the effulgence of its motion. The bird is harbinger, creator. It rises from the waters "Shedding white rings of tumult"—shedding light, white circles of perfect harmony —and the dance of its being, its "building high," enacted in the poem's movement, is an upward vortex, while the "tumult" is its cry of birth and creative play as well as a reminder of the downward vortex, the chill and darkness, the "rest," from which it has ascended. This light-giving flight brings to view—may be said to create—the Statue of Liberty and is, in itself, an act of liberty, the free action of the spirit over the "chained bay waters. . . ." Accordingly, as the imagery of the last stanza indicates, it is a paradigm of the bridge.[43]

Seagull and statue intertwined: the importance of this bright wonderful image is stressed by the brevity of its appearance. "Liberty" also "forsake[s] our eyes" with the departure of the gull; it, too, becomes "apparitional." And what was actual thereby becomes

42. *The Prelude*, I, 10; "Spring," *Walden*; P, 74. Claude Bragdon compared the "people of the fourth dimension" and the "birds of the air. . . ." See Ouspensky, *Tertium Organum*, p. 6.

43. The time is winter; the bay may be frozen, as in "Voyages V." In any case, the image is one of limitation reminiscent of what the sea "keeps" in "At Melville's Tomb."

Jean Guiguet says: "The gull, in the first verse of 'Proem,' prefigures the final image of the ideal bridge to which the poet addresses himself. . . ." *L'Univers poétique de Hart Crane*, p. 91; my translation.

visionary, a presence to be pursued, like the woman of "The Harbor Dawn." We are permitted only a glimpse of the goddess, the first in the poet's pantheon to be presented, although historically she may be the last, assuming all that Crane invests in the more prominent Mary and Pocahontas.[44] "Liberty" stands in the harbor welcoming the voyager, a supreme image of homecoming for Crane, who spoke his double need—for response and imaginative freedom, security and risk—in "To Liberty":

> Out of the seagull cries and wind
> On this strange shore I build
> The virgin. . . .[45]

And just as the image of the ascending gull recalls the moth of his earliest poem, so these lines of explicit comment on the initial stanza of "Proem" recall "C 33" and the fledgling poet's justification and devotion: "O Materna! to enrich thy gold head / And wavering shoulders with a new light shed." At the beginning of *The Bridge*, the poet, looking to sea, counts on poetry, an energy of the self, to liberate him and to bring him home.

Turning on "Liberty," the poem itself describes a curve like the "inviolate curve" of the gull and quickly enacts a momentous transition from space to confinement, imaginative liberty to routine, reality present (beheld) to reality lost (remembered, imagined in interior space, longed for)—from dawn, that is, to "day," the working day, which fails the expectations of the dawn by being dark. With remarkable compression, the second stanza places us in the business world of "Faustus and Helen" and "Recitative." And the gull, who in its flight "forsake[s] our eyes" (and all the affirmative possibilities of the self), is now assimilated to "sails," an image as white and fleeting ("apparitional") that evokes the spacious past of discovery and sea adventure (the world of "Ave Maria" and "Cutty Sark") and, in the context of an office worker's reverie, represents the deepest longing of the soul. What the "inviolate curve" of the gull intends and the sail summons us to

44. Crane most certainly was aware of Williams' association of Venus and "Liberty"—that is, associations of America, discovery, beauty, renewal, and imagination—in "St. Francis Einstein of the Daffodils," *Contact*, no. 4 (Summer, 1921), 2–4.
45. P, 180.

is deferred ("filed away" covers it too) until we are freed, as in "Faustus and Helen," from the routine that characterizes modern civilization (suggested also by paper work, finance, skyscrapers, and machinery). Then we may seek the "world dimensional," that "somewhere / Virginal perhaps, less fragmentary, cool." [46]

Only with this pursuit in mind does the poet distinguish himself from the "multitudes" for whom he speaks, and then in order to propose an object worthy of their desire. Though the first three stanzas represent a diminution in intensity of seeing—from beholding to dreaming to fantasizing passively—there is no diminishment of its necessity. The poet subscribes to the belief, from Proverbs, that where there is no vision the people perish. When he thinks of "cinemas" it is not only because he associates "panoramic sleights" with the gull's vanishing flight, but because, even though they ultimately cheat the multitudes, they show their inextinguishable desire for the true magic of revelation. Though in their removes from the source (object) of vision—the light of some "flashing scene / Never disclosed"—the multitudes are in Plato's cave, they are also in church—the church that the movies, especially remarked in the twenties, had become.[47] Their attitude ("bent toward," where "bent" is read as "kneel" and "toward" is read as a transcendental preposition) is religious, albeit secular and parodic, and prepares us for the revelation of the bridge, a true object of devotion, which the poet, moving from darkness to light and from disappointment to fulfillment, discloses in all of its radiant splendor:

> And Thee, across the harbor, silver-paced
> As though the sun took step of thee, yet left
> Some motion ever unspent in thy stride,—
> Implicitly thy freedom staying thee!

46. Crane's revision of the last line of the stanza, though not accepted by Caresse Crosby in the Black Sun edition, is more appropriate because it includes an entire day and opens out, in a way similar to that of "Faustus and Helen," to a world of possibility.

47. See Alan Trachtenberg, *Brooklyn Bridge: Fact and Symbol* (New York: Oxford University Press, 1965), p. 154; William Carlos Williams, "Light Becomes Darkness," *Spring and All*, pp. 59–60.

As the great modern art of illusion, the cinema called attention to the illusory nature of art.

The image is vital, not mechanical: the bridge, an organic structure, has what Louis Sullivan called "mobile equilibrium"; and as a roadway for the sun it is an arc of the cosmic circle. And it recalls the dawn-bringing gull of stanza one. "Thee" rhymes with "Liberty." The poet, in showing us the path of the soul to reality,[48] restores the epiphanic glory of the beginning. Again the poem is at peak, and now the bridge becomes its focus, to be variously characterized in the next five stanzas and invoked in the concluding two.

Before turning to these stanzas something more should perhaps be said about the third stanza. It works to distinguish the poet from the "multitudes" but, as "Van Winkle" shows, its imagery carries his private burden. The most notable thing about it is the violated curve of desire, the terrible want always frustrated (refused: "Never disclosed"), a pattern of expectation and disappointment first traced in the poet's case in his boyhood. In "Van Winkle," where memory flashes it out of his own dark depths, he remembers

> . . . the Sabbatical, unconscious smile
> My mother almost brought me once from church
> And once only. . . .

> It flickered through the snow screen, blindly
> It forsook her at the doorway, it was gone
> Before I had left the window. It
> Did not return with the kiss in the hall.

In this episode, the poem—and the poet's quest—has its origin. "Forsake": "forsook." And in considering the bridge to which he directs our attention, it may help us understand the deification and celebration of this answerer.

Stanzas five to nine are a litany—a catalog somewhat in Whitman's fashion—of the attributes and occasions of the bridge. In the first, the bridge provides a platform for spiritual release, in this instance the death leap of the "bedlamite" who has fled the subway (the "Tunnel," or inferno of industrial civilization and of isolation), ascended the parapets of the bridge, and there, "shrill

48. Whitman, Preface (1855), *Leaves of Grass*.

shirt ballooning," like a gull, taken flight. The concluding line—
"A jest falls from the speechless caravan"—is Whitman-like in its
matter-of-fact tone and cadence, and perhaps in its ambiguity.
For "jest" may refer to the bedlamite as well as to the kind of re-
mark called forth in moments of extremity. That it "falls," in con-
trast to the "ballooning" shirt—both arrested in the instant of the
poet's own "flashing scene"—conveys a positive value even though
the negative is present. "To die," as Whitman said, "is different
from what any one supposed, and luckier." [49]

The next stanza maintains the values established in stanzas one
and four. Significantly, the bridge is set against the artifacts with
which the poet defines modern civilization: Wall Street, a dark
confining metallic space associated with the mechanical by the
image of the acetylene torch—that is, by the busy construction of
skyscrapers, these conveyed in the images of "rip-tooth" and of
towering (yet "cloud-flown": gull-abandoned) derricks. The bridge,
again, is not presented in its mechanical but in its vital aspect.
Though it is a part of the scene (seen), the very center of it, it
belongs to another world: to the eternal, spiritual, pristine, spacious,
natural world of the "*North* Atlantic," the cool new world of the
harbor dawn, as the further contrast of "noon" and "afternoon"
suggests.[50] And even now, in the frenzy of modern life, the bridge
responds to the spirit ("breathe") and is "still," at peace.

Crane wrote Waldo Frank that, in "Atlantis," which he was
again working on in January 1926, the bridge was becoming "a
ship, a world, a woman, a tremendous harp. . . ." [51] It is world
and ship here, and both are related to each other. "Cables breathe"
is descriptively accurate in respect to the actual bridge, just as
"flashing scene," in an earlier stanza, is in respect to the movies of
that time. Crane is invariably true to the actual, and his metaphors,
accordingly, are never far-fetched. In the context of ocean setting
("North Atlantic"), "cables" acquire nautical significance, and
animated by "breathe" (breath), they evoke the image of sails. And
so the bridge is a ship—sailing ship, and gull—and the world it

49. "Song of Myself," § 6.
50. My italics.
51. *Letters*, p. 232 (January 18, 1926).

belongs to is both natural (spiritual) and past. The bridge is a curve of time, simultaneously past-present-future. It exists in the present as a vital presence of the past, and the future it portends will possess values—new only because rediscovered—that are associated with the past.[52]

The progression of this litany is most clearly one of increasing religious identification; of mounting fervor, too, culminating in stanza eight and subsiding in the wonderful peace of stanza nine. In stanza seven, the weakest, the bridge is asserted to be a redemptive agency—again because vital ("Vibrant"). The referents are vague ("that heaven of the Jews," "guerdon," "accolade"), but evoke religious and archaic associations, chiefly those of chivalric times, and do the work of transition. What the poet asserts, however, is what he hopes to receive ("reprieve and pardon"). Syntactical parallelism and rhyme indicate what is important to him: "Accolade thou dost bestow"; "Vibrant reprieve and pardon thou dost show." The bridge neither withholds nor hides, and its accolade is conferred by embrace.

Such is the logic by which the bridge becomes the answerer of stanza eight and the holy mother of stanza nine. In stanza eight the wonder of

> O harp and altar, of the fury fused,
> (How could mere toil align thy choiring strings!)

is heightened by the immediate recollection of Blake's great poem to creation, "The Tyger," no image of which is employed by Crane, the association being achieved instead at a deeper level by "fury fused" and the interrogatory character of the parenthetical exclamation. Blake's poem speaks in these lines for Crane's awareness of the terrible but joyous energies and awful grandeur of art, of the difficulty of synthesizing (to use his theoretical word for "fuse") the contraries of experience. It speaks for Roebling's achievement and that of his own "song." By joining the mechanical (the forge of creation) and the natural (the tyger), Blake's poem also confirms the mysterious double nature of the bridge, Crane's tyger,

52. Kenneth Burke considers the poem nostalgic. See "Doing and Saying: Thoughts on Myth, Cult, and Archetypes," *Salmagundi*, no. 15 (Winter, 1971), 119.

burning brightly in the darkness of the next stanza, but in a way moderated perhaps by the moderating stanza of Blake's poem:

> And when the stars threw down their spears,
> And water'd heaven with their tears,
> Did he smile his work to see?
> Did he who made the Lamb make thee?

The evocation of divinity is powerful in Crane's lines—"Terrific," used in the sense of awe-inspiring, is fitting. For the bridge, framed by divinity, is also the instrument with which we entreat divinity: an instrument of religious celebration ("harp and altar") and the "threshold" from which the prophet, pariah, and lover launch their petitions—the "pledge," "prayer," and "cry" whose answers, imputed here, are assured in the next stanza, which concludes the sentence begun by the poet's outcry.[53]

Now with the coming of night the masculine divinity of creation becomes the feminine divinity of love, or rather we see this aspect of divinity's nature, a nature similarly presented in "Ave Maria." Night overtakes the poem without our knowing it, but, as in "Faustus and Helen," it is a time consecrated by woman. Not Helen, however, but Mary is associated with the "traffic lights," which move across the bridge, delineating it—"immaculate sigh of stars, / Beading thy path"—even as the continuous movement "condense[s] eternity," reveals the radiant bridge fully, in its supreme office: "And we have seen night lifted in thine arms." This image of the mother, recalling the pietà, is among the greatest in Crane's work. It is the culminating image of his litany and is presented as the revelation hitherto undisclosed ("we have seen"). In the curve of lights from pier to pier, the bridge, which is more commonly recognized as spanning the abyss, is represented as sustaining the darkness of the world. Its most powerful meaning for Crane—he ascribes eternity to it—is in its upholding arms.

And so he invokes it in his dark time. The concluding stanzas

53. The use of "threshold" offers an opportunity to mention Joseph Stella, whose "The Brooklyn Bridge (a page of my life)" is the richest single gloss on Crane's "sentiments" regarding the bridge and their appropriateness, especially to Crane's generation. The essay is reprinted in *transition*, no. 16–17 (June, 1929), 86–88; see *Letters*, pp. 333–34 (January 24, 1929), for Crane's request to reprint the essay and use a Stella painting of Brooklyn Bridge for a frontispiece.

may be considered separately, even though they fulfill the develop-
ment of the litany, because in them the poet speaks *in propria
persona*, thereby focusing the poem, hitherto focused on the
bridge, on himself—on his own position in respect to the bridge
and his need for its spiritual agency. At the end of the poem we
find him awaiting the dawn of its beginning. (He is not waiting
passively, but, as "I waited" suggests, humbly.) We have moved
through an entire day—the temporal span of *The Bridge* (as also of
"Song of Myself")—and now move out of the darkness into the
rest of *The Bridge*. We stand beneath the bridge, in its shadow, not,
as at the end, in "Atlantis," on it; for "the darkness," as Crane
maintained, is part of the poet's business: [54] the condition and
point of departure for a journey, a trial, a passage into light. The
time is probably late December, past Christmas (the "fiery parcels"
of the brightly lit Manhattan skyline are "all undone"), and past
midnight. Yet the winter solstice, the darkest time, portends the
light, just as Christmas portends redemption and the gentle, puri-
fying snow (submerging "an iron year") the blessing of love.

Of these hopeful changes—of the vital process that brings them to
pass—the bridge is guarantor, an eternal wakefulness ("O Sleep-
less") overseeing the restless movement of history ("the river").
Always in motion, it has life, a cosmic energy like that of the sun,
which earlier "took step of thee" and whose diurnal course over
the continent is now represented by its "inviolate curve": "Vaulting
the sea, the prairies' dreaming sod." Again the bridge figures as part
of the circle of life; and it is an awakener, not merely vaulting the
prairie but bringing forth—the hope of *The Seven Arts* critics—its
hidden life. Its magnitude and height above us comport with
divinity, but so does the dovelike nature of its spirit ("sometime
sweep, descend" recalling the seagull), which the poet, finally, pe-
titions: "Unto us lowliest sometime sweep, descend / And of the
curveship lend a myth to God."

With this personal request, psychological-spiritual meanings are
added to the geographical points (east and west) of the poem.
The poet asks for intervention of spirit, for his own quickening by
the divinity he recognizes and celebrates in the world. For the act

54. *Letters*, p. 260 (June 20, 1926).

of descent empowers the poem, "a myth to God" ("descend" rhymes with and controls the meaning of "lend"); it complements the upward flight of the seagull, a "curveship" too. And these visible motions of spirit, like the poem the poet wishes to create, are the "concrete *evidence* of the *experience* of a recognition"; they are instances of "the real connective experience, the very 'sign manifest' on which rests the assumption of a godhead." [55] We should not invest "myth" too heavily, certainly not with the religious and philosophical expectations of Crane's friends. The poem is concerned with myth but is itself not necessarily mythic. Nor is it religious, though Crane said that "the very idea of a bridge . . . is a form peculiarly dependent on . . . spiritual convictions." [56] It does not aspire to anything so grand (and doctrinal), but merely to poetry, an "affirmation of experience," [57] and an affirmative experience of the kind Williams rendered in "The Wanderer":

> And with that a great sea-gull
> Went to the left, vanishing with a wild cry—
> But in my mind all the persons of godhead
> Followed after.[58]

"Proem: To Brooklyn Bridge" is an invocatory prayer—an equivalent perhaps of the traditional invocation to the muse—that also does the work of Whitman's "Inscriptions." It introduces us

---

55. *Letters*, p. 237 (March 17, 1926).
56. *Letters*, p. 261 (June 20, 1926).
57. *Letters*, p. 351 (May 22, 1930).
58. *The Collected Earlier Poems of William Carlos Williams* (Norfolk, Conn.: New Directions, 1951), p. 3. What is revealed to the wanderer is central to Crane's poem:

> It is she
> The mighty, recreating the whole world,
> This is the first day of wonders! [p. 4]

For Crane's debt to Williams' poem, see John Unterecker, "The Architecture of *The Bridge*," *Wisconsin Studies in Contemporary Literature*, III (Spring–Summer, 1962), 9.

See also Thomas A. Vogler, "A New View of Hart Crane's Bridge," *Sewanee Review*, LXXII (Summer, 1965), 382: "The poem labors to move from a state of desire to one of conviction, to see in the curve of the Bridge the arc of a rainbow promise not dependent on any text or tradition, but on the poet's own power to see into the nature of things."

to the poet's themes and to the "thematic anticipations" noted in part by Frederick Hoffman.[59] More formally integrated with the poem than "Inscriptions," it does more. In many significant ways it is a single version of the entire poem: an instance of its situation, duration, landscapes, mediating consciousness, poetic (symbolic) action, and "logic of metaphor." In naming the bridge, it centers and localizes the poem, establishes a point in history and geography, in time and space; and in invoking the bridge, it begins the symbolization upon which the success of the poem depends. No more ludicrous than the Eiffel Tower, the bridge is a symbol, of the order of Whitman's "grass," that acquires meaning by participating in concrete situations. In speaking of the frequently expressed wish of overcoming the "meaningless life of our industrial society . . . [by] introducing value through creating new symbols," Dorothy Lee addresses the problem Crane recognized in writing "Proem": "symbols in themselves have no value, and they cannot convey value to a situation. Only after they have participated in a situation can they have value, and then only in so far as the situation itself holds value." Since individual experience initiates this acquisition of meaning, the poet, for whom the bridge already possesses meaning at the beginning of the poem, speaks for himself and enables us, by means of the poem (to invoke, in this instance, is to evoke), to enter his experience and come into his meanings. And since a symbol "grows in meaning, and even changes in meaning," he will present the bridge in various situations, as he does so exemplarily in "Proem" by using the cubist technique of shifting perspectives, a technique that brings much together in the name of the bridge and represents one of the ways in which the entire poem, the poet's journey of consciousness, becomes a totality of meaning, the "Word" of a simultaneously apprehended "logic of metaphor" as well as the warrant of his identification with life.[60]

"O clemens, o pia, o dulces Maria." With these words of Columbus' prayer, William Carlos Williams concluded "The Discovery of

59. *The Twenties: American Writing in the Postwar Decade*, rev. ed. (New York: Collier Books, 1962), p. 264n.

60. "Symbolization and Value," *Freedom and Culture* (Englewood Cliffs: Prentice-Hall, 1959), pp. 84–85. See P, 261–62; Trachtenberg, *Brooklyn Bridge*, pp. 153–55; *Letters*, p. 140 (July 21, 1923).

the Indies," a chapter of *In the American Grain* that Crane prob-
ably read when it first appeared in *Broom*, in March 1923.[61] His
"Ave Maria," a dramatic monologue of the returning Columbus,
also concludes with a prayer, one that celebrates God's work in the
discovery even as it speaks the mariner's thankfulness for home-
coming to Spain after the terrible trials of passage. Placed in respect
to homecoming rather than, with Williams, to discovery, the prayer
(and the prayerful nature established by the title of the poem)
provides a transition from "Proem." For like the poet of "Proem,"
Columbus, isolated and alone, is represented as enduring a dark
time and petitioning divine help; he has found the New World
("It is morning there") but now, like the dawning world of
"Proem," it has been lost in the darkness of the present and, even
for him, has become "apparitional," a wonderful event of the
past. The homeward voyage to report the discovery ("I bring you
back Cathay") is depicted as a test of faith, an act decreed by God,
who "dost search / Cruelly with love." In every respect, all the
more so in its time of difficulty, "Ave Maria" shows the Christian
orientation provided by what critics of modern secularism and dis-
integration, like Waldo Frank, called the medieval synthesis. It
offers a contrast to the present in *The Bridge* ("A period that is
loose at all ends, without apparent direction of any sort") [62] at the
same time that Columbus, the only person in the poem other
than the mother of "Indiana" who is permitted the autonomy of
monologue, becomes an example of the kind of discovery and heroic
perseverance which by imaginative identification the poet assimi-
lates to himself.

The presence of Columbus is perhaps inevitable in a poem so
much concerned with the redemption—or rediscovery—of America.
(This, in fact, is the theme for which Columbus is spokesman in
the concluding dialogue with Cervantes in Waldo Frank's *Virgin*

61. *Broom*, whose staff Matthew Josephson joined in November 1922, published
part II of "Faustus and Helen" in January 1923, along with Williams' "The Destruc-
tion of Tenochtitlan." As one of the magazines that educated Crane, it is interesting
to note a picture of Brooklyn Bridge by Joseph Stella, in the November 1921 issue,
and the always prominent discussion of the Machine. Williams' essay, published in
March 1923, though revised for *In the American Grain*, which Crane also read, ends
in the same way.

62. *Letters*, p. 110 (December 24, 1922).

Spain, whose title refers to Mary, to Spain, the immaculate "mother of beginnings.") [63] When Crane first outlined *The Bridge* for Otto Kahn, he began it with Columbus and moved forward chronologically—and dialectically—through Pocahontas and Whitman, its three major figures.[64] He did not seem to consider the disjunctions of time that he later employed nor the movement of consciousness that contained them. Yet this is what makes "Ave Maria" both a historical starting point and a present occasion in the mind of the poet. Though the monologue, in language suitable to the speaker (sometimes, as with Williams, in words from Columbus' journal), presents a world of its own distant from the poet, it is still immediately there, known in its language by the "contact," as Williams would say, it affords. The separateness of that world—the differing conceptions of deity, cosmos, geography—marks its distance, conveys the poet's sense of time, though in his dream it is timeless. And in its placement between "Proem" and "The Harbor Dawn," the episode belongs to the poet; it is not merely the formal beginning of a poem on America but the first episode in the poet's act of remembering (remembering, awakening, and discovering, for much of his discovering is remembering); it is his historical "ground," something still vital in which he participates, something very much related to the present time and to his concerns. For it is a historical representation of loss—what better example of discovery, loss, even "betrayal"?—a loss also told in "Proem" and "The Harbor Dawn" and subsequent parts of the poem.

When we say that "Ave Maria" is a historical starting point we mean not only that here, with Columbus' discovery, American history begins but that here is the beginning of "history" in America. This is the sense in which Claude Lévi-Strauss uses "history" when he remarks, in *Tristes Tropiques,* that until the discovery "the New World was spared the agitations of 'history'. . . ." [65] For "history" is an intrusive force, one that Crane, with the

63. "The Port of Columbus," *Virgin Spain* (New York: Boni & Liveright, 1926), pp. 295–301; see also *Our America* (New York: Boni & Liveright, 1919), p. 28: "America is a mystic Word. We go forth all to seek America. . . ."

64. *Letters,* p. 241 (March 18, 1926).

65. See "The Doldrums," where Lévi-Strauss ponders the discovery, in *Tristes Tropiques,* trans. John Russell (New York: Atheneum, 1965), p. 78.

particular sensitivity to its consequences shown by other writers of his time, identifies when he says, in the context of the lost (or hidden: overlaid) timeless world of the Indian, "always the iron dealt cleavage!" [66] Columbus, according to Lévi-Strauss, "risked the only total adventure yet offered mankind," but in doing so he introduced "history," opened America to the "shallowness which characterizes the history of the New World in modern times." [67] He betrayed it to the ravaging greed (symbolized by the westward movement, the gold rush, the railroad, and the skyscraper) against which, in "Ave Maria," he warns Ferdinand ("Yet no delirium of jewels!"; "Rush [not] down the plenitude").[68] Columbus, then, begins a history of spoliation and loss at the same time that he reminds us, if only in the phrase "Indian emperies," of a primitive world antedating "history," a world whose "lesson," Lévi-Strauss tells us, "may even come to us with a millenary freshness. . . ." [69]

Its lesson—of "contact" (Williams), harmony (Frank), sacrality (Rosenfeld)—came to Crane with millenary freshness; [70] and by manipulating time, the very element that destroys the work—myths, religions—of man, he tried to bring it to us. To treat time disjunctively is to negate its linearity, its irresistible historical dimension, the "viewpoint" that Crane told Otto Kahn one could get in "any history primer." He preferred "a more organic panorama, showing the continuous and living evidence of the past in the inmost vital substance of the present." For the "purely chronological," he said, was "ineffective from the poetic standpoint"—that is, would not enable him to do what he wished to do in the poem: recover time and, with it, the sacred ground, or possibility, of a new beginning.[71]

At the end of *Virgin Spain*, the "history" begun by Columbus

66. P, 66. In *Our America*, Frank says that the fatal weakness of the Indian was that "he knew not iron" (p. 125).

67. *Tristes Tropiques*, pp. 81, 240.

68. This warning is addressed to the King, thereby stressing the "masculine" compulsion to conquest: the rape of the New World.

69. *Tristes Tropiques*, p. 392.

70. See Williams' *In the American Grain* (New York: New Directions, 1956); Frank, "The Land of Buried Cultures," *Our America*; Rosenfeld, "Indian Corn Dance," *The Dial*, LXXXI (December, 1926), 529–34. Neither the primitive element in modern art nor the influence of Lawrence should be neglected.

71. *Letters*, p. 305 (September 12, 1927).

ends with the disappearance of the White Towers of America; as the sun sets in the west, the sky in the east is "*suddenly aflame wth sunrise.*" Crane may have acknowledged this apocalypse by calling the concluding poem of *The Bridge* "Atlantis." Yet his expectation of the dawn, though as great as Frank's, was never expressed in such Wagnerian fashion. It depended, instead, on radical change in perspective, on awareness of the circular rhythms of man and nature, on the realization that, as Lévi-Strauss learned, "The golden age which blind superstition situated behind or ahead of us is *in us.*' " [72] The possibility of a new beginning for which Crane speaks is underwritten by the mind and nature, by the similarity of *experience* so often emphasized by the logic of metaphor of his poem—for example, in the hierophany of the seagull's flight experienced by the poet in "Proem" and that of the " 'The Great White Birds' " experienced by the Indians in "Ave Maria."

In speaking of his own "pioneering" in *The Bridge*, Crane explained to Otto Kahn that, in what followed "Ave Maria," he was working backward from the present (or down) to "the nature-world of the Indian." When he said that he was treating the "Myth of America," he meant both the recurrent pattern—the impulsion—of our "history" and the mythic, or aboriginal, world beneath it.[73] This is the double aspect, represented in *The Bridge* by the interplay of linear and circular imagery, to which he refers in telling Waldo Frank that "to handle the beautiful skeins of this myth of America—to realize suddenly, as I seem to, how much of the past is living under only slightly altered forms, even in machinery . . . is extremely exciting." [74] Much of the excitement of writing (and reading) *The Bridge* comes from discovering this new world. For Crane's passage, like Whitman's in "Passage to India," is "back . . . to primal thought"; his is the voyage of the "mind's return, / To reason's early paradise. . . ." And perhaps his passage follows that of Columbus because, in Whitman's poem, Columbus ("History's type of courage, action, faith") is said to have opened the way to the greater work of the poet—to those reconciliations

72. *Tristes Tropiques,* p. 392.
73. *Letters,* p. 305.
74. *Letters,* p. 274 (August 19, 1926).

and reunions whose all-inclusive example is that of "Nature and Man . . . disjoin'd and diffused no more." That Crane turned to Mexico after completing *The Bridge* is understandable; there he actually reached, as he once said of "The Dance," "the pure mythical soil . . . at last!" [75]

Crane's conception of Columbus owes something to Williams (the "wonder-breathing" discoverer, not despoiler, of Beautiful Thing) and something to Waldo Frank (the "mystic mariner" overwhelmed by "faith, not fear"). But it owes most to Whitman, to "Passage to India" and perhaps to "Prayer of Columbus." Of more significance than the verbal evidence—"rondure," "teeming," "athwart," for example—is the fact that Columbus' prayer in "Ave Maria" is in spirit so much like Whitman's apostrophe to God in section eight of "Passage to India," a poem in which the poet celebrates both the sacrality of the universe and the soul's desire to go beyond, to voyage forth and come to rest in God. To reach, to return to, "affection's source" is Whitman's goal; he can only be satisfied by "love complete," as he says in the stanza from which Crane took the epigraph to "Cape Hatteras":

Reckoning ahead O soul, when thou, the time achiev'd,
The seas all cross'd, weather'd the capes, the voyage done,
Surrounding, copest, frontest God, yieldest the aim attain'd,
As fill'd with friendship, love complete, the Elder Brother found
The Younger melts in fondness in his arms.

A similar desire for the assuagement of the "trembling heart" concludes "Ave Maria" and is expressed in lines that visually reach forward into the poem and are recalled once more (in "O Hand of Fire") at the close of "The Tunnel." For the poet they mark the beginning and the end of the rediscovery of America—and the soul's voyage—whose ecstatic goal is reached in "Atlantis."

And then Whitman confirms for the poet, in "Cape Hatteras," the faith (the trust) of which so much of the poet's journey is a

---

75. In a letter to Edna Lou Walton, he said that he was "penetrating to a new kind of world in the psychology of the Indians. . . ." The finest letter of his Mexican experience tells of his participation in an Indian ritual at Tepoztlán. *Letters*, pp. 389, 380–83 (November 27, September 21, 1931).

test; confirms the faith in a meaningful, living universe of which Columbus provides the first touchstones. As a historical figure, Columbus may be said to represent the religious consciousness of medieval Christianity; for him the "medieval synthesis" is still a fact of experience, not a phrase to designate the falling-away of subsequent history. Of him, as a historical figure, it is perhaps sufficiently accurate to say that "being dedicated to divine will, [he] holds a vision of God that is integrated within the life he enacts, giving him the sense of a living universe and the sense of his own mission within the divine whole." [76] But in the poem, in the poetry, it is otherwise: it is his renewed sense of a living universe, his sense of the cosmos itself as hierophany—this is his vision of God—that sustains his faith and steadies his dedication. [77] Twice— on the return voyage and the voyage out—he is tested at sea, by chaos; and the monologue that tells of the stormy return and homecoming concludes with the prayer, a celebration of the mystery and power of God and of the glory of his universe. Here Columbus tells of the passage out—"through night our passage"— whose wonderful culmination certified the hierophanies he had witnessed (the corposant, "Teneriffe's garnet," the "teeming span" itself) and, considering "all that amplitude that time explores," was *his* discovery of cosmos. [78] The discovery is revelation ("where our Indian emperies lie revealed") and accordingly, he says, "faith, not fear / Nigh surged me witless. . . ." Like the Indians who are moved by his ships to sacral awareness, he is moved by the dawn that discloses the New World, moved by his presence at creation: "I, wonder-breathing, kept the watch,—saw / The *first* palm chevron the *first* lighted hill." [79] And a similar sense of cosmos—of order, of motion, and energy and the splendor of creation—is expressed in the brilliant lines that remind us of the poet's apostrophe to the bridge in "Proem" and of the epigraph from Plato

76. Jerome W. Kloucek, "The Framework of Hart Crane's *The Bridge*," *Midwest Review* (Spring, 1960), p. 15.

77. See Mircea Eliade, *The Sacred and the Profane: The Nature of Religion*, trans. Willard Trask (New York: Harcourt, Brace & World, 1959), p. 12.

78. Columbus, according to Crane, was to represent "Conquest of space, chaos." *Letters*, p. 241.

79. My italics.

that introduces "Atlantis" and the greater apostrophe of that poem:

> This turning rondure whole, this crescent ring
> Sun-cusped and zoned with modulated fire
> Like pearls . . .
>
> . . . .
>
> This disposition that thy night relates
> From Moon to Saturn in one sapphire wheel:
> The orbic wake of thy once whirling feet,
> Elohim, still I hear thy sounding heel! [80]

Perhaps this explains the dramatic issue of the monologue: the return voyage to "bring you back Cathay"; not riches, as Crane explained to Otto Kahn, but the "word" (of a morning world) that had been revealed to Columbus ("For I have seen now what no perjured breath / Of clown nor sage can riddle or gainsay"), "Cathay," which Crane said was a "symbol of consciousness, knowledge, spiritual unity." [81] The voyage to the New World is the ultimate trial of faith—wherever one discovers cosmos there is a new world—and Columbus is a hero of faith. Allusions to Captain Ahab's blasphemous voyage (corposants, compass, "gleaming fields") underscore his achievement; and he is especially important to a poet for whom such a victory is one of trust and involves Mary (mother), God (father), friends ("Be with me, Luis de San Angel") and perhaps lover ("Dark waters onward shake the dark prow free," which recalls "Voyages VI").

More resonant than any lines in the poem are those that evoke the ultimate world that answers the voyager:

> . . . the far
> Hushed gleaming fields and pendant seething wheat
> Of knowledge. . . .

They recall the lines of Watts's hymn that Bildad sang as the *Pequod* plunged into the open seas ("Sweet fields beyond the

---

80. Eugene Paul Nassar says of these lines that the "historical Columbus' beliefs are maintained . . . but Crane's doubts are also." "Hart Crane's *The Bridge* and Its Critics," *The Rape of Cinderella: Essays in Literary Continuity* (Bloomington: Indiana University Press, 1970), pp. 156–57.

81. *Letters*, p. 241.

swelling flood, / Stand dressed in living green"), lines that Ishmael said never sounded more sweetly to him, "full of hope and fruition." And they recall the lines of Ceres' blessing in *The Tempest* cited by Crane in a letter to the Browns from California: "Spring come to you at the farthest / In the very end of harvest." [82] How wonderfully they summon for us the earthly paradise that Columbus believed he had found, the "verdant land" from which Ishmael said we should never push off, the "fresh, green breast of the new world" that Nick Carraway, in *The Great Gatsby*, said "had once pandered in whispers to the last and greatest of all human dreams": all the images we cherish of Mother Earth, the sacred body risen from the sea, the "plenitude" to be worshiped, not violated or profaned. For the gleaming fields are cosmos (and beauty and knowledge), the bright living world created anew from the waters of chaos, darkness, and death. We may even, in considering the "pendant . . . wheat / Of knowledge," recall the evocation of the golden-haired Venus at the close of "Voyages." [83] These images move us, and they move the poet, who, in the dream of "Ave Maria," is about to enter the "waking dream" of "The Harbor Dawn," where he himself discovers the New World by imaginatively possessing Powhatan's daughter.[84]

Philip Horton justified Crane's use of the epigraph from Seneca because Columbus himself had cited it to show that he had fulfilled "an ancient destiny." [85] But it confirms the poet's destiny as well. For "all of the terms of his quest," as Thomas Vogler says, "are symbolically interchangeable with those of Columbus' quest." [86] Columbus' monologue is the poet's dream, which explains the most notable things about it: that the passage home provides the dramatic setting of the discovery; that the chaos that tests the "word" is under the dominion of a cruel Hebraic God, the father whose hand is fire and whose love requires the intercession of the mother

82. Melville, *Moby-Dick*, ch. 22; *Robber Rocks*, p. 85 (February 22, 1928).

83. "Knowledge" may be glossed in terms of the Renaissance attribution of it to Venus and in the Freudian meaning of discovery. Consider also "Landscapes projected masculine, full-sized and golden," in Whitman's "Song of Myself," § 29.

84. Pocahontas, Crane said, represented the "natural body of America—fertility, etc." *Letters*, p. 241.

85. *Hart Crane*, p. 196.

86. "A New View of Hart Crane's Bridge," pp. 384–85.

("O Madre María"); and that the mother to whom the poet appeals in "Ave Maria" is the tutelary divinity of his vision and its object, the paradise he wishes to discover and the homeland to which he wishes to return. Discovery is recovery because, as the poem tells us, the poet has been there before.

With "The Harbor Dawn," *The Bridge* returns to the scenario of "Proem," to the "harbored room," where a central imagination of the poem occurs.[87] This section of the poem incorporates the previous sections—the present landscape of "Proem" and the prayer of "Ave Maria," which is answered here—and also opens out into the quest of the rest of the poem. Of all of Crane's poems of the enclosed interior world, "The Harbor Dawn" is perhaps the finest and most remarkable. It reminds one especially of "Stark Major," the action of which is divided between "The Harbor Dawn" and "Van Winkle." But it not only treats a similar theme of possession and loss with more assurance, it places it (which also accounts for its success) within "this history," within the private history or flow of reverie that comprises *The Bridge*. Here, in the genesis of reverie, which Gaston Bachelard says is under the sign of the *anima*, is the genesis of the poem.[88] And more because of difference than likeness—because of the growth and greater poetic power of "The Harbor Dawn"—it reminds one of "Interior." The "harbored room" no longer protects the self from the world. The intimate space the poet occupies is open to the world, almost coextensive with it, and the secret of the self and the imagination—their erotic awakening—is not withheld but enacted.

Had Crane followed a chronological sequence, he would have begun with "Ave Maria" and followed with this imagination of beginnings, with the birth or dawn of consciousness out of the "blackness" or cosmic darkness of sleep. The "darkling harbor" precedes the auroral harbor of "Proem," and the "tide of voices" that the poet hears "midway in [his] dream" includes Columbus'. So placed, "The Harbor Dawn" would have served in the way "Loomings"

---

87. Bernice Slote speaks of the "harbored room" in "Views of *The Bridge*," in James E. Miller, Jr., Karl Shapiro, and Bernice Slote, *Start with the Sun: Studies in the Whitman Tradition* (Lincoln: University of Nebraska Press, 1960), p. 157.

88. P, 116; *The Poetics of Reverie*, p. 62.

does in *Moby-Dick*—a chapter alluded to in "white surplices, be-shrouded wails" ("there floated into my inmost soul," Ishmael says, "endless processions of the whale, and, mid most of them all, one grand hooded phantom, like a snow hill in the air").[89] Nearer the outset we would have learned the profound personal motive of the poem.

Antecedent to all the action of *The Bridge* is the primordial elemental world, the fog that encloses the enclosed (hence "harbored room") and figures forth both a soft protected childhood world and a child's sense of cosmicity. The fog itself slumbers on a sleepy seascape.[90] Cosmos and consciousness are assimilated to each other. The fog world is not only the cosmos in a nebular state ("Somewhere out there in blackness steam / Spills into steam and wanders, washed away") but the "dream land" of which Crane told his mother in a letter from Columbia Heights—and a "hidden world." [91] Dream is a beginning, and the dream is of beginning: of the emergence of the self, its identification, as Whitman would have said, out of the float of existence; a dream of love in which the self begets itself by possessing (in this instance, being possessed by) the "me myself," the soul or spirit of its deepest being, the very precipitate (fog: woman) of the cosmos; and a dream of completeness from which awakening is loss, compelling the need to go in search of the self's "ideal."

This fable is familiar, as in the work of Williams, where the woman or "beautiful thing" he pursues is also America, and Crane calls attention to it by placing "The Harbor Dawn" within the sequence of five poems entitled "Powhatan's Daughter" and by using as an epigraph the passage from Strachey on Pocahontas that Williams quoted in *In the American Grain*.[92] But its special

89. *Moby-Dick*, ch. 1. The imagery, even "wails" (a pun but also a rhyme), recalls "As apparitional as sails" in "Proem."

90. Bachelard, *The Poetics of Reverie*, pp. 108–9.

91. *Letters*, p. 193 (November 16, 1924); see also a less happy account of fog in *Letters*, p. 198 (February 10, 1925).

92. Crane may have used the passage as it was copied out by Kay Boyle in a review of Williams' book in *transition*, I (April, 1927), 139–41. In *In the American Grain* it appears in "The May-pole at Merrymount," where Williams explains the Indians' attitude toward "wantonness" in considerng the Puritans' revenge on Mor-

interest, especially since Crane emphasizes the dark pagan girl rather than the Christianized woman (the light lady) of legend, is its heavy burden of spirituality. Though presumably Pocahontas, the woman of the poem comes from the spirit world ("white surplices," "beshrouded," "veils," "sheath of pallid air"). She is no emanation of earth, or is an earth mother more by right of Crane's association of her with Hertha than with Pocahontas.[93] She belongs to the poet's past, his hidden world of childhood (the "long, tired sounds" are also "voices" of memory), and one recalls her presence in the cool, enveloping world of Crane's early poems. The North Atlantic, established in "Proem" as a place of spirit, is now a dream world of fog, the fog that is associated later with bird and sky and purity, and it is again contrasted with the busy, "modern" present; and when, in the third stanza, the poet falls into deepest sleep—the all-permitting unconscious—it is to be wholly possessed by the "pallid air" whose "cool arms" enfold him. Even without the images ("veils," "dim snow") that, in "Van Winkle," are clearly associated with the poet's memory of longing for his mother's love, we recognize the impelling force of the imagination that has created this dream.

The poem itself both disguises and reveals this. Its movement and imagery are so exact, the experience so well rendered, so controlled, that we tend to overlook its disturbing features.[94] We note the poet's humor in the "alley-upward" pun on "Alley-oop," [95] the irony of his reference to Prufrock's world ("The fog leans one last moment on the sill") and the "mistletoe of dreams." But what are we to make of the inset, italicized lines? Do they depict only

ton's sexual license. With this in mind, it is interesting to note Crane's remark to his mother: "while you are naturally an inbred Puritan you also know and appreciate the harmless gambols of an exuberant nature like my own." *Letters*, p. 193.

93. For Crane's use of Pocahontas, see Slate, "William Carlos Williams, Hart Crane, and 'The Virtue of History,' " pp. 503–5; Philip Young, "The Mother of Us All: Pocahontas Reconsidered," *Kenyon Review*, XXIV (Summer, 1962), 391–415. Crane's reference to Hertha (*Letters*, p. 305) reminds us of his reading of Swinburne—of "Mater Triumphalis" and "Hertha," which employs the images of tree, hair, star, and brow, and treats Hertha as the source of all things, even the gods.

94. The images themselves do not "blur," as Crane said. *Letters*, p. 306.

95. R. W. B. Lewis, *The Poetry of Hart Crane*, p. 291.

the sexual climax that awakens the poet to consciousness—the consciousness of loss that he anticipates in "now, before day claims our eyes"? They remind us of the similarly inset, italicized lines of "Faustus and Helen," especially since they should, in the context of the fog-spirit world, represent the "somewhere / Virginal perhaps, less fragmentary, cool." But they are startlingly erotic, and confusing. They evoke Pocahontas, the dark lady (the "smoky" soil), and, in addition, are homoerotic.[96] The gloss notes suggest confusion: "*Who is the woman with us in the dawn?*" But the poet, who has fulfilled a profound wish (consider again the import of the straining to hear at the beginning of the poem), seems to know, and the advent of day is disturbing to him because it awakens him to this unacceptable knowledge. The line immediately following the inset lines answers the "*—with whom?*" of the gloss note that appears to accompany it. "The window goes blond slowly. Frostily clears" is unusual both for the flatness it suddenly introduces and the impact of "blond," the only word in the poem that seems strange or strained. It depicts accurately the earliest morning light and, as a pun on "blind," fulfills the claim of "before day claims our eyes." [97] But its force is owing to the fact that its reference is maternal and that "frostily" is a sharp (North Labradorian) transformation of the "snowy hands" of the previous stanza—an image itself suggesting importunity, freighted with so much recollection of Joyce's "The Dead" and already telling the poet what the completed poem does, that "the time had come for him to set out on his journey westward." [98] With the awakening introduced in this line, the energy of the poem collapses, the intimate space empties, becomes vast and lonely, and the poet's soul is abandoned and cold like the gulls of this auroral world. To awaken from love is a loss comparable to that of being born (the sun is "released," the gulls are "aloft"); and it is a loss for which the poet feels guilty, feels maternal disapproval, perhaps because his imagination of love has not been exclusively hers, and paternal threat in the "Cyclopean"

96. The imagery of hands and eyes as well as the symbolic burden of Pocahontas will be associated with Whitman in "Cape Hatteras."

97. R. W. B. Lewis considers this pun in *The Poetry of Hart Crane*, p. 290. Even the pun may be associated with the mother: see "blindly" in "Van Winkle," where "forsook" also picks up "foresake our eyes" in "Proem."

98. "Cyclopean" also supports the journey motif.

cityscape, because it is both usurping and impure.[99] It is understandable then that, while recognizing the sentimentality, he wishes to linger with the fog, take refuge under the all-permitting magical "mistletoe of dreams," and in that dream put to rest—and thus wittily enclose the poem in sleep—the star that summons him to the "waking west."[100] For this dream of love is unattainable except in dreams, the disturbing private quest most fully revealed in "Three Songs," a quest whose fulfillment is possible only when it is imagined in terms of Pocahontas.[101] According to Crane's scheme of "love-motif" and the ages of man, "The Harbor Dawn" represents the "sowing of the seed"—a metaphor that prefigures both a process of growth and the harvest of "gleaming fields and pendant seething wheat. . . ." The poet is his own creator and, having given birth to himself in this poem, moves forward to young manhood in "The Dance," where the backward search for the "pure mythical and smoky soil" reaches its goal.[102]

Where "The Harbor Dawn" enacts a dream, "Van Winkle" enacts memory, another—a later and necessary—stage in the truancy to time that marks both the poet's discovery of America and awakening to the present. Rip Van Winkle, whom Crane said was "the 'guardian angel' of the journey into the past," is a familiar figure of our literary past (here a "usable" past) who speaks for the poet's desire to resist change by remaining asleep.[103] To do so is "childish," and the poet knows that Rip is a child—a child he admonishes in the way he himself undoubtably was: "Keep hold of that nickel for car-change, Rip,— / Have you got your *'Times'*—? / And hurry along, Van Winkle—it's getting late!" It is just this need to hurry, to be up and doing in behalf of "the immanent tasks of the

99. Isn't this poem a "spring of guilty song"? "Sirens," a fitting pun in this fog-enclosed world, recalls "Faustus and Helen."

100. The imagery evokes many associations: Christmas, the winter season of the poem, the Nativity (Mary, Jesus, the journeying wise men), the setting star of westward destiny.

101. The ambiguity is suggested by Kloucek's characterization of the dream: " 'Madre Maria' becomes the mysterious, vague archetypal female figure who makes him conscious of Desire and inspires him to go forth upon his quest." "The Framework of Hart Crane's *The Bridge*," p. 16.

102. *Letters*, pp. 306–7.

103. *Letters*, p. 306.

day," [104] the success that Rip forgot (*"And Rip forgot the office hours, / and he forgot the pay"*), that, in conjunction with the poet's sense of a radiantly fresh, open, and inviting world, prompts his memory. The gloss notes explain the appeal of that vista: *"Streets spread past store and factory—sped by sunlight and her smile. . . ."* And though Rip is the "guardian angel," it is *"she"* who *"shall take you by the hand. . . ."* The poet is moved to memory by a profound desire, by *"her smile,"* just as in the first version of the opening quatrain—it was perhaps the first verse of *The Bridge* to be composed—he is moved by the "joint piracy," the *voyage* permitted by the open road.[105]

Because the stress of the present summons the stress of the past (the unfinished situation), the poem is neither as buoyant as Crane indicates in his letter to Otto Kahn nor as it superficially seems.[106] Like Irving's tale, its treatment is humorous, or tries to be, but its undercurrent is not—and we are reminded of the sad, comic child figure of "Chaplinesque." The hurry to be off to work reminds the poet of "Times earlier, when you hurried off to school," a task that was unhappy too, though he doesn't say so but merely sets it against the music of the hurdy-gurdy, associated at the start with the appeal of the open road. His comment ("It is the same hour though a later day") conveys the sense of loss that comes with time—the quickened time of hurry and the time of history which commands progress ("hurry along . . . it's getting late!")—conveys the loss of yielding childhood and the pastoralism that accompanies it to the demands of the adult, urban world, and it opens his memory of childhood, when, as he realizes now, he had possessed the past, the historical childhood of America that parallels his own. This memory of the past is of conquistadores, whose determination, grandly represented by Cortes' horsemanship as well as his own sentimental childhood identification, he wittily deflates in Eliot's fashion ("Firmly as coffee grips the taste"). It is sentimental and enticing, as the presence at the threshold of Rip Van

---

104. *Letters*, p. 306.
105. See *Letters*, p. 123 (February 12, 1923). The image of being taken by the hand relates to that of the open road. See Whitman's "Song of the Open Road."
106. *Letters*, p. 306.

Winkle, who dreamed of Henry Hudson, indicates—and the content, too. For he remembers the historical figures who fit his (the child's and to some extent the man's) ideal of the feminine and the masculine, of mother and father: "There was Priscilla's cheek close in the wind, / And Captain Smith, all beard and certainty. . . ." These especially evocative lines render the child's sense of intimate tenderness and protective strength, and thus become the measure of the disturbing memories of father and mother to which the logic of memory eventually leads. Priscilla, we note, is a light lady, and though Captain Smith is mentioned where we might expect John Alden, Pocahontas is only vaguely present, perhaps as a hint of sexuality—the imperious kind Crane associated with his father. In the context of the stanza, Rip, who is introduced here, may also be the child of these parents, the child with whom the poet identifies in the jingles or interior songs where, ironically in tune with the hurdy-gurdy, he acknowledges—and also criticizes in a parental way—his remissness and its consequences.[107]

Now the hurdy-gurdy (the "grind-organ"), even when the jingle speaks of forgetting, provides a music of memory, and insists on the difficult, hesitant work of remembering. It functions in the manner of the street piano in Eliot's "Portrait of a Lady," where the young man says, "I remain self-possessed / Except when a street piano, mechanical and tired / Reiterates some worn-out common song. . . ."[108] And at first it awakens two incidents of childhood play, the stoning of garter snakes and the launching of toy airplanes—prefigurements of the serpent and the eagle, symbols of the time and the space he has begun to enter. These incidents—images—are related to each other in memory just as later, in "The Dance," they are related in (and by) the dance of imagination. But the image of the snake is the more prominent and persistent not only because it has sexual import (both of sexual discovery—the *revelation* which recalls "Proem"—and of sexual experience, which recalls "The Harbor Dawn") but because, as a symbol of time, the snake figures here as a symbol of memory, and the incident of the boy's prodding

107. The consequences are severe: not only failure but social displacement. The Van Winkle who "sweeps the tenements" may be a Negro. The jingle contains a threat of the kind Crane felt in working for his father.

108. Stanley K. Coffman, Jr., "Symbolism in *The Bridge*," *PMLA*, LXVI (March, 1951), 75.

it with a stick speaks also for the present activity of the poet's mind.

On one level—that on which the poet imagines himself as Rip— the image of the snake "flash[ing] back," an image of revelation, carries over in Rip's awakening (from his "harbor" dream) and being *"made aware."* He is confused, as well he might be, by the *"here"* of the present and the *"there"* of the past (his dream); and he is slowly made aware—in the split in his identity, too—that the revelation of his dream (*"He . . . swore he'd seen Broadway / a Catskill daisy chain in May"*) is no longer the case.[109] This dream of the pristine pastoral world is an equivalent of the poet's dream in "The Harbor Dawn." It is the child's version of the adult's dream, reverberates with its meaning of possession and loss, and, still vivid in memory, compels the truancy to the present (*"she is time's truant"*) by which the poet recovers both the "Appalachian Spring" and Pocahontas in "The Dance."

On another level, the jingle itself is an example of memory "that strikes a rhyme out of a box. . . ." For even as the logic of memory moves to its end, to the most important, deepest memories of childhood, the poet is aware of the process, oversees it, as he had overseen the dream of "The Harbor Dawn"; what is remarkable is the art—the self-possession—with which he uses his dreams and memories, being true to them, letting them inspire the poem, yet managing them. He is aware of the revelatory power that "strikes" and "splits" and that neither box nor glass can confine. And in addition to this, he is aware of the fact that the memories so revealed—memories tightly closed in the self—are problematical. These memories, as Thomas Vogler says, are the most important in *The Bridge:*

> Is it the whip stripped from the lilac tree
> One day in spring my father took to me,
> Or is it the Sabbatical, unconscious smile
> My mother almost brought me once from church
> And once only, as I recall—?

109. R. W. B. Lewis relates the splitting of Rip Van Winkle's name to the confusion of past and present. (*The Poetry of Hart Crane*, p. 294.) It might also be related to the parental conflict that resulted in Harold Hart Crane becoming Hart Crane.

Unlike the other memories, these take an interrogative form and direct our attention to "it," to which both refer. And Vogler, who notes this, explains them: "In the image of his father, he is asking if *this* is his equivalent to the Elohim of Columbus; he may even be asking the psychological question whether this is the source of his need to find now, in his adult life, some means of assimilating this early experience into a pattern of benignity. With the mother's smile, Crane [the poet] is asking the same two-part question. Is this the best he can find for his own 'Maria' or is this the real source of his need for such a figure?" The latter memory is the more insistent:

> It [the smile] flickered through the snow screen, blindly.
> It forsook her at the doorway, it was gone
> Before I had left the window. It
> Did not return with the kiss in the hall.

This memory, already adumbrated in Rip's recollection of the Catskill daisy chain, is one of loss, of something fleetingly seen, with wonderful revelatory force, and lost. The memory is not marked, as Vogler says it is, by a "feeling of hesitancy and doubt. . . ." [110] The emphatic words are "once," "once only," "forsook," "gone," "did not return." Focused here is the sense of loss that belongs to memory and that envelopes the poem, and the feeling is one of irrevocability. Though childhood is the happy time recalled by the music of the hurdy-gurdy, its deepest memory is of the loss of complete love, a loss whose inevitability is recognized but still deeply felt by the poet. This, as the poem shows, is the moving force of both his dream in "The Harbor Dawn" and his subsequent truancy. In *The Bridge*, R. W. B. Lewis observes, "it is 'the lost mother'—rather than, as more normally in the epic tradition, 'the lost father'—whom the poet needs, longs for, and journies far in search of." [111] Yes, when he (Rip) enters the subway, it is not to go to work but to find a way back to the past. He is moved by the vision of love he had once seen on his mother's face, "*sped by sunlight and her smile*. . . ." [112]

110. "A New View of Hart Crane's Bridge," p. 387. Yet Crane is true to his childhood by presenting happier images of it: Priscilla, Captain Smith, the sunlit world, the hurdy-gurdy.

111. *The Poetry of Hart Crane*, p. 296.

112. I say "vision of love" because even though the poet cannot dissociate it from

The hurry of "Van Winkle" is translated into the speed of the initial verses of "The River," and the poet is transported by train, not subway, "From tunnel into field. . . ." He has, in Paul Rosenfeld's words, begun his "trip to the Indian," to the sacred center. Like Rosenfeld, he has taken the "Limited," and as Williams says of the protagonist of *The Great American Novel*, "Over the great spaces of New Jersey, Pennsylvania, Ohio, Indiana he sped in the Pullman car." [113] The rush characterizes the "20th Century" as well as the poet's eagerness to flee it and return to the heartland, and homeland (to which Crane was many times compelled to go), the place, according to Crane's scheme, of "Youth" and, in the work of writers such as Sherwood Anderson and F. Scott Fitzgerald, of adolescent America. Crane speaks of the train as a "psychological 'vehicle' for transporting the reader to the Middle West," but it is also a vehicle for transporting him to the past, to an earlier condition; and the "cultural confusions of the present" rendered at the start are both an image of the " '*Times*,' " of the East, and the experience of quickly passing sensation rushing into sensation by which the present is displaced—a displacement whose achievement and consequence are represented in the juxtaposition, in the first part of the poem, of the third and the two preceding stanzas. [114]

In these virtuosic stanzas, futurism and dada, the most advanced expression of the modern, are used to repudiate it. And in them Crane repudiates the poetry of advertising advocated by Matthew Josephson as well as the success to which he sometimes hoped copywriting would lead him. The office hours that Rip forgot were probably to be spent in an advertising agency, and having forgot, or having shed them in the rush of the train, the poet finds himself not on Avenue A but with the hobos beside the track. He is one

---

his mother, he knows—or so he represents it—that it is something greater than she is, something not within her power but, like grace, granted her. Yet the memory, like that of "Porphyro in Akron," unites love and resentment.

113. "Indian Corn Dance," p. 529; *The Great American Novel* (1923), reprinted in *American Short Novels*, ed. R. P. Blackmur (New York: Thomas Y. Crowell Co., 1960), p. 325.

114. *Letters*, p. 306. Crane mentions both the New York Central and the Erie railroads, both of which served Cleveland, the latter passing en route through Warren and Garrettsville, Ohio. See John Baker, "Commercial Sources for Hart Crane's 'The River,' " *Wisconsin Studies in Contemporary Literature*, VI (Winter-Spring, 1965), 52.

of the "left-overs of the pioneers," part of the detritus of culture—not only of modern culture but of the history of spoliation of which it is an expression.[115]

For the train that rushes *"past the din and slogans of the year"* follows the old westward course, its speed a coefficient of spoliation, and the slogans tell some of the essential history from the time of the discovery to the present. Men came to America with "patents," grants or privileges, and so staked their claims; they came in a "delirium of jewels" and, forgetting the warning of Columbus, "Rush[ed] down the plenitude. . . ." The "patent names" (patented names: "Tintex," "Japalac") serve the same function. Men stick them on signboards but now their stakes and claims are weak and unenduring, like the "new playbill ripped / in the guaranteed corner. . . ." [116] So much for "Go West, Young Man, Go West," a slogan of another year that still resounds with the imperative of success. Phrases like "all over" tell the double story of conquest and its end—or the end of the dream of the West, referred to again in "dream to ticking dream," "spends your dream," and "Poised wholly on its dream."

Nothing is adventitious in these stanzas because, besides the superficial value of their imitative form, they render the poet's experience, his train of associations as the Limited leaves the station.[117] They show his quick mind, are a parody—sometimes an ad man's perversion—of the "logic of metaphor," and they imitate the very thing the poet ponders and later depicts by dividing "20th Century" from "Limited," the dissociation of sensibility. "Certain-teed Overalls" plays cleverly with "all over" and "guaranteed corner," and still speaks for the rural hinterland, perhaps for the incredulous boobocracy, as "lands sakes!" suggests. (The rural voice is heard again in "can you / imagine," with equally dire overtones.) The rush of signs establishes a kind of indiscriminate equivalence, a visual roar. A playbill calls up Bert Williams and his routine at

---

115. *Letters*, p. 306.

116. The slogans of the year are layered; beneath the new playbill is an old one for Bert Williams, who died in 1922. See Baker, "Commercial Sources for Hart Crane's 'The River,'" p. 49.

117. L. S. Dembo, who considers the "dangers" of imitative form, says that these stanzas "do not reflect the theme of the section; namely, that 'iron dealt cleavage.'" (*Hart Crane's Sanskrit Charge*, p. 69.) But that is exactly what they do.

the National Winter Garden (a part of the troublesome present the poet is leaving behind?).[118] And the patter of "Minstrels," already evoked in the first line by the tune of "The Darktown Strutters Ball," [119] merges into an advertisement for "Mazda" lamps, which, in turn, suggests the inventor, who had once been a telegrapher. But "the telegraphic night," in connection with "coming on," also speaks of imminent darkness and prepares for the "wires," which, as much as the railroad, have conquered the continent and subverted the dream, and for the later image of the train's taillights fading from view. These associations of light and darkness, of Spenglerian doom and salvation, gather in the poet's image of the modern hero—"saint"—the wizard-inventor, whose synthetic substitute for religion is made obvious in the synthetic name-making of "Thomas a Ediford" and in the trinity of "SCIENCE-COMMERCE and the HOLYGHOST. . . ." Guided by Edison and Ford, unmindful of the "teeming span" in which Columbus trusted, we race down the night, like Ahab on his rails of steel, toward the orgiastic future that beckoned to Gatsby.

Contributing to the success of these stanzas are the quick comic turns of the run-over lines and the colloquial speech. For example: "EXPRESS makes time / like SCIENCE—." Yes, science creates categories of time and, technologically, has speeded it up. ("The world moves by so fast these days!," Crane wrote in "The Great Western Plains," an earlier poem anticipating "The River.") [120] And in a sense in keeping with the major theme of spoliation, "makes time," as Thomas Vogler says, is a "degrading sexual pun"—science makes time by overcoming space, by raping the body of America.[121] In doing so, as what follows bears out, science destroys the spiritual wonder of contact with the eternal present (the unity of space-and-time, the eagle and the serpent), interrupts the slower, natural rhythms of agrarian, or pastoral, life. Its achievements are "breath-

---

118. John Baker says that Bert Williams, the Negro vaudevillean, a "loser" on the stage, anticipates the hobos. "Commercial Sources for Hart Crane's 'The River,' " p. 49.

119. R. W. B. Lewis discusses the jazz rhythms of the poem in *The Poetry of Hart Crane*, p. 297.

120. He had also used capitalization in his Cummings' parody, "America's Plutonic Ecstasies."

121. "A New View of Hart Crane's Bridge," p. 388.

taking," not "wonder-breathing," the dissociation that accounts for the spiritual hunger of the "left-overs" and leads to the confusions—the easy equation of incommensurables of such terrible consequences to Gatsby—exploited by advertising men like Bruce Barton and promulgated by the radio, the inventive wonder of the twenties: "COMMERCE and the HOLYGHOST / . . . WALLSTREET AND VIRGINBIRTH. . . ." The humor here is broad, like that of Sinclair Lewis in *The Man Who Knew Coolidge*, and telling.[122] The "HOLY-GHOST / RADIO" *is* a spiritual medium, wireless, yet "connecting ears"; and it brings us not only the pitch for patent medicines (and the sermons and the lectures that edified Lowell Schmaltz) but such marvels as contacting Byrd at the North Pole.[123] Linked with the train by "roar," the radio, too, despoils, supplants, filling with its noise ("a hash of noise," to cite Crane's characterization of the modern city in "Porphyro in Akron") the pastoral space evoked by "As You Like It" and the allusion to sermons in stones and books in the running brooks.[124] The "20th Century" is indeed "Limited," in the poet's view very much what critics like Eliot and Joseph Wood Krutch said it was—a time of dissociation, vulgarization, and profanation.

These verses, a collage of voices ending in the upward cadence of a sardonic question, speak for themselves. But they are also answered by the flat comment of the poet, who has shifted his point of view—the perspectivism is modernist—and now, standing with the hobos beside the track, sees the 20th Century Limited roar by. "Still hungry," carried over from the culinary meaning of "as you like it . . . eh?," is the dissatisfaction stressed in this comment; and it is not, quite so much as it might be for us, a jibe at the consumption ethic, but at the profound failure of modern technological society to nurture the spirit. As a machine, the train is a ready substitute for Henry Adams' dynamo. For what the men hunger for is represented by the Virgin, by the nativity symbolism of "three ["wizen"] men" watching (not following) the star (tail-

122. It is also a part of the closely woven fabric of the poem, recalling "Down Wall" in "Proem" and "Madre Maria" in "Ave Maria."

123. For comment on the national excitement over Byrd—and Lindbergh—see Edmund Wilson, *The Shores of Light*, p. 526.

124. The passage from *As You Like It*, II, i, 16–17, also speaks of "tongues in trees," anticipating the "singing tree" in "The Dance."

lights). The "VIRGINBIRTH" of the previous stanza is appropriated to this context, which also recalls the Christmas symbolism with which "The Harbor Dawn" and "Proem" end. But whatever hope is raised by these symbols is foreclosed by the tunnel-vortex into which we now see the train rushing, its lights "slip-/ping gimleted and neatly out of sight."

This Spenglerian doom, depicted again in the river's death in the sea, encloses the poem, which, with "Quaker Hill" (where the train similarly figures), is most concerned with the pastoral and most nostalgic. And now, in keeping with its historical burden, the poem acquires a narrative quality at times like that of Stephen Vincent Benét's *John Brown's Body*, and the verse, according to Crane, "settles down to a pedestrian gait," though meditative might better describe it.[125] Without violating the poet's voice, other voices speak through it, voices connected with hunting, fishing, river towns, harness-racing—with oral tradition and vernacular culture, and with those, like Anderson and Sandburg, who had used it in a literary way. As a collage of folk materials and as a historical and geographical catalog, it is sometimes perilously close in sentiment to the *American Heritage*. Yet however much it exploits Sandburg ("Caboose Thoughts," for example) and Williams (in the allusions to Boone and Burr in *In the American Grain*), it does serious work by enabling the poet to spell out the nature of his identification with the "ancient men." [126]

As important as the sacral knowledge he imputes to them (to call the hobos "ancient men" invests them with spirit, creates a mystique of the hobo comparable to that of Jack Kerouac's) [127]—as important is their resistance to the world of progress and speed whose very instruments—*slow* freights, to be sure—they nevertheless use. They represent, as the "But" insists ("But some men take their liquor slow"), the antithesis to, the rejection of, progress; their retrograde character is indicated by slowness, by the fact that they "count" and "reckon" time in terms of natural cycles and

125. *Letters*, p. 306.

126. Faulkner, who comes to mind with "the last bear," may have been prompted by this section of *The Bridge* to write "The Bear." How is it Richard Brautigan missed the reference to " '—For early trouting' "?

127. Also, by way of "ancient clown" and "Chaplinesque," they figure, in a context of authority, as defenseless children.

rhythms, a religious mode, according to the poet, who interjects "—Though they'll confess no rosary nor clue—," an allusion to the faith expressed in "Ave Maria." [128] And yet they are inadequate embodiments of the spiritual liberation to which the poet aspires, for all the imagery of birds ("bird-wit," "sped high," "loose perch") not to be compared with the seagull of "Proem." He recognizes the limitation as well as virtue of their "bird-wit," the fact of their being "blind baggage" and "Blind fists of nothing, humpty-dumpty clods," the profound sadness of a free life which isn't free—caught as it is in the other time, marked by the impurity of history, moved by compulsion—and the arrested development. In the passage where he both most closely identifies with them and rejects them, he places them (with Eliot's help) in the waste land of his childhood; no longer are they associated with the pastoral but with the industrial world, the "empire wilderness of freight and rails" to which the poet's father's cannery, like Crane's, belonged:

> Behind
> My father's cannery works I used to see
> Rail-squatters ranged in nomad raillery,
> The ancient men—wifeless or runaway
> Hobo-trekkers that forever search
>
>   . . . .
>
> Each seemed a child, like me, on a loose perch,
> Holding to childhood like some termless play.

In this waste-land world of men, the presence and threat of the father are strongly felt. He, not Dame Van Winkle, is the scourge of these Rip Van Winkles ("wifeless or runaway") who pass the time in much the same way as Rip did at Nicholas Vedder's, though their "nomad raillery," perhaps because of the pun, is forced rather than pleasantly spontaneous; and the poet voices the father's disapproval in "Blind fists of nothing, humpty-dumpty clods"— the last phrase itself full of the threats and fears of childhood. Homelessness and insecurity—the necessity of holding on—are what the poet identifies with: the feeling of orphanage born of the

128. In respect to the Machine, their dilemma is like that of the poet, for whom the wires "strung to a vast precision" may suggest, and compromise, the symbol of the bridge.

double need to cling and yield, to keep the good ("termless [time-less] play") of childhood and to give it up for work, the up-and-doing of manhood.[129] And he identifies with these child-men because, like him, they "forever search" for the mother whose absence, notable in this stanza, becomes presence in the two stanzas that follow.

The verses move with the poet's argument, in slow periods of alternating realism and sentiment, and now these desperate men are said to "*have touched her, knowing her without name. . . .*" Lacking that knowledge, they are blind (powerless to create a vision), yet they touch and "lurk," as the blind do, and represent the contact—return to sources—that may be redemptive in the "telegraphic night": "Yet they touch something like a key perhaps. / From pole to pole across the hills, the states / —They know a body under the wide rain. . . ." And now, for the first time in *The Bridge*, the great valley of the continent (from the Rockies to the Smokies, from the Dakotas to Louisiana) is delineated as a woman, an "immensity" that contains them (they are not lost) and whose "breast" they know.

"Body" and images of contact ("her body bare," "I knew her body") are conspicuous, in keeping with the sexual import of "trod" in "As I have trod the rumorous midnights, too," the initial line of a passage describing the poet's imaginative possession of Pocahontas. One tends to place the experience in the poet's youth rather than in an immediate past because he introduces it in an old-fashioned romantic way, vaguely reminiscent of Poe (the midnight, the "circuit of the lamp's thin flame," the parenthetical exclamation). But it may be the latter, or both, the romantic being merely a way of acceptably revealing the poet's eroticism. Unlike the hobos with whose experience the poet compares his own, his is not one of actual contact with the land but of imagination or memory, contained within the "rumorous midnight" of his room and prompted by his reading and the sounds from without. For them the land may be said to evoke the female, for him the female to evoke the land. The night, of course, is "rumorous" of her—one recalls

129. "Loose perch," an appropriate spot for men of "bird-wit," may call up Ishmael, another orphan and wanderer, by way of "loose fish." See *Moby-Dick*, ch. 89.

Crane's attempt on returning home to write a poem "about a child hearing his parents quarreling in the next room at midnight" —and what the poet hears in the sounds of trains has as much to do with his as with the American past.[130] The "wail" of the trains in the blizzard recalls the "beshrouded wails" of "The Harbor Dawn" and the situation of that poem. The "wail" belongs to her "distances"—"distances I knew were hers," the poet says, the line conveying a knowledge like that of the syntactically similar "I knew her body there. . . ." And it becomes, in a rising series, the crying of a child (of papooses, linked also to the Indian world by the equestrian imagery, though the imagery is more significant for the sense of loneliness it awakens) and the screaming of the child that, syntactically, belongs also to the "redskin dynasties," the terror of whose warfare, or extermination, provides an image of both the child's hysteria and imagination of sexuality. These, he says, are "dead echoes"—the still-sounding echoes of the past, of that time (those wonderful "Nights" of childhood) when he "knew her body there [bare]," when, to be comforted, the screaming child had perhaps been "brought" to its mother's bed. Then, in infancy, he had known her, "Time like a serpent down her shoulder, dark, / And space, an eaglet's wing, laid on her hair." Then he had been one with her, consummately so, even though the image of the "lamp's thin flame," to be compared with the fiery dance of the next section, already evoked by the "redskin dynasties," tells us it was with the ineffectual passion of a child.[131]

The poet's concern with sources, his recognition that the echoes he has heard belong to his deepest being, to the unconscious, is of more importance than his imputed awareness of *"the myths of her fathers"* in the following stanza on the "old gods" dozing in pools under the Ozarks, though the reference to myth contains the clue he will take up in "The Dance." [132] The poem works on its stated level, but not well enough; and after the memorable stanza on

130. *Letters*, p. 39 (April 26, 1920). In his boyhood and youth, Crane often traveled by train with his mother.

131. Crane's workmanship is so close that one suspects him of using the lamp in contrast to the Mazda light bulb. Here, as elsewhere—with "key," for example —the obviousness troubles one.

132. "Under" and "below," which describe layers of history that are coeval in time, also describe the psyche.

childhood it falters because the poet is unable to push the poem any farther in that direction and resorts to folk materials more sentimental—and awkwardly, more loosely composed—than those of the early stanzas. The genuine sense of the deepest, hidden levels of experience, of the kind of consciousness or unconsciousness involved in myth (the "dark gods" of Lawrence, their natural elemental power injured by "iron," if not castrated, driven underground), is weakened by our disbelief—the gods are not so easily propitiated—and by the enormity of "eatage" in the rhyme "eatage-cleavage." Less bad but no less disturbing is the consistent chiming rhyme of the next stanza, where the poet returns to the initial level of meditation on trains and tramps.

In the morning hours (the profoundest parts of the poem occur at night) the train reaches the Mississippi, where, like the Ohio and other tributaries, it merges with the larger flow of history. This essential work the verses accomplish at much expense: the image of the iron giant, the folklore of railroad and river, the appeals to the passengers to sense the River's presence and, having done so, to acknowledge the common fate. Yet even more than the invitation to "gaze . . . below" and "hum *Deep River*" (the theme song, the "liquid theme" of liberating the spirit from slavery and death), the Chaplinesque image of the "ancient clown" confronted by "Authority" provides the transition to the celebrated concluding quatrains.

For the train, by bringing the poet to the River, confronts him with limitation and prompts his despairing vision of history and human life. Having seen his childhood self in the hobo (as, earlier, he had identified the punishment of social displacement with the Negro), the River for him has the special import of victimage. To be arrested, or out of time, like the hobos, does not spare one the defeat of time: "Down, down . . . / They win no frontier by their wayward plight, / But drift in stillness. . . ." Time brings them down, and they can no more win their goal (the frontier, the pristine mother) in time than the poet can by growing up. Time defeats this dream, "spends" it— and them. For they experience the death—the loss and powerlessness—of self ("What are you, lost, within this tideless spell?") and do not find, as the echo of "Repose of Rivers" suggests ("You will not hear it as the sea"), any recompense at the end. They suffer the unredemptive "Passion" of history, are "tortured" by it because they must not only share it, but, in sharing the common fate, recapitulate it. Thus they become their "father's father" and know the sexual "passion" (marvelously described in geological terms) of the Father of Waters, the great despoiler, spender, of the continent. They must acknowledge the jungle sexuality of advancing life—their sexuality—which is attributed to them in the illusions to De Soto: not only in "one whose eyes were buried long ago," which refers to the spending of his dream, but in the opening "Down, down," which, levying on Williams' account of De Soto's contest with the "She" of the continent and the evocation of his death ("Down, down, this solitary sperm . . ."), connects sexuality (the desire to possess America) with death.[133] Sexuality: this, for the poet, is one of the horrors of time, of growing up, of adult awareness—a fact of his condition that he faces directly in "National Winter Garden" but still cannot happily accept. And so history, now like a dying old man raising himself from bed, comes to an *end*, meets the "Gulf" (gulf), finds "No embrace . . . but the stinging sea. . . ."

What the poet desires cannot be won in time, not, at least, by the masculine imperatives of conquest and success which fill this vision of history. He does not assent to the kind of masculinity associated with the train and with industrialism—with his father's world.[134] The "ticking dream," the dream of time, spends one meaninglessly in a "Passion" that does not, to recall the goal of "Legend," win "the bright logic." But he has another dream. As Crane explained to Mrs. Simpson, "The River" opens "the door

133. In commenting on *In the American Grain*, Williams remembered that "the chapter on De Soto was used by Hart Crane in 'The Bridge'—he took what he wanted, why shouldn't he—that's what writing is for." *I Wanted to Write a Poem: The Autobiography of the Works of a Poet*, reported and edited by Edith Heal (Boston: Beacon Press, 1958), p. 43. Williams overlooked Crane's other borrowings: from ch. 9 of *The Great American Novel*, where De Soto figures again, and, perhaps of most importance, from "The Wanderer," where the poet is baptized in history, in the "filthy Passaic": "Again into the older experiences, / And so backward and forward, / It tortured itself within me. . . ."

134. The masculine stress of this section is announced in the play on the Trinity: Father, Son. . . .

to the pure Indian world. . . ." [135] This is the world of "The Dance"—of poetry.

The journey back, when seen under the aspect of the feminine in "The Dance," is a journey to the beginning rather than to the end, to an awareness (such as will again have to be achieved in "Cape Hatteras") of ever-recurring life, not nihilistic death. To reach the pure Indian world is to come to the sacred center, the source of life—and poetry. Crane was never more sure or true to the intensity of his own art than when he named this section of the poem, for, as Susanne Langer says, "in a world perceived as a realm of mystic Powers, the first created image is the dynamic image; the first objectification of human nature, the first true art, is Dance." [136] The realm of the dance is the symbol-making realm, the realm of creation, of the first created images. Here the root metaphors of human consciousness are born of immediate, seminal contact with the world—here, as the gloss note reminds the returning traveler, *"you shall see her truly—your blood remembering its first invasion of her secrecy. . . ."*

By going back the poet fulfills a profound wish: he enters a world where sexuality—the generative process enacted in the corn dance, the hierogamy of vegetation myth—is one with poetry, the birth of song.[137] He discovers the "infancy" of language, when, as Emerson observed, "it is all poetry; or, all spiritual facts are represented by natural symbols." [138] But in entering this mythic world (using, as Crane explained, the symbols the Indian himself would have understood),[139] the poet identifies with the Indian because he represents best all that being a man and a poet means for him. In this section, as elsewhere, the poet treats history as the "apologue or parable of [his] being and becoming"; [140] he chooses to treat this

135. *Letters*, p. 303 (July 4, 1927).

136. *Problems of Art: Ten Philosophical Lectures* (New York: Charles Scribner's Sons, 1957), p. 12.

137. Williams commented on the "superb corn dance of the Chippewas [that] symbolizes the generative processes" in *In the American Grain*, p. 157.

138. *The Complete Works of Ralph Waldo Emerson*, I, 29.

139. *Letters*, p. 307.

140. *The Complete Works of Ralph Waldo Emerson*, II, 66. See also "History": "If the whole of history is in one man, it is all to be explained from individual experience" (p. 4).

episode of prehistory as a parable of "Manhood"—that is, of voca-
tion. The Indian enables him to tell of the origin, vision-quest, and
sacrificial office of the poet. The sachem–medicine man stands for
a different conception of manhood than that evoked by Cortes or
the captain of industry, or for that matter by Rip Van Winkle and
the hobos; he is not unlike but more mature than the chivalrous
poet of the early poems. With him the poet moves over the con-
tinent in a different manner—his discovering is life-giving, not
death-dealing—and undergoes a Passion of a different kind than
that of "The River." The Indian vindicates the poet; he fulfills
the conditions that Crane set down in "Legend." And though he
suffers a ritual marriage-death very much in keeping with the poet's
fearful imagination of sexuality, the ritual—the dance—represents
the poetic act, and the poet's recognition of the eros of imagina-
tion, the fact that for him poetry is profoundly sexual in origin and
end, is his only way of knowing the mother and of having his
being at the heart of the world.

The masculine and feminine elements of the cosmos figure im-
mediately in the question with which the poet begins the poem:
"The swift red flesh, a winter king— / Who squired the glacier
woman down the sky?" They introduce the first three stanzas, in
which the poet's mythic awareness of the still-active vegetative
process speeds him—in a way other than that of the railroad:
arrow-like, arcing like a bridge—from the waste-land present, which
here seems past, to the mythic past, which becomes present. With
the six concluding stanzas, concerned also with the poet's present,
but deepened, awareness of the hierogamy genteelly alluded to in
"squired," they frame and insist on the recurrence of the central
mythic narrative. This the poet makes his own by means of identifi-
cation and the telling—and it is his myth, the paradigm of the
journey of "Powhatan's Daughter," which he can here—how secure
his formal means!—confidently celebrate.

Like the poet of "The Harbor Dawn," the Indian has known a
bride of whom he must now go in search. Her virginity belongs
to the winter season, the season of "The Harbor Dawn" and of
the poet's memory of his mother in "Van Winkle" and "The
River," and much of the poem is recalled in "bed," "broken play,"
"veil," and "virgin May" (a pun on Virgin Mary). Mother as well

as bride, she is the "glacier woman," the earth in its winter with-
drawal or death (hence lost), whom the Indian must discover and
waken into life. That is the task and trial of his manhood: the
function of the dance, as of poetry, is to make the unresponsive
earth, the North Labradorian mother, "answer," to call the world
into speech and thus redeem its nothingness ("High unto Labrador
the sun [son?] strikes free / Her speechless dream of snow").[141]

The Indian's journey from east to west represents the course of
the sun, of the natural seasons and those of human and Indian
tribal life. In his youth, the vernal time, he enjoys her streams
(the "neighing canyons," the "torrent," of other stanzas); he knows
her in her youth as well as his, innocently, romantically, in her
lunar aspect (as Diana, chaste, "fleet," but not, as in classic myth,
unmoved by love). He experiences a playful love like that of the
beginning of "Voyages II" ("What laughing chains the water
wove and threw!") and a sense of cosmicity such as Thoreau knew
when drifting on Walden Pond and fishing for the stars ("I learned
to catch the trout's moon whisper; I / Drifted how many hours I
never knew"). But this period of happy dependence ("laughing
chains"), of unconscious union, passes with the waning of the
moon; passively ("watching") he sees his loss in her withdrawal,
when, more likely, as the image of the moth joined with the star
"swinging . . . alone" suggests, it is he who, under the imperative
of growth, like the moth of Crane's earliest poem, has "take[n]
wing." In any case, this moment of recognition of lost innocence
and separation is marked by a sign, the single, lonely star (already
in the poet's dream of "The Harbor Dawn") whose bleeding into
dawn portends the Indian's destiny, his Passion and apotheosis.[142]

With the advent of manhood the Indian undertakes a more
arduous journey into the world, an ascent reminiscent of Thoreau's

141. As with William Carlos Williams, discovery has sexual meaning. The gloss
note speaks of the *"invasion of her secrecy. . . ."*

In the Orphic sense, the function of poetry is to call the world into being. "Gesang
ist Dasein" ("Song is being"), Rilke's statement in the third poem of *Sonnets to
Orpheus*, applies also to Crane's awareness of the nature of poetic activity. See Gerald
L. Bruns, "Poetry as Reality: The Orpheus Myth and Its Modern Counterparts,"
ELH, XXXVII (June, 1970), 263–88.

142. I speak of "Passion" because of its use in "The River" and its depiction in
"Legend" and "Lachrymae Christi."

in *A Week*, to the source, the "Appalachian Spring!" ("One white veil gusted from the very top" and "inaccessible smile"—a geographical description of the curving mountain range, referred to in "The River" in "yonder breast"—again identify it with the mother.) By ascending the mountain, Thoreau was rewarded with a vision (literal enough) of the pure upper world in which he wished to have his being; the Indian, too, is rewarded by a "wonder-breathing" experience that certifies his vision-quest. By exposing himself to the elements (the "mystic Powers") and by yielding to their rhythms ("the padded foot / Within,—I heard it; 'til its rhythm drew"), he becomes one with them; and by means of this intense experience (his world is magical: "wisped of azure wands") he both envisions and enacts the titanic—thunderous, cyclonic, volcanic—storm that constitutes the Passion it will become his destiny to fulfill. The experience of the vision-quest purifies him ("Siphoned the black pool from the heart's hot root!"), identifies him ("Know, Maquokeeta, greeting"), and gives him his mission ("know death's best"). To this point the mythic actuality of the poem is impressive: for both the Indian and the poet, the vision experience creates its own reality.

The Indian's office, like the poet's, is to "restore," to summon the powers of renewal by the ritual enactment in the dance of the process of death-and-life, destruction-and-creation. He is enjoined to dance at the moment of the storm's most destructive fury. "Restore" is yoked to "relent": by means of the dance he is to initiate change, the metamorphosis attributed to his snakelike nature ("casts his pelt") and demanded in the ritual cries of "Sprout, horn! / Spark, tooth!" His office is to "Lie to us" only in the sense that the dance itself, an effective agency, is, the poet knows, as impermanent as poetry or myth or religion. But in a culture where its agency is accepted—where natural and human powers are believed to be inseparable—it is possible to "dance us back the tribal morn!" The phrase, the opening for so much doubt about the efficacy of the "myth" of *The Bridge*, is no more inadvertent than the imagery of industrialism and industrial agriculture in "A cyclone threshes in the turbine crest," and the difficulties it raises are probably due to Crane's predilection for compressing meanings rather than to modern skepticism about what the poem is doing. These troublesome phrases merely call attention to one of the themes Crane wished to treat in "The Dance": the "conflict of the two races" and the "extinction of the Indian," a historical event that the Indians themselves, even as they prepare to meet it, recognize as inalterable.[143]

By identifying with the Indian, the poet identifies with his defeat as well as with the sacrifice by which Pocahontas, the Earth Mother, is served. He sees himself as sacrificial victim, and what he fights is represented by the tribe (society) itself. This is the point in the poem at which he calls attention to his identification with the Indian ("I, too, was liege"), an act, interestingly, of separation that permits him to double the intensity of the experience by observing it for us ("I heard . . . ," "I saw . . .") in the spirit of Whitman's "I am the man, I suffer'd, I was there." [144] The social dimension of the ritual asks us to note his resistance, the death by fire at the stake by which he "Surpassed the circumstance, danced out the siege!"—and to note also that this is a ritual of atonement for some "sin," perhaps the sexual violence of the storm in stanza fourteen, which, again, represents not only the consummation of an earlier phase of Maquokeeta's dance but the jungle warfare of the races and the ruthless extermination of the Indian in the Darwinian century.[145] Sexual trespass, however, is the prominent feature, dramatized by the retribution demanded by "Spears and assemblies" and the "black drums thrusting on," the latter recalling the "black pool at the heart's hot root." And though the Indian's immolation is erotic, it is also the Passion which purifies and spiritually translates him, a death he willingly accepts. In this ecstatic consummation, the Indian fulfills the destiny foretold in his youth, becomes the star that "bled into the dawn." He spends himself out (to use the applicable words of "Legend") and, purified by this sexual yet purgatively redemptive act, can "kiss" the destiny he desires, the "bright logic" depicted here in the "one white meteor, sacrosanct and blent / At last with all that's consummate and free. . . ." Like the gull's "inviolate curve" in "Proem," the

143. *Letters*, p. 307.

144. "Song of Myself," § 33.

145. The ritual is composed of several rituals, just as the Indian, tribally speaking, is many Indians, from the eastern seaboard to the southwestern desert.

meteor's plunge traces the spirit's deepest motion, the desire for absolute freedom (he has become the "moon / Of his own fate") and for absolute homecoming—"There" (in the timeless precincts of pure being), "where the first and last gods keep thy tent." Like the "curveship" of the bridge, it is the signature of the mythic consciousness—the imagination— that redeems time.

And so it is in the concluding stanzas, where the poet, in the present, addresses the star, the eternal witness of history—of fallen Indian and rising modern civilization—and of natural recurrence, the "infinite seasons" that restore Maquokeeta's "bride immortal in the maize!" Freedom from the limiting perspective of time: that is the gift granted by the Indian's ritual attendance on Pocahontas, by the vision-quest and the fulfillment of its behest ("know death's best"), both of which are recalled in "path thou knewest best to claim her by." Imaginatively, the poet, too, has followed these paths—they are the paths of poetry—and now, in the finest stanzas of the poem, he experiences as his own, in a natural language warming into the loveliness of the "Song of Solomon," the living presence, the immortal, inviolable bride vouchsafed by myth:

> High unto Labrador the sun strikes free
> Her speechless dream of snow, and stirred again,
> She is the torrent and the singing tree;
> And she is virgin to the last of men . . .
>
> West, west and south! winds over Cumberland
> And winds across the llano grass resume
> Her hair's warm sibilance. Her breasts are fanned
> O stream by slope and vineyard—into bloom!

In this landscape—it is his equivalent of the "gleaming fields and pendant seething wheat" of "Ave Maria"—myth takes the lineaments of his deepest wish. He frees the North Labradorian ice, transforms the "glacier woman" into a blooming bride and a warm, responsive, nourishing mother whom the winds of his creative spirit give voice. And for him the reality is so powerfully present, he wonders if, in fact, the Indian is still not there, in union with his bride, "her perfect brows to thine?" This vision, which the concluding stanza tells us is consummatory for the poet, is what the dance of poetry realizes for him. This is what poetry, the work of his manhood, makes possible, the achievement of the "strong prayer." And so he can now legitimately claim identity with Maquokeeta:

> We danced, O Brave, we danced beyond their farms,
> In cobalt desert closures made our vows . . .
> Now is the strong prayer folded in thine arms,
> The serpent with the eagle in the boughs.

The last line reminds us of the intimate memory, in the previous section, beyond which the poet could not go, and it points ahead to the closing lines of *The Bridge*, where the images of serpent and eagle figure again in a passage as conclusive as this one, the pinnacle of the poem.

With "Indiana"—its name still resonant of the previous section —we return to time, re-enter history. Historically, "Indiana" treats another episode of the westward movement, one that evokes the trek overland ("wagon-tenting," "the long team line") at the same time as it reveals, by restricting the narrative to the gold rush, the unworthy goal in which Columbus' vision reached an end. "Indiana" does not take us to the "Golden Gate"—Colorado is far enough—and it makes another music than that of the "gold arpeggios" the poet hears in "Van Winkle," as the opening image of the morning glory (pun) "furl[ing] in its song" at dusk tells us it will. Delusion and failure are the burden of its song, and the kind of resignation for which the Robinsonian touchstone is "We found God lavish there in Colorado / But passing sly." The backtrailing ("The long trail back") is also of historical importance, representing a terminus for the old but a beginning for the young—the second pioneering and hope of true possession, as Waldo Frank had said in *Our America*, in terms of the frontiers of art.

For the poet, who identifies with Larry, the departing son to whom the mother speaks in this ballad-like monologue, history has as much personal significance as it does in "The River." His westward journey, or return, discovers a mother to whom neither the gloss note ("*and read her in a mother's farewell gaze*") nor her account of maternal acknowledgment by the squaw transfers the erotic values he seeks in Pocahontas.[146] Though the sentimentality of the poem may be attributed to her, the emotional deadness is also his, for his journey has been no more successful than hers. The pioneer mother does not approximate his ideal and fails him, betrays the Columbian dream for which he must now search elsewhere. In depicting her, he reveals the troubled source of his poetic quest.

That this accounts for Crane's difficulty with the poem does not seem unwarranted. He told Otto Kahn, in September 1927, that this section of the poem was "well-nigh done." [147] But it was not completed until the final work of composition two years later, and then its scenario was altered in the most significant way. Originally, the monologue was to be that of the farmer; now it became his wife's. This change better fitted the theme of "Powhatan's Daughter," and it balanced the masculine-dominated "The River" with a feminine correlative. The latter, however, subverts the former, for the mother is a figure of history, a tributary of time, and, as much as the father, an exponent of westering success. The imagery of her monologue—"claims to stake," for example—recalls "The River," and in her reiterated "too late" we hear the admonition of "Van Winkle" and remember that Rip fled the importunity of his wife (or mother, since he is more child than man).

Now the difficulty Crane had with both versions of the poem—a difficulty increased by his honesty and awareness of the poem's importance—is due to its theme: a son's farewell, his leaving home. The first version may allude to his break with his father in 1922–23, though the unenthusiastic account of the poem in the letter to Kahn suggests its irresolution. This is not the case with the completed version because the change in narrator accommodates the more conclusive break with his mother in 1928. Like Grace Crane, the mother of "Indiana" is under the ambivalent sign of gold. She has gone west, as Grace Crane had gone to Hollywood, a "visionary" in pursuit of an illusion ("A dream called Eldorado was his [God's] town"); now she is old and defeated—has lost her dream, her husband, her son. The parallel with Grace Crane is evident also

146. See Whitman's "The Sleepers" for the anecdote of the squaw.
147. *Letters*, p. 307.

in the portrait of a woman self-pitying ("I'm standing still, I'm old, I'm half of stone!"), reproachful ("As once my womb was torn, my boy, when you / Yielded your first cry"), possessive ("First-born, remember— / . . . —all that's left to me of Jim"), and curiously uncertain of her relation to her son ("You, Larry, traveller — / stranger, / son, / —my friend—").[148] From what we know of Grace Crane, the portrayal is just, perhaps cruel but not vindictive.

For there is, as William Carlos Williams noted, "sweetness . . . and great charm in *Indiana*. . . ."[149] And Crane projects the poet's deepest necessity in the last desperate plea of the pioneer mother ("Oh, hold me in those eyes' engaging blue; / There's where the stubborn years gleam and atone,— / Where gold is true!"; "Write me from Rio . . . and you'll keep your pledge; / I know your word!") and in her declaration of constancy ("oh, I shall always wait"). Her plea recalls that of the poet to his lover in "Voyages III" and especially "Voyages IV," and this may explain better than "race," which Crane offered as a reason, why he thought that, "observed in the proper perspective, and judged in relation to the argument or theme of the Pocahontas section as a whole, the pioneer woman's maternalism isn't excessive."[150] Her maternalism is the counterpart of the poet's need, expressed in his memories of childhood, to hold on. And the mother asks of her son to become for him what Crane actually made of his mother: an ideal, the true gold of the "gleaming fields" envisioned by Columbus. By the end of "Powhatan's Daughter," not Pocahontas but the mother, for whom she has all this time been surrogate, emerges, even speaks, giving him his role. To her, we feel, he gives his "pledge" and "word," while she assuringly promises an ultimate haven. But the dominant presence of the mother also makes us aware of the poet's earlier imaginative violation of the inviolable (when Crane spoke of "race" perhaps he had in mind the transformation of dark into light lady that maternity as well as the presence here of the white pioneer woman achieves). She is the goal of the search, an object never to be possessed; and even though she is not depicted as want-

148. For further comment, see my review of *Voyager* in *JEGP*, LXIX (April, 1970), 326.
149. "Hart Crane (1899–1932)," p. 4.
150. *Letters*, pp. 357–58 (November 21, 1930).

ing in love, her love is "Too lichen-faithful," to cite the complaint of "Voyages I," and the son must leave her as had the poet the mother of that poem—must "drop the scythe [associated with the "gleaming fields"] to grasp the oar. . . ." Nothing is of greater consequence to the poet than leaving home, that is, the imaginative world of "Powhatan's Daughter," for the wider, fearful world represented by the sea and by contemporary industrial urban (eastern) life. That is where we find him at the beginning of *The Bridge* and that is where we find him in turning to "Cutty Sark"; and what has intervened may be read as explanation, for as Crane told Otto Kahn, "this section ["Indiana"] is psychologically a summary of 'Powhatan's Daughter' in its entirety." [151]

The structure of *The Bridge* indicates a turning: from the most extensive, deeply cherished section, a world primarily of dream and memory closely knit and threaded by gloss notes, to the many subsequent sections, the episodes, or fragments, of the poet's journey-quest in the modern world. "Cutty Sark," the title of the third section, calls us to sea (and to sailing ships and drink), and its epigraph from Melville's "The Temeraire" provides us an exact resonance to the poet's nostalgia for the past he is about to relinquish as well as readies us for the "derelict sailor," [152] whose story and situation tell us what we need to know of this interval in history. The old sailor is Larry briefly come to port, a Bulkington still in search of the gleaming fields beyond ("I can't live on land—!"); and, as Jean Guiguet says, "This old Melvillean sailor— and perhaps Coleridgean also—is a double of the poet, and his encounter is without doubt more important as an interior adventure than as a fortuitous exterior coincidence." [153] With his talk of Leviathan, of the "spiracle," of the whiteness that killed his time, the sailor is clearly Melvillean, a son of *The Pequod*. But he has been on other nineteenth-century voyages, that of *The Ancient Mariner* as well as those of Poe's *The Narrative of Arthur Gordon Pym* and Baudelaire's "Le Voyage." The latter, in fact, is as important to the poem as *Moby-Dick*, for its references to Eldorado

---

151. Cited by Dembo, *Hart Crane's Sanskrit Charge*, p. 82.
152. *Letters*, p. 307.
153. *L'Univers poétique de Hart Crane*, p. 86; my translation.

and the Promised Land connect directly to "Indiana" and much of it recalls the Columbian theme. The derelict sailor is the drunken sailor (for good reason) who, Baudelaire said, was an "inventor of Americas"—"Ce matelot ivrogne, inventeur d'Amériques / Dont le mirage rend le gouffre plus amer?" There is also a Baudelairean concern with time and eternity ("Berçant notre infini sur le fini des mers"), and the poem itself, in which Crane said that "the old man of the sea (page Herr Freud) suddenly comes up," may have been suggested by the third part of "Le Voyage":

> . . . quelles nobles histoires
> Nous lisons dans vos yeux profonds comme les mers!
> Montrez-nous les écrins de vos riches mémoires,
> Les bijoux merveilleux, faits d'astres et d'éthers.
> . . . .
> Dites, qu'avez-vous vu? [154]

Toward the sailor, whom he befriends, the poet's attitude partakes very little of Baudelaire's irony, though the poem itself is intrinsically ironic. His attitude is more compassionate—one thinks of the projective sympathy of "The Wine Menagerie"—partly because the sailor is his double, and it is more philosophical after the fashion of Melville, whose conclusion to "The Fountain" (chapter 85 of *Moby-Dick*, referred to by "spiracle") provides the theme developed fugally in the poem: "Doubts of all things earthly, and intuitions of some things heavenly; this combination makes

---

154. Translations by Edna St. Vincent Millay are:
> Mad, drunken tar, inventor of Americas . . .
> Which, fading, make the void more bitter, more abhorred.
> * * *
> Cradling our infinite upon the finite sea. . . .
> * * *
> . . . —your eyes
> Are deep as the sea's self; what stories they withhold!
> Open for us the chest of your rich memories!
> Show us those treasures, wrought of meteoric gold!
> . . . .
> Tell us, what have you seen?

Robert Lowell's rendering, in *Imitations*, brings out the meaning of the first line: "discovering new Americas." His translation, incidentally, seems to be mediated by his reading of Crane. For "Herr Freud," see *Letters*, p. 268 (July 29, 1926).

neither believer nor infidel, but makes a man who regards them both with equal eye." Being double, the poet entertains his skepticism and faith, his Melvillean despair and his Whitmanian hope; he is true to the complexity of his experience.

The poet's "interior adventure" takes place past midnight, in the "cooler hell" of a waterfront saloon. It is vaguely reminiscent of Ishmael's adventures in New Bedford and, like it, is a prelude to what follows. Here he meets a man whose presence, marked by height, "a nervous shark tooth," and conspicuous distant green eyes, is surrealist in quality. He *is* the old man of the sea and he bears its stigma. A sailor of another time—another left-over—he has, like Ahab and Pip in *Moby-Dick* and Kurtz in *Heart of Darkness*, been spiritually destroyed by the horrible experience to which the sea admitted him.[155] Now, moved to speech by the song of the mechanical piano, whose lyric expresses the deepest wishes of both men and accompanies the movement of reminiscence, he relates the essential episodes of a journey to nihilism. The most important episode, prompted by the song started by "somebody's [Rip's] nickel" in the pianola, from the pun on wing in "*Ala*"(on consummate freedom: gull and sailing ship; and on its loss: the albatross of Coleridge and Melville), and from the play on "time" ("sails *on* time," "*beating* time," "*keep* time") [156]—the most important episode concerns the overwhelming experience of eternity, of an icy white vastness that for him as for Ishmael "shadows forth the heartless voids and immensities of the universe, and thus stabs us from behind with the thought of annihilation. . . ." [157] "That / damned white Arctic killed my time," he says, with just enough similarity in cadence to remind us of "dat ole davil, sea," the refrain of Eugene O'Neill's *Anna Christie* (1921). But for the poet, who perhaps has all the while followed his own reverie on "*rose*" ("*dreams weave the rose!*") and who is after all in a waterfront

155. On sharks—and the cannibalism of life—there is considerable comment in *Moby-Dick*, Queequeg's remark fixing its drift: "de god wat made shark must be one dam Ingin" (ch. 66). Eliot called attention to Conrad's story in the epigraph to "The Hollow Men" (1925), and Fitzgerald, in *The Great Gatsby* (1925), characterized Wolfsheim not only by his name but by his cuff buttons made of human molars. Darkness in Crane has Conradian reverberations.

156. My italics.

157. *Moby-Dick*, ch. 42 ("The Whiteness of the Whale").

section like that of "The Harbor Dawn," only, as is fitting at this stage in his journey, on the other side of the Brooklyn Bridge, the sailor's talk tells of his own North Labradorian experience, of a "glacier woman," unanswering, beyond his powers of stirring to speech.

This double nature pertains to the subsequent elements of the sailor's story. Prompted by *"drums,"* he tells of working in tropical, primitive Central America. But running the donkey engine on the Canal (the Passage to India) and selling kitchenware in Yucatán (whose native population is Mayan) have confirmed rather than lifted his despair. He is a waste lander for whom there are no saving illusions. The very myth of the plumed serpent that *"drums"* evokes for the poet of "The Dance" means nothing to him: "have you seen Popocatepetl—birdless mouth / with ashes sifting down—?" [158]

The way in which "Cutty Sark" serves as a portmanteau section, as resumé and prefigurement, is evident most in what follows the longest portion of song:

> *Rose of Stamboul O coral Queen—*
> *teased remnants of the skeleton of cities—*
> *and galleries, galleries of watergutted lava*
> *snarling stone—green—drums—drown__*

Crane identifies the song with the voice of eternity and with the theme of Atlantis.[159] In this instance and that of the song's conclusion both "The Tunnel" and "Atlantis" are clearly prefigured. The image of *"watergutted lava"* as well as the sequence of *"green–drums–drown"* tells the sailor's course and fate, only, as happens here, the "machine that sings" may start something else. The image of the "Rose," now connected with "Queen," prompts the ejaculation (*"Sing!"*) that stands apart from the sequence to which it may belong and in immediate relation to the sailor's exclamation, " '—that spiracle!' " And this takes us back to another aspect of Melville's chapter on "The Fountain," Ishmael's reflections on mist and rainbows: "For, d'ye see, rainbows do not visit

158. For Crane's use of Amerindian myths, see Deena Posy Metzger, "Hart Crane's *Bridge*: The Myth Active," *Arizona Quarterly*, XX (Spring, 1964), 36–46.

159. *Letters*, p. 307.

the clear air; they only irradiate vapor." In conjunction with the sailor's protestation (" 'I can't live on land—!' ") and the subsequent image of the risen Atlantis ("ATLANTIS ROSE"), what may be said to be woven (*"dreams weave the rose!"*) is an image of the "lovely leewardings" that moved Ahab and that the poet of "Voyages" called "Belle Isle."

This maternal development of the theme of eternity is verified and glossed by the poet:

> I saw the frontiers gleaming of his mind;
> or are there frontiers—running sands sometimes
> running sands—somewhere—sands running . . .
> Or they may start some white machine that sings.
> Then you may laugh and dance the axletree—
> steel—silver—kick the traces—and know—
>
> ATLANTIS ROSE. . . .

The frontiers of his mind, that to which the sailor is compelled, unite the "gleaming fields" of "Ave Maria" and the pioneer mother's injunction to her son to hold her in "those eyes' engaging blue," where, she says, "the stubborn years gleam and atone. . . ." But the dream of the rose, already compromised by the suggestive title of the song—"Stamboul Nights"—is, as the fable of Atlantis and other testimony of quest also indicate, never to be realized. Aware of this, the poet's thought recovers the sailor's despair and nihilism. An image of the sands of time, their "running" reiterated, fills his mind—an image of the vortex, of the sands in "Passage" that "troughed us in a glittering abyss," of the "dead sands flashing" of "Voyages V." And yet, as the sailor's response shows, this death-dealing experience (*"drown"*) "may start some white machine that sings"—may liberate one from the "traces" of time into a cosmic-centered ecstatic motion of being, the condition declared in *"Sing!"* Evoked by "steel—silver—," that gloriously white machine is the bridge, invoked in "Proem" and celebrated in "Atlantis" and alluded to in "ATLANTIS ROSE." The bridge is centered movement (dance) and song, and the radiant being both express and call into being; and it is not only a machine that sings but what it sings (" 'Make thy love sure—to weave whose song we ply!' ").[160] Poetry, woven as it is woven here and throughout *The Bridge*, is the machine that sings and, for the poet, makes being possible, creates a welcome space even in the abyss of time. In Baudelaire's words ("Berçant notre infini sur le fini des mers"), it "cradles our infinite upon the finite sea," summoning both the consoling meaning of Whitman's "Out of the Cradle Endlessly Rocking" and the bitter meanings (of "berçant") of vain hopes and deceitful nurture. The occasion of poetry is doubt and despair, and the poet does not deny the brevity of its conquest. The song stops abruptly. There is a consummatory moment when, as in "The Dance," the furious ecstasy of dance and song pushes back the vortex or claims it for its own: "ATLANTIS ROSE *drums wreathe the rose.*" But loss and suffering and longing for forgetfulness follow: "*the star floats burning in a gulf of tears / and sleep another thousand—.*" Resumptive and premonitory, these lines are suspended, unhappily broken, like the poet's reverie, for want of a rhyme. Unlike Rip, the poet is not permitted the refuge of sleep and dreams but is reminded of the flat actuality of his situation. (It is represented by the emptiness of the white space on the page.) His facetious remark on the Statue of Liberty ("the dawn / was putting the Statue of Liberty out—that / torch of hers you know—") is a dispirited recognition of all he invoked in "Proem." But, along with the next isolated, lonely line ("I started walking home across the Bridge . . ."), it reminds us of, as it locates us at, the center of the poem. And the bridge does not fail him, even though the vision it affords him, so much in the romantic spirit of "The Bridge of Estador," may be taken for a Rip-like evasion of the present.

For depressed as he is, he is "started" (startled) by his walk upon the bridge and becomes a "machine that sings." And the beautiful poem he sings—Crane called it a "cartogram" and Jean Guiguet calls it a "nostalgic litany"—even as it opens an adventurous space and celebrates the "apparitional . . . sails" of "Proem," is valedictory.[161] It confirms the poet's sympathy with the derelict sailor by evoking the great era of clipper ships but it also adds the poet's emphasis to the "no more!" of the epigraph. He is on his way

160. P, 114.
161. *Letters*, p. 283 (January 7, 1927); *L'Univers poétique de Hart Crane*, pp. 59, 67; my translation.

"home." He is at the center, at the turning. Hereafter, the past is at his back.[162]

Homecoming is told (in the nautical sense) in "Cape Hatteras." The epigraph from "Passage to India" may be read as a gloss note to "Cutty Sark" as well as an advertisement for this and the subsequent sections *of The Bridge.* And "Cutty Sark" may be read as a prologue, rehearsing the theme that the homeward journey enacts —the theme, simply stated, of Melvillean despair and Whitmanian hope, whose resolution is homecoming. What follows "Cutty Sark" is notably spatial—simultaneous—in design. The voyage mentioned at the opening of "Cape Hatteras" is treated again in "Southern Cross," and all of the sections, without regard to time, though not without regard to development, belong to an experience whose spatial presentation may be described as the superimposition of "Cape Hatteras" on "Atlantis." Then the epigraph, fulfilled at the end of "Cape Hatteras" and spoken for again at the end of "The Tunnel," is doubly fulfilled:

> The seas all cross'd, weather'd the capes, the voyage done,
> Surrounded, copest, frontest God, yieldest, the aim attain'd,
> As fill'd with friendship, love complete, the Elder Brother found,
> The Younger melts in fondness in his arms.

Then we have visually represented the kind of liberating yet protected experience Crane associated with the bridge (Bridge): "And I have been able to give freedom and life which was acknowledged in the ecstasy of walking hand in hand across the most beautiful bridge of the world, the cables enclosing us and pulling us upward in such a dance as I have never walked and never can walk with another." [163]

"Cape Hatteras" ("weather'd the capes") is the longest section

162. In instructing Caresse Crosby to place a photograph—by Walker Evans— between "Cutty Sark" and "Cape Hatteras," Crane said, "That is the 'center' of the book, both physically and symbolically." *Letters,* p. 347 (December 26, 1929). The photograph of barges and tugs also indicates the nature of the turning. See Gordon Kay Grigsby, "The Modern Long Poem: Studies in Thematic Form," unpublished doctor's dissertation, University of Wisconsin, 1960, p. 320.

163. *Letters,* p. 181 (April 21, 1924). An indication of how closely this experience was associated with the Bridge and with Whitman are the Whitmanian words, chiefly "answered" and "flood tide" (from "Crossing Brooklyn Ferry").

of *The Bridge,* one of the most ambitious and, in some aspects, one of the least successful. "A kind of ode to Whitman," as Crane said, it follows Whitman's practice of thematic and incremental development and treats "Time and Space and Death," the themes of "Passage to India." [164] But even with its long lines the verse is markedly different from Whitman's perhaps or partly for the reason that Crane could not follow—the reservation is significant—a poet whose "faults as a technician and . . . clumsy and indiscriminate enthusiasm" he admitted. And if this acknowledgment of faults is "somewhat beside the point," as he said in his high estimate of Whitman's achievement,[165] it indicates another constraint: the criticism of Whitman by Tate and other of his friends, the depressing effects of which the poem recalled and forced him to work through. Of all the sections of the poem, this section was a test case; Crane took it up during his stay in France and finished it only under pressure of completing *The Bridge.* This, and the fact that in it he again addressed the aspects of modern civilization— war, machinery, spiritual emptiness—that questioned his faith, may account for much in the texture and tone of the verse (often working from the norm of blank verse) that recalls "Faustus and Helen."

"Cape Hatteras," like "Ave Maria," is better read with Whitman's "Passage to India" in mind. Common to both sections of *The Bridge,* it now helps us recognize in Whitman the poet-discoverer who follows the "great captains and engineers," who, after the futile conquest of space and time and the betrayal of Columbus' morning world, discovers realms of consciousness and justifies the world—the ways of God—to man. Granted his pre-eminent role in the present stage of history, it is fitting that a poet becomes the poet's guide on his journey.[166] And it is fitting, too, that this

---

164. *Letters,* p. 308.

165. P, 263. A more important reason is Whitman's open line and openness. Crane is not confessional in the way of either Whitman or, to provide another measure, Allen Ginsberg. Crane finds himself in tension, perhaps for the reason that, as Robert Lowell says of his need for the difficult and complicated, "more can perhaps be said thrusting through complication." Dudley Young, "Talk with Robert Lowell," *New York Times Book Review* (April 4, 1971), p. 32.

166. How challenging to his critics—and to himself! Originally Crane did not

poet leads him back, for his is a voyage of the soul's homecoming.

In "Cape Hatteras" the poet enters the waste-land world, confronts it, and declares against it. He begins with cosmic darkness and ends by celebrating the light—"Easters of speeding light." In this way the poem enacts Crane's Donnean text, " 'Make my dark poem light, and light.' " [167] Its theme, like that of "Faustus and Helen," is resurrectional; the mystery it addresses is that of death-and-life, Whitman's central concern—and Williams' too, whose last poems, written in awareness of death, "celebrate the light":

> Light, the imagination,
>> and love,
>>> in our age,
>> by natural law,
>>> which we worship,
>>>> maintain
>> all of a piece
>>> their dominance.[168]

The poem—and the act of writing it, living in it—is a gathering of faith. In it, as in "Ave Maria," doubt is transformed, cosmos restored, and the poet is prepared to journey onward into the further dark. And this transformation, in spite of flaws in the verse that suggest strain, is not merely rhetorical; it is a meditative work of possession, comparable to that which filled the poet's dream with Columbus.

The poem opens with a prelude, with a cosmic event spoken of in the present, still in process: phenomena, astral, geological, evolutionary, that qualify—by containing—the space-and-time, world-conquering feats of modern times.[169] Though "ghoul" strikes the motif that figures in the poem, the prelude speaks also for resurrection—for the rainbow that at the close of the poem arches the "Cape's ghoul-mound": the cape sinks while the mountain range

---

sketch this Virgilian role for Whitman, though, by placing him after Columbus and Pocahontas, he suggested his pre-eminence. *Letters*, p. 241.

167. *Letters*, p. 176 (March 1, 1924).

168. "Asphodel, That Greeny Flower," *Pictures from Brueghel and Other Poems* (New York: New Directions, 1962), p. 180. Crane's first notation of Whitman's significance concerns "death, disunity . . . immortality." *Letters*, p. 241.

169. Crane's awareness of the cosmos is one of his distinctions.

rises. But this change brings death to species, like the dinosaur, unable to accommodate it—opens an evolutionary naturalistic vista, even for man with his powers of adaptation, not necessarily auspicious. Change and transformation concern the poet, who has now turned to the present, and his fear of and resistance to them account for the meaninglessness the imagery now conveys. The universe itself is depicted in volcanic terms applicable to the machine ("Combustion at the astral core"), the representative agency of change, chaos, and death in the modern world. And we are suddenly in a world of energies, whose changes are as unaccountable and dreadful to the poet as the "convulsive shift of sand," the vortex of space and void of time they create.

The "but" that introduces the rest of the stanza speaks for another measure of time, for the speed with which we "round the capes," speed by, and overlook the universal and cosmic; it does not alter the logic of feeling. We travel to evade the fearful nothingness of our own cosmic awareness. Our voyage—so Baudelairean —is trivial, a passage to India miscarried, for we recall only the picturesque—"how the priests walked—slowly through Bombay." [170] Yet it brings us home, it is a return; and in this sense the India to which we have taken passage is America. Or so it is for the poet, whose previous verses warrant his confession of Columbian desire:

> knowing us in thrall
>> To that deep wonderment, our native clay
>> Whose depth of red, eternal flesh of Pocahontas—

The poet reads Whitman because he is enthralled by Whitman's theme, identified here with Columbus' "wonder-breathing" discovery of the new world, and because Whitman, the Elder Brother, is—here and in the work of the poem—identified with Pocahontas. But the poet also reads Whitman because Whitman had anticipated him. As Whitman says in "Crossing Brooklyn Ferry," "Others . . . look back on me because I look'd forward to them. . . ." In this miraculous poem, Whitman creates the supreme bridge—demonstrates that "It avails not, time nor place—distance avails not / I am with you. . . ." And the realization of Whitman's presence—

170. "Slowly" calls to mind the hobos in "The River."

What gods can exceed these that clasp me by the hand, and with
voices I love call me promptly and loudly by my nighest name as
I approach?

What is more subtle than this which ties me to the woman or man
that looks in my face?
Which fuses me into you now, and pours my meaning into you?

—the realization of this is what "Cape Hatteras" most successfully
achieves. This, and Whitman's faith that change is not destruction
but an ever-renewing ("Urge and urge and urge, / Always the pro-
creant urge of the world").

The poet accepts Whitman's terms in "Crossing Brooklyn
Ferry." He calls him by his "nighest name," but mostly, at the
start, to tell him of all that has now overlaid the "continental
folded aeons, surcharged / With sweetness," those modern con-
quests of space and time, some already treated in "The River,"
that have not contributed to "love complete" but to the egocentric
predicament of "The Tunnel" ("a labyrinth submersed / Where
each sees only his dim past reversed") and the annihilation—iso-
lation and instrumental reduction—of the self (space, now one
with time, "consumes us with its smile"; man sees himself "an
atom in a shroud" and "hears himself an engine in a cloud!"). As
Joseph Wood Krutch at this time also maintained, in *The Modern
Temper* (1929), science progresses by clarifying—and narrowing—
our sight at the expense of necessary "illusions" and real satisfac-
tions ("while time clears / Our lenses, lifts a focus, resurrects / A
periscope to glimpse . . ."). Among its results are pragmatism
("the dream of act"), spiritual arrogance, political tyranny, the
destruction and death of war.

But just as the poet's dismay balances on his belief that the "star-
glistered salver of infinity"—the signs of the cosmos in "Proem"
and "Ave Maria"—can never be "subjugated" (only "conjugated":
in the fertile marriage of language), so the genial taunt of his sub-
sequent appeal to Whitman is balanced by appreciation:

> "Recorders ages hence"—ah, syllables of faith!
> Walt, tell me, Walt Whitman, if infinity
> Be still the same as when you walked the beach. . . .

The initial phrase refers to the poet himself, to what he has just done; and it puts in question the faith Whitman expressed in "Crossing Brooklyn Ferry." (The passage tells the persistent doubt that troubled Crane, the "skepticism" he knew had to be worked through. "If only America were half as worthy today to be spoken of as Whitman spoke of it fifty years ago there might be something for me to say," he wrote to Frank of his distress over "materials," "—not that Whitman received or required any tangible proof of his intimations, but that time has shown how increasingly lonely and ineffectual his confidence stands.") [171] But the phrase is also the title of a *Calamus* poem in which Whitman asks to be remembered as "the tenderest lover" whose happiest days were spent in the countryside "wandering hand in hand" with his friend. Accordingly, while serving to deny the "similitudes" of materials between past and present, it affirms the deeper "similitudes" of experience, expressed finally by Whitman's faithful acceptance ("Sea eyes and tidal, undenying, bright with myth!"), that bind him to the poet.

For the poet answers his own question about infinity by referring to those poems of Whitman that confirm his very experience of the anguish of existence and the trials of faith. He reminds us of "Out of the Cradle Endlessly Rocking" (using details of it to clarify his poem: Whitman hears the "messages of surf" to which the travelers have not attended) and he reminds us of other "Sea-Drift" poems: "As I Ebb'd with the Ocean of Life" (with its questionings, its images of the wrecked, castaway self and the dispirited poet, its appeals to father and mother), "Tears" (so full of darkness and desolation, the poet's other self a tearful "ghost"), and "On the Beach at Night Alone" (where the poet, his faith in cosmos restored as he watches the stars, proclaims the "similitude" that "spans" all things, "and always has spann'd, / And shall forever span them and compactly hold and enclose them").

And though the Whitman who "walked the beach / Near Paumanok—your lone patrol—and heard the wraith / Through surf . . ." is also a celebrant of the city, the poet of Mannahatta ("For you, the panoramas and this breed of towers"), he remains for the poet a poet of nature, of an organic universe ("Of you—

171. *Letters*, pp. 261–62 (June 20, 1926).

the theme that's statured in the cliff").[172] Because of this, his open road ("free ways still ahead") points backward in time, leads away from the city to "Connecticut farms, abandoned pastures"—to "Quaker Hill"—to the "competent loam" and the "something green" (like the "bright green weed" Thoreau, at Walden, found at the bottom of the frozen pond) that declare everlasting life.[173] So Whitman, lonely, tested, and faithful like Columbus, is needed, again like Columbus, to guide us out of the "labyrinth" (now chiefly Wall Street, center of our "empire wilderness"), to our still-undiscovered or unpossessed "empire," the "gleaming fields" spoken for in Whitman's gleaming eyes—eyes as much as Columbus' (or Melville's) familiar with the sea, yet "undenying, bright with myth!" Whitman's eyes are neither restricted in focus nor "bicarbonated white by speed," and their "gleam," we learn later, also involves the fire of responsive love. The myth that brightens them is the natural one developed by the poet in terms of Pocahontas, the organic myth of life-and-death that promises renewal—and something more, equally important to the poet (and often neglected in talking about Crane's "vision"), the prospect of love and community:

> O, upward from the dead
> Thou bringest tally, and a pact, new bound,
> Of living brotherhood! [174]

Cosmos (and poetry and song), as the epigraph to "Atlantis" indicates, is a work of love, and community, the risen Atlantis, is its counterpart. Cosmos is a sign of love, and love—the deepest similitude in the experience of these poets—answers all enigmas, stills all doubts.

Now, in what follows, this vision is challenged by the poet's awareness of its absence, by his sense of the enormities of modern life. A demonic landscape countervails the apocalyptic landscape

172. See: ". . . thy lines, rife as the loam / Of prairies, yet like breakers cliff-ward leaping"—a characterization of organic theme and movement.

173. Thoreau is also evoked by "Saunterer," which, according to Wright Morris, is "ill-suited to Thoreau" but perfectly fitted to Whitman. *The Territory Ahead* (New York: Atheneum, 1963), pp. 49–51.

174. For Crane's belief in the communal nature of art, see *Letters*, p. 260. Crane alludes to Ezra Pound's "A Pact," *Lustra* (1915).

of "Powhatan's Daughter," now represented by Whitman.[175] In the relevant phrase of Henry Adams, the poet is acutely aware of the "two kingdoms of force," of the industrial world and the pastoral world it supplants; and though the protraction of the poem may be explained by the poet's desire to surpass "Faustus and Helen," it is better explained by his need to give body to his recognition. With the first line ("The nasal whine of power whips a new universe") we enter the kingdom of the dynamo, whose force, Adams said, was "wholly new" and "anarchical"; and, as we do, we remember—because the poet uses the old imagery, both natural and historical, to describe the new—the kingdom of the Virgin (of Pocahontas), whose sexual power only Whitman among American artists, Adams claimed, insisted on.[176] And almost immediately, in such phrases as "New verities, new inklings," in such questions as "Towards what?," in such images of the vortex as that of the whirling "bobbin-bound" dynamo, and of meaningless dance, as the axle and the "oilrinsed circles of blind ecstasy," we are aware of doom, of the Icarian destiny and futuristic debacle the poem describes in the culminating death dance of the airplane's vortical descent and total destruction. Clearly, the "Skygak" has not heeded Whitman's warning ("Passage to more than India! / Are thy wings plumed indeed for such far flights?") and, in failing his "Sanskrit charge / To conjugate infinity's dim marge— / Anew . . . ," has mistakenly "unleash'd" his "bent." [177] His death, unlike that of the Indian brave, is meaningless:

> down gravitation's
> vortex into crashed
> . . . . dispersion . . . into mashed and shapeless debris. . . .
> By Hatteras bunched the beached heap of high bravery!

We remember the "wrecks of skeletons" that Whitman did not fail to mention in "Passage to India" as well as the debris of spirit in "As I Ebb'd with the Ocean of Life," both appropriate to the

175. I follow Northrop Frye's use of these terms in *Anatomy of Criticism: Four Essays* (Princeton: Princeton University Press, 1957).

176. *The Education of Henry Adams* (New York: Modern Library, 1931 [1918]), pp. 379–90.

177. A skygack is a bridge-builder. See *Letters*, p. 272. See "Passage to India," § 9.

"ghoul-mound," where the poet has told of death and of the doom of doom in which he seeks the promise of new life.

At this juncture of the poem, he turns again to Whitman, who, for all of his knowledge of death, has kept the faith, "held the heights" of life:

> O Walt—Ascensions of thee hover in me now
> As thou at junctions elegiac, there, of speed
> With vast eternity, dost wield the rebound seed!

The imagery is of upward motion, resurrection, spiritual ascent (a bird is suggested by "hover"), and possession. Unlike the pilot, who "sowest doom," Whitman "wield[s] the rebound seed!"—that is, the life-generating and -sustaining vision born of descent-to-death, of dying in order to be reborn. He has not avoided death but entered it, has, as he counsels in "Passage to India," "Sound[ed] below the Sanskrit and the Vedas," has, in the slightly modified words of *Moby-Dick*, "look[ed] deep down and . . . believe[d]." [178] Whitman's faith is as unfailing as the natural phenomena, the miracles upon which it relies: the tides, "the competent loam, the probable grass. . . ." His "leaves of grass" "tally" it, for, as he himself says,

> The smallest sprout shows there is really no death,
> And if ever there was it led forward life. . . .[179]

And even now, having died and passed the barriers of death, he is —so the poet addresses him—"there beyond," eternally, livingly present, a witness whose songs assure us by the presence they create ("Be it as if I were with you. [Be not too certain but I am now with you.]") that death is deathless.[180]

The proof for the poet is also in the movement of the verse, in the vernal passage following his tribute to Whitman, the "Mourner," the repository of all our war-inflicted deaths.[181] Not only does it recall "that spring / When first I read thy lines," it

---

178. For faith in seeds, see Williams' *Paterson*. The quotation from Melville is from "The Gilder," ch. 114—an important chapter for Crane.

179. "Song of Myself," § 6.

180. "Full of Life Now," *Leaves of Grass*.

181. "Vigils" invites us to read, as part of the poem, such moving poems as "Vigil Strange I Kept on the Field One Night."

tells of spring, of life breaking into the fullness of summer and the richness of fall. And it tells of the poet's sense of cosmicity, of his "Appalachian Spring"—how, like the Indian brave of "The Dance," only with Whitman as a guide, he ranged the continent and discovered Pocahontas, beheld the transformation of the "glacier woman" ("White banks of moonlight came descending valleys") and heard the "thunder's eloquence"; and how, finally, he fulfilled his destiny, a westward one, and reached the "hill" (a resplendent "Quaker Hill") "crowned" by the golden autumn— the heart's goal, the "gleaming fields" of home.[182]

The prospect of homecoming opened by this remembered (imagined?) landscape is confirmed by the "Angelus" (as in "Ave Maria") that echoes in "*Panis Angelicus*" and by Whitman's "Nazarene and tinder eyes" (as in "Lachrymae Christi")—"Eyes tranquil with the blaze / Of love's own diametric gaze, of love's amaze!" [183] Not Whitman's greatness but his nearness, his sunlike hopeful presence in the familiar world, matters to the poet, who is heartened by him to continue the task he himself began, the task evoked by our recollection of "Proem" and "Ave Maria":

> Evasive—too—as dayspring's spreading arc to trace is:—
> Our Meistersinger, thou set breath in steel;
> And it was thou who on the boldest heel
> Stood up and flung the span on even wing
> Of that great Bridge, our Myth, whereof I sing!

The arc of the dawn—and of spring—is rainbow-bird-bridge, interrelated symbols of new life, freedom, and spirit. And here Whitman, who at the end of "Song of Myself" relinquishes himself to the elements, is resurrected by the poet and, perhaps with

182. In the earlier passage "Glacial sierras" and "wand" tell of Whitman's agency in calling Pocahontas to life. "Trembling hill" recalls the "trembling heart" of "Ave Maria"; "crowned" transforms the golden harvest into hair. And both remind us, as John Unterecker has reminded me, of "The Harbor Dawn" ("a forest shudders in your hair").

183. This passage of "Ave Maria" recalls Whitman's "Sea-Drift" poems. "*Panis Angelicus*," a not wholly felicitous coinage, accords Whitman divinity and vaguely summons Dionysus in the evocation of Pan. Considering the phrase in the fashion of Kenneth Burke—remembering, too, Whitman's "wand" and life-awakening sunlike role—one derives "*Penis Angelicus*," a meaning of genuine import in the poem and not far-fetched for the poet who wrote the 1855 Preface.

some slight hesitancy and irony, hailed as the deific life-giver of America. By setting "breath in steel," he began the continuing work of American poets ("breathing into the proud, material tissues, the breath of life," he said in "Democratic Vistas"), and by launching the "span" ("span of consciousness"), he began the supreme work of restoring cosmos, for which, in the image of "boldest heel," he is associated with Elohim.[184]

Though the poet briefly reminds us of his struggle with doubt ("Years of the Modern! Propulsions toward what capes?"—the first phrase identifies another significant Whitman poem), the "Vedic Caesar," Whitman, with his faith in grass, has won his own. In proof of which he, too, sets breath in steel by transforming the airplanes, the previous symbol of death-dealing machinery, into "Easters of speeding light," angelic adventurers on the "Open Road" of man's endless passage. But admirable as this transformation is as an expression of restored faith in man's spiritual exploration, it seems suspect to invest it in machines. Whitman's vision is not reclaimed by the airplanes' flight but by the poet's own vision of it—by his own resurrected spirit and inspirited imagination, by his association of it with seagull and bridge. This is the "heritage" Whitman bestows.[185]

Of this, the "rainbow's arch" is the seal. It surmounts the "Cape's ghoul-mound," the scene of the poet's sea-drift situation, as later the bridge surmounts the tunnel; declares a joyous outcome, not a desolate one such as that of "Stark Major"; and transforms a waste of darkness and death into "Belle Isle." And transferred to the "aureole" around Whitman's head, it is the seal of his presence as well as pastoral sainthood. Now "Recorders ages hence" speaks for the similitude of love enacted by the gesture of hands with which the poem closes. By reminding us in the playful assumption of halo of "Crossing Brooklyn Ferry," the poet reminds us of what he assures Whitman: that he is present and will continue to be for

184. Crane said that Whitman, "better than any other, was able to coördinate those forces in America which seem most intractable, fusing them into a universal vision which takes on additional significance as time goes on." P, 263.

185. Apollinaire, alluded to earlier in "alcohol of space," daringly employs the airplane in "Zone" (1912), *Alcools*. Joseph Stella speaks of the "verse of Walt Whitman—soaring above as a white aeroplane of Help . . . Keeping me awake with an insatiable thirst for new adventures." "The Brooklyn Bridge," p. 87.

"ages hence." With his hand (no "Hand of Fire") in his, he accepts the open road, and nothing so conclusively achieves Whitman's presence as this pledge of love, the poet's answer to the petitions at the end of "Song of the Open Road":

> Will you give me yourself? will you come travel with me?
> Shall we stick by each other as long as we live? [186]

Is the final "so—" "hesitant, or at least questioning," as Thomas Vogler says, and should we read the final lines conclusively in the spirit of warning in "Whoever You Are Holding Me Now in Hand" ("The way is suspicious, the result uncertain, perhaps destructive")? Vogler appreciates the function of "Cape Hatteras" in the design of *The Bridge*. "Whitman's equanimity in the face of death and catastrophe," he believes, "is what Crane needed at this stage of his quest, and would need even more in the final transition from 'The Tunnel' to 'Atlantis.'" [187] But the poet has such equanimity at this transition because "Cape Hatteras" exists for him simultaneously with "Atlantis"—the "ghoul-mound" surmounted by the rainbow is another symbol of the risen Atlantis —and because he himself has achieved more than equanimity. He has achieved what Whitman said, in the poem just cited, was the one thing needed and for the poet perhaps the most difficult thing —trust. The way the verse ends calls up and contrasts with the endings of "Ave Maria" and "Indiana," with the "Hand of Fire" of the one and the uncertain "—my friend—" of the other; and it reminds us of the hard lesson of love Ishmael learns on first meeting Queequeg and awakening in his embrace with dreadful memories of his childhood experience of "the supernatural hand." [188] The way the poet now goes in "Three Songs" is dark but Whitman's love (and example: for the way requires an initial freedom from one's self, its confession) permits him to enter it, retrospec-

186. See also "Of the Terrible Doubt of Appearances."
187. "A New View of Hart Crane's Bridge," pp. 394–95.
188. *Moby-Dick*, ch. 4. Ishmael remembers the punishment of his stepmother. The transformation that occurs here and in Crane's poem recalls Whitman's "And I know that the hand of God is the elderhand of my own." I cite § 5, "Song of Myself," in *Leaves of Grass* (1855) because of the association of this line with "Passage to India."

tively, as it were, and to acknowledge fully the erotic nature of his quest. Like Whitman his perturbations are chiefly sexual. What he fantasized in terms of "Madre Maria" and Pocahontas he now confronts directly, and nothing shows better the present aspect of the poem or the poet's honesty ("perfect personal candor," as Whitman says) [189] than his descent from the ideal to the actual.

This descent accounts for the terrible bitterness that characterizes "Southern Cross" and "National Winter Garden." Like Leander, alluded to in the epigraph from Marlowe's *Hero and Leander*, the poet is now a voyager in quest of love (and in need of a bridge), whose trip, prefigured in "Cutty Sark," is a tragedy. Love has made him a voyager, as it had the poet of "Voyages," and in its pursuit he has gone to the ends of the world—has crossed all the seas and weathered the capes and returned empty-hearted. The force of his desire, confessed at the start, measures his bitterness as well as what John R. Willingham calls his "male restlessness": "I wanted you, nameless Woman of the South, / No wraith, but utterly. . . ." [190] And this confession suggests the reason for his failure: not that the woman he desires is nameless but, as her sexual possession in the waking dream of "The Harbor Dawn" has told us, too well known and forbidden to name. So even now he would purify his desire by likening himself, a lonely sufferer, to the Southern Cross and by depicting, in its ascent from "the slowly smoldering fire / Of lower heavens" to heavens "High" and "cool," his own wish to "take night." Moreover, the constellation with which the poet identifies establishes the ideal reference that permits him to direct the bitterness of emotional impasse from himself to the fallen nature of woman.

Again the woman he desires is not nameless but unanswering. Whatever name he calls ("Eve! Magdalene! / or Mary, you?"), her name is Mother. Each song considers her in one of her aspects, or rather defines, in a curve of feeling rising from misogyny, the poet's attitudes toward her. Here she is Eve, the mother of us all, and for the poet, in his sexual revulsion, a "simian Venus"—someone whose jungle nature recalls Eliot's "Whispers of Immortality"

---

189. Preface (1855), *Leaves of Grass*.
190. " 'Three Songs' of Hart Crane's *The Bridge*: A Reconsideration," *American Literature*, XXVII (March, 1955), 65.

and "Sweeney among the Nightingales." The poet depicts her after her fall, significantly in terms of his own dispossession from the garden (of childhood) and therefore not without some sympathy:

> homeless Eve,
> Unwedded, stumbling gardenless to grieve
> Windswept guitars on lonely decks forever;
> Finally to answer all within one grave.

The stress is on "homeless" and "gardenless"—she is connected with the sea, the vast space the poet himself has entered—and on an unbiblical detail, the "Unwedded[ness]," the act of separation, that accounts for her plight. Expulsion from the garden of home, from whatever infant paradise the poet imagines, has been the irreparable disaster, its relation to his awareness of sexuality told in "Unwedded" and "stumbling" and, more fearfully for him and the death she answers with, in the image of the guitar, which belongs here, not only by right of its association with lonely lament but with the incest theme of Melville's *Pierre*.[191] We may read the last line to mean that Eve ultimately answers for all she has done by one death. But "answer," an obsessive word, established in its primary meaning by "call" and by the poet's insistent desire, tells us that her answer to all, and to all desire, is the sexual embrace of death itself—"within one grave," the very vortex of her sex.

These associations, carried over to the next stanza by "wake," explain the poet's almost overwhelming disgust. For now, in what has suddenly become the present, with the poet himself at sea, returning from his (Columbian) voyage, he recognizes in his "backward vision," in the wake of the ship, the true nature of his course and its futility and emptiness. His vision is indeed backward (as he more fully acknowledges in "National Winter Garden"), and the "Kiss" of what he sees is the kiss of death, terrible beyond im-

---

191. The guitar motif, common in cubist paintings, most immediately recalls Picasso's "Le Vieux Guitariste" (1903). Mr. Ronald Johnson informs me that an article, "The Psychology of the Guitar," explaining, among other things, its sexual meaning, appeared in *Arte Joven* during Picasso's editorship.

agining, touching what is most sensitive and vulnerable: "Eyes crumble at its kiss." All his affirmations, his visions of the ideal, the structure of dreams, his very being, disintegrate:

> Its long-drawn spell
> Incites a yell. Slid on that backward vision
> The mind is churned to spittle, whispering hell.

The experience is as painful as the line that tells it. The mind, losing itself, surrealistically imaged, becomes its disgust. With reversal, everything becomes demonic.[192]

To this the poet's recourse—repetition suggests its typicality—is to consider desire within the context of the ideal. Now his own smoldering passion, figured in the "Cross," acquires the values of pure possession. His suffering becomes virtuous. Momentarily he restores himself ("It is blood to remember; it is fire / to stammer back") by turning to the world of "Legend," "Lachrymae Christi," and "The Dance"—and, as we see in the ellipsis and dash (". . . It is / God—your namelessness"), by leaping to the conclusion of "Possessions." But the "wash" is still the "wake" from which no Venus is born:

> All night the water combed you with black
> Insolence. You crept out simmering, accomplished.
> Water rattled that stinging coil, your
> Rehearsed hair. . . .[193]

Medusa emerges from the black sea of the poet's unconscious. Eve is the "terrible mother" whom Jung associates with the fear of incest, the witch of "Rapunzel," alluded to in "Virginia," who keeps the poet from attaining not phallic mastery but the ideal.[194] It is she whom want of love produced ("Wraith of my unloved seed!"); she who destroys the ideal ("The Cross, a phantom, buckled—dropped below the dawn") and who, having turned all

192. The images of reversal recall the labyrinth of "Cape Hatteras" and prefigure the even more demonic landscape of "The Tunnel." They may have been prompted by "the dark backward and abysm of time" in *The Tempest* (I, ii) as well as by Crane's own experience. See *Letters*, p. 280.

193. See "The Bathers." "Stinging" is often used by Whitman to describe the sea, the "fierce mother."

194. Frye, *Anatomy of Criticism*, p. 196.

hope to stone, to unattainable stars, now drowns them in her light.[195]

Although the poet admits, in "National Winter Garden," that his disgust originates in his own lust, he still displaces it, in this instance on the burlesque queen whose nature, like Eve's, he considers to be that of a prostitute-Medusa. He also displaces it, even as he recognizes it, by seeing her dance as a parody of the dance in "Powhatan's Daughter." The title of the poem, identified with the Houston St. Burlesque (Minsky's) in the Black Sun edition of *The Bridge*, is parodic too, since it tells of much that makes "the burlesque of our lust" so terrible for the poet: a winter dance in an artificial garden, and one, significantly, that is of national character. The situation as well as the episode of the poem are "modern replicas," to use William Carlos Williams' phrase for his own (and Joyce's and Eliot's) way of contrasting past and present. Yet the poet who by these means would distance what disgusts him is an unwilling participant, stirred as much as anyone by a still-powerful erotic ritual—one that struck the audience, a contemporary observed, with "a kind of awe, as if before priestesses of Venus. . . ." [196]

The theme and virtuosity of the poem remind one of "Faustus and Helen II." But "National Winter Garden" stands to that poem as "Southern Cross" stands to "North Labrador," the earlier poem providing a measure of the deeper experience and more openly expressed understanding of the latter. The poem involves us in general humanity, for what the poet depicts speaks for Eve's "spawn," for us as well as for him. We, too, follow the "outspoken buttocks" with our "bandy eyes," and we are objects of revulsion when he describes the oppressive, crowded theater as "one flagrant, sweating cinch." Besides expressing a harsh avid vulgarity and the motion of hips in its rhyme with "clinch," "cinch" conveys, as in "it's a cinch," an easy success, the vulture-like assurance of passive men, fantasizing in the presence of captive prey. The subsequent image of food ("And while legs waken salads in the brain") is

195. "Phantom" is significant here as a vague reminder of the poet's situation and vision at the end of "Cutty Sark." With the concluding image of dawn in "Southern Cross," it provides a connection with the Statue of Liberty in the earlier poem and Cathedral Mary in "Virginia."

196. Wilson, *The Shores of Light*, p. 281.

appropriate, a surrealist evocation of an appetite both gross ("she's a dish") and fastidious, hungry for something fresh and green; and it represents the double nature of the poet's own infantile fantasy of ideal (romantic) possession:

> You pick your blonde out neatly through the smoke.
> Always you wait for someone else though, always—
> (Then rush the nearest exit through the smoke).

The sharp observation, marked by "neatly," is Laforguean. The poet knows that here, as in the previous line, he is describing an idea of love that, whether in girlie magazines or burlesque shows, is secured by distance and passivity. He picks his blonde, as in the practice of the brothel, but his action, supported later by the parenthetical thought, has another end. He picks his blonde *out* of the smoke, out of what is becoming for him infernal. For even though he picks her in the way of the brothel, he does so regretfully and still with longing, always waiting, faithful to some other, earlier golden-haired ideal, whom "blonde" identifies with the submerged maternal image of "The Harbor Dawn." And when the image clarifies his sexual confusion, the logic, noted by "Then," takes a romantic turn, the poet imagining himself a chivalric rescuer, or even better, since the poem depends upon this association, the deliverer of Persephone from Hell.

This thought—and the continuing regret evoked by "Always" and the effectively delayed "begins" of the next stanza—permits him to remain even as the vegetative myth it recalls prompts him to set the dance against the primitive ritual, to see in it the "cheapest echo," a burlesque. Yet his response is equivocal, of the kind expressed by "And shall we call her whiter than the snow?," where, in answer to desire, the burlesque queen momentarily becomes Pocahontas ("virgin to the last of men"), only, in answer to his troubled awareness of this, to be depreciated by the sneer in "whiter." As he follows her dance to its culmination, he is acutely aware—because unable to resist its spell or overcome the disgust it provokes—of just those details that transform her into Medusa; and at the end, fascinated by her "whirling strands" and mounting "snake rings," he "wait[s] that writhing pool," waits, expectantly and fearfully as the repetition of "wait[s]" tells us, for the penalty of forbidden love, the vortex, the very death of sex itself. The brilliant stanza depicting this develops from and contrasts with stanza two ("And while legs waken salads in the brain"):

> We wait that writhing pool, her pearls collapsed,
> —All but her belly buried in the floor;
> And the lewd trounce of a final muted beat!
> We flee her spasm through a fleshless door. . . .[197]

For it tells us that even more fearful than sexuality is isolation and unresponsiveness ("who knows her smile?"), the death or spiritual nothingness of empty sexual climax, of unshared love. This worst and most saddening way of sexual release—its origin, he knows, is in romantic love—is for him the truest gauge of modern lapse from the erotic universe represented in vegetative myth. It is the profoundest reason for his disgust.

Not "flesh" but the want of contact with it is what we flee. And so, as he says, we desperately return: "Yet, to the empty trapeze of your flesh, / O Magdalene, each comes back to die alone." Even though the trapeze is empty—the image evokes the empty space as well as the abyss; it suggests the gymnastics of the dance and the bridge it fails to be—or even though each imaginatively fills it and "dies alone" in a death compounded by the Elizabethan pun, he comes back because the lust she burlesques is after all a manifestation of "faith," of desire for life. The perverse is compensated by a powerful reverse action: "Lugs us back lifeward." She brings us back, to life and to the source of life, because she represents the original, the maternal object of desire, the flesh from which we have been separated; and she compels us to return because we have never been satisfied.[198] "Bone by infant bone," with its burden of heavy stress, tells of the difficulty of that birth but also expresses the ache of loss felt from infancy and, since the phrase summons it, "the anguish of the marrow" that Eliot attributed to Donne—the fact that "No contact possible to flesh / Allayed the fever of the bone." [199]

197. Noting the solemnity of the audience, Wilson explains: "this vision of erotic ecstasy, when they see it unveiled before them—though they watch it with fascination—frightens them and renders them mute." *The Shores of Light*, p. 281.

198. See Gaston Lachaise's statue, "Dynamic Mother."

199. "Whispers of Immortality."

The seasonal course or upward curve of "Three Songs" is also a backward one: the rebirth of idealism in "Virginia" is achieved by renunciation of desire or, rather, by willingness to return to the purer, because ineffectual, condition of childhood. The title does not name but describes the character of the girl addressed in the poem. It transforms what it recalls: by way of her native state, Pocahontas (of the "red, eternal flesh") becomes the Virgin, the Mary of the poem. To similarly innocent ends, the poet employs the fairy tale of Rapunzel and the popular song "What Do You Do Sunday, Mary?" [200] The former is not an analogue so much as an awakener of childhood wishes and fears and, mostly, happy endings; the latter, no longer risqué, becomes *song*, a child's (no Columbus') lighthearted clear—how clear!—prayer to the Virgin ("blue-eyed Mary"). Longing is not denied ("I'm still waiting you—": Mary is the blonde of the previous poem) nor sexuality forgotten ("Let down your golden hair"), but nothing is insistent and everything, discordant elsewhere, is reconciled. How charming this urban-pastoral world! [201]

Its queen is Mary, the good country girl whom the city cannot sully (her smile protects her) and who, like the flowers in the window boxes of tenements, fills the daylight world of this poem with the fragrance, color, and radiance of springtime innocence:

> High in the noon of May
> On cornices of daffodils
> The slender violets stray.
> Crap-shooting gangs in Bleecker reign,
> Peonies with pony manes—
> Forget-me-nots at windowpanes. . . .

The flowers of this lovely verse evoke young love, the shy girls and the still-uncertain boys of some *West Side Story*. "Pony manes" summons the world of childhood and recalls the frisking Pocahontas of the Strachey epigraph. Raised to nobility by "reign" and "Prince Street," the crap-shooters are lovely boys like those of

200. For the libretto of Irving Caesar's song from the musical comedy *Poppy* (1923), see Brown, *Robber Rocks*, pp. 110–11.

201. I use Paul Goodman's term. See *The Empire City* (New York: Macmillan, 1964), p. 341. Note also his remark: "to enjoy the things of the present it is necessary to be touched by love" (p. 343).

William Carlos Williams' "Horned Purple"; and, since "Peonies with pony manes" is appositive and "pony manes" also recalls the "wild ponies' play" of "Episode of Hands," an innocent homosexuality, or a sexuality not yet wholly differentiated, becomes part of the scene—to be contrasted, for example, with the lust of the poet who enters Bleecker Street in "Possessions." [202]

And raised up by the imagination of this poem, Mary is Williams' "Beautiful Thing," the Kora (Persephone) the poet rescues from Hell, by means of art "lift[s] . . . out of the ruck. . . ." [203] Both the inviolable beauty of the self and the object of its devotion, she is the enviable freshness of a renewed world, the spring or innocence for which Crane longed when, in a letter to William Slater Brown, he remembered Ceres' speech in *The Tempest* ("Spring come to you at the farthest / In the very end of harvest").[204] With her appearance the city is redeemed; suddenly it is "Spring in Prince Street." With her "claret scarf" she recalls the "skil-/ful savage sea-girls / that bloomed in spring" in the poet's vision of the pennanted clipper ships in "Cutty Sark"; she, too, is a figurehead and, in point of time, belongs to the poet's past.[205] And with her blooming the plenty of Ceres' blessing is before us in the outdoor marketplace: the exotic harvest of land and sea, the green gleaming figs and the oysters, symbols at once of sexuality and fecundity, and of orally satisfied desire. In the world restored in this poem she is the "shore beyond desire":

> O Mary, leaning from the high wheat tower
> Let down your gold hair!

—the goal of ultimate fulfillment, the "far / Hushed gleaming fields and pendant seething wheat" that Columbus hoped to reach.[206]

Neither demonic woman nor sportive pagan, Mary is a light lady, an object of sexuality made ideal by unattainability. She be-

---

202. .The initial line of the cited passage recalls "High unto Labrador . . ." in "The Dance."

203. *Kora in Hell*, p. 11.

204. Brown, *Robber Rocks*, pp. 84–85. Ceres' speech celebrates a marriage.

205. In this respect, she is like Daisy in Edmund Wilson's *I Thought of Daisy*.

206. The high tower establishes for this passage something comparable to the last two stanzas of "Royal Palm."

longs to the world of childhood and chivalry as well as to a culture
in which the Virgin is discounted. She is never to be possessed,
only idolized and worshiped:

> Out of the way-up nickel-dime tower shine,
>> Cathedral Mary,
>>> shine!—

She is out of the way, and it is enough, it seems, that she light
the poet's way. She is a *light* lady, brightening those dawns that in
"Cutty Sark" and "Southern Cross" were full of darkness. What
Helen meant to the poet of "Faustus and Helen" she means to
the poet of *The Bridge*. Hopefully, with her light he will be spared
the shipwreck of the voyage of love and find his way home.

This wonderful evocation of harmony—of all that ideally per-
tains to the pastoral world—is purchased by retrogression. It per-
mits the poet a salutary interval of radiance (to be compared
with "Atlantis") but, as the imploring note and critical awareness
at the end of the poem suggest, it cannot keep him long from the
darker way of his journey. With sudden transition, the evocation
of spring confronts the evocation of the actual autumnal landscape
of "Quaker Hill," where the pastoral is treated elegiacally in recog-
nition of the fact that what it so easily seemed to transform in
"Virginia" has transformed it.

And it is treated elegiacally because it is a moralized landscape
representing the poet's maturer attitudes and their difficult attain-
ment, attitudes that the epigraphs immediately identify with the
courage to accept the assaults of experience and the loss of ideals.
Here, as elsewhere in *The Bridge*, the poet so fully understands the
"influences" he acknowledges that he may be said, in the Buberian
sense, to converse with them.[207] But more than most, Isadora
Duncan and especially Emily Dickinson are present—have presence
—because, as women, they bond "Three Songs" and "Quaker
Hill" and have a high place—the highest, I think—in the poet's
gallery of women. As artists, knowing the spoliation of experience
and mastering it, they speak authoritatively to him, belong to an
order just as generative and comforting but superior to the ma-

207. I am indebted to Mr. Michael Lynch for making me attend to this con-
versational aspect of poetry.

ternal. Their peers are not to be found in *The Bridge* but in *Paterson:* they stand with the Abbess Hildegard and Madame Curie.

That Crane remembered Isadora Duncan at the time he was composing "Quaker Hill"—the last section to be completed—was not fortuitous. In 1928 he had read Isadora Duncan's *My Life*, published the year before, the year of her death. The book moved him ("a very sad but beautiful book," he said, noting also that "her career would be impossible now") and seems to have awakened his memory of her reception in Cleveland nearly a decade before. Almost certainly it corroborated for him the high regard in which she was held by the Stieglitzians—all the more so because at this time Waldo Frank had placed her in a group of pioneering artists that included Crane.[208]

With Emily Dickinson the case was different. She was a fiber of his being: he had addressed a sonnet to her and she had become an exemplar, associated in his mind with Blake, of the value of the "intuitions" (imagination).[209] How much she belonged to his poem—to his consciousness—and to this juncture of its course may be seen by reading "To Emily Dickinson":

> You who desired so much—in vain to ask—
> Yet fed your hunger like an endless task,
> Dared dignify the labor, bless the quest—
> Achieved that stillness ultimately best,
>
> Being, of all, least sought for: Emily, hear!
> O sweet, dead Silencer, most suddenly clear
> When singing that Eternity possessed
> And plundered momently in every breast;
>
> —Truly no flower yet withers in your hand
> The harvest you descried and understand
> Needs more than wit to gather, love to bind.
> Some reconcilement of remotest mind—
>
> Leaves Ormus rubyless, and Ophir chill
> Else tears heap all within one clay-cold hill.

208. *Letters*, p. 322 (March 28, 1928); "Our Arts: The Re-Discovery of America: XII," *New Republic*, LIV (May 9, 1928), 347.
209. *Letters*, p. 324 (April 17, 1928).

The poem is no less true to Emily Dickinson by being so true to Crane. The apostrophe with which it opens is in fact a declaration of recognition—of their hard task, its justification and reward. Like the poet of "Three Songs"—and of *The Bridge* in its entirety —Emily is distinguished by a desire impossible to satisfy, a hunger (appropriately) which she nevertheless feeds and makes her "endless task." That her hunger is for assurance of "Eternity" ("one shore beyond," to cite "Ave Maria") and accordingly "endless" need not be insisted on. For what matters most is that, even though unanswered, she keeps desire alive and *dares* to make it her task— the "labor" of poetry—and so, in poems, dignifies the self-generated activity of art. And Emily "bless[es] the quest" by teaching the poet that "The dream," as Williams says in *Paterson V*, "is in pursuit!"—that the activity is itself an end, justification, and reward, achieving, as it does in the making of and *in* poems, the ultimately satisfying condition of "stillness," the "Being" that is both the "all-feeling" noted by Melville and of all feeling at once the best and most impossible to decree.[210] And what the poet wishes to tell her is that her poetry works this miracle of "stillness" for him. She is the "sweet, dead Silencer" because her "singing" both quiets the noise of the abyss and consoles him in his dread—is itself, in his experience, the "Being, of all, least sought for," the "Eternity" of which she sings, that still, radiant moment ("suddenly clear") in which "momently" (stressed in the poem) possessing and plundering (exact words in Crane's lexicon of emotion) cease to be violent extremes of the heart in yielding to an occasion of central joy.

By being true to the perilously balanced experience that for Crane defined the human condition—and by making it eternally present—Emily has achieved the immortality of art ("Truly no flower yet withers in your hand"—again how skillfully Crane brings together flowering-withering and introduces "hand" to define the special context of experience). But this freshness (recalling "Virginia") is also virginal, the result, in this instance, not of willingness but of lack of the answerer she desires. Emily's poems are true—note the shift to present tense—because she, like the

210. *Herman Melville*, ed. Willard Thorp, p. 393.

questers of *The Bridge*, has "descried" the "harvest" (the gleaming fields beyond) but not been permitted to gather it. Her universe, like theirs, is one of radical estrangement (distance) from the ideal, and nothing she can do or that can be done brings the "reconcilement" which, the syntax tells us, lies only within the power of someone else. Emily's world and the reason for her song are not unlike those of the poet of "North Labrador," who now, in images recalling her poems as well as his, depicts the desolation of lovelessness. Without the "reconcilement of remotest mind"—what infinite reaches of space "Eternity" opens! how terrible the need for anchorage expressed by the use of the substantive and in the determined *m*'s and *t*'s!—even the possession of Ormus and Ophir, fabulous places of the Orient, cradles of religion and sources of gold, would be valueless, empty, and cold.[211] And the poet's tears—the tear in which he travels in "The Wine Menagerie" and those that, in "Legend," he wishes to string into "some constant harmony"—would be "heap[ed]" up, like the wreakage in "Cape Hatteras," becoming themselves the "clay-cold hill," the grave of all (and of the "Being, of all") he desires, the closed-in space of death.[212]

The enclosure with which this poem ends speaks for the sense of foreclosure, the diminishment rather than harvest of autumn, in "Quaker Hill." This poem, which Crane mistook for an " 'accent mark' " perhaps because in its historical aspect and nostalgia it is comparable to such characteristic works of the time as Van Wyck Brooks's "Old America," presents a personal landscape of anxiety and a moment of tragic realization—one of the finest moments, perhaps the unsurpassed moment, of *The Bridge*.[213] That this landscape belongs not to memory but to the present, that it is

211. The imagery speaks covertly for two reconcilements, one with Crane's mother, the other with Emil Opffer ("Ophir").

212. "All within one clay-cold hill" is echoed in "all within one grave" in "Southern Cross." Crane may have remembered Emily Dickinson's "For Each Exstatic Moment," which ends with "And Coffers heaped with Tears!"

213. *Letters*, p. 347; *Letters and Leadership* (New York: B. W. Huebsch, 1918). I use "tragic" in the sense defined by Clark Griffith, *The Long Shadow: Emily Dickinson's Tragic Poetry* (Princeton: Princeton University Press, 1964), pp. 6–7. Griffith places Dickinson with Melville, and what he says of the criticism of her poetry puts the case for Crane as well.

identified by name and local detail, that the poet's meditation on it is broken by bitterness and precipitate need for change—all this, and the feeling one has throughout that the poet-of-the-poem is about to become the poet-in-the-poem, contribute to its anxiety. We need not know how much hope Crane invested in "the dear hills of Connecticut"—for the homeless impecunious wanderer this was the "Promised Land"—we simply feel it in the evocation of loss.[214]

This is not the bucolic poem we perhaps expect it to be. The cows pasturing on the grassy hill do not prompt an idyll but rather a melancholy meditation on time. By recalling Whitman's remarks on animals ("I think I could turn and live with animals, they are so placid and self-contain'd")—and Whitman is also recalled by "halo" and the animal faith in organic process—they tell us of the poet's agitation.[215] He has not yet achieved their equanimity—the perspective that never "withers," the Dickinsonian perspective toward which his meditation moves—because he is still burdened by unreconciled and unvented griefs. The poem is his mourning labor.

Of these griefs, the first and most immediate, establishing the situation of the poem, is the failure of friendship, or community. The Robinsonian cadence of "And they [the cows] are awkward, ponderous and uncoy" awakens it, and the poet treats this theme, appropriately, with Robinsonian acumen and irony.[216] Again no knowledge of Crane's life at Patterson, New York, is needed to insure the full force of the poet's sense of discord and betrayal. The friends with whom he presses cider and with whom he drinks and gets drunk are, as he himself admits to being, distrustful and wanting in love, boastful of "faith in other men" yet—how neat the reversal, how bitter—ready to "stalk down the merriest ghost." But the bitterness, while partly self-directed, is mostly toward those vengeful friends who, by denying vision—the "apparitional" called

214. The phrase is from a letter in Brown, *Robber Rocks*, p. 85, which also provides the best guide to this landscape. For a more recent account, see "Quaker Hill, Where Lowell Thomas Is Patriarch of the Quiet Celebrities," *New York Times* (November 10, 1968), 90.
215. "Song of Myself," § 32.
216. We remember "Mr. Flood's Party."

up by "ghost" as well as by "old Mizzentop, palatial white" of the next stanza—undermine the work of *The Bridge*.

And meanwhile, there "above them," as he observes with muted irony, stands "Old Mizzentop," the nautical-named abandoned hotel (if not the shipwreck of a dream, its stranding), itself a stoic, patient visionary, such as the poet, too, must learn in view of change to become. For even now, in response to diurnal change, it reflects in the "loose panes [pains]" of its (tearful and empty) eyes the "gleam" (the "harvest" of the sonnet to Emily Dickinson) and upholds "still," like her, "some dream" through (in spite of) and throughout time, whether its changes are natural or human ("Through mapled vistas, cancelled reservations!").[217]

Yet the endurance (and wishfulness) this suggests to the poet falters before the mordant realization that height is no guarantee of vision and that perspectives wither:

> High from the central cupola, they say
> One's glance could cross the borders of three states;
> But I have seen death's stare in slow survey
> From four horizons that no one relates. . . .

Even the vision of cosmos granted from the "central cupola" is discounted—"they say" makes it apocryphal—and even if we grant its possibility and accept the allusions to something beyond death in "cross the borders of three states" (states of being as in answer to the riddle of the sphinx), we are forced to estimate its power to assure us by the difference between "glance" and "slow survey," the hasty and the deliberate.[218] "But" introduces the reality of the present and the authority of the first-person experience of the poet, who, like Tiresias in *The Waste Land*, sees and tells what "no one relates": that death fills the world, the lack of meaningful relation making it a chaos; that where there is no vision the people perish; that absence of vision is death.[219] Now the poet sees that the windows "staring out" are "death's stare." And in keeping with

217. By association with crucifixion, "crown" suggests suffering, too; "gleam" has a Robinsonian resonance, and the autumnal season calls up his "The Sheaves" (1925), a poem of some relevance to *The Bridge*.

218. See "Cape Hatteras," where Whitman is said to have "passed the Barrier that none escapes. . . ."

219. The numbers in the immediately following lines identify them with chaos.

the waste-land mood and his vantage between past and present, the testimony he sees is of the kind that dismayed Tiresias:

> Weekenders avid of their turf-won scores,
> Here three hours from the semaphores, the Czars
> Of golf, by twos and threes in plaid plusfours
> Alight with sticks abristle and cigars.

This passage is as brilliant as Eliot's on the typist and the "small house agent's clerk"—and bold, considering the fact that the poet, so demonstrably acknowledging Eliot, proposes a different resolution. It turns the poet's meditation to history, to the spoliation of the land, associated with the railroad and telegraph of "The River" as well as with the "suburban land agent," and thus accords with the sordid sexuality that Tiresias sees.

The sharp contrast (of perspectives) supports the poet's declaration, "This was the Promised Land"—a declaration whose bitterness perhaps resonates with the recollection of the "improved infancy" these hills "promised" in "Passage." The previous pastoral and communal evocations define the nature of "Promise": the virgin land of the agrarian dream, a place of vista and freedom, yet reposeful, having a slower natural way of life (as recalled in "The River") as well as the shared life of community suggested by cider-making.[220] The promise is related to the dream associated with the old hotel and to the loss of "kinsmen and the patriarch race." It is not specified so much as indicated by what has betrayed it: the railroad which, in turn, has opened the land to a new discoverer, the "persuasive suburban land agent," who not only subverts it to money values but vulgarizes it by introducing the meretricious forms of urban "community." Nowhere in Crane's work, not even in "The Tunnel," which reaches back to tell the community promise of this landscape, is the revulsion to the city, or better, to what Benton MacKaye at this time called the "metropolitan invasion" of the "indigenous environment," so strong and controlled—saved by irony.[221]

220. Cider-making joins two pastoral landscapes, that of Patterson, New York, and that of William Sommer's Brandywine.

221. *The New Exploration: A Philosophy of Regional Planning* (New York: Harcourt, Brace and Co., 1928).

As a poem of perspectives should be, and is, especially in the line on which the poet's meditation pivots: "What cunning neighbors history has in fine!" This line both comments on the community of the previous stanza and introduces, with an effective echo of Eliot's "Gerontion" ("History has many cunning passages, contrived corridors / . . . Guides us by vanities"), the poet's thought on the conqueror worm, which already signals his need to descend. "Mortgages" here, perhaps because of its relation to bug and table, reminds one of the conclusion of *Walden*, though in contrast to Thoreau's, the poet's thought is not hopeful—he has yet to undergo the equivalent of Thoreau's winter, though perhaps he is asking questions ("Who," "What," "Where") of the kind Thoreau asked in "The Pond in Winter." The ironies, directed by the sneer of "in fine" (in short, and in the end), move toward futility, and, with the questions, which may also parody the threefold thunder of *The Waste Land*, express the querulousness of the poet, who at this point acknowledges only death, not its agency in renewal.

Yet in answering the last question ("Where are my kinsmen and the patriarch race?") he recognizes that death, in ending conflict, is not unlike the state of resignation it would be well for him to achieve. The ironic tone is suddenly dispelled by "The resigned factions of the dead preside. / Dead rangers bled their comfort on the snow"—direct statements that relieve the tension, express letting-go and, especially in the second line, the attractiveness and comfort of death, a death whose private import and connection with the remainder of the stanza is disclosed by "rangers" (see "Indiana") and the curious satisfaction of bleeding one's comfort, of ultimately spending out the self "on the snow," in an acceptably cool, pure, and all-accepting landscape. (Perhaps this line reinterprets "And she is virgin to the last of men. . . .") But this confrontation with the land—this easeful death—is no more possible than the childhood wish that awakened it. The poet's destiny is otherwise, and, as the allusion to the work of "Powhatan's Daughter" tells us, it is a *poet's* destiny, one that he must now take up even as the poem engages itself. His destiny demands descent: "However hopeless it may seem, we have no other choice," Williams concluded the chapter called "Descent" in *In the Amer-*

ican Grain; "we must go back to the beginning. . . ." [222] So the poet turns to the bitter ground of the past in his present, to the ground of his poetry, to all that, terrible as it is, he must "shoulder" —the word plays against the happier summons of Whitman's "Shoulder your duds, dear son"—in order to continue his task.[223]

> Shoulder the curse of sundered parentage,
> Wait for the postman driving from Birch Hill
> With birthright by blackmail, the arrant page
> That unfolds a new destiny to fill. . . .

These lines, with those on friendship, account for the sense of loss that fills this landscape. Neither complaint is petulant: the poet utters both in defense of his vocation, his very being. And by making them known—their candor and bitterness presses us toward autobiographical supposition—he acts to accept his experience, "unhusks the heart of fright," and truly begins the purgative-redemptive work of the poem.[224]

The transition to this work is designated by "So" and by the interrogative statement of its necessary nature, which, rhetorically, demands the "Yes" with which the poet four times answers, affirming his willingness to "descend." The art of these stanzas is superb, balanced on negation-and-affirmation, on the double perspective of hawk-and-worm, on the double need to release and protect one's being. And these stanzas are filled with beauties, with resonant cadences and allusions, and with the very music—the urgent, elegiac, heart-made music—of the "throbbing throat":

> So, must we from the hawk's far stemming view,
> Must we descend as worm's eye to construe
> Our love of all we touch, and take it to the Gate
> As humbly as a guest who knows himself too late,
> His news already told? Yes, while the heart is wrung,

222. *In the American Grain,* p. 215.
223. "Song of Myself," § 46.
224. This passage refers to both Crane's parents' divorce and his own break with his mother; to the legacy from his grandmother that his mother tried to withhold; to the correspondence that he always awaited desperately and impatiently and, in this instance, hoped would bring news of an open future for his work. The last clause is heavily compressed; perhaps the least available meaning is that suggested by "unfolds," which recalls "And fold your exile on your back again" in "The Wine Menagerie." The equivalence of "unfolds" and "unhusks" should be noted.

Arise—Yes, take this sheaf of dust upon your tongue!
In one last angelus lift throbbing throat—
Listen, transmuting silence with that stilly note

Of pain that Emily, that Isadora knew!
While high from dim elm-chancels hung with dew,
That triple-noted clause of moonlight—
Yes, whip-poor-will, unhusks the heart of fright,
Breaks us and saves, yes, breaks the heart, yet yields
That patience that is armour and that shields
Love from despair—when love foresees the end—
Leaf after autumnal leaf
                    break off,
                              descend—
                                        descend—

The new destiny, it seems, requires the revocation of the past, the
relinquishing of the transcendental vision associated here with
Whitman and Thoreau but even more with the moth's vortical
flight in Crane's earliest poem. Descent is a movement from past to
present whose exigence is defined by the Robinsonian cadence of
these lines and the recollection (awakened by "Gate") of both
"Luke Havergal" and the Blakean epigraph to "The Tunnel." Yet
neither past nor transcendental vision is denied: the poem places
them within its complex experience, the "while" that includes every-
thing. For descent—acceptance of mortality and the attendant
anguish—is the necessary condition of "transmuting silence." The
worm, named only now, reminds us opportunely of the "worms" in
"Lachrymae Christi," "tunneling / Not penitence / But song. . . ."
And every "Yes" affirms the acceptance of pain as the price of its
opposite. So "while the heart is wrung" ("twist[ed]" by doubleness
as in "Recitative") we are asked (enabled) to "Arise" (like the
"Poor streaked bodies" of "The Wine Menageries"); and by ac-
cepting this "sheaf of dust," the communion wafer of the poem,
we are invited by the poet to enter the communion—community—
of suffering and (thereby) find the strength to *lift* the "throb-
bing throat" (like the birds of "Out of the Cradle Endlessly
Rocking" and "When Lilacs Last in the Dooryard Bloom'd" re-
sponding to the loss of love and to death) in an "angelus" or
celebration of our own painfully incarnated spirit.

The song we lift is also the one we hear. Our voices, too, join in the angelus, whose "stilly note / Of pain" moves us by the almost unendurable purity of its Keatsian beauty. (The pain of Emily and Isadora is rightly associated with Keats's "Ode to a Nightingale," all the more so because we recall the allusion to violation in *The Waste Land*.) And the song, so full of pain, the poet's *cri de coeur*, is the tragic-redemptive agency that saves by breaking. By "unhusk[ing] the heart of fright," it discloses the terror at the heart of the world and frees the poet's heart of fright. Thus it prepares the seed-heart for new life, ever new in its vulnerability, yet now, in the harvest of this experience, enabled to endure, without being wholly overwhelmed by despair, the death most feared, of love.[225]

With the subsidence of the stilly note that filled the night with moonlight, the poet, too, is ready to let go. Taking the form of falling leaves, the shaped verse and the rhymed closure tell us this and that, like Thoreau, whose "Autumnal Tints" is perhaps alluded to, the leaves have taught him how to die—to die, as the shaped verse also reminds us, not in the meaningless way of the pilot in "Cape Hatteras," but in order to "conjugate infinity's dim marge — / Anew. . . ." [226]

Visually, these lines descend into "The Tunnel"—into the city and into the tomb—but even now anticipate "Atlantis" because the falling leaves, a phase of the natural process, anticipate spring. If we consider the immediately preceding sections of *The Bridge* as adumbrations of Northrop Frye's theory of myths—"Virginia" representing the mythos of summer and "Quaker Hill" that of autumn—"The Tunnel" may be said to represent the mythos of winter and "Atlantis" the mythos of spring.[227] When Crane first outlined *The Bridge* for Otto Kahn, he designated this poem "Subway" and said that its subject matter comprised "the encroachment of machinery on humanity; a kind of purgatory in relation to the

225. "Heart" is reiterated as insistently as "yes."
226. "They that soared so loftily, how contentedly they return to the dust again, and are laid low, resigned to lie and decay. . . ." Thoreau's sentence contains several images of the poem; it also expresses the faith in process that distinguishes Crane from Emily Dickinson.
227. *Anatomy of Criticism*, pp. 158–239.

open sky of [the] last section. . . ." [228] Clearly these sections are
related: "Tunnel," which evokes encroachment (spatial limitation)
and darkness, suggests, where "subway" need not necessarily, a
journey directed toward outcome. Tomb is womb—the abyss does
become a fertile darkness—and its horror, as Maud Bodkin says of
Dante's Hell, is "made bearable for the reader by the fact that
interest is concentrated upon a forward movement." [229] The night
journey of the poem predicates day: ascent, rebirth, renewed pow-
ers, cosmos.[230] And the poet knows this even as he makes descent a
trial of faith. He knows that "the darkness is part of his business,"
that what he postponed in "Van Winkle" he must now undergo.[231]
This is his Columbian voyage—its demonic character connects it
with the voyage of "Southern Cross"—one, however, whose glo-
rious outcome is assured by the Blakean epigraph under which it
is made. For the poem from which the epigraph comes is "Morn-
ing," a celebration of merciful liberation and light.[232]

What most distinguishes the poet's from Columbus' voyage is
that it not only tries the mind but takes place within it. His
"Columbus Circle" belongs to psychological geometry. This de-

228. *Letters*, p. 241.
229. *Archetypal Patterns in Poetry: Psychological Studies of Imagination* (Lon-
don: Oxford University Press, 1934), p. 136.
230. Not only in terms of the seasons and of night and day but in their move-
ment, these sections, each a complementary arc, describe a circle:

"Atlantis"   Bridge
"The Tunnel"   Subway

231. *Letters*, p. 260.
232.

> To find the Western Path
> Right thro' the Gates of Wrath
> I urge my way;
> Sweet Mercy leads me on:
> With soft repentant moan
> I see the break of day.
>
> The war of swords & spears
> Melted by dewy tears
> Exhales on high;
> The Sun is freed from fears
> And with soft grateful tears
> Ascends the sky.

This poem revives the soft and tearful world of Crane's earliest poems.

fines its modernity, though the form the voyage takes—the night journey —is as old as the profound need it expresses. "Before any great task that begins a new life and calls upon untried resources of character," Maud Bodkin explains in the case of Aeneas' night journey, "the need seems to arise for some introversion of the mind upon itself and upon its past—a plunging into the depths, to gain knowledge and power over self and destiny." [233] *Introversion of the mind upon itself and upon its past* is a description as applicable to *The Bridge* as it is to "The Tunnel." But what especially marks "The Tunnel" is the degree and duration of descent—the near madness of entering the "interborough fissures of the mind"— and its dramatic position in the total sequence of the poem.[234] Within the journey of *The Bridge*, this is *the* journey, being the longest deferred and the most necessary to make—a journey, incidentally, that stands comparison with those of the subway poems of other poets of the time, whether in modernist treatment, range of feeling, or depiction of the isolated, unsupported self.

The journey begins in a nighttime urban landscape like that of "Faustus and Helen." We are at the center of the entertainment world. But the poet's response is not that of a lover for whom the city is woman. The serial character of the opening lines tells us— and by way of vaguely reminding us of the opening lines of "The River"—that the poet is adrift in experience, passive, merely observant; and what he sees—and having seen imagines he will see— and how he sees it tell us that he is dispirited and displaced. Whatever excitement the first few lines may initially summon, especially in the case of "mysterious kitchens," is soon dispersed by the sour and weary feeling of *déjà vu* that dominates the stanza. "Performances, assortments, résumés"—yes, *résumés*. The poet has "search[ed] them all" [235] and learned *at* heart "each famous sight"; and they are no more the revelation, the Edenic reality, he seeks than the garden in the third act of the play—that cheat, reminiscent of the movie-goers' situation in "Proem," practiced here not on the poet's credulity but on his undiminished expectancy. Not

233. *Archetypal Patterns in Poetry*, pp. 124–25.

234. "Interborough" introduces a mad wit as well as conveys the sense of tangle, added depth, and darkness.

235. Like Tiresias, in *The Waste Land*, he has "foresuffered all."

only that expected betrayal—how much it depends on his hope for the sudden opening into creation depicted in "Voyages VI"!—but the bedroom situation he imagines, presumably to shield himself with the superior Laforguean attitude of boredom, disclose his desperation. The garden is "dead" because Eve, as we learned in "Southern Cross," has been evicted; the curtain rises on nothingness because the "lounged goddess" is no longer there. And he is as disconsolate as the similarly situated poet of "Porphyro in Akron," as lonely and insecure as the child he recollects in "The River" ("perched" prompts this), and therefore eager—"Mysterious kitchens" seems out of place otherwise—for the warmth and pleasure and maternal presence with which, in "Porphyro in Akron," the Italian household is associated.

Even the imagery of light does not transfigure this city scape. Though "Up Times Square to Columbus Circle lights / Channel the congresses" establishes us in the brightest place in the world, it carries the darker undertones of "The River" as well as—and most important—of Whitman's "Chanting the Square Deific." This poem introduces Jehovah ("I am Time"), the implacable father and judge ("I will have that man's life") whose presence in "The Tunnel" is clearly specified at the end ("O Hand of Fire"); it introduces Jesus, the suffering son, who fills "résumés" with the woe of "Many times have I been rejected . . . and many times shall be again" and whose role suggests that of the poet ("Wending my way . . . with hope and all-enclosing charity"); it introduces Satan ("Morose . . . full of reminiscences, brooding . . ."), whose underworld the poet is about to enter; and, finally, it introduces the presence felt most by absence, the mother, "Santa Spirita" (not "Spiritus Sanctus"), who is everything the poet desires: the breath of his life ("breather, life / Beyond the light, lighter than light, / Beyond the flames of hell, joyous, leaping easily above hell"), of the cosmos ("Life of the great round world, the sun and stars"), and of his poem ("Breathe my breath also through these songs"). Accordingly both the city is dark and the poet is powerless. The city of his poem has long since undergone the "Reflective conversion . . . / At your deep blush. . . ." Words such as "post-illusional" and "afterwards" define its character—or "late midnight," which Crane associated with the subway and the materials of the poem.[236]

Perhaps the most significant indication of the poet's state of being is his precarious identity, the dissociation represented by the way he addresses himself. This is not merely a Prufrockian device, though the poet's passivity and indecision are Prufrockian, nor is the use of the second person to be construed chiefly as a reference to the reader, implying a common humanity. The split is genuine and manifests itself in weariness and, increasingly, in anomie. The curious expression ("let you") in the indented, or most interior, passage conveys the want of will to will for which the sense of monotonous recurrence ("as usual") is again the immediate sign. He has descended the subway before, and, like Jesus greeting the (ascending) apostles, has entered the tomb with nothing more perhaps than a perfunctory salute, a cheery hello. The humor of the imagined situation is Laforguean by way of "Prufrock" ("I am Lazarus . . ."): a grim humor, the flimsiest of defenses. For "subscription praise / for what time slays," with its echoes of "Voyages II" and Emerson's "Brahma," is satanic in its mockery of faith. And though indecision itself is characteristic, his "usual" predicament, to be ended finally by the discomfort of the cold weather—

> But you find yourself
> Preparing penguin flexions of the arms—
> As usual you will meet the scuttle yawn:
> The subway yawns the quickest promise home

—it seems to be well founded in his fear of the "scuttle" (associated with the bedlamite in "Proem") and in his desire for but uncertainty of reaching "home." [237]

And he takes precautions, not only those of self-diminishment and avoidance but that of "metaphysical" attitude. By counseling "Be minimum, then" he hopes to distance vulgarity. He puts on a seventeenth-century armor which is not proof from injury but, as we see in the passages contrasting his meditation with what he overhears, another sign of the disintegrating self. There was a time,

236. *Letters*, pp. 274–75 (August 23, 1926).

237. "Promise" qualifies the phrase as does the recollection of "sleep the long way home" in "Voyages V," which it concludes.

in "The Hive," when, for the milk and honey of love, he suffered the "hiving swarms"; now he prepares to swim against them. And he moves carefully, too, to the left of the revolving door, the vortex. Yet what he avoids—the vertiginousness, the momentary death of being "boxed," the "naked" feeling of exposure—is the very sexuality of entrance depicted in "And down beside the turn-stile press the coin / Into the slot." Reality so brilliantly rendered— "The gongs already rattle" is the final, signal instance—becomes surreal. Suddenly the entire passage becomes sexually overwrought. The composure of the verse is belied. The vulgarity against which he arms himself is his own—his sexuality.

On this we hear the commenting voice of his deepest, most in-terior consciousness:

> And so
> of cities you bespeak
> subways, rivered under streets
> and rivers. . . .

Not white cities, but sunken cities . . . rivers . . . sewers . . . history . . . humanity . . . the abyss. . . . But the thought runs off, lulled by the sensations of moving underground (again bril-liantly rendered, by woven, enclosing cadences vaguely Eliotic) and by the complementary, iterated desire to be "underground," though the poet's awareness of "the sound / of other faces" in-dicates that his almost vacant absorption in the "monotone" is not complete, that he is still responsive, willing, in fact, to attend the sounds that appear to break in on him. Each passage of overheard conversation (one thinks of Prufrock's "I have heard the mermaids singing, each to each. / I do not think that they will sing to me") begins in an intrusive way; and each has an appropriately frag-mentary or jerky form. Each is presented directly in the vernacular —that is part of the affront—and each is vulgar. And though each seems inconsequent, it isn't, its consequence having been deter-mined by the attention of the listener.

The first ("Let's have a pencil Jimmy") may have been sug-gested by Williams' "Shoot it Jimmy!" just as the method of collage may have been suggested by "Rapid Transit." [238] It seems

238. *The Collected Earlier Poems of William Carlos Williams*, pp. 269, 282.

to be spoken by a traveling salesman, and everything in it, as Thomas Vogler points out, refers to a previous section of *The Bridge*: "Jimmy was the father of Larry in 'Indiana' and the pioneer he represented is living now in a fallen garden ('Floral Park') in the city ('Flatbush'). 'The Fourth of July' is a flashback to the political beginnings of the nation ('I'm a / Democrat,' insists the continuation of Larry in 'Cutty Sark'), and the 'pigeon's muddy dream' is a reminder of the dream-vision of the 'Strange bird-wit' or mythic consciousness of the earlier poem. The salesman is mobile, like the tramps, and sees his vision 'night after night' of 'the girls all shaping up.' The whole passage is a burlesque of vision as 'it used to be' for the poet." [239] And it is also a burlesque that includes within its range of reference Sinclair Lewis ("Floral Heights" in *Babbitt*) and E. E. Cummings (in the context, "Fourth of July" recalls "Next to of Course God America I"), contemporary writers who may be said to have found in art—in burlesque—a way of fending contemporary life. And burlesque in another sense, for as much as anything the poet responds to the summary, vulgar remark, "the / girls all shaping up."

This prompts both the "metaphysical" revulsion of the passage beginning "Our tongues recant like beaten weather vanes" (which vaguely summons the unrelated horizons of "Quaker Hill" as well as the concluding verse of "National Winter Garden") and the subsequent conversation in which the strong echo of the pub scene in *The Waste Land* is joined (deliberately—for the art is deliberate) to the image of the swinging gate, the symbolic substitute for the "trapeze" in the previously noted poem:

> "what do you want? getting weak in the links?
> fandaddle daddy don't ask for change—IS THIS
> FOURTEENTH? it's half past six she said—if
> you don't like my gate why did you
> swing on it, why *didja*
> swing on it
> anyhow—"

One cities this passage less for the importance of its transparent

---

Crane may have accepted the challenge of the first poem, which ends, "They can't copy it"; and he may have had in mind Cummings' "Jimmie's got a goil."

239. "A New View of Hart Crane's Bridge," p. 402.

sexuality (the malapropism of "weak on the links" identifies it with the suburban activities of "Quaker Hill") than for the focus to which it brings the poet's profound concern with the relation of sexuality and art. For this reason none of the allusions to other poets is trivial. And no poet is of such importance as Eliot, whose theory of dissociated sensibility the poet here enacts, with Eliot himself as a spokesman for one part of his divided being. Contemporary urban life, vulgarity, sexuality—to "descend" is to meet with these and experience revulsion. Yet only by meeting—accepting—them can the poet, whose many references to earlier sections of *The Bridge* make this section a test of materials, "launch into praise" and thereby complete his poem in an "ecstatic" and "positive" way.[240] This is the impasse of feeling and thought that, again at the deepest level of consciousness, verbal-erotic play—the salutary, Cummingsesque "And somehow anyhow swing—" breaks.[241]

But only momentarily, for repetition renews disgust and, as the circular images indicate, becomes itself a cause of incipient nightmare. Not only the sexual nausea expressed by "and love / A burnt match skating in a urinal," but the awareness of the mind's own tunnel-like aspect—these, and the Dickinsonian dread of "presentiment," show the poet at the point of madness reached in "Southern Cross" ("Slid on that backward vision / The mind is churned to spittle, whispering hell").[242] It needs very little to overwhelm him, just the realization of his presentiment, or perhaps *this* realization, which, though the briefest of overheard conversations, tells him that Mary, the ideal he had again raised up in "Virginia," has been despoiled.

With this the poet briefly enters the "hades in the brain," that surrealistically evoked place whose talisman is the dissociated self —the "swinging" head severed from the body. This hallucinatory experience, we learn, is not unusual, always apparently associated by the poet with Poe, with the haunted mind and death. Yet what is immediately most notable about it, at least in this instance, is

240. *Letters*, pp. 94, 114, 117.
241. In this context, "swing" may also refer to:
> Something it swings on more than the earth I swing on,
> To it the creation is the friend whose embracing wakes me.
>
> Whitman, "Song of Myself," § 50
242. See Emily Dickinson's "The first Day's Night had come."

its power to reintegrate the self by stirring its indignation. Even as the poet tells his despair, he begins to surmount it by the mockery of his questions. But his despair, we note, is public, turning on the poet's place in society. This may be a sufficient explanation of why he meets Poe's visage in the subway, but it is not the only reason, the deepest reason from which the thought of Poe, so skillfully presented in terms of his own work as well as the work of Blake and Hopkins, may divert him. The poet seldom complains about his difficult role; maybe he does so because Williams did in "Rapid Transit." [243] But he does complain about want of love, and this is a reason Williams stressed in treating Poe in *In the American Grain*. Crane admired this book and felt corroborated by the fact that Williams "put Poe and his 'character' in the same position as I had *symbolized* for him in 'The Tunnel' section." But that is not as significant as the corroboration he must have felt in such conclusive statements as "the one earthly island he found where he might live in something akin to the state he imagined, the love of his wife, had to be single and inviolate" and "Had he lived in a world where love throve, his poems might have grown differently." [244]

For more than any other reason the absence of love is associated with madness and death and, as in what follows, brings the poet to a "dead stop." After the rising inflections of the questions addressed to Poe, the sudden flatness of the isolated lines—the deadpan humor of "For Gravesend Manor change at Chambers Street" and the passivity rendered by "The platform hurries along to a dead stop"—indicate exhaustion. With the stopping of the train, the poet's thought stops, the poem stops; the moment is empty, as it often is at this juncture, when the train, awaiting transfers, stands ready to make the descent under the river, under the bridge itself.

243.   To hell with you and your poetry—
           You will rot and be blown
           through the next solar system
           with the rest of the gases—
           What the hell do you know about it?

244. *Letters*, pp. 277–78; *In the American Grain*, pp. 231–32. The chapter on Poe, originally intended to conclude the book, was Williams' literary directive to his generation.

But not empty for long. Anticipation of dread, told by the poet's wistful imagination of redemption, fills it:

> The intent escalator lifts a serenade
> Stilly
> Of shoes, umbrellas, each eye attending its shoe, then
> Bolting outright somewhere above where streets
> Burst suddenly in rain. . . .

As he follows those who have been released from the "heart of fright," he thinks of the "stilly note / Of pain" and of those who, unlike the office workers undone by death in *The Waste Land* ("each man fixed his eyes before his feet"), find again, in the explosive instant of birth, the open innocent world whose advent is only announced by the thunder in Eliot's poem. But for him there remains the "heart of fright," the scream and roar of the descending "demented" train (self), and the letting-go, like the falling leaves at the end of "Quaker Hill" (recalled by "Newspapers wing, revolve and wing," which also figure the gull's consummate freedom), that is the necessary condition of the miracle of rebirth.

When he abandons himself and descends most deeply into his situation—the self-and-world rendered so clairvoyantly—he discovers within it a "Materna": [245]

> And does the Daemon take you home, also,
> Wop washerwoman, with the bandaged hair?
> After the corridors are swept, the cuspidors—
> The gaunt sky-barracks cleanly now, and bare,
> O Genoese, do you bring mother eyes and hands
> Back home to children and to golden hair?

The ironic echoes of Blake and Eliot and the interrogative form qualify the poet's recognition, which, we note, is not overwhelmed by sexual disgust. He attends the "Wop washerwoman" not only to fix clearly the homeward—and childhood—direction of his Columbian journey but to fill his world with a necessary presence, one associated with the gratifying experience of "Porphyro in Akron." And just as the Italian woman of that poem is not debased by being part of a world of illicit pleasure, so here the washerwoman is not demeaned by her work. She cannot be said to be

245. See "C 33."

an "ideal"—she is no "Cathedral Mary"—but Eve traveling in the underworld, a woman who, like Emily Dickinson and Isadora Duncan, has known tragedy, has been hurt by life ("bandaged"), a life, moreover, connected with the daytime masculine urban world of history. And since she redeems this sordid world by her nighttime cleaning—in this respect "she is virgin to the last of men"—it is not unreasonable to believe that she brings "mother eyes and hands / Back home to children and to golden hair"— not unreasonable at all when these resonant sustaining lines so eagerly wish to establish her there.

And her maternal presence is needed to help the poet, who, in "unhusk[ing] the heart of fright," relieves the trauma of his emergence. As in Crane's earliest poems this is depicted as a birth throe, and more than any other passage of the poem is truly demonic— filled with derision at the very hope of birth and poetic utterance and with diabolic enormities of cosmic proportions. The poet's imagination of birth, projected in terms of a hostile technological universe, is bound by death, by the "hideous laughter" carried over to the "muffled slaughter of a day in birth," by the evil practiced on innocence that this and the subsequent and related "cruelly to inoculate the brinking dawn" suggest, by the science-fictional antennae piercing the very heavens, which again seem to violate the natural, as do the final enormities of false nurture and cosmic abandonment. The horror of modern urban society is extreme, compounded for the poet by his sense of infantile impotence and helplessness ("O caught like pennies beneath soot and steam"). Yet his agony, whose ultimate cause and cry is told by "shrill ganglia / Impassioned with some song we fail to keep," is beneficent ("Kiss of our agony"), the very cry of birth. Now the "Daemon" of this journey, hitherto demonic, fulfills his better nature, or, rather, permits its concurrence, and in that instant, descent becomes ascent, death life, nay yea:

> And yet, like Lazarus, to feel the slope,
> The sod and billow breaking,—lifting ground,
> —A sound of waters bending astride the sky
> Unceasing with some Word that will not die . . . !

The participials promise home; for the poet, as the expectant calm of the verse assures us, is about to enter the natural world of earth, water, sky—and poetry.

At this point "Atlantis" might have followed, for the thought of the bridge has been with the poet since the beginning, when the thought of theaters was undoubtedly associated in his mind, as it was in "Proem," with the bridge. His night journey has been a journey "East," to the light, to home, to the bridge.[246] And not only is this journey a paradigm of psychic distress and restoration, of doubt-and-death and faith-and-rebirth, it is a paradigm of creation to which the concluding celebratory poem attests. (Playing on the Blakean poem of creation alluded to in an early line, one might say that his journey is "Out of the Square, [to] the Circle burning bright. . . .") In this regard, the sexuality of the poem is doubly significant, for the journey itself, beginning with the minimal person swimming against the swarm, depicts the self-generativity of art, the breeding with the self, in the chaos and darkness of the unconscious, that brings forth form. The poet's anguish, at every level, has to do with the making of poems. "The Tunnel" tells us of the terrors of creation; and even the concluding verse, which provides an interval of calm and preparation, reminds us that agony is always—endlessly—the condition of poetry. ("On what wings dare he aspire?" asks Blake. "What the hand dare seize the fire?")[247]

The initial lines of this verse convey the quiet relief of repossessing the self-and-the-world. They restore our sense of a state of existence between the despair of "The Tunnel" and the exaltation of "Atlantis."[248] Now, as never before in The Bridge, the poet is at home in the harbor of his world ("thy harbor, O my City"). He accepts this world in the spirit of Williams' "The Wanderer," heeds the tugboat whistle, which "stove up the River"—that is, destroys history or time, as he himself begins to do, paradoxically, by counting "the echoes assembling" (as in "Recitative").[249] And

246. See Bodkin, *Archetypal Patterns in Poetry*, p. 52.

247. The best glosses on this are William Carlos Williams, *A Voyage to Pagany* (New York: Macaulay Co., 1928), pp. 125–27, and Whitman's "The Sleepers."

248. These lines recall Psalm 23, especially "he leadeth me beside the still waters. He restoreth my soul. . . ."

249. See Stella, "The Brooklyn Bridge," p. 88. Originally this part of "The Tunnel" was a part of "Atlantis." See Weber, *Hart Crane*, p. 426.

that "galvanic blare," usually associated with other urban noise, is a Wagnerian fanfare that interpenetrates and fills the world with music. "Thumbing the midnight on the piers" anticipates the harp of the bridge, and the "tympanum of waters" prepares for the full orchestration of "Atlantis." Whether of light or sound, the images bespeak a darkness no longer dismaying but expectantly attended.

But all of this, we realize, is recounted in the past tense. It has already yielded to a present that is otherwise—that is troubled by thoughts of time, of "Tomorrow." For the poet recalls the entire journey he has this day taken and will perhaps take again:

> And this thy harbor, O my City, I have driven under,
> Tossed from the coil of ticking towers. . . .
>   Tomorrow,
> And to be. . . .

And, like Hamlet, he ponders his existence, which may not be the timeless, innocent being he experiences "Here at the waters' edge," his true Cathay and repose of rivers, but the non-being, or death, of the city whose temporal dominion as well as "smoked forking spires" he has tried to flee.[250] And so, acknowledging the doubleness of experience—this is his agony and gathering force—he turns once more to poetry.

"Atlantis is the poem of the poem that the poet "gatherest"— the sunken world the imagination raises up or, better perhaps, all that the imagination raises up from the sunken world when, to cite the poet's tragic awareness in an early version of the poem, "love / From terror lifted, stanchions the heart's pain." It is everything said of the bridge in "Proem":

> O harp and altar, of the fury fused,
>
>   . . . .
>
> Terrific threshold of the prophet's pledge,
> Prayer of pariah, and the lover's cry. . . .

That it is a full version of the kind of ending Crane sometimes declares at the end of shorter poems ("Possessions" and "Recitative," for example), that it renders a consummate experience—attains a peak and subsides in repose—meanwhile containing or admitting

---

250. I cite "smoked forking spires" because "Tossed" recalls the distress of "Possessions."

all that it overcomes, is a measure of its achievement. It is the poem that all that has gone before it permits him to write, the sign that the poet's journey has been purgative-redemptive and that what he discovers has fulfilled his Columbian dream.

In the earlier versions of the poem—as in the last—the insistent theme is love answered. The poet, having found in the bridge the "expansive center, purest moment," wishes to "hold consonance / Kinetic to [its] poised and deathless dance." The bridge sometimes figures as "our answering world, / Recreate[d] and resonantly risen in this dome"; and in one version the agony that gives it birth is explicitly sexual, treated somewhat in the mythic way of sun and ice in "The Dance," while in another, the bridge is the "white nativity" that breaks through the "glittering thighs" of a North Labradorian landscape. In still another version, the upward motion of the cables is depicted as "drawing love"—in a passage, connected with the confidences of youth, whose ending recalls "Voyages III"; "The dance is chosen, the steep ways evoked!" Throughout these versions desire is held in tension—intensified, poised—by fear (of transience as well as overreaching) and by the poet's awareness that what he seeks is inevitably compromised by the unsteady nature of man ("steady as the gaze incorporate / Of flesh affords"). In the first version, which deserves to be quoted in its own right as well as for its central place in Crane's imaginative endeavor, desire is matched by the use of the subjunctive:

> And midway on that structure I would stand
> One moment, not as a diver, but with arms
> That open to project a disk's resilience
> Winding the sun and planets in his face.
> Water should not stem that disk, nor weigh
> What holds its speed in vantage of all things
> That tarnish, creep, or wane; and in like laughter,
> Mobile yet posited beyond even that time
> The Pyramids shall falter, slough into sand,—
> And smooth and fierce above the claim of wings,
> And figured in that radiant field that rings
> The Universe:—I'd have us hold one consonance
> Kinetic to its poised and deathless dance.[251]

251. For all early versions, see Weber, *Hart Crane*, pp. 425–40.

The imagery, situation, and world of this poem are familiar by now—perhaps they remind us of all the poems that have made them familiar to us—but as the germ of "Atlantis," as the poem was later called, perhaps the thing most noteworthy is the Shakespearean voice, the voice of Gonzalo in *The Tempest*, which the poet borrows to sing his own golden age.

"Atlantis" identifies a myth of redemption, restoration, return, and it is associated in the epigraph with Plato, not only because he relates the legend of the sunken—fallen—civilization in the *Timaeus* and *Critias* but because its restoration may be considered the advent of cosmos. The spirit in which Crane employs it is best expressed by Thoreau in *Walden*: "the coming in of spring is like the creation of Cosmos out of Chaos and the realization of the Golden Age." [252] This accords with *The Tempest*, where restorations (of relations in power and sex) are manifold and, equally important, achieved by the agency of imagination. Crane associated Atlantis with the Isle of Pines, his own island paradise and place of imaginative achievement.[253] But in naming the poem "Atlantis" he universalized the pattern of experience presented in the poem and made it the burden of man's historical consciousness; he related the poet's personal desire for redemption with that of society or civilization. Not for himself alone did he perform what Joseph Campbell calls "the modern-hero deed . . . of questing to bring to light again the lost Atlantis of the coordinated soul." [254]

And since in ways most important to him Atlantis figures prominently in Blake's prophecies, he used it to call attention to the mythic function attributed to the bridge in "Proem" and "Cape Hatteras"—to connect it with a myth of redemption but also to apprise us of "myth," which serves the need of redemption as poems do, and of the imagination that creates them. Crane was neither ignorant nor careless in identifying redemption with a work of man. The bridge of his poem as well as the poem itself is, as Louis Sullivan said of the arch, a form of limitless plasticity and imaginative use that may be viewed "both as a triumph over

252. "Spring," *Walden*; and note Thoreau's quotation from Ovid, the source of Gonzalo's speech in *The Tempest*.
253. *Letters*, pp. 255–56.
254. *The Hero with a Thousand Faces* (New York: Pantheon Books, 1949), p. 388.

an abyss and as the very crystallization of that abyss itself"—"a form so much against Fate, that Fate, as we say, ever most relentlessly seeks its destruction." [255] Following Frederick Hoffman, we may speak of its myth as "intrinsic," that is, as "secular," residing in its own organic character and "not dependent upon past dogmas. . . ." [256] Crane himself defined myth in this way when he told Gorham Munson that Plato no longer lives because of the "truth" of his statements but because of the poetic way ("the architecture of . . . logic") in which he organized them—a point he made not to discredit Plato but to defend his own "reorganizations of chaos" from the prescription of what he felt to be the inadequate systems of thought and belief of his time. [257] To have chosen the bridge as the organizing symbol of his experience of nature, history, and art was a master stroke of imagination. Crane's high originality is that he found a sufficiently "modern" symbol, a mechanistic yet organic form, adequate to the task of gathering his themes and of affirming what modernism, in its traditionalist or theological variety, disclaimed: natural order (the meaningfulness of process) and human agency. He would have agreed with William Carlos Williams, who, commenting on the kind of modernism exemplified in "St. Francis Einstein of the Daffodils," said that "It is always spring time for the mind when great discoveries are made"—and would have added, as Williams undoubtedly intended, when great poems are (being) written. [258] To restate Thoreau in the spirit of another age: The creation of Cosmos out of Chaos brings in spring, the golden age. The "vernal strophe[s]" of "Atlantis" perform this glorious work.

By inverting "span of consciousness," a phrase from "Cape Hatteras" linking the bridge with the "Open Road" of experience (an idea presented at the beginning of *The Bridge* in the initial

255. *Kindergarten Chats and Other Writings* (New York: George Wittenborn, 1947), p. 124.

256. Crane himself provides these terms ("Swift peal of secular light, intrinsic Myth"); Hoffman considers their significance for a time concerned with "tradition" and "experiment." *The Twenties*, p. 273.

257. *Letters*, pp. 237–40 (March 17, 1926). The issues presented here will be treated in Chapter V.

258. Cited by John Malcolm Brinnin, *William Carlos Williams*, University of Minnesota Pamphlets on American Writers, 24 (Minneapolis: University of Minnesota Press, 1963), p. 20.

stanza of "Van Winkle"), one may characterize the concluding poem. *Consciousness of span:* an experience of the bridge itself which is the experience the creation of the entire poem (itself a span) makes possible. At the end of the poem, the poet finds himself neither beneath the bridge, as in "Proem," nor on it, as in "Cutty Sark," where it affords a prospect for visionary experience, but within its space, enclosed by it, caught up in the dance of its motion, sound, and light. To borrow a phrase from "Cutty Sark," he is within "some white machine that sings," and the "ATLANTIS ROSE" of that poem is the song of this experience—a possession of such intensity and imaginative fullness that, even with—or because of—the concomitant awareness of what is being overcome, it answers, for its duration, the poet's need for love.

Though "Atlantis" serves the "symphonic" function of recapitulation, it is best considered, in its relation to "The Tunnel," as rendering an antithetical experience: creative experience, the moment of a poem's creation. Of one of the earlier versions Crane noted the "sheer ecstasy," and of a later version he said that he had "attempted to induce the same feelings of elation, etc.—like being carried forward and upward simultaneously—both in imagery, rhythm and repetition, that one experiences in walking across my beloved Brooklyn Bridge." We may cite Crane because the poem realizes these intentions. The strands of the poem do converge—to such an extent that felicitous exegesis is difficult, gainsaying Crane's belief that the symphonic form provided "some liberation for my condensed metaphorical habit. . . ." [259] And elation is induced, with a forceful stress that reminds one of the "Ode to Joy" at the end of Beethoven's *Ninth Symphony*—which is perhaps what Herbert Leibowitz had in mind when he called "Atlantis" a "choral paean." [260]

Creation is ascent, a difficult, terrifying kinesis, a dance. And so the poem insistently carries the poet upward, not merely by reiterated word ("Onward and up") but by its arc-like cadences of aspiring effort and cessation, a sexual rhythm the pattern for which is established by the syntactically parallel quatrains of the opening stanza. The verbal imagery is notable and its energy tremendous,

259. *Letters*, pp. 141, 232.
260. *Hart Crane*, p. 139.

lifting the poet ever higher until the "white seizure" of creative experience, of song, releases him in the self-transcendence that figures here, as in "Proem," in the image of ascending bird ("Kinetic of white choiring wings . . . ascends"). But the upward motion, represented by the arcing cable strands of the bridge, gives direction to an experience that becomes a "white seizure" by virtue of other things as well: the responsiveness to experience that the poet's synaesthesia and sense of interpenetration indicate, and the willingness, in abandoning himself to this experience, to permit his deepest thoughts—thoughts previously associated with the bridge—to fill his mind. For creation, as it is so well depicted by this poem, overcomes not by denial but by lifting up. Space (all space: "seven oceans") and time (all history), darkness, and terror are acknowledged in—exist in the very tension of—the imaginative act that surmounts them. And the poet whose poem renders this experience is glad, but, in Emerson's words, "glad to the brink of fear." [261]

For convenience the poet's deepest thoughts may be indicated by the metaphors Crane spoke of in relation to the bridge: "a ship, a world, a woman, a tremendous harp. . . ." [262] These metaphors of voyage, cosmos, love, and celebration are related, converging finally in the "white seizure," which becomes "Thou Bridge to Thee, O Love," where love, like the enclosing bridge itself, becomes the "whitest Flower, O Answerer of all. . . ." This is the supreme moment of the poem, a consummation, at once imaginative and erotic, of all the poet's experience in *The Bridge* ("this history"): the moment of rapture and radiance. In this moment ("Now while . . .") the poet, centered in the flower, is at the very heart of "the radiant field that rings / The Universe":

> Now while thy petals spend the suns about us, hold—
> (O Thou whose radiance doth inherit me)
> Atlantis,—hold thy floating singer late!

The urgency of the poet's plea to "hold" (to stay and to enclose) is one with the experience so exquisitely rendered by "spend" (com-

261. *The Complete Works of Ralph Waldo Emerson*, I, 9. The state of feeling is of the kind conveyed by the phrase "Terrific threshold" in "Proem."
262. *Letters*, p. 232.

bining a sense of cosmic centrality and generation, of spinning as well as incredible lavishness) and "inherit" (which picks up the latter meaning of "spend" and adds to it the poet's bestowal of self, his ultimate spending).

The image of the flower and of the vortex suggested by spinning, the image of the "floating singer" and his petitioning voice not only remind us of "Voyages" but show us the extent to which Crane's poetry is a single work in which the themes of the earlier poems are taken up and developed. The voyage, hitherto treated in "Ave Maria," "Cutty Sark," "Cape Hatteras," and "Southern Cross," becomes prominent now but with much that derives from "At Melville's Tomb" and "Voyages"—and properly so, since *The Bridge* seeks another, no less tragic but more affirmative account of experience than the Melvillean one of those poems.

The cry of history—"labyrinthine" recalls the psychic depths of "The Tunnel," "cordage" the violations of experience of "Voyages I"—the cry of all the water-borne, whether on ocean, tide, or river, is " 'Make thy love sure. . . .' " What history "calls," filling the universe of time and space, the bridge ("their dream") "answers"; but not without the poet's recognition of the terror that intervenes on the voyage whose end, he also realizes, has been in the beginning. We note the "frosted capes" and "bequeaths" of the third stanza, which, with "eyes . . . strung with rime" and the agony of their lifting ("Pick biting way up . . .") in the fourth stanza, remind us of "At Melville's Tomb." So does the shipwreck of Jason and the Argonauts, which figures here not only to depict the poet's own heady but frightening experience aloft, on a pier of the bridge, but to remind us of the pattern of myth in which other voyages—that of *The Pequod,* of the *Santa Maria,* and of *The Bridge* (the ship of poetry, established by the pun on "rime")— participate. And Jason's voyage is suddenly prominent because by means of it the poet acknowledges his deepest reason for voyaging: to find love, the arduous and dangerous undertaking, for which a marriage-task myth, the quest of the golden fleece and the slaying of the dragon, are fitting.

Now the shipwreck ("splintered in the straits"), representing what hitherto had been the end of the voyage, is recognized as a phase of a more complex experience, one likened to that of "The

Dance" and of "The Tunnel," an experience of "death" that yields "life"—that here, "From gulfs unfolding, terrible of drums," yields the "Vision-of-the-Voyage," the bridge, the white "Paradigm" of love. By way of the vortex and the dance the poet achieves this answer because he has learned what he had failed to learn in "Voyages": to live fully in his situation and thereby come through it, to use poetry not as an object, a transcendent refuge against further experience, but as an activity, a dance and discipline of experience. Though the ending of "Atlantis" explicitly recalls that of "Voyages VI," it is not of a transcendental kind. (Crane himself said that "this section seems a little transcendental in tendency . . . but . . . the pediments of the other sections will show it not to have been.") [263] *The Bridge* is a span of consciousness, the way of experience, which Emerson said opened to surprise and self-recovery.[264] By following this way the poet makes his long way home.

His voyage of discovery is one of return:

> We left the haven hanging in the night—
> Sheened harbor lanterns backward fled the keel.
> Pacific here at time's end, bearing corn,—

The passage recalls the desperate voyage of *The Pequod*, Ahab's transcendental madness and monomaniacal flight from all havens astern, at the same time as it tells of the poet's realization that the repose he seeks, the "hushed gleaming fields," the golden fleece of his quest, has been there from the beginning, awaiting his return. Bringing him home, his own voyage shares the circularity—imaged in the "circular, indubitable frieze" of the bridge, itself an arc of the circle, a pathway of the sun—that supports his intuition of cosmos. The line in its entirety ("And still the circular, indubitable frieze") recalls the opening line of Keats's "Ode on a Grecian Urn" ("Thou still unravished bride of quietness")—a fitting association to the themes of permanence and change and art; and it reminds us that for the poet "bride" and "bridge" are cognate. Having traveled the circle of experience, he finds himself again at the beginning, in that moment when time (to cite Thoreau), by means of its own

263. *Letters*, p. 233.
264. "Experience," *The Complete Works of Ralph Waldo Emerson*, III.

lapse, has recovered itself—in the springtime of the "vernal strophe" and the "lark's return," in the happy time, before discord and separation, of the "chrysalis" and the feminine and masculine harmony of "stitch and stallion glow," and in the very opening of creation, like that envisioned in "Voyages VI," when cities, hitherto demonic and associated with "dust and steel," themselves participate in the wonderful delirium of natural restoration and seasonal fulfillment:

> With white escarpments swinging into light,
> Sustained in tears the cities are endowed
> And justified conclamant with ripe fields
> Revolving through their harvests in sweet torment.

The transcendental dream of white buildings and of gleaming fields (as expressed in "Ave Maria") is now something vouchsafed only in time and at the heavy cost of its experience ("Through the bright drench and fabric of our veins"; "through blinding cables"; "through spiring cordage"). The bridge is not a transcendental object but a "Pledge," like the rainbow in Genesis IX, 12–17: a "covenant with creation . . . to all the life that quickens mortal things . . . with all the life that beats in mortal creatures upon earth." It is the pledge or "prophecy" of creation, of renewal; of the "fresh chemistry" and the "wrapt inception and beatitude" of a natural world of mortal creatures and things; of the very experience "Atlantis" realizes—that, to cite "Song of the Universal," the poem of Whitman most prominent in this section, of "Love like light silently wrapping all, / Nature's amelioration blessing all." It declares what we feel throughout the poem, the "recovered innocence" through which, Thoreau said, "we discern the innocence of our neighbors." [265] And it is something that only men themselves can raise up, and only a "myth to God," the very thing whose making becomes a sign of faith in cosmos, "this quenchless faith / In Thy ensemble," as Whitman says, "Belief in plan of Thee enclosed in Time and Space. . . ."

This is the faith for lack of which the poet, in the very ecstasy of its assurance, asks pardon for "this history." But even so—even

---

265. "Spring," *Walden*. See also Melville, *Moby-Dick*, ch. 94 ("A Squeeze of the Hand").

in the moment of reconciliation—it remains a troubled faith because it is, after all, a faith in the glory men earn for themselves in that time whose fullness also ebbs. The flower will not hold. The dawn, with its dews and rainbows, reddens the bridge into a "Bridge of Fire," reminding the poet not only of the providence Columbus saw in "Teneriffe's garnet" but of the trial of art and life he has endured and will endure again. The "orphic strings" sound the "One Song" of tremendous poetic achievement but remind the poet of the necessary descent into Hades and the terror of the backward glance. And even the "Whispers" that answer the question with which he responds to the wonder of his experience ("Is it Cathay . . . ?") are "antiphonal," perhaps, as this image recalling "Recitative" suggests, blending, but only momentarily, into affirmation—affirmation enclosing skepticism, as Emerson says—an irreducible yea-and-nay. "Whispers," too, raises some question of certainty, but it is a word, from Whitman, of assurance, and the context in which it figures now is spiritual and heavenly. Yet uncertainty is intended because it is part of the experience and also because in the moment of presumably greatest certainty the interrogative form makes us earn, at the highest pitch, our certainty of certainty.

> Is it a dream?
> Nay but lack of it the dream,
> And failing it life's lore and wealth a dream.
> And all the world a dream.

This conclusion to "Song of the Universal" is the analogue of the closing lines of "Atlantis" in which we may now hear other resonances. "Whispers" takes us back to "C 33," as does "pity"; and "rainbows," as in "Voyages VI," is also associated with the "Materna" of that early poem. The serpent and the eagle recall the fulfillment of "The Dance." And "Whispers antiphonal . . . swing" evokes the motion of the bridge, another kind of trapeze than that of "National Winter Garden," the answerer of the poet's cry for love. Its alternating motion, especially in connection with "Whispers," reminds us of "Out of the Cradle Endlessly Rocking," another poem about love and poetic vocation. But to solace love's loss, the bridge does not whisper the delicious word "death," though the poet knows that consolation. Instead, in the face of death, it whispers the solace of love. And this is its achievement, the reason for all that is celebratory in Crane's work. *The Bridge* is the signal instance of Crane's ability to find "the means as a maker of poems to deliver the central erotic content of all our imaginations with unusual power and fullness." [266]

266. Warner Berthoff, letter to the author, January 26, 1969. In reminding us of "The Dance," "Atlantis" reminds us that poetry, like dance, may vitalize space by eroticizing it. The significance of this for us is developed by Martin Pops, who points out that dance, by making us body-conscious, unites us with others and fills the impoverished spaces that, when alienated, we inhabit. In this regard, Crane's epigraph from Plato is especially meaningful because it speaks for what, in one view, is the impelling desire of *The Bridge*: not only to create cosmos, but to restore the cosmic dance that Pops says was "untuned in the breaking of the circle. . . ." That ecology is "[our new] metaphor for [such] vitalized space" is something Crane would have readily appreciated. See "The Rape of Sleeping Beauty: Dance in Our Time," *Salmagundi*, no. 15 (Winter, 1971), 12.

It is naive to think, as Susan Jenkins Brown does, that Crane was untroubled by the critical response to *The Bridge*. He did not begin to study Dante for idle reasons—he took up the corrective so highly regarded by his critics. Nor was the following remark, in a letter written shortly before his death asking for an opinion of "The Broken Tower" ("about the 1st [poem] I've written in two years"), merely casual: "I'm getting too damned self-critical to write at all any more." [1] Criticism, we must remember, was part of the milieu of his work, and he closely attended it because much of it, written by poets and writers (Pound, Eliot, Williams, Tate, Winters, Frank), addressed the difficulties of poets in the modern world. Having learned so much from it—having made the issues it defined so much the substance of his work—he could not easily dismiss its strictures, and all the more so since his intelligence was of the healthy kind that admitted doubt.

To read the criticism of *The Bridge*—of Hart Crane—from our present vantage is, to say the least, an astonishing experience. How could Allen Tate, Yvor Winters, and R. P. Blackmur, the critics whose opinions of Crane and his work went almost uncontested until recently, have been so unaware of the merits of the *poem* and the tough genius of its maker? How could critics so well versed in Eliot's work find it so difficult to make formal sense of *The Bridge*, and, being poets themselves, to enter the dimensions of the poem? They had the "time and familiarity" that, Crane told a reviewer of

1. *Robber Rocks*, p. 120; *Letters*, pp. 356, 406 (September 30, 1930; Easter Sunday, 1932).

The Bridge, had helped him discover the unity of *The Waste Land* and would help others discover the unity of his "complicated" poem. But then, though Tate and Winters knew Crane's "too well-known biography," of more importance in understanding their response is the fact that criticism is always of its moment—that the criticism as much as the writing of *The Bridge* belongs to the history of modernism.[2]

Crane never disputed Eliot. Eliot was his teacher, a "beloved predecessor," to borrow Pasternak's generous phrase. As Crane told Tate at the beginning of their correspondence, Eliot, "our divine object of 'envy,'" was not someone to reject but to "absorb," to work "*through* . . . toward a *different goal*." He was especially pleased when Eliot accepted "The Tunnel" for *The Criterion*, and Eliot, he said, inspired his reading of Dante. By placing him within his poem—and from the beginning he is a significant voice in Crane's work—Crane honored him.[3] Yet Eliot, ironically, had prepared the generation of critics who discounted Crane's achievement.[4] He had given them the idea of dissociation of sensibility, a psychological idea that served the purposes of immediate cultural description—it was witnessed by much in "modern" life—and of historical interpretation. Like "lowbrow" and "highbrow," Van Wyck Brooks's terms for what Santayana called the "two mentalities" in America, it was a ready critical instrument and equally useful in dramatizing the "ordeal" of the artist. Adopting this idea, Tate and Winters, Crane's first critics, treated him as a representative figure whose "ordeal—he was said to suffer the limitations and failure of the romantic sensibility—provided an instructive, "cautionary" example.

The chief objection to *The Bridge* is already present in Tate's Foreword to *White Buildings*. It is Crane's ambitiousness, which we learn by the end of the essay has nothing to do with a poetry "at

2. *Letters*, p. 350 (April 22, 1930); P, 21. Nine sections of *The Bridge* appeared in periodicals prior to the publication of the book. There is no evidence that time and familiarity altered the early opinions of these critics.

3. *Letters*, pp. 90, 308, 356.

4. Crane anticipated their response when, speaking of Eliot, he told Munson: "But in the face of such stern conviction of death on the part of the only group of people whose verbal sophistication is likely to take an interest in a style such as mine —what can I expect?" *Letters*, p. 236 (March 5, 1926).

once contemporary and in the grand manner" but with a fault "common to ambitious poets since Baudelaire," the fact that "the vision often strains and overreaches the theme." What this means exactly, in terms of the poems in *White Buildings,* is never made clear because Tate, as his reference to Whitman indicates, is looking ahead to Crane's uncompleted poem ("The great proportions of the myth [of America] have collapsed in its reality. Crane's poetry is a concentration of certain phases of the Whitman substance, the fragments of the myth"). But what he means in this respect is clear, at least to readers of *The Sacred Wood,* in his conclusion: "It [the common fault] appears whenever the existing poetic order no longer supports the imagination. It appeared in the eighteenth century with the poetry of William Blake." [5]

Eliot's short essay on Blake is in some ways the model for much of the criticism of Crane. Take, for example, the assignment of praise and blame: Blake is "only a poet of genius" where Dante is a "classic." This distinction rests on Eliot's view of Blake as a "naked man," a Robinson Crusoe, one whose "philosophy, like his visions, like his insight, like his technique, was his own"; it rests, even when Eliot acknowledges the historical necessity, on his distrust of the poet who "needs must create a philosophy as well as a poetry." Dante wisely "borrowed" his philosophy and so was spared "the certain meanness of culture" Eliot notes in Blake, a poet outside "the Latin traditions." Blake remained only a genius because "what his genius required, and what it sadly lacked, was a framework of accepted and traditional ideas which would have prevented him from indulging in a philosophy of his own"—a deficiency that contemporary poets may avoid because, as Eliot observes, "we are not really so remote from the Continent, or from our own past, as to be deprived of the advantages of culture if we wish them." [6]

If we wish them. Crane's early critics seem as much disturbed by what they consider needless balkiness as by the challenge of his genius. They address him as a schoolboy who, as Munson, citing Arnold and Eliot, says, " 'did not know enough.' " Blackmur summarizes their objection when he says that Crane was an extreme

5. *White Buildings,* pp. xi–xviii.

6. "William Blake," *Selected Essays* (London: Faber and Faber, 1951), pp. 317–22; originally published in *The Sacred Wood* (1920).

case of the "predicament of immaturity." His genius is indubitable ("of a high order," Winters says) but its "flaws"—in a muddy yet transparent statement—"are . . . so great as to partake, if they persist, almost of the nature of a public catastrophe." "Poetic order" (Tate), "system" (Munson), "adequate ideational background" (Winters)—deficient in these, Crane, according to Munson, is "a 'mystic' on the loose," and his work, according to Winters, is "a form of hysteria." [7] So much, in sum, for individual talent without tradition.

Of course it was not that Crane was wholly without learning— though his meager formal education is usually noted—but that he had, as Blackmur claims, the "wrong masters," had submitted to deleterious influences. Yes, he had read Eliot but "not, so to speak, read the Christianity from which Eliot derives his ultimate strength. . . ." The advantages of culture, of all that Crane might have gained from the Continent, from Latin traditions, from philosophy, are reducible to Christian culture—the kind of culture or "system of disciplined values" that would have provided him the "faith [and] discipline to depend on" he was said to lack.[8] And that Crane, whose poem has its foundation in an awareness of the bankruptcy of all "systems"—he said that "the great mythologies of the past (including the Church) are deprived of enough façade to even launch good raillery against"—that he refused the advantages and subscribed instead to the radical American modernism associated with the "tradition" of Whitman and Stieglitz is chiefly what accounts for the vehemence of his critics.[9] More than a decade ago, Gordon Grigsby put the matter of orthodoxy in criticism with salutary directness: "Criticism of *The Bridge* has been strongly affected from the start by the simple fact that Crane does not share the ethics or the religion of the majority of his critics." [10]

7. Munson, "Hart Crane: Young Titan in the Sacred Wood," *Destinations* (New York: J. H. Sears and Co., 1928), pp. 160–77; Blackmur, "New Thresholds, New Anatomies," pp. 301–16 (originally published in 1935); Winters, "The Progress of Hart Crane," *Poetry*, XXXVI (June, 1930), 153–65.

8. Blackmur, "New Thresholds, New Anatomies"; Tate, "American Poetry since 1920," *Bookman*, LXVIII (January, 1929), 507; F. O. Matthiessen, "Harold Hart Crane," *Dictionary of American Biography*, supp. 1, XXI (New York: Charles Scribner's Sons, 1944), 207.

9. "General Aims and Theories" (1925–26), P, 218.

10. "The Modern Long Poem," p. 251.

And not only the ethics and the religion but allegiance of place. For Crane stands with Paul Rosenfeld, a cosmopolitan critical spokesman of the Stieglitz circle, who concluded *Port of New York* by offering another reading than Eliot's of the "Falling towers" of *The Waste Land*, one more in accord with Crane's "Atlantis": "We had been sponging on Europe for direction instead of developing our own, and Europe had been handing out nice little packages of spiritual direction to us. But then Europe fell into disorder and lost her way, and we were thrown back on ourselves to find inside ourselves sustaining faith." [11]

Now this is heresy too, and fatal, as Tate argues in an obituary essay on Crane. Alluding to Brooks's thesis about the failure of American artists, Tate maintains the contrary:

> If there is any American life distinct from the main idea of western civilization, their failure has been due to their accepting it too fully. It is a heresy that rises in revolt against the traditional organization of the consciousness—for which the only substitute offered is the assertion of the will. We hear that Americans are not rooted in the soil, that they must get rid of the European past before they can be rooted. That is untrue: the only Americans who have ever been rooted in American soil [Southerners, according to Southern Agrarians] have lived on the European system, socially and spiritually.

That Crane was not a Southerner Tate points out elsewhere, though he may have had this in mind when he said that Crane's early life and education fitted him to be the "archetype of the modern American poet"—a role, we are told, he filled with admirable "integrity" and "courage" by carrying his work to "its logical conclusion of personal violence." Crane's suicide, Tate believes, was "morally appropriate" and significant as "a symbol of the 'American' mind," because, like Crane's, this mind, as the quotation marks indicate, is dissociated or isolated from *the* tradition. And Tate believes—it is the real point of contention—that Crane misunderstood the grounds of Eliot's pessimism and that instead of

11. *Port of New York: Essays on Fourteen American Moderns* (New York: Harcourt, Brace and Co., 1924), p. 295. In reply to Munson, with whose awareness of "spiritual disintegration" he was in sympathy, Crane said that he doubted "if any remedy will be forthcoming from so nostalgic an attitude as the Thomists betray, and moreover a strictly European system of values, at that." *Letters*, p. 323 (April 17, 1928).

refuting him exemplified Eliot's "major premise": "that the integrity of the individual consciousness has broken down." [12]

This conclusion was arrived at in another way by Winters, who said that Crane's master and model was Whitman and that "Mr. Crane's wreckage" (*The Bridge*) demonstrates "the impossibility of getting anywhere with the Whitmanian inspiration." Tate attributes the failure of *The Bridge* and Crane's inability to continue his work to the "framework" of the poem, which, he believes, Crane himself knew was "incoherent." Such views, even granting Winters' and Tate's attention to the poem, are compromised by the threefold assumption that a poem (especially one of epic proportions) must have a framework, presumably outside of itself, that there is a correct framework ("framework of accepted and traditional ideas," to cite Eliot again), and that in choosing the wrong framework (if anything romantic or Whitmanian can be called a framework) one is sure to fail. (*The Bridge*, Winters said, not knowing he was pointing in the direction of a different truth, "has no more unity than the *Song of Myself.* . . .") Tate assumes an "intellectual order"; like the "framework," it is there for those disposed to take it. And his account of Crane's place in recent literary history, where Crane is set against but in a succession from Rimbaud, follows from it. For Crane, he says, coming "at the end of the romantic movement, when the dissociation [of the inherited intellectual order] is all accomplished, struggles with the problem of finding an intellectual order. It is the romantic process reversed, and the next stage in the process is not romanticism at all." The futility and failure of misdirection are the burden of these remarks on the struggle of the modern. Yet seen from another side these remarks might be said to define and approve the courageous enterprise of one who understood and fully accepted the modern condition.[13]

12. "American Poetry since 1920"; "Hart Crane and the American Mind," *Poetry*, XL (July, 1932), 211–16. Tate had also developed these views in reviewing *The Bridge*: see "A Distinguished Poet," *Hound and Horn*, III (July–September, 1930), 580–85.

13. Winters, "The Progress of Hart Crane"; Tate, "Hart Crane and the American Mind." Leslie Fiedler points out that "the failure of *The Bridge* was interpreted not as Crane's failure, but as Whitman's" and that Whitman was regarded "not only as a bad 'influence' but even as a bad poet, the founder of an inferior

Crane's sensibility, aesthetics, and poetry are decidedly modern, for they are all characterized by distrust of absolutes (intellectual orders or systems) and respect for experience and by an intelligence both intelligent and resilient enough to remain skeptical and to include skepticism in its "stab at a truth." [14] The "confusion" in Crane's work is not inadvertent, as Tate and others believe, but deliberate; it belongs to that "extraordinary insight into the foundations of his work" that in other respects Tate said Crane had.[15] To those in quest of certainty, Crane's vision is disturbing because it is "doubtful" or double; it is not a vision of either/or but of both/and. As Gordon Grigsby maintains, in a study of *The Bridge* that in many ways remains the essential pioneering work, "this doubtful vision, far from ruining the poem, is in fact one of its chief sources of strength"; and as Eugene Nassar insists, in a recent study that considers only the "posture toward experience" presented in the verbal texture of *The Bridge*, the poem "dramatizes a dualistic experience of life," a complex response to complexity that is not " 'idealistic,' or 'affirmative,' or 'platonic,' or 'mystic,' or 'epic,' or, for that matter, wholly 'tragic,' "—though these elements may be included in it.[16] Crane's letters and essays on poetry support these views; they have the vigor and acuity of one who is pressed to define and defend them. And the single proposition they advance reminds one of another American who has a place in "the revolt against formalism" and whose words, slightly altered, exactly express it: "The life of poetry has not been logic: it has been experience." [17]

Crane's summary statement of this crucial issue is his best, de-

---

tradition." "Images of Walt Whitman," *Leaves of Grass: One Hundred Years After*, ed. Milton Hindus (Stanford: Stanford University Press, 1955), p. 70. See also Karl Shapiro, *Essay on Rime* (New York: Reynal & Hitchcock, 1945), pp. 51, 66.

14. P, 220. Crane may be said to be modern in the sense employed by Irving Babbitt, who identified the modern spirit with "the positive and critical spirit, the spirit that refuses to take things on authority." *Rousseau and Romanticism* (Boston: Houghton Mifflin Co., 1919), p. xi.

15. "Hart Crane and the American Mind," p. 211.

16. "The Modern Long Poem," p. 254; *The Rape of Cinderella*, pp. 144–45.

17. Oliver Wendell Holmes, Jr., *The Common Law* (Boston: Little, Brown and Co., 1881), p. 1. "The Revolt against Formalism" is the subtitle of Morton White's *Social Thought in America* (New York: Viking Press, 1949), which treats repre-

livered with the declarative force of a poet for whom aesthetics and ethics, poetry and being are one, and with the assurance of a poet who has informed himself and put what he knows to the test. The third paragraph in an article on "Modern Poetry," this statement is the logical conclusion to brief descriptions of the situation in poetry—of the rebellion, already over, that had moved in "a classic direction," and of the tradition of rebellion (he has in mind the early phases of what Harold Rosenberg calls "the tradition of the new") that is now, he feels, of little importance to the "serious artist." What matters to the serious artist is outlined in the following:

> The poet's concern must be, as always, self-discipline toward a formal integration of experience. For poetry is an architectural art, based not on Evolution or the idea of progress, but on the articulation of the contemporary human consciousness *sub specie aeternitatis*, and inclusive of all readjustments incident to that consciousness and other shifting factors related to that consciousness. The key to the process of free creative activity which Coleridge gave us in his *Lectures on Shakespeare* exposes the responsibilities of every poet, modern or ancient, and cannot be improved upon. "No work of true genius," he says, "dares want its appropriate form, neither indeed is there any danger of this. As it must not, so genius can not, be lawless: for it is even this that constitutes its genius—*the power of acting creatively under laws of its own origination.*" [18]

This is Crane's reply to his critics, to those who perhaps did not appreciate, as much as he did, the view of poetry advanced by I. A. Richards in *Principles of Literary Criticism;* who had not fully grasped, as he had, that the "architectural" aspect of poetry, like that of a cubist painting, refers not only to the way an art work is made but to the artist's conception, the imagination of the work, which Coleridge's notions of genius and organic form confirm; and who did not value, to the extent that he did, the "process of free creative activity" nor accept so willingly as a responsibility of art the "articulation"—the double meaning is intended—of "the

---

sentative thinkers, such as Dewey and Veblen, who attacked "abstractionism" and insisted on "life, experience, process, growth, context, function" (pp. 12–13).

18. P, 260. The quotation from Coleridge is accurate except for the italics.

contemporary [immediate, always changing] human consciousness." [19] Here, as in the work of Williams, whom Crane's declaration calls to mind, the poet is given the fundamental tasks of "unbound thinking" and of bringing the immediate world to form.[20]

Crane's definition of the poet's concern—"self-discipline toward a formal integration of experience"—also tells us of the function poetry had for him. He was a poet by necessity, having need of a discipline, not of denial but of inclusion, that provided enough security to permit the risk of growth. The first lesson of art and psychology he reports having been taught by Carl Schmitt was one of balance ("There is only one harmony, that is the equilibrium maintained by two opposite forces, equally strong"), a lesson, it seems, that did not omit the caution to maintain the vital or dynamic condition of constant "inward struggle." [21] For the discipline respected experience, required, as he told William Wright, the "development of one's consciousness even though it is painful." [22] The moments of equilibrium that Crane reports are those ecstatic ones of love (a "thrilling and inclusive" experience that "reconciled" him), of "inspiration" (as, when under ether, he "felt the two worlds . . . at once"), and of art, when, by inward struggle, he achieved a "consistent vision of things." [23] Balance, integration, synthesis—interchangeable words for Crane—characterize these moments and provide the touchstone of his appreciation of Donne

19. For Crane's appreciation of Richards' book, see *Letters*, p. 314 (December 19, 1927).

20. *Selected Essays of William Carlos Williams* (New York: Random House, 1954), p. 163. For Williams, "the poet thinks with his poem. . . ." See *The Autobiography of William Carlos Williams* (New York: Random House, 1951), pp. 390–91, and for a characteristic criticism of systems, pp. 360–61. And see Stanley Burnshaw, who says that poetry is "an open area . . . the only field of discourse in which thought can participate in its entirety." *The Seamless Web: Language-Thinking, Creature-Knowledge, Art-Experience* (New York: George Braziller, 1970), p. 107.

21. *Letters*, p. 5 (January 5, 1917).

22. *Letters*, p. 19 (June 17, 1919). Giving up the therapy of Christian Science and having fewer "denials" was part of it. See *Letters*, pp. 14, 15 (March 11, April 2, 1919).

23. *Letters*, pp. 49, 92, 267 (December 22, 1920; June 1922; July 16, 1926). See also, on the need for "a strong critical faculty," *Letters*, p. 245 (April 5, 1926).

("at once sensual and spiritual, and singing rather the beauty of experience than innocence") and, to cite another example, of Fielding, whose attitude toward society and life he found "more 'balanced' " than Hardy's.[24] They explain his quarrel with Matthew Josephson, who refused "to admit the power and beauty of emotional intensity" (both means and end where "fury fused"). And they also explain his reservations concerning Eliot, whose "poetry of negation [was] beautiful" but one-sided in not acknowledging that "one *does* have joys," that there are "positive" emotions.[25] To balance Eliot's pessimism by presenting "these other moods" was one of Crane's objectives in *The Bridge*. "I tried to break loose from that particular strait-jacket, without however committing myself to any oppositional form of didacticism," he told Selden Rodman, who had reviewed it. "Your diffidence in ascribing any absolute conclusions in the poem is therefore correct, at least according to my intentions. The poem, as a whole, is, I think, an affirmation of experience [that is, of the possibility of a more inclusive experience and of experience itself as an "absolute"], and to that extent is 'positive' rather than 'negative' in the sense that *The Waste Land* is negative." [26]

How well this statement substantiates itself by demonstrating the quality of mind it declares—a quality of mind that put Crane in opposition to most of his friends and critics. What he objected to early in Josephson became the prominent theme of his letters and essays on art: "he tries to force his theories into the creative process. . . ." [27] To Munson, who asked that his poems provide philosophical and moral "knowledge," Crane answered that he had misunderstood his "poetic purpose" and had proposed "such ends as poetry organically escapes. . . ." For poetry, he said, does not provide knowledge unless by knowledge one means simply "the

24. *Letters*, pp. 68, 300.

25. *Letters*, pp. 106, 89, 71 (November 1922; May 16, 1922; November 26, 1921); P, 46. In the passage on Eliot, Crane may be referring, in "it is hard to dance in proper measure," to Williams' *Kora in Hell*, an appropriate book. For intensity, see *Letters*, p. 302.

26. *Letters*, p. 351 (May 22, 1930). For "absolute" experience, see P, 221; *Letters*, p. 302.

27. *Letters*, p. 65.

concrete *evidence* of the *experience* of a recognition." His intention was neither to oppose "any new synthesis of reasonable laws which might provide a consistent philosophical and moral program for our epoch" nor to use poetry "to delineate any such system." But he was disinclined to follow Munson in search of system because system itself was, in fact, the chief obstacle to poetry. "The tragic quandary . . . of the modern world," he said in a statement that accords with the central idea of Ortega's *The Modern Theme,* "derives from the paradoxes that an inadequate system of rationality forces on the living consciousness." [28] When Crane told his mother—this context is also significant—that "the freedom of my imagination is the most precious thing that life holds for me,—and the only reason I can see for living," he spoke his deepest truth. For system, too, betrays, and poetry is prior to all system. [29]

Crane's replies to Winters and Tate cogently argue this point. To Tate he protests Winters' "arbitrary torturings—all for the sake of a neat little point of reference," and to Winters he protests Munson's desire for "some definite ethical order." He tells Winters that in his own case he has not attempted "to reduce" his code of ethics "to any exact formula"; that he cannot trust, as Winters does, "to so methodical and predetermined a method of development"; that to do so makes a "commodity" of experience and frustrates "the possibility of any free realization. . . ." In response to Tate's review of *The Bridge,* he tells him that critics like Genevieve Taggard and Winters are no longer interested in "poetry as poetry" but in finding some "cure-all," and, with evident weariness, simply remarks that "so many things have a way of coming out all the better without the strain to sum up the universe in one impressive little pellet." [30]

Though Crane withstood the arguments of his friends, he never convinced them that "truth has no name," a lesson they might also have learned from his poetics and, explicitly, from "A Name for All," a late poem available to them in *The Dial.* In this neglected poem he treats the naming, inevitable to writing, whose limitations

28. *Letters,* pp. 237–40.
29. *Letters,* p. 189 (September 14, 1924).
30. *Letters,* pp. 288, 298–302, 353 (February 24, May 29, 1927; July 13, 1930).

the "logic of metaphor"—or, more evocatively, the "dynamics of inferential mention"—enabled him to overcome.[31]

> Moonmoth and grasshopper that flee our page
> And still wing on, untarnished of the name
> We pinion to your bodies to assuage
> Our envy of your freedom—we must maim
>
> Because we are usurpers, and chagrined—
> And take the wing and scar it in the hand.
> Names we have, even, to clap on the wind;
> But we must die, as you, to understand.
>
> I dreamed that all men dropped their names, and sang
> As only they can praise, who build their days
> With fin and hoof, with wing and sweetened fang
> Struck free and holy in one Name always.

In this poem the poet's dream of redeemed mankind is a dream of poetry as a liberating field of natural life. We name, but what we name, having the winged life of spirit and imagination, escapes us, cannot be fixed. We name—in the name of rationality—out of envy of freedom, for rationality is vindictive, a will to power feeding on what Nietzsche called *ressentiment*. We even try to imprison the wind! And as the negative condition implied by "sweetened fang" tells us, our own fury to name makes nature red in tooth and claw. And only when we ourselves become the objects of a similar death do we begin to "understand"—not know, but understand—an understanding, alas, that, coming too late, is irremediable. And so the poet dreams of a better world and a better poem, of the peaceable kingdom of life ("For every thing that lives is Holy"),[32] where men drop their names or chains, or, rather, are "Struck free" by doing so *and* by entering a different realm of being and language, the totality of interpenetrated freely living things, or the poem whose form, paradoxically, is all-inclusive, a "Name" for all.[33] This liberation is poetry because it frees us to sing and to praise—and to love. And it belongs to the new space we find

31. *Letters*, p. 240; P, 221–22.
32. Blake, "A Song of Liberty," *The Marriage of Heaven and Hell*.
33. This poem—what its vision both enables and is of—is closely related to "The Wine Menagerie."

in the "poetry of reality"—the space in which "things, the mind, and words coincide in closest intimacy"—a space best contrasted with the empty space of "North Labrador," for now the "Name" for all the poem creates in its immanent space is God, in the sense for Crane that a poem is a "myth to God." [34]

The central importance of Crane's quarrel with his friends becomes clearer when we realize that he is repudiating the notions of mimetic form and correspondence truth. For him the poem is not to be judged by anything external to it: its form is organic in the primary sense of self-originating and its "truth" is nothing absolute but the coherence of meanings generated by its language. He explained this to Munson when he told him that "Plato doesn't live today because of the intrinsic 'truth' of his statements: their only living truth today consists in the 'fact' of their harmonious relationship to each other in the context of his organization. This grace partakes of poetry." And he indicated what he meant by "architecture"—how it relates to organic form, to "logic of metaphor," to the use of "build" in "A Name for All"—when he spoke of the "architecture of [Plato's] logic" as "poetic construction." [35]

Crane first employed the phrase "logic of metaphor" in a letter to Stieglitz, the import of whose work for his own he had begun to understand at the time he was beginning *The Bridge*. The phrase occurs in a passage praising Stieglitz for being an "indice of a new order of consciousness" and is connected with freedom of the imagination and the need, in using the imagination to transform "the great energies about us," of "perfecting our sensibilities" and thereby "contributing more than we can realize (rationalize). . . ." (Here is the germ of his discussion, in "Modern Poetry," of the way in which the machine must enter poetry: not by external but by inner appropriation, by surrender to and assimilation of the "sensations of urban life" which will later permit the connotations of the machine to "emanate from within," to form a "spontaneous . . . terminology of poetic reference. . . .") And this is the reason Crane complained to Stieglitz that he had "to combat every day those really sincere people, but limited, who deny the superior logic of metaphor in favor of their perfect sums, divisions and sub-

34. Miller, *Poets of Reality*, pp. 1–12.
35. *Letters*, p. 238.

tractions." (Harriet Monroe was such a person to whom he explained in detail, by glossing Eliot's and his own poetry, how the "dynamics of metaphor" worked and why this "logic" was necessary as a "connective agent" in the poet's pursuit of "added consciousness and increased perceptions," of "fresh concepts, more inclusive evaluations.") [36]

The phrase "superior logic of metaphor" refers to an earlier letter in which Crane had tried to describe Stieglitz' art—how he used the camera as an instrument of "apprehension," how the speed of the shutter enabled him to make the moment eternal, to arrest the essences of things by suspending them on "the invisible dimension whose vibrance has been denied the human eye at all times save in the intuition of ecstasy." He, too, by means of this logic, would make poetry an instrument of "consciousness," of an "absolute" experience, of radiant apprehension or illumination— that "peculiar type of perception" which, he said, was capable of "apprehending some absolute and timeless concept of the imagination with astounding clarity and conviction." In the previously cited passage on Plato the "fact" is just this presentness, the direct communication of the thing itself made possible by "poetic construction," or by the two aspects of the "logic of metaphor" that permit the poet who employs it to make this stunning impact: the fact that this logic is "organically entrenched in pure sensibility"— in the reader's as well as the poet's—and the fact that the poem it constructs is "a name for all"—strikes the reader as "a single, new *word*, never before spoken and impossible to actually enunciate, but self-evident as an active principle in the reader's consciousness henceforward." This logic operates at a deeper level than "pure logic" and transcends its limits. By using it the poet not only serves the "truth of the imagination" and gives form to its "living stuff" but lives, like the soaring bird of "Forgetfulness," in the fullness of its freedom.[37]

36. *Letters*, pp. 137–39 (July 4, 1923); P, 262, 234–40.
37. *Letters*, p. 132; P, 263, 235, 221–22. In an introductory comment on Mina Loy, William Carlos Williams speaks of making poems and recalls "the time of James Joyce's *Ulysses* when the Word was made." *Lunar Baedeker & Time-Tables: Selected Poems of Mina Loy* (Highlands, N.C.: Jonathan Williams, 1958). Crane, of course, was familiar with Mallarmé's notion that "poetry fashions a single new word which is total in itself. . . ." See also, for its relevance to this chapter, Roland

The overreaching and incoherence that Tate found in Crane's poetry—particularly in *The Bridge*—follow from Tate's failure to appreciate or grant the nature of the "logic of metaphor." This logic is the means by which the poet builds the poem from the inside out, creates the field of meaning upon which its coherence depends—the field of meaning, however, whose "expanding resonances of implication" also keep the poem forever open.[38] Whether excluded from the poem by their own beliefs or by insufficient attention, Crane's early critics were confused by the fact that "poems . . . are steadily engaged in the work of con-fusing, for the paradigm of poetry—metaphor—pervades its every act." They forgot, it seems, that what Crane called the "logic of metaphor" is the logic of the imagination, and that the imagination, expressing our deepest being, always seeks unification, always seeks "a name for all," for the reason Crane did: because "The poetries of speech / Are acts of thinking love. . . ."[39]

Even before the assumptions underlying the early criticism of *The Bridge* were questioned, close examination of the poem proved untenable the verdict of its incoherence. The poem was found to have the structural elements of other large modern works: a persona or central subjective consciousness, lyric design or thematic form, and symbolic narrative. Crane himself called it an "epic of the modern consciousness," spoke of its symphonic form, identified the architectural aspect of the "logic of metaphor" ("reflexes and symbolisms," "interlocking elements," "strands . . . interwoven") and of its episodic construction, and noted in the se-

Barthes, "Is There Any Poetic Writing?," *Writing Degree Zero*, trans. Annette Lavers and Colin Smith (London: Jonathan Cape, 1967).

38. I am indebted to J. Hillis Miller for this phrase and for the lecture on Wordsworth from which I gleaned it on February 11, 1971.

39. Burnshaw, *The Seamless Web*, pp. 18, 194. The concluding lines are from Burnshaw's *Caged in an Animal's Mind* and so doubly remind us of "The Wine Menagerie."

Much of the argument of the foregoing sections, I was pleased to find, was anticipated by Robert Creeley in "Hart Crane and the Private Judgment," written in 1953, published in 1960, and only now readily available in *A Quick Graph: Collected Notes & Essays*, ed. Donald Allen, Writing 22 (San Francisco: Four Seasons, 1970), pp. 75–87. The short review of Crane's *Letters* (pp. 88–91) is also instructive.

quence of poems "a certain progression." Criticism has substantiated him and shown him to be " 'a master builder,' " as Otto Kahn hoped he would be, " 'in constructing *The Bridge* of your dreams, thoughts and emotions.' " [40]

Though such characterizations of *The Bridge* as Otto Kahn's or Crane's ("epic of the modern consciousness") have always embarrassed critics, they are accurate and valuable in indicating the deliberate building-up or construction of the conception of the poem—that in which its form is cubist or "synthetic"—and its special modernity—that, say, where it differs from *The Waste Land*, a poem in which modern elements of form are also employed.[41] The poem is an epic of *modern* consciousness. It is that epic, first, in an anti-epical sense, for the modern poet is no more the hero of an epic action than he is a discoverer like Columbus. If we follow the progression of the epic hero from the *Aeneid*, with which Crane compared *The Bridge*, to recent "epic" works, we arrive, as Thomas Whitaker says, "at the modern poet's often ironic celebration of himself as hero-everyman, who performs universal imaginative acts . . . in an ambiguous cosmos where history must be discovered and values renewed." [42] But the very scope of this enterprise deserves to be called epic. The space in which the poet journeys is an infinitely larger space than any traversed before —the space of consciousness, at once of self, world, and word, a new field of discovery. Here the heroic deed, the culturally redemptive act, the particularly modern exploit is performed. Crane called it the "conquest of consciousness," meaning also that the conquest is achieved by consciousness alone.[43]

The poem itself is the imaginative action that performs this

40. *Letters*, pp. 306, 125, 176, 241, 305, 340, 232. Stanley Coffman, Bernice Slote, and Lawrence Dembo were among the first to appreciate the poem's coherence. Grigsby, "The Modern Long Poem," is the fullest early study and the most useful.

41. Crane noted the synthetic form of *Winesburg, Ohio* and of Stieglitz' photographs, and pointed out the relation of poetry and cubism in "Modern Poetry." Here the important statement for his own work is the following: "both media were responding to the shifting emphasis of the Western World away from religion toward science. Analysis and discovery, the two basic concerns of science, became the conscious objectives of both painter and poet." P, 212, 260; *Letters*, p. 139.

42. *Letters*, p. 309; *William Carlos Williams* (New York: Twayne, 1968), p. 129.
43. P, 222.

daring exploit. By means of the "logic of metaphor" the poet creates the space or world of the poem, the field of meaning through which he journeys. "Proem," which establishes the bridge as an artifact of the real world as well as the center of the space of the poem, calls the field of meaning into being. As the poet moves within the field, which he also continues to create (explore) as he goes and which, in turn, permits us at each stage to possess all of the poem at once, each episode, or state of consciousness, is actualized (like a Whiteheadian "event") out of the field.[44] (Crane was true to the nature of the poem when he said that there might be additional episodes: the materials are already there, in the field of meaning.) Each episode presents directly rather than symbolizes a different kind or stage of consciousness. All contribute to the "world dimensional" of the poem, the world in which the poet, after the fashion of Satan in the epigraph from *The Book of Job* that prefaces *The Bridge*, goes to and fro in the earth and up and down in it, enacting in his movement the doubleness and balance that distinguish so many elements of the poem. To follow him is to learn of heaven and hell, of vast continents and seas, of immense elemental energies (nebular, volcanic, meteorological) and processes (diurnal, seasonal, vegetative), of evolutionary and human history.[45] It is indeed to know the constituents of chaos—and of cosmos.

The movement of the poem is both circular and linear, the latter dividing at "Cutty Sark," another central point, marked by the bridge. In the simplest terms, the initial movement, which is prompted by the poet's dream of discovery, of beginnings and "making new," and of loss, is essentially inward, backward, and downward; always in the present, its focus is on the past, on childhood and youth, on the pastoral condition, on the early ground of

44. Crane read Whitehead's *Science and the Modern World* early in 1926, when he was beginning *The Bridge. Letters*, p. 235 (March 5, 1926).

45. Again, because he was concerned with "framework," Tate was mistaken about Crane's use of American history. He did not see that it functioned within consciousness and not as plot, and that Crane actually included—was aware of—the decisive, representative events. ("A Distinguished Poet," p. 582.) Denis Donoghue perpetuates Tate's view in *Connoisseurs of Chaos*, p. 48. Like Williams in *In the American Grain*, Crane shows us in *The Bridge* how the poet takes up tradition, makes the past "usable."

self. The second movement, turning on the losses expressed in "Indiana" and "Cutty Sark," is essentially outward, forward, and upward; its focus is on the present, on manhood, on the urban condition, the new ground of self. Both movements contribute to the symbolic narrative, to the profound journey into the self and the world that teaches the poet that the losses the self has experienced in its history ("this history"), like the losses America has undergone in its history, can be redeemed only by imagination—by the effort of the poet to do what he actually does in the spaces of the poem: enter his experience and rescue it with art. For the journey is also one of faith in which beliefs as polar as the Christianity of Columbus and the nihilism of the old sailor are entertained but set aside for tragic natural acceptance. From primitive myth, from the poems and example of Whitman and Emily Dickinson, the poet learns to accept the natural world of time, of process, and to accept the natural self, whose willingness to live in the world empowers the imagination.

By following a diurnal course and by returning to the bridge at the end of the poem, the journey becomes circular. As "Atlantis" closes the circle and brings the purgative-redemptive journey of consciousness to an end (or another beginning), the poem finds its center. Now, in the interpenetration of the threefold space suggested by its title—the bridge as representative artifact of the world or physical space, the bridge as poem or verbal space, and bridging as the action of the self in the space of consciousness—the poem completes its journey to love. Bridge becomes bride in the marriage of self and world consummated by poetry (poetry is marriage, Williams says).[46] And in this radiant ecstatic moment of consciousness the poet knows the power by which poetry achieves this end—discovers the "gleaming fields . . . / Of knowledge" and briefly takes possession of the kingdom "naked in the / trembling heart. . . ."

When we recall "Porphyro in Akron" and "The Bridge of

---

46. "In Praise of Marriage," *Quarterly Review of Literature*, II (Winter, 1944–45), 145–49; see Miller, *Poets of Reality*, p. 225, for this touchstone, "Words are the best marriage-place of mind and world"; and see Robert Edward Brown's topo-analysis, "Walk in the World: A Journey in the Space of William Carlos Williams' *Paterson*," unpublished doctor's dissertation, University of Rochester, 1970, p. 59, where marriage is said to be the "ceremonial image of Williams' aesthetic."

Estador"—even "For the Marriage of Faustus and Helen"—we realize better the difficult resolution of modernist allegiance Crane achieved in *The Bridge*. To be reminded by it so often of Williams is a measure of the distance Crane had come as well as an indication of his particular modernity. We think of *The Bridge* less in relation to *The Waste Land* than to *Paterson*, and chiefly for the reason that both offer us a myth of the imagination, and one that is inalienable from place: the "myth" of America is itself "modern," for it is a myth of discovery, of discovering (entering) our world, the ground of our being—or recovering it, making new. Like *Paterson*, *The Bridge* reminds us that "again is the magic word" and that for a culture as for art the difficult thing is "to begin to begin again, / turning the inside out. . . ." Both poems represent the making by which we begin ("To make, that's where we begin"); they invite "the recreators." [47]

And both exemplify the kinds of journey the self must take in order to liberate the imagination and overcome the dissociations of self and world (space) and self and history (time) involved in making new. Immanence, interpenetration, continuity characterize the worlds of these poems; in them such discontinuities of modern experience as the metaphysical (natural/human/supernatural) and the temporal (past/present/future) are surrendered. [48] The circularity of form in these poems derives from the recurrence of natural process. So does the faith in vital renewal—the reverence for generative feminine force, the sacramental sense of the world. To enter these natural worlds is to know cosmicity again ("outgrowing the child's world does not imply abandoning what it stands for") [49] and to know that love moved the poets of these poems to seek salvation not for themselves alone but for society and by the grace of their own imaginations.

47. *Paterson* (New York: New Directions, 1963), pp. 162, 167; *A Voyage to Pagany*, pp. 129–30. Philip Furia interprets both poems in terms of Williams' aesthetic in "The Beast That Was and Is Not and Yet Is: A Study of the Imagery of Hart Crane's *The Bridge* and William Carlos Williams' *Paterson*," unpublished doctor's dissertation, University of Iowa, 1970.

48. For these and other discontinuities, see Monroe K. Spears, *Dionysus and the City: Modernism in Twentieth-Century Poetry* (New York: Oxford University Press, 1970), pp. 10–34.

49. Northrop Frye, *Fearful Symmetry: A Study of William Blake* (Princeton: Princeton University Press, 1947), p. 236.

For neither poet, finally, are the imperatives of imagination religious or visionary. Cubist better describes them. The poet of *A Voyage to Pagany*, who, in meditating on making new, not only remembers Whitman but confesses his envy of modern French painters, might as readily be Crane as Williams. For Crane employs the "logic of metaphor" more in the manner of a cubist than a symbolist.[50] Condensed metaphor is not used to evoke a reality beyond the senses but to present an object clearly to the senses by way of simultaneous perspectives of meaning. In this fashion Crane moves around the object. (Ideally, by completing the circle, he would make the word a Word—though not quite in Mallarmé's sense.) Or he uses this logic to achieve the "interpenetration of dimensions" one finds in cubist painting.[51] And Crane's vision is also cubist, comporting with the kind of apprehension and presentation he found in Stieglitz' photographs, the kind of vision for which he turned for corroboration to Blake, and we may too: "vision represents the total imagination of man made tangible and direct in works of art." [52]

Crane's achievement in *The Bridge* was canceled for him by the curious consequence that, having found in *The Bridge* what Williams had in *Paterson* ("an image large enough to embody the whole knowable world about me"), he had, he felt, closed out his poetic future.[53] What was he to do next? And this anxiety of creators was compounded by other things: by the hostile criticism of respected friends and by a misunderstanding of his work so egregious that the "failure" of the poem was connected with the break-

50. *A Voyage to Pagany*, pp. 131–32. For Crane's turning from the symbolist tradition, see Haskell Block, "The Impact of French Symbolism on Modern Poetry," *The Shaken Realist: Essays in Modern Literature in Honor of Frederick J. Hoffman*, ed. Melvin J. Friedman and John B. Vickery (Baton Rouge: Louisiana State University Press, 1970), p. 216. For Crane's painterly description of *The Bridge*, see *Letters*, p. 305.

51. See Mina Loy, "Communications" [on Gertrude Stein], *The Transatlantic Review*, II (September, 1924), 307.

52. Alfred Kazin, Introduction, *The Portable Blake* (New York: Viking Press, 1946), p. 17.

53. *The Autobiography of William Carlos Williams*, p. 391. On Crane's "fullness of experience," see Robert Lowell, in an interview with Frederick Seidel, in *Robert Lowell: A Collection of Critical Essays*, ed. Thomas Parkinson (Englewood Cliffs: Prentice-Hall, 1968), p. 32.

down of American society in the Great Depression. His immediate reaction, as we saw, was to study Dante and, as he explained in applying for a Guggenheim fellowship, to study, in Europe, "characteristics of European culture, classical and romantic, with especial reference to contrasting elements implicit in the emergent features of a distinctive American poetic consciousness." [54] The prose of application forms does not obscure the central issue: he would go to school to tradition but without wholly giving up his stake in the matter. Yet when the fellowship was granted he altered his plans in keeping with the direction of his genius; he turned to Mexico, where, on arrival, he found the poets "busy aping . . . Paul Valéry, Eliot,—or more intensely, the Parnassians," heedless of the indigenous culture that had brought him there ("there is a soil, a mythology, a people and a spirit here that are capable of unique and magnificent utterance").[55]

To fathom this indigenous culture might be dangerous, as he said, but the danger Crane faced in Mexico was of another kind. Coming to it without a pattern (" 'You cannot heed the negative— so might go on to undeserved doom,' " he records Hans Zinsser telling him in "Havana Rose," " '. . . must therefore loose yourself within a pattern's mastery that you can conceive, that you can yield to—by which also you win and gain mastery and happiness . . .' ")—having as yet no pattern with which to discipline himself, his energies went undirected, exploded in violent disintegration, providing, one might say, a parodic (demonic) version of his intensity as a creator.[56]

Whether this descent would finally have proved fruitful is difficult to say. Crane himself described the ambivalence and peril of his situation when he wrote in "Purgatorio" that "I am unraveled, umbilical anew"; and in "The Broken Tower," which is related to the previous poem, he told of a similar unraveling, spending out, and breaking down as well as the humble restoration he had newly found in love. But both poems, the first not quite finished and the second brilliant, but perhaps overwrought, exhibit the diffi-

---

54. *Letters*, p. 354 (August 29, 1930).
55. *Letters*, p. 372 (June 13, 1931).
56. *Letters*, p. 371; P, 188–89. See *Letters*, p. 124, on the need, at the outset, of "some channel forms or mould into which I throw myself at white heat."

culties of creation. The poet may be reborn, but, as Crane feared—and fear itself contributed to its realization—he may no longer have creative force enough to begin anew. And what would he do then? How could he continue to exist as a poet, or to exist at all, since poetry was his only way of being in the world?

Everything—the loss of financial security on which he had counted, the shame he felt for his behavior, the responsibilities of family and love—fed this overwhelming anxiety. We may measure its extremity by the way in which Crane chose to end it, but perhaps the only thing we should say about his suicide is that he had already contemplated it in the spaces of poetry—that for him, as Kenneth Burke says of suicide, it may have been "the act of rebirth reduced to its simplest and most restricted form (its least complex idiom of expression)." [57]

57. *The Philosophy of Literary Form: Studies in Symbolic Action* (Baton Rouge: Louisiana State University Press, 1941), p. 39.

Index